Athletes Breaking Bad

Athletes Breaking Bad

Essays on Transgressive Sports Figures

Edited by JOHN C. LAMOTHE and
DONNA J. BARBIE

McFarland & Company, Inc., Publishers
Jefferson, North Carolina

ALSO OF INTEREST AND FROM MCFARLAND

The Tiger Woods Phenomenon: Essays on the Cultural Impact of Golf's Fallible Superman (edited by Donna J. Barbie, 2012)

LIBRARY OF CONGRESS CATALOGUING-IN-PUBLICATION DATA

Names: Lamothe, John C., editor. | Barbie, Donna J., editor.
Title: Athletes breaking bad : essays on transgressive sports figures / edited by John C. Lamothe and Donna J. Barbie.
Description: Jefferson, North Carolina : McFarland & Company, Inc., Publishers, 2020 | Includes bibliographical references and index.
Identifiers: LCCN 2020023266 | ISBN 9781476677088 (paperback : acid free paper) ∞
ISBN 9781476639536 (ebook)
Subjects: LCSH: Transgression (Ethics) | Sports. | Athletes—Biography.
Classification: LCC BJ1500.T73 A84 2020 | DDC 175—dc23
LC record available at https://lccn.loc.gov/2020023266

BRITISH LIBRARY CATALOGUING DATA ARE AVAILABLE

ISBN (print) 978-1-4766-7708-8
ISBN (ebook) 978-1-4766-3953-6

© 2020 John C. Lamothe and Donna J. Barbie. All rights reserved

No part of this book may be reproduced or transmitted in any form or by any means, electronic or mechanical, including photocopying or recording, or by any information storage and retrieval system, without permission in writing from the publisher.

Front cover: (left to right) Barry Bonds (Jim Accordino), Hope Solo (Andre Borges/Agencia Brasilia) and Dale Earnhardt (Darryl Moran)

Printed in the United States of America

McFarland & Company, Inc., Publishers
  Box 611, Jefferson, North Carolina 28640
    www.mcfarlandpub.com

Acknowledgments

I remember exactly when the idea for this book was first mentioned. It was around the time my coeditor, Donna J. Barbie, was finishing up her collection on Tiger Woods, a book that I contributed to, and we were sitting in her office chatting about sports. To this day, I don't know what made her suggest that the two of us work together on a book, but I practically leaped out of my seat at the opportunity to work with my mentor and friend. We started tossing around ideas. I honestly don't remember who first suggested the topic of bad boys in sports—it seemed to grow organically out of our shared ideas about sports culture—but I do know that once it was mentioned, we both knew we wanted to bring this book to life.

Years passed as we worked on other projects. We had innumerable conversations about other issues, but we would often end those conversations by saying, "We really need to do that bad boys book." Finally, the stars aligned, and we were able to focus on the project. Once that happened, things moved quickly because we had so many supportive individuals around us, people who deserve acknowledgment.

We need to give a heartfelt "thank you" to Lynnette Porter. Not only did Lynnette contribute a fantastic essay about Johnny Weir, but she also volunteered to index and proofread the entire book, a chore she claims to enjoy immensely. Her extracurricular activities may be suspect, but her aid and feedback on the book were invaluable. We would also like to thank all the contributing writers. You all were a joy to work with. We consider you all colleagues and friends and look forward to working with you on other projects in the future.

A special acknowledgment goes to the faculty of Embry-Riddle Aeronautical University's Humanities & Communication Department. Your collaboration makes projects like this a reality. In particular, we want to thank Steven Master, Sarah D. Fogle, Andy Oler, Chad Rohrbacher, and Wesley Dunning, whose sports-related conversations not only informed this book but also made coming to work more enjoyable.

Last, but far from least, I personally want to thank my wife, Mandy. Her eagle eye during proofreading caught countless errors that had slipped through my careful editing. More than that, she has supported me in everything that I do, and I couldn't have accomplished this—or so many other things—without her in my life.—J.C.L.

Table of Contents

Acknowledgments — v

Introduction: Coding and Decoding "Badness"
DONNA J. BARBIE *and* JOHN C. LAMOTHE — 1

"Not Good for the Sport"? Fabulous Figure Skater and Controversial Critic Johnny Weir
LYNNETTE PORTER — 9

John Daly: Golf's *Enfant Terrible*
DONNA J. BARBIE — 28

Nothing but the Truth: The Rise and Fall of Marion Jones
BROCK T. ADAMS — 44

Lessons from #LochMess: Ryan Lochte in Our Rush-to-Judgment Culture
STEVE MASTER — 61

Diego Maradona: The Hand of God
ISMAEL LOPEZ MEDEL — 80

Barry Bonds v. Alex Rodriguez: Don't Hate the Player; Hate the Steroid-Manufactured Game
BROCK T. ADAMS — 95

No Coward: Hope Solo Battles Against the Status Quo, Injustices and, Sometimes, Her Own Poor Decisions
JOE GISONDI — 112

The Book of Dale Earnhardt: Beyond the Intimidator's Last Lap
TERESA MARIE KELLY — 127

"Often an Eyeful, Sometimes an Earful, but Always a Handful":
Dennis Rodman, Quintessential NBA Bad Boy
   SARAH D. FOGLE   146

Reframing Jameis Winston: Fan Response When Players
Go "Bad"
   JOHN C. LAMOTHE   162

When "Bad Boys" Resist, "Good Ol' Boys" Revolt: Colin
Kaepernick's NFL Protest
   TAYLOR JOY MITCHELL *and* JESSICA MCKEE   175

Ronda Rousey from Badgirl to "Femininely Badass"
   JOSEPH M.M. ALDINGER   194

The Rise, Fall and Rebirth of "The Baddest Man on the Planet":
Bad Boy Mike Tyson
   BRANDY MMBAGA *and* NICK MMBAGA   208

About the Contributors   221

Index   225

Introduction

Coding and Decoding *"Badness"*

Donna J. Barbie and John C. Lamothe

At their basic level, sporting events are about numbers: wins and losses, percentages and points, shots and saves, clocks and countdowns. Athletes are initially assessed by these indicators, proving that they are worthy of attention and high praise. As David Andrews and Steven Jackson note in *Sports Stars: The Cultural Politics of Sporting Celebrity*, the sporting arena is "considered to be fundamentally meritocratic," and sporting celebrity typically is a "corollary of performative excellence" (8). However, sports narratives—expert commentary before, during, and after games; athlete interviews and press conferences; family and friend discussions around the television; and fan debates in online forums—quickly leave the realm of statistics and enter into mythos. Those narratives, the stories we tell and retell, sometimes for decades, make sports dramatic and compelling.

Just like any great drama, sports imply conflict, not just battles on the field of play, but clashes of personalities, goals, and strategies. Conflict creates heroes, elite athletes who measure up to cultural expectations and serve as role models for present and future generations. Graeme Turner contends in *Understanding Celebrity* that sports stars, particularly males, are expected to embody the heroic, serving as emblems of how life should be lived (83). However, sporting conflict also prompts tales of villainy, and in those narratives, players who miss the mark are exposed and even renounced. As Turner notes, heroism is often defined "in relation to the transgression of the accepted norms of conduct" (83–4). Sometimes, an athlete is defamed for a game or possibly a season, but occasionally players break from social expectations so often or in such a dramatic fashion that they are labeled "bad."

Although the idea may seem paradoxical, athletes must be great before they can be *bad*. From Dale Earnhardt, Sr., and Dennis Rodman to Ronda

Rousey and Marion Jones, sporting history has been punctuated by elite athletes—players at the top of their sport and well known in popular culture—who transgress norms and expectations. Whereas average professional athletes typically escape sustained media attention, those who achieve greatness are celebrated. Elite athletes, nonetheless, are also vulnerable to close scrutiny that can result in harsh judgments, and sometimes they are branded as bad for a variety of reasons, including the place they hold within the sport and larger culture.

Such assessments are neither linear nor simple, however. A great many athletes, both male and female, from a variety of sports, have been branded for myriad reasons: because of egregious behaviors on and off the field of play, because they break laws or rules or social norms, because they have bad relationships with the sports media or fans, or because they do not represent the ideals the culture expects of sports figures. Although "badness" may be forced upon some athletes, other players not only embrace the moniker, but actually cultivate that reputation. Regardless of the circumstances, Chris Rojek argues in *Celebrity* that cultures often view notoriety as "charming" and even "extremely seductive" (172). In essence, notorious sports figures can find themselves more highly celebrated because of their transgressions.

In this collection, contributors examine notorious sports figures through the lens of their purported badness. Authors explore the behaviors and factors that have qualified players to be deemed bad, and they analyze and sometimes deconstruct the premises that have resulted in branding. In other words, the contributors "break down bad." These commentaries allow us to analyze and critique important aspects not only of the sporting world, but also of the larger culture. What does it say about our heroes and villains? What does it communicate about gender and sex and race? How does it reveal the values we hold and the hypocrisies we avoid acknowledging? All of these concepts are wrapped up in the question of what constitutes badness in sports. This collection explores elite bad boy players and their place in both the sporting world and broader culture. Each essay focuses on a central figure, and in one case a comparison of two figures, within a specific sport, as a means to explore larger sporting and social issues.

A Note About Language

Because this book centers on "bad boys" in sports, that concept begs analysis. Typically more than simplistic models of badness, bad boys often carry a cultural cachet. They cross boundaries and break the rules, but in doing so, they are also given a wink and a nod as free spirits, rebels, and rugged individuals. In sum, they are "cool." In many ways, bad boy is more in line with "bad ass" than it is with just being bad, and many individuals from a variety of entertainment and celebrity industries have capitalized on that image. Of course, bad boys often maintain a precarious liminal space. Without regularly reinforcing the bad boy persona through speech, actions, or image, they lose their "edginess" and drift back toward the mainstream. At the same time, bad boys can go too far—be too extreme, too incendiary, or too insensitive—and move into the realm of being just bad; they lose their coolness and instead can be despised, feared, or pitied. The sports figures in this book maintain various positions along this spectrum and sometimes shift positions throughout their career or depending on the audience.

However, we recognize that the term "bad boy" can also be problematic because the signifier may be read as gendered male without a female equivalent. Although "bad girl" may relay similar images as bad boys in certain social groups, the female version is often sexualized, a connotation that does not apply (or to a much lesser degree) to bad boys. In the Ronda Rousey essay, nonetheless, the author uses "badgirl" (no space) as an equivalent term for a female bad boy. Throughout this book, "bad boy" is not gender-specific, but rather a reference to a person's position within a sport or culture. In other words, a bad boy—a person who has crossed particular boundaries—can be either male or female.

Secondly, the word "boy" is tied to a history of racial bigotry. Although "bad boy" is often disconnected from race, overt references to "boy" within racial contexts are both vulgar and hurtful. For the most part, within this text, "bad boy" remains disconnected from race; however, several essays directly address the role that race plays in such labeling. That issue is explored most deeply in the essay on Colin Kaepernick.

What Sports, Which Athletes, and What Order?

It would be easy to fill a book with examples of elite athletes who have broken laws or committed violence on or off the field. Oftentimes, those kinds of acts are the first that come to mind. Similarly, we might have focused exclusively on male athletes from professional football, basketball, and baseball as those sports receive the majority of media coverage in the U.S. However, doing so would have presented a narrow spectrum of subjects. Within every sport, players cross lines, but what constitutes boundary-crossing is as varied as the sports themselves. We have included essays on players who committed violent or illegal actions, but other essays focus on athletes who have been labeled "bad for the sport" because of what they say, how they dress, what they do when they are not competing, or because their behaviors do not reflect gender expectations.

4   Introduction

The centerpiece of each essay is a well-known, elite athlete, and in an effort to address the important nuances of bad boy athletes, we have included a wide variety of sports. Popular contact sports, like football and boxing, are more obviously connected to potential bad boys, but even sports like figure skating and swimming have produced notorious players. Because crossing lines into villainy is not confined to male athletes, several essays comment on infamous female athletes. Most importantly, every essay addresses a variety of social and cultural issues—from the impact of the media and fans; to issues such as cheating, legacies, expectations, addictions, and lying; to the role that race, gender, sex, or social class plays in labeling heroes and villains.

Although a number of organizational strategies might have worked well for this collection, we have ordered the essays on a scale of physical aggression that players typically enact during play. Moving from the least to most potential physical aggressiveness, the book begins with figure skating, golf, track and field, and swimming and ends with essays focused on sports where player aggression is a given or even a necessity, including football, mixed martial arts, and boxing. Certainly, the order is arguable; in fact, we debated the merits of various configurations (as all good sports fans love to do), but putting aside the nitpicky questions of whether golf is less physically aggressive than swimming, the overall structure achieves our goal of widening the definition and examination of badness in the sporting arena.

The Essays

Lynnette Porter's "'Not Good for the Sport'? Fabulous Figure Skater and Controversial Critic Johnny Weir" examines two-time U.S. Olympian and three-time national figure skating champion Johnny Weir as a unique bad boy. The exceptionally driven and hard-working Weir is unlike other athletes who have broken laws or stirred up controversy arising from such socially unacceptable behaviors as excessive alcohol consumption or gambling. Instead, the "flamboyant" Weir's gender performance on the ice, as well as content during interviews, prompted commentators to raise questions about his sexual orientation. Ultimately a number of critics brand him as "bad for the sport."

In "John Daly: Golf's *Enfant Terrible*," Donna J. Barbie features one of the most infamous bad boys in golf, a sport that typically requires physical and mental discipline. Literally leaping into celebrity as a rookie by winning the 1991 PGA Championship, Daly came to be known for his powerful swing and his antics on the course. Daly, whose nicknames include "Wild Thing," is the consummate example of a sports celebrity whose untamed appetites for food, tobacco, drink, women, and gambling disrupted his personal life and his professional career. Barbie claims that Daly's worst transgression was squandering the natural talent that could have taken him to greater heights.

"Nothing but the Truth: The Rise and Fall of Marion Jones," written by Brock T. Adams, constitutes a rhetorical analysis of Marion Jones and the dichotomous roles she played in the sporting community. After becoming the most decorated woman in track and field history at the 2000 Summer Olympics in Sydney, Jones fell from grace as a participant in one of the most notorious drug scandals in contemporary sports, the BALCO performance-enhancing drug schemes. Adams highlights how the sprinter's "win at all costs" attitude and actions shocked the world, and he argues that her adamant denials of involvement with BALCO not only cheated the sport and the fans but also forever tarnished her once flawless reputation.

Steve Master's "Lessons from #LochMess: Ryan Lochte in Our Rush-to-Judgment Culture" notes that cultivating a reputation as a bad boy doesn't necessarily require years—or even weeks—of misdeeds, as evidenced by American swimmer Ryan Lochte. Lochte's misstep, a booze-fueled misadventure at a gas station during the 2016 Summer Olympics in Rio de Janeiro, will forever stain his career as the second greatest swimmer in history. Master explores how and why an event that was not a crime—and, contrary to initial reports, not much of a cover-up—tarnished decades of accomplishments and whether we expect too much of our Olympians' personal conduct and too little from our news media's often sensationalized Olympics coverage. According to Master, the intellectual laziness and *Schadenfreude* exhibited by the public during the scandal was no less irresponsible than the swimmer's party night gone awry.

Ismael Lopez Medel's "Diego Maradona: The Hand of God" examines soccer's bad boy Diego Armando Maradona and his fandom's fanaticism, a phenomenon that goes beyond anything the sport has previously witnessed, even twenty years after his retirement. Lopez Medel asserts that Maradona's story reveals the profound cultural importance of soccer, as a significant aspect of the social fabric of not just Argentina, but also the world. Raised in poverty and a culture of hopelessness, Maradona embodied Argentinian pride as he led his teams to victory. Lopez Medel asserts that Maradona's phenomenal professional career was overshadowed by personal issues that included Mafia connections, drug abuse, house arrests, alcohol excesses, accusations of domestic abuse, tax evasion, controversial opinions, and radical political choices.

"Barry Bonds v. Alex Rodriguez: Don't Hate the Player; Hate the Steroid-Manufactured Game" by Brock T. Adams is a critical analysis of the similar, but significantly divergent, baseball careers of Barry Bonds and Alex Rodriguez. Although Bonds and Rodriquez were both exposed for their involvement in taking performance-enhancing drugs, Bonds, baseball's all-time home run king, became the sport's bad boy. Adams argues that Bonds, despite his greatness on the field, was pilloried in the baseball community because of his contentious relationship with his teammates and the media. A-Rod, on the other hand, was able to restore his reputation by cultivating an image of repentance and sincerity through his media savvy. Comparing and contrasting these two sports greats reveals the critical role the media plays in determining the good and bad in sports history, the way celebrities respond to and manage their public personas, and ultimately how we think about heroes and villains in contemporary culture.

In "No Coward: Hope Solo Battles vs. Status Quo, Injustices and, Sometimes, Her Own Poor Decisions" Joe Gisondi investigates how the media has covered Hope Solo, a world-class athlete, both on and off the soccer field. Gisondi contends that many female athletes act similarly to men on the field, displaying confidence, cockiness, happiness, and displeasure, and contends that those identical behaviors in women often evoke harsher criticism from journalists and fans. At least a few sports commentators have tried equating the fight Solo had with her cousin to the violent actions of Ray Rice and other NFL players—even though the acts are not similar in any way. This essay addresses the double standards in perceptions of female athletes in general, and of Hope Solo in particular.

"The Book of Dale Earnhardt: Beyond the Intimidator's Last Lap," written by Teresa Marie Kelly, analyzes why the "Intimidator's" on-track reputation endeared him to racing fans and emerged as an integral element of NASCAR culture. Kelly asserts that Earnhardt's tragic death in Daytona completed his public transformation from bad boy to folk hero and illustrates how portrayals of Earnhardt in contemporary works, including commercials, dramatized accounts, documentaries, and fiction and nonfiction, allow his legend to grow and thrive nearly two decades after his last lap.

"'Often an Eyeful, Sometimes an Earful, but Always a Handful': Dennis Rodman, Quintessential NBA Bad Boy," written by Sarah D. Fogle, features the NBA's Dennis Rodman, a player who embodies all the elements of the quintessential bad boy. He is a rule breaker both on and off the court, and he has used his body and image as a way to challenge societal norms. Even after his retirement from professional basketball, Rodman continued to make headlines as a professional wrestler, with his run-ins with the law, his gender-bending behaviors, and as a "basketball diplomat" with North Korea.

John C. Lamothe's "Reframing Jameis Winston: Fan Response When Players Go 'Bad'" examines the highs and lows of one of college football's recent bad boys to place a spotlight on how fans construct and defend their athletic heroes, often reimagining the dominant narratives along the way. Winston won the Heisman, led his team to a national championship, and brought home a truckload of other awards and accolades, but outside of Tallahassee, Florida, Winston most often is remembered for his off-field antics and troubles with the law. While the rest of the college-football community cringed at his poor decision making, the fan base for the Florida State Seminoles embraced Winston for his on-field excellence and tried to downplay his actions with rationalizations and even talk of conspiracy theories.

"When 'Bad Boys' Resist, 'Good Ol' Boys' Revolt: Colin Kaepernick's NFL Protest," coauthored by Taylor Joy Mitchell and Jessica McKee, analyzes how and why Colin Kaepernick has become the NFL's most controversial bad boy. Mitchell and McKee argue that Kaepernick gained that status precisely because his player position offends the dominant narrative that black athletes do not have the intellectual capabilities to make the calls—whether on the field or in the streets. Reviewing wide-ranging sports commentary and the history of athletic protest, the authors compare Kaepernick to the "Golden Boy" quarterback and reveal how the cultural invasiveness of racist ideology has reduced Kaepernick's body and his protest, villainizing him within football culture for speaking out against social inequalities.

Joseph M.M. Aldinger's "Ronda Rousey from Badgirl to 'Femininely Badass'" examines how the "rowdy" Ronda Rousey carefully crafted her badgirl image. Aldinger argues that Rousey not only constructed her persona, but also simultaneously created new cultural possibilities by resisting current power structures. Describing two different types of females, Rousey defines the "Do Nothin' Bitch" (DNB) and the "Femininely Badass" woman, the latter concept arising from the fighter's understanding of autonomy. Aldinger asserts that in creating clearly delineated categories, Rousey relegates DNBs to the classification of disabled figure/body.

"The Rise, Fall and Rebirth of 'The Baddest Man on the Planet': Bad Boy Mike Tyson," coauthored by Brandy Mmbaga and Nick Mmbaga, examines some of the events and processes that led to Tyson's bad boy persona. Although they acknowledge the egregious behaviors that contributed to his branding, Mmbaga and Mmbaga argue that the media played a significant role in creating and reinforcing his reputation. This essay notes that Tyson's life and reputation have included several phases as he ascended early in his career, descended after serious personal and professional transgressions, and reemerged over time through a different medium. Because this last phase happens infrequently among fallen athletes, Tyson's story is particularly compelling.

As this book illustrates, a great many elite athletes have been branded *bad*, a moniker that has adhered for myriad reasons. Although different behaviors have contributed to this designation, some common characteristics and themes are evident. All of the athletes possess the natural talent and physical skill that helped them reach the highest levels of their sport. Many, like Diego Maradona and Ronda Rousey, arose from humble beginnings and were forced to deal with difficult childhoods and formative years. Such circumstances certainly contributed to their perceptions of the world and to shaping their warrior mentalities. Several, including John Daly and Jameis Winston, were ill-prepared to deal with sudden fame, and that led them to overindulge in an array of excesses. Invariably, those excesses had a negative impact on their accomplishments. A number, including Mike Tyson, Dale Earnhardt, and Dennis Rodman have used their bad boy image to great effect by compounding both their financial and celebrity capital. A considerable number of athletic bad boys, including Johnny Weir, have been viewed as "other" within their sport and the broader culture because of race, gender, or sexual orientation. Cultural stereotypes made them more vulnerable to negative perceptions and judgments. Some athletes, like Colin Kaepernick, Hope Solo, and Ryan Lochte, simply couldn't manage to say the "right" thing when the microphones and cameras were pointed their way. Although it is clear that some threads tie these athletes together, each is unique, with individual stories that are worthy of exploring.

Works Cited

Andrews, David L., and Steven J. Jackson. *Sports Stars: The Cultural Politics of Sporting Celebrity*. Routledge, 2001.

Rojek, Chris. *Celebrity*. London: Reaktion Books, 2001.

Turner, Graeme. *Understanding Celebrity*. SAGE Publications, 2014, www.sk.sagepub.com.ezproxy.libproxy.db.erau.edu/Books/understanding-celebrity-2e.

"Not Good for the Sport"?

Fabulous Figure Skater and Controversial Critic Johnny Weir

Lynnette Porter

When thinking about a bad boy in sports, the first figures that might come to mind are macho he-men who go out brawling or have a series of scandalous sexual relationships. They may drink to excess or abuse drugs. They may seem belligerent, unrepentant, violent, rude, sexist, racist, or homophobic. Potentially worse for their careers, they may periodically display qualities that spectators do not like to admit their sports heroes have. Until a bad boy breaks the rules of the game or the law of the land, however, he can continue to be notorious and suffer no financial or legal consequences that really matter to die-hard fans or sports officials.

Yet another definition of bad boys in sports is more difficult to measure because only public perception, not the official rules nor the law, determines who is deemed "bad" and for what reason. Athletes who deviate from their sport's (or society's) norms may suffer consequences because they act or look "different" from what fans and sports officials expect to be associated with a specific sport. These bad boys develop a reputation based on their identity. Their professional reputation may become tarnished when fans or officials do not support their personal choices based on who they are.

One athlete who exemplifies the latter definition of a bad boy is figure skater Johnny Weir. His public persona is controversial, even if he is serious about figure skating and a good sport on camera. During his career as a figure skater with Olympic aspirations, he was "hardly the pro-jock-gone-wild who gets tangled in a web of drugs/violence/gambling," but he also was "not as demure as he appears on skates" (Strauss). Weir's "bad"ness instead revolves around his sexual orientation and gender identity. Speculation about whether

Weir is gay fueled much of the media's interest in the figure skater. In his autobiography, *Welcome to My World* (2011), written before he retired from figure skating, Weir explains that he preferred to have his public identity reflect his artistic athletic performances, not his sexuality, gender identity, or sexual orientation. Despite consciously crafting a unique on-ice presence that led to public assumptions that he is gay long before he officially came out, Weir only said during interviews that he was just being himself.

As a world-ranked figure skater, Weir earned national (U.S. Champion 2004–2006) and international (2001 Junior World Champion, World Championship bronze 2008, and Grand Prix medalist 2009 and 2010) titles and awards. Despite his success, the media often focused on his gender performance instead of his skating performance. His identity, rather than his status as a highly competitive and competent skater, put Weir into the bad boy category and led critics to question if he is good for the sport.

From early in his career, Weir defied the image many Americans in general and the U.S. Figure Skating Association (USFSA) in particular wanted to represent them on the world stage. In the U.S., the USFSA regulates figure skating as a result of its membership in the International Skating Union and on the U.S. Olympic Committee (U.S. Figure Skating Association). The USFSA also promotes the sport's reputation as being genteel, classy, and as artistic as it is athletic. Although pairs skating or group competitions are included within competitive figure skating, it is primarily perceived as an individual's sport, one that is expensive and elitist. Middle-class or blue-collar parents who hope their children may one day be successful Olympians often have to scrimp paycheck to paycheck or take a second job to pay for ice time and costumes. Thus, they, in particular, are likely to help ensure their children behave as expected, on and off the ice. USFSA officials and judges, as well as coaches, keep tabs on skaters throughout their amateur career, and the U.S. skating community is very insular. The illusion, if not the daily off-ice reality, for many American figure skaters is that, in addition to athleticism, their sport requires good sportsmanship, perfection in appearance, and avoidance of any controversy.

At least in part, a skater's success may hinge on reputation (such as how far someone like Weir tends to push the traditionally accepted boundaries of "masculine" costumes or skating style). Those skaters who abide by the officials' or judges' expectations may be more successfully scored when their and their rivals' quality of performance is very similar during a competition. After all, in an artistic sport like figure skating, judges have wiggle room to score a performance's creative merits and rank the "complete package" of art and athleticism required for an award-winning routine. The final determination of a performance's success "all hangs on the subjective judgment of a diverse team of judges, and not on the statistically-certain number of times [an athlete has] crossed a goal line or put a ball into or through a net" (Benton). Although competition medalists often exceed expectations for completing difficult technical elements, the most successful skaters are also exalted for their "acceptably" creative expression and idealized persona on the ice. These skaters are perceived as "good for the sport" and represent the Olympic gold standard for skating insiders as well as fans.

Perhaps that is why, decades after the 1994 attack on figure skater Nancy Kerrigan, her story, as it intersects with Olympic rival Tonya Harding's, still captures the public's imagination as such a deviation from USFSA protocol— as well as an illegal physical assault. The shocking injury to Kerrigan as she left a practice session (Longman, "Jealousy on Ice") diverges widely from the expected narrative of gentility, friendly competition, and the ideal that the best skater should win.

Kerrigan cultivated the image promoted by the USFSA and embraced by the viewing public, whereas Harding—cast as the villain later banned from the sport—never met expectations for an Olympic hopeful.

A 2017 Oscar-nominated film, *I, Tonya*, purports to be the true story of bad girl Harding, whose life as an abused child and beaten wife framed her career as a figure skater. From the start, her family's limited budget could not accommodate the expensive requirements for a national champion or an Olympic star. One scene depicts Harding confronting disdainful judges about her low scores at competitions; she later hears "off the record" that she does not present the proper image to be a world-class (or classy) skater representing the U.S. Her confrontational anger, rough language, and home-made costumes made her a bad girl within figure skating long before her husband's accomplice swung a bat at Kerrigan's knee. *I, Tonya*, in particular, portrays Harding as a victim, not only of her home life but also of the (for her) unrealistic expectations of the USFSA who wanted to give fans and the American public the perfect ice princess as Olympic medalist.

Those expectations heavily imply that successful American skaters must dedicate their lives to skating, be gracious winners or losers, and withstand public pressure to be anything less than graceful, athletic, and appropriately artistic. Those who want to remain in the good graces of the USFSA are interested in doing their best but also following the protocol of gentility important to the way the public perceives figure skating. Figure skaters should stand out because of their athletic artistry and expertise, not because they seem socially "other," not only from other skaters but from public "norms."

Johnny Weir has often failed to meet public or USFSA "norms" on or off the ice. As a result, during competitions he could not capitalize on the judges' wiggle room in scoring because of his "feminized" appearance or flirtatious wiggle during a televised performance broadcast to the world. To some fans and critics, he seemed not to live up to his athletic promise as a medal winner because he chose not to live up to the USFSA's or public expectations for male skaters.

Being "good for the sport" also involves representing the U.S. during international competitions and illustrating to the world—on or off the ice—the class, sense of fair play, dedication to the sport, and ability to win expected of U.S. athletes. The values that U.S. champion figure skaters are expected to uphold reflect upper-class ideals, gender politics, a long history of competition and tradition, and the personal biases of fans, coaches, judges, and USFSA officials. United States' values are as much on display as world-class figure skating. Despite Weir's dedication to figure skating, resulting in being named to two U.S. Olympic teams, bias against him has manifested because he insists on being who he is—even during performances when Olympic gold is on the line. During a pre–Olympics interview in 2010, Weir admitted that "If I was out to please 10-year-old girls and their 45-year-old mothers in Boise, Idaho, I could play the game and be nice and make my voice deeper. But I don't see the point. I'm not alive for 10-year-old girls and their 45-year-old mothers in Boise, Idaho—or Colorado Springs, Colo[rado]," where the USFSA is based. During the media promotion leading to the 2010 Winter Games, Weir also claimed that the skating federation promoted Evan Lysacek, a more "manly" skater known for his athletic, rather than artistic, performances (Schwarz), as a subtle punishment for Weir's behavior. Unlike Harding, however, Weir has never portrayed himself as a victim of bad press and unfair expectations. Instead, he praises his family for giving him the confidence to speak his mind and be exactly who he is, whether on the ice, during an interview, or, later, in a broadcast booth.

When broadcasters or sportswriters identify a bad boy of figure skating, the definition shifts from merely being a controversial figure. The label is based primarily on perceptions of a skater's gender identity or sexual orientation. Being a bad boy in figure skating has become defined by a male skater's perceived lack of American-defined masculinity and his inappropriateness to serve as a role model for youth who want to succeed in his sport and as a representative of what the U.S. stands for when its athletes participate in an Olympics.

The Development of a Bad Boy: Masculinity (or Perceived Lack of) in Figure Skating

Weir began skating at the relatively old age of 12. However, he was a prodigy who taught himself how to perform a double axel jump by watching Olympians Kerrigan and Oksana Baiul on television. Perhaps from these women's performances Weir also first developed his sense of dramatic flair in style and costume that he would incorporate when he began competing. From the start, Weir stood out for his natural athleticism and ability to see a jump performed and replicate the move himself. As a result, he acquired a professional coach early in his teens and won his first senior national title at 18 (Weir 22–31).

Weir also stood out for the public persona he cultivated off the ice. He always has been disturbingly uncensored when talking with the media. Early in his career, he described his costume as "an icicle on coke" and a "Care Bear on acid"; after these quotations were published, the skating federation duly slapped Weir on the wrist because he mentioned drugs in interviews taking place during a U.S. national championship. The unspoken message to Weir was that "skaters should be seen—preferably doing a triple salchow—and not heard" (Strauss). As might be expected within the elite figure skating community, USFSA took Weir to task for being outspoken and personifying what one journalist described as "the grandest hopes and most nightmarish fears of his sport's governing officials" (Shipley).

Figure skating is, again, unlike many other sports. An NFL star, for example, most likely would never be officially reprimanded for such a benign reference to drugs. After all, Weir was not advocating drug use or confessing to the media that he snorted coke or dropped acid. He was merely describing his costumes—albeit with unique word choices. Nonetheless, the USFSA frowned upon the image Weir was presenting to the media, which contrasted the wholesome ideal the federation promotes.

That Weir is outspoken about figure skating and enjoys elaborate costumes is only part of the problem leading to his being classified as a bad boy. He also seems questionable because he has excelled in a sport that fails to comply with traditional forms of masculinity. Even those who recognize the physical demands of skating may think of the sport as "feminine" because of its emphasis on artistic requirements. Especially around the time of the 2010 Winter Games, which pitted Lysacek and Weir not only against other internationally ranked skaters but each other, figure skating was trying to appear more "masculine" in order to appeal to a broader audience. Lysacek embodied the "masculine" ideal better than did Weir. Lysacek knew how to play the game, was dating ESPN's Hottest Female Athlete 2006 (Tanith Belbin), and wore a plain black bodysuit during performances. Thus, unlike Weir, he fit the public expectation of a "masculine" figure skater (Schwarz).

Part of Weir's preference for showmanship likely was fostered in the early 2000s, when the novice figure skater began performing at national competitions. At that time, skaters were encouraged to develop characters through costume, body language, and musical interpretation. Furthermore, since the 1970s, sequins and spandex have become the norm, and male figure skaters either have embraced such costuming and performance style or fought against them. In a "sports world that worships manliness," some figure skaters, such as two-time Olympic silver medalist Elvis Stojko, chose to insert martial arts moves into routines and select pounding music for competition performances. Olympian Michael Weiss' routines "advertised his masculinity so insistently" that audiences might not have been surprised if the skater had worn a t-shirt "stained from an oil change, a box of Marlboros rolled up in a sleeve," and sported a skull tattoo (Caple, "Johnny Weir is a Real Man"). Lysacek followed in their manly footsteps.

To further illustrate the contrast between Weir and other recent U.S. male Olympic figure skaters, an example of pre–Olympics publicity emphasizes athleticism rather than artistry and implies the skater's masculinity—a trend that continues since the Lysacek-Weir on-ice rivalry. Before the 2018 Winter Games, a *New York Times* article about national champion Nathan Chen noted that his costume for the long program is "a unitard that has no sequins, giving Chen the unadorned athletic look of a bobsledder or speed skater"—who are apparently more visually masculine than a figure skater (Longman, "Why Nathan Chen"). Although the article only mentions sequins once, its title, "Why Nathan Chen Shuns Sequins," quickly attempts to separate Chen from association with sequin-wearing male figure skaters, such as Weir, and to align him more desirably with "masculine" male athletes.

Thus, skaters like Stojko, Weiss, Lysacek, or Chen provide a "masculine" model of how male figure skaters should look or what kind of professional image they should convey through performance. Their masculine "look" is more closely aligned with the aerodynamic, form-fitting attire typically worn by male gymnasts, whose sport is perceived by the public as more masculine than figure skating. Gymnastics is also unlike figure skating in that it "is not built for show. The gymnasts wear uniforms, not costumes." Furthermore, "the artistry of gymnastics has diminished in recent years" through a greater emphasis on strength and power (Meyers), a shift similar to that advocated through the performances of Stojko, Weiss, Lysacek, or Chen. Lysacek's desire to make figure skating more athletic with dynamic stunts and aerodynamic attire (and thus more akin to a sport like gymnastics) resulted in Weir commenting during an interview that "If [Lysacek] doesn't want to skate to music that's pretty and wear a pretty costume, then go rollerblade or skateboard or do one of those extreme sports" (Schwarz). For Weir, artistry is key to his sport.

In his most memorable performances, Weir created characters like a fallen angel, graceful swan, or Jesus Christ. He wore spectacular costumes covered in see-through mesh, feathers, fur, and lots of sequins, as well as make-up applied heavily enough that spectators seated rows back from the ice could see it. Aided by these props, Weir employed appropriate facial expressions and style of movement (e.g., gentle and graceful, aggressive and powerful) to get across his interpretation of a character, especially in the footwork sequences or lead-ins to jumps or spins.

A 2006 *Washington Post* article, for example, begins with a description of Weir's crimson-streaked hair and costumes "with a massive sequined broken heart ... sheer purple fabric, off-the-shoulder necklines ... a silver-and-white cascade of glitter and sparkle ... [and] a red glove [named Camille] on his right hand" (Shipley). Comments such as this, which focus on appearance many spectators thought of as feminine (or at least not masculine), led the media and the public to question Weir's sexual orientation throughout his skating career.

As Tamar Z. Semerjian and Jodi H. Cohen noted in their study of issues facing queer figure skaters,[1] "male figure skaters such as Johnny Weir have been able to display not only characteristics typically identified as feminine but camp performances." Throughout his career as an athlete, Weir was in his element in the "highly performative space of figure skating," although judges, critics, and many television viewers had difficulty accepting Weir's performances and costumes that significantly differed from other male skaters."

A prime example is Weir's long (free) program at the 2010 Winter Games, where his fans, more than the judges, appreciated his performance. A YouTube video shows Weir skating flawlessly, receiving zero deductions from his score. His graceful moves and powerful jumps and spins are choreographed to the music. His black-and-white costume, although sequined and meshed, is more conservative than most of his outfits but evokes both the angelic (through a white top with cutout areas and the illusion of feathers) and the fall (through dark trousers and skates). In particular, Weir's balletic glides and graceful hand gestures capture the essence of the angel before the fall. When the music's pace increases to indicate the fall, so do Weir's emotional intensity and skating speed, and the audience begins to clap in time to the faster beat. After each jump or combination of jumps in the final minute, the audience cheers and applauds. At the end of the five-minute emotional journey for both Weir and his audience, the tearful kneeling skater pumps his fist before standing to wave to his fans. On camera, Weir insists on wearing the crown of red roses given to him by a fan, even though his coach tries to take it from him, and he holds a huge bouquet of red and cream roses. When the scores are read, the audience groans, but Weir brushes off his fifth-place ranking (at that point in the competition; he ultimately finished in sixth place). Instead, he smiles, stands, and waves to the crowd ("Johnny Weir—FS 'Fallen Angel'").

In his autobiography, Weir described his coach's reaction to similar low scores for his 2010 Olympic short program, featuring both classical music and a "dirty rumba" in which Weir not only nailed his jumps but also "wiggled

[his] butt and started to give major face…. [He] flirted with the audience and the judges" (Weir 247). Fans cheered wildly, but the judges ranked him far down the list of potential medal winners. Weir recounted that his coach told him, "Of course they did this to you. Don't be shocked. Just deal with it. The people love you and respect you" (Weir 248).

Weir has celebrated his "otherness" from fellow skaters and emphasized his "free to be me" choices in the way he represents himself as a U.S. athlete, even if that differs from the way that the American public, other male skaters, USFSA officials, or judges believe a representative of the U.S. should look or behave. On camera after his final career performance, Weir's "otherness" from the skaters with whom he was competing was apparent. Unlike his competitors, he chose to wear a wreath of roses during close-ups, where his make-up was also more obvious. His grace on the ice was evocative of ballet, which, in the U.S., is not considered a "manly" occupation. Although Weir clearly came across as a talented athlete, he was perceived by critics as being less "traditionally masculine" than other male singles skaters, including Lysacek. Gold-medal-winning Lysacek, for example, skated powerfully but not balletically and showed exuberance without tears at the conclusion of a flawless performance ("Vancouver 2010"). Needless to say, he did not don a rose crown, and, in close ups, his facial stubble and lack of visible make-up made him seem more "masculine" and more "typically" representative of U.S. men.

The artistry that endeared Weir to his fans also led sportscasters to question not only his masculinity but whether skating can be a real sport if it is basically a "girls'" artistic activity. To the sport's gender critics, the difference between men's and women's figure skating—more jumps with more rotations, less artistry—is not enough of a distinction to make figure skating "masculine." Even when ESPN sportswriter Jim Caple appeared to defend figure skating as an Olympics-worthy sport before the 2010 Winter Games, he could not resist poking fun at its lack of masculinity. Caple wrote that "figure skating requires a level of strength, balance and agility that few other athletes can match. Imagine leaping high and powerfully enough to spin your entire body four revolutions, then landing flawlessly on a quarter-inch metal blade and continuing to skate." He added that this description is only of one jump, which is often followed by another and another or with spins. Skaters glide forward or backward with apparent ease, unlike spectators like Caple, who have a difficult time imagining "doing anything on ice without falling on your ass." Yet, two paragraphs later, Caple concluded his description of figure skating by listing its other attributes: "Of course, it would be a lot easier to argue that figure skating is as manly as, say football, if it weren't for the costumes. And the sequins. And the glitter. And the makeup. And the judges. And the kiss-and-cry zones where the skaters sit nervously and wait for their scores while holding stuffed animals and flowers tossed by fans" (Caple, "Johnny

Weir Is a Real Man"). *Masculine* is not a term that sportswriters, or even some fans, might use when speaking about male American figure skaters.

A study published in 2016 helps explain why people who identify with sports like U.S. football may have difficulty understanding or accepting figure skating or skaters. Woojun Lee and George B. Cunningham's study measured "the association among sexual prejudice, sexism, gender, and identification with different sports" (469), specifically, football and men's figure skating. As might be expected, more respondents identified with football rather than skating. Lee and Cunningham's results indicate that those who identified with football are more likely to be more sexually prejudiced. They were "significantly unlikely to identify with men's figure skating" (Lee and Cunningham 467). Women more often identified with men's figure skating, a finding supported by the composition of Weir's international fan base. Furthermore, football, as described in this study, represents assertiveness, violence, and traditional forms of masculinity; "figure skating largely lacks these characteristics" (Lee and Cunningham 469). This study is especially interesting in light of the USFSA's attempt to broaden figure skating's audience so far as to include NFL fans. Yet, as one *Seattle Times* reporter reminded fans in preparation for the 2010 Olympics, "While figure skating tries to become more mainstream and looks for some love from the NFL-loving fans, while it tries to 'masculinize' its sport, it shouldn't forget about athletic showmen like Johnny Weir. He is too good and too charismatic to be ignored" (Kelley).

A range of published interview comments from 2014 onward highlight Weir's perceived difference from "masculine" skaters and the "norms" figuring into mainstream sports (e.g., NFL) fans' expectations of athletes representing the United States. A 2014 *BuzzFeed* article cited a U.S. coach and former Olympian (who wanted to remain anonymous) saying that "Europe has more masculine-type skating" and "no straight man wants to see a man in sequins or crap like that." More specifically, he mentioned Weir as a top skater who was so "flamboyant" that "he was bad for the sport, really, because for a while he was ... the face of the federation." He added that he knew lots of people who "would not turn on the TV and watch [figure skating] because of that. That's a problem" (Braverman). "I don't need to see a prima ballerina on the ice," announcer Mark Lund once proclaimed in discussing Weir (Schwarz). A flamboyant ballerina is not a masculine image most Americans can support, much less when it is compared with that of a pro football player.

Weir's presence at national championships and international competitions encouraged sportscasters to wonder whether "Johnny Weird" is male or female because of his choice of sport and his artistic expression. Many male sportscasters' definition of *masculinity* varies from Weir's, which might be best described as representing a global rather than national outlook. As a result of his travels, Weir recognizes that his masculinity more closely meets other nations' standards. In the U.S., Weir commented during an interview, a male ballet dancer would "get beat up and left on the side of the road," whereas in Russia he is revered as "what a man is." Especially in Japan, Weir reported, masculinity equates to "making sure your hair is completely gelled and coiffed and that you're dressed and decked to the nines." Weir's assertion is that masculinity is "what you make it out to be. Here in the U.S., not everyone feels the same way" (Zeigler). By setting himself up at the opposite end of the "manliness" scale created from the expectation that masculine athletes are more like football players, Weir reinforced his critics' belief that he could never fit into the traditional sphere of men's sports or, in truth, be a "real man."

Two Australian broadcasters covering the 2010 Winter Games questioned Weir's masculinity and his sexual orientation. They first said that male figure skaters do not leave anything in the locker room, prompting a quip of "or in the closet." Later they teased that the skating competition was going poorly because "the organi[z]ation found out one of the ice dancers wasn't gay." The broadcasters then critiqued male figure skaters' costumes to determine which athlete was not gay, ending with a photo of Weir wearing a rose crown and carrying a bouquet. The broadcasters exclaimed "but it definitely wasn't this guy" ("These 2 Aussie Commentators").

In a subsequent on-air commentary in Canada, one sportscaster asked his partner whether he thought Weir lost points during the "Fallen Angel" program "due to his costume and his body language." Without specifically commenting on the judges' decision, the second sportscaster replied that people will "think all the boys who skate will end up like him. It sets a bad example," leading to the follow-up comment that Weir "should pass a gender test at this point" ("The 2 Canadian Sportscasters").

Such comments support the "rugged man" or football player model of masculinity and indicate no socially acceptable deviance from this "norm," especially in sports. That Weir participates in figure skating, which already invites questions about male-gender appropriateness because of its artistry, only exacerbates many sportscasters' criticisms. Weir, however, refuses to be (queer)baited by this type of media coverage. Instead of showing anger or embarrassment at these comments, Weir used the opportunity to turn media scrutiny into a way to serve as a role model, especially for LGBTQA+ youth.

Weir as a Role Model

During a press conference that Weir called after 2010 Winter Games sportscasters' questions and jibes about his sexual orientation and gender, he bemusedly pointed out his facial stubble as one proof that he is a man. Weir then turned his possible public embarrassment or victimization into a statement of empowerment for young people who feel "other" or outside social expectations of who they should be. He told the media that "I hope more children have the same opportunities as me [sic] and the same sort of parents I did, who taught me to be an individual, gave me freedom and taught me to believe in myself. I hope more young boys and girls grow up to have that bedrock of support from their families" (Caple, "Seizing the Olympic Day"). Instead of simply addressing the broadcasters' comments for self-vindication, Weir saw an opportunity to potentially help future generations. Because "[e]ven my gender has been questioned," Weir wanted his situation "to be public because I don't want 50 years from now more young boys and girls to have to go through this sort of thing and to have their whole life basically questioned for no reason other than to make a joke." Weir added that people should not be defined by gender, sexual orientation, or race but by their values (Bierly). By speaking out in this way, Weir is good for his sport because he uses his celebrity and notoriety to support young people who are questioning their sexual orientation or gender identity.

Weir is gay and sees himself as a role model for young people who feel "other" from their peers; however, that combination does not make him the ideal "gay role model" that others would like him to be. Just as in figure skating, Weir does what he thinks is best, but that means he frequently has confronted critics who want him to fit their expectations of a role model.

In 2011, Weir formally came out in his autobiography, *Welcome to My World*. The dozens of media articles announcing his "news" often republished photographs as examples of his "gayness." CBS included a likely titillating-to-readers statement that Weir "once posed for a photo shoot in a skirt and stilettos" ("Johnny Weir, Figure Skater") but added that, throughout his career, he had rebuffed questions about whether he is homosexual because he does not want to be labeled for who he inherently is but because of what he does. However, the media persist in featuring "gay" photos of Weir to draw readers into their articles. Out of all the potential photographs to include with their online February 2018 article initially published in *Impact* magazine, Lambda Legal chose one of Weir wearing only fur briefs and stilettos, his hair in an up do, and his hands defiantly on hips ("Sass on Ice"). The photo of Weir wearing a crown of red roses similarly has been used in articles discussing his sexual orientation, as if these images provide visual evidence that, during his figure skating career, he was gay, just as the public suspected.

Weir has often been criticized for not coming out publicly much earlier in his figure skating career, especially as an Olympian, because that would have made a greater statement than waiting until his competition days were over. Before and during the 2018 Winter Games, the media praised figure skater Adam Rippon and skier Gus Kenworthy as the first openly out athletes to compete in the Olympics. Weir posted what became a highly controversial tweet beginning with the innocuous statement that he was "happy that there are out representatives of the LGBTQ community" competing in the Games. The controversial next line—"I never 'came out' in sport because being gay was something born in me & had nothing to do with my skating. I never came out as white"—led to immediate social media backlash. Weir then removed this tweet. In a series of follow-up posts, Weir reiterated that he was "thrilled" to see publicly out athletes compete in the Games, he was not publicly out when he competed as an Olympian, and living one's truth in public is a brave act. Finally, Weir tweeted that "I wear my sexuality the same as I wear my sex or my skin color. It is something that simply is and something I was born into. I never 'came out' in sport because I didn't imagine it as a great secret," and it had nothing to do with his ability to skate (Reynolds).

Some critics may question Weir's timing of his official coming out announcement in his autobiography, which was published a year after Weir's performances at his final Olympics, the 2010 Games in Vancouver. After all, if he did not feel the need to come out as "white" because his race is an inherent part of him, why did he then eventually decide to come out as "gay" and publicly announce another inherent part of who he is? The publicity surrounding the publication of his book helped Weir keep his name in the media as his figure skating career was winding down before his retirement in 2013. Thus, cynics might suspect Weir's motive for "revealing" his sexual orientation in 2011 had little to do with seeking greater public acceptance for everyone in the LGBTQA+ community and more with gaining media attention for himself and his post-figure skating projects.

Despite Weir's nonchalance about coming out because it was, for him, a non-issue, U.S. figure skating has not always been a welcoming sport to gay athletes. In 1996, Rudy Galindo, an openly gay singles skater, won gold at the U.S. National Championship and a bronze medal at Worlds. In a 2018 interview about the history of figure skating, Galindo reiterated the difficulty of being a gay role model when it was not politically correct.

> I was told by the authorities within my sport to skate in a certain masculine way.... My sometimes controversial costumes were hyper-analyzed by authorities in the sport.... As the power brokers within my sport tried to contain me, I was equally steadfast in attempting to break through the barriers and show the world who Rudy Galindo truly was, and is to this day [O'Callaghan].

Galindo added that his isolation because of others' expectations made him feel like "an island in an open sea" (O'Callaghan). Weir faced similar scrutiny during the time before gay Olympians like figure skater Rippon were openly celebrated. Even if Weir insists that the timing of his "coming out" had nothing to do with his skating career, the fact remains that he was under enough scrutiny for "being himself" without having to live up to expectations as a gay role model or even more backlash because he had become "officially" gay. He may not have wanted the extra controversy or expectations in an already highly scrutinized public life.

Weir offers another explanation for the timing of his "coming out" announcement. In his autobiography, he discussed that backlash does not motivate him to change; he does not bow to pressure from others to do something he does not believe is right for his life. He emphasized that "All the gay websites couldn't figure out why I was such a jerk that I wouldn't talk about it. But pressure is the last thing that would make me want to 'join' a community" (Stewart). In other words, he stubbornly waited to announce his sexual orientation to the media when it suited his purpose, not the gay community's.

Weir also did not bow to public pressure in the weeks leading to his official debut as a permanent NBC sports commentator covering the 2014 Winter Games in Sochi. To people who wanted to use the Olympics as an opportunity to highlight "Russia's oppressive anti-gay laws, Weir's defense of the games—and criticism of calls to boycott them—[were] jarring," especially to the LGBTQA+ community and its supporters. Additionally, some anti-gay activists, fearful that a gay man would be discussing gay figure skaters on NBC, "convinced themselves that the Olympics are no longer safe for children" (Ohlheiser). Yet, to Weir, simply being a gay athlete or broadcaster at the Olympics was a powerful symbol. His presence would send a stronger message than a boycott that hurt athletes, not the Russian government. It would rebuff anti-gay activists because he would be as professional as any straight broadcaster. Furthermore, he responded personally to the call for him to stay home from the Games. He emphasized that Olympic athletes have "all given up our lives for the Olympics.... I would never want my life's work to come down to a boycott" ("Gay Olympian to Athletes").

However, Weir can admit when he has been politically naïve. After meeting gay activists in Russia, Weir learned a great deal more about Russian oppression of non-heteronormative citizens. As a result, while in Sochi covering figure skating for NBC, he hosted a filmed-in-secret documentary, *To Russia with Love,* in which he interviewed Russian gay activists. The documentary is described as examining "human rights through the lens of two generations of LGBT athletes" (Schweigert). During the filming, Weir met a young activist who talked openly about his struggles in Russia. Because of this encounter, the former U.S. Olympian said the activist "was able to lift my rose-colored glasses" about "a country that I *love* so much." [Weir is a well-known Russophile.] Weir began to "understand something that I knew I had to fight for with this film" in the hope that many people would see it and become better educated about Russia's legal stance on homosexuality and its repercussions (Schweigert). Throughout his public life, Weir has decided how and when to fight for change. Along the way, he often becomes a role model, if not the ideal gay role model the LGBTQA+ community would like him to be.

Weir as a Bad Boy Broadcaster and Reality Television Star

Weir's decision to be himself as a figure skater—despite the very real possibility of professional disapproval and harsher judging—has been extended to his celebrity image as a sports commentator and reality show star. However, in these roles, Weir's "flamboyance" pays off and can generate greater ratings because viewers want to see what he is wearing or how his hair is styled.

As a figure skater, Weir was featured in coverage by every network around the world that recorded and commented upon competition performances. As but one commentator on one U.S. network (or one host or guest on a cable network show), Weir does not achieve such global coverage. Nevertheless, the media still describe Weir's fashion choices and the height of his coif as often as they report the quality of his comments about skating. He is still considered controversial and "other," but this time NBC, in particular, uses Weir's image to attract audiences who otherwise might not follow the network's sports coverage of figure skating or even other events, like the Kentucky Derby, where Weir's fashion-statement attire and comments are part of the show.

To gain a younger viewing audience and perhaps greater ratings, in 2018 NBC gave the coveted live Olympic figure skating coverage to Weir and former Olympic gold medal figure skater Tara Lipinski, thus relegating longtime figure skating commentator and genial Olympic figure skating gold medalist Scott Hamilton to the NBC Sports Network show *Olympic Ice*. Ever the good sport, Hamilton noted that "Johnny and Tara were just this phenomenon [beginning during the 2014 Winter Games broadcasts], and no one was going to stop them.... They were such a breath of fresh air" (Hurley). Whereas Hamilton has continually looked to the positive aspects of every skater's performance and has represented his country, sport, and NBC as an upstanding, non-controversial presence, Weir may be what the network needs to woo a larger audience or different segments of the viewing public. On national network television covering a sport that has lost popularity since its heyday in the 1990s and 2000s, Weir brings an edge that a commentator like Hamilton lacks. During the 2014 Winter Games, the *New York Times* classified Hamilton as a skating "enthusiast" who balances technical analysis with "flowery praise," whereas Weir was deemed a "fresh voice" who converses easily about technical scores and banters conversationally with Lipinski (Sandomir).

However, this type of friendly comparison was absent when Weir and Lipinski took over primetime coverage in 2018 and Weir's controversial comments made headlines. To some viewers, Weir might again be "bad for the sport," this time as a highly critical commentator. As might be expected, a sports blogger (Barstool Sports) termed Weir an "Olympic bad boy" for being "too mean to figure skaters" during his on-air commentary. Weir's critiques were brutally frank during the first skating event, when he duly noted that Nathan Chen, the rising star expected to be the best chance for the U.S. to win an individual gold medal, failed to meet expectations during the team skating event. "That's the worst short program I've ever seen from Nathan Chen," Weir said. His criticism resulted in a tweet-storm by fans who claimed Weir was too harsh. Yet, other fans praised Weir for being honest about an event in which several skaters, including Chen, fell; they preferred Weir to tell it like it was (Sobel). In response to the controversy and media coverage regarding his performance as a broadcaster, Weir tweeted "I'm a commentator, not a 'complimentator'.... I would never be able to do my job without telling the truth about every aspect of figure skating and the performances" (Root).

Weir's harsh criticism was a broad departure from the more comforting style of NBC commentators like Hamilton, who has become the sport's elder statesman. Hamilton's public persona as a married father, Christian, Olympian, and cancer survivor make him a more sympathetic figure than in-your-face Weir. Unlike Hamilton, who well represented the USFSA during his career as a good sport, successful athlete, and skater whose personal style did not court controversy, Weir has often been at odds with the USFSA and its preferred public persona for its skaters. Because figure skating has maintained a more genteel reputation than most other sports, Weir's harsh criticism rankles viewers accustomed to a classy, softer style of public commentary about fellow skaters.

Weir's critical approach to commenting about Olympic figure skating was only one reason viewers either loved or hated him. His style and on-air persona also received opposing reviews. *The Advocate* discussed Weir's fashion as much as his role as commentator and returned to the term *flamboyant* more than once: the statement "Adorning high fashion, gender non-conforming outfits at the events and unapologetically criticizing the performances in South Korea, Weir has come under fire for being too flamboyant" follows a photo caption that "When someone as proudly flamboyant as Weir headlines a network's Olympics coverage, feathers are bound to be ruffled" (Sobel). In coverage of the controversy about Weir's criticism of Chen's performance, *Vanity Fair* (which may be expected to highlight fashion over sport) added that many television viewers "just appreciated [Weir's and Lipinski's] carefully coordinated fashion efforts"; after all, "Weir's outfit choices have been known to be flashy since his days at the 2006 and 2010 Olympics" (Weaver). Weir knows how to calculate what his fans want and how best to express himself, even if (or especially because) it might generate attention.

Allure, another fashion magazine, interviewed Weir—although the publication likely would not have featured other sports commentators in a fashion piece. In an article entitled "Olympic Legend Johnny Weir Reveals the Secret to His Gravity-Defying Hair," Weir discussed fashion and explained that he does not wear lipstick on air because "there's a really fine line between drag, masculine, and feminine. I really like to blur all of those lines, but if I did the full lip and I had my mascara and the hair, it's just too much" (Kallor). Such revelations indeed may be too much for viewers who already tend not to like Weir's role as NBC commentator. Nevertheless, this statement also reveals Weir's calculating nature when it comes to how far he can push a controversial public image at a specific time or for a specific audience. Additionally, being "flamboyant" and keeping his fans and the viewing public entertained are increasingly an expectation if Weir is to maintain his celebrity status as an NBC commentator or a reality television star. Comments about his makeup and hair are one way to attract attention and maintain a controversial image.

Especially when Weir takes on reality television roles, he embraces a public expectation of "gayness" and plays to the audience. His television guest appearances include *Say Yes to the Dress*, in which he tried on a wedding dress during friend and future broadcasting partner Tara Lipinski's bridal appointment ("His Opinion"). He and Lipinski commented on fashion for *Access Hollywood* during their 86th Academy Awards coverage and for NBC's coverage of the Kentucky Derby (since 2014) and the 2016 Summer Olympics. During *Access Hollywood*'s announcement of the duo's upcoming role as fashion commentators, the show's executive producer Rob Silverstein enthused that "Fashion—and our show—is about fun, and they're fun." Silverstein added that Weir and Lipinski are successful because "they're authentic, and authenticity sells" (Kaufman). What was once perceived as bad boy behavior in figure skating is part of a lucrative post-skating career in which "flamboyance" is expected and desirable as being "authentic Weir." On television, being "bad" is very good for Weir's career.

Because Weir is no longer a figure skater performing as a U.S. representative at international competitions, he and NBC can more specifically market his fashion-forward image and a definition of masculinity that differs from many American viewers'. The network even gave Weir a "bedazzled headset" to wear during broadcasts (Kallor). The media seem happy to embrace Weir's television persona now that he is not the face of the USFSA or one of only a few U.S. athletes representing the country at the Olympics.

Weir has acknowledged that "I am outlandish and flamboyant and all those things.... There was a focus on all that in my [figure skating] career, which I am fine with, but there also was little attention paid to how hard I actually worked" ("Johnny Weir's 16-year Career Over"). He added that he wished people had emphasized his effort and tenacity "as much as my characters and my costumes." He concluded that he gave everything to his sport, a trait that he believes more accurately describes him and his work, whether on the ice or for NBC.

Unlike other "bad" athletes discussed in this book, Weir is portrayed in the media as either a groundbreaking role model or a true bad boy. The media seem to recognize no gray area, and tweet wars between Weir's fans and detractors ignite when he is on air. Whether Weir is a bad boy or how bad he seems depends on one's concern with gender, a black-or-white masculine/feminine dichotomy, or the importance of determining and then meeting a U.S. public standard for masculinity. Social constructs change over time—what is defined as "masculine" or "feminine" by one generation may not be supported by the next. However, Weir is a constant. Since the beginning of his figure skating career, he has determined how he will look during a performance and discuss himself and his career in a public forum. He seems comfortable with himself and often sees no need to filter his opinions. He is outspoken, even if his comments or tweets get him in trouble and generate more controversy. He is an ally and role model for many youths because his gender and sexual orientation have been challenged publicly. He also is savvy and calculating as he develops his post-skating image as a fashion-influencing celebrity. In short, Weir is simply himself, no matter what anyone thinks of him or expects him to be. In a post–2018 Olympics interview, Weir summarized the philosophy that guides him: "[S]howing your true colors is the most important thing that we can do in our lives.... [N]o matter how weird you are, how different you are, how eccentric, how flamboyant.... Feel free to live uniquely. Feel free to be special because life's so short" (O'Malley). From a perceived bad boy, this empowering philosophy is not so bad after all.

Note

1. The term *queer* has many connotations. In Semerjian and Cohen's study, they made *queer* an inclusive term that could be based on sexual orientation, self-identification, or lack of identification with a heteronormative identity.

Works Cited

Barstool Sports. "Olympic Bad Boy Johnny Weir Already in Trouble for Being Too Mean to Figure Skaters on Air." *Barstool Sports*, 9 Feb. 2018, bars.to/Vu6u/O9GjW825oK.

Benton, Nicholas F. "Johnny Weir Has Prevailed." *Falls Church News-Press*, 17 Feb. 2010, fcnp.com/2010/02/17/johnny-weir-has-prevailed/.

Bierly, Mandi. "Johnny Weir Responds to Commentators Who Questioned His Gender, Example He Sets." *Entertainment Weekly*, 25 Feb. 2010, www.com/article/2010/02/25/johnny-weir-olympics-gender-example/.

Braverman, Blair. "Why Is the World's Gayest Sport Stuck in the Closet?" *BuzzFeed*, 31 Jan. 2014, www.buzzfeed.com/blairbraverman/why-is-the-worlds-gayest-sport-stuck-in-the-closet?utm_term=.urbx4Rx1A#.ispnYWn39.

Caple, Jim. "Johnny Weir Is a Real Man." *ESPN*, 15 Jan. 2010, www.espn.com/espn/eticket/story?page=100114/johnnyweir.

———. "Seizing the Olympic Day." *ESPN*, 24 Feb. 2010, www.espn.in/olympics/winter/2010/columns/story?columnist=caple_jim&id=4943488.

"Gay Olympian to Athletes: Don't Boycott Winter Olympics." *Here & Now with Robin Young and Jeremy Hobson*, 2 Aug. 2013, www.hereandnow.legacy.wbur.org/2013/08/02/gay-olympian-weir.

"His Opinion." *Say Yes to the Dress*, season 8, episode 7, TLC, 7 June 2012. www.tlc.com/tv-shows/say-yes-to-the-dress/full-episodes/his-opinion.

Hurley, Laura. "How Scott Hamilton Feels About Losing His Announcing Spot to Johnny Weir and Tara Lipinski." *Cinema Blend*, Feb. 2018, www.cinemablend.com/television/2317182/how-scott-hamilton-feels-about-losing-his-announcing-spot-to-johnny-weir-and-tara-lipinski.

I, Tonya. Directed by Craig Gillespie, performances by Margot Robbie, Sebastian Stan, and Allison Janney, 2017.

"Johnny Weir, Figure Skater, Comes Out as Gay." CBS, 7 Jan. 2011, www.cbsnews.com/news/johnny-weir-figure-skater-comes-out-as-gay/.

"Johnny Weir—FS 'Fallen Angel,' 2010 Olympics." YouTube, uploaded by Elena Vasileva, 23 Aug. 2017, www.youtube.com/watch?v=PI98au8CMqA.

"Johnny Weir's 16-year Career Over." *ESPN*, 23 Oct. 2013, www.espn.com/olympics/figureskating/story/_/id/9866174/johnny-weir-retires-16-year-skating-career.

Kallor, Amber. "Olympic Legend Johnny Weir Reveals the Secret to His Gravity-Defying Hair." *Allure*, 26 Mar. 2018, www.allure.com/story/johnny-weir-interview-beauty-secrets.

Kaufman, Amy. "How Billy Bush Got Tara Lipinski and Johnny Weir an Oscars Gig." *The Los Angeles Times*, 25 Feb. 2014, www.latimes.com/entertainment/movies/moviesnow/la-et-mn-oscars-tara-lipinski-johnny-weir-access-hollywood-20140224-story.html.

Kelley, Steve. "Figure Skating's Flamboyant Johnny Weir Must Be Taken Seriously." *The Seattle Times*, 16 Jan. 2010, www.seattletimes.com/sports/figure-skatings-flamboyant-johnny-weir-must-be-taken-seriously/.

Lee, Woojun, and George B. Cunningham. "Gender, Sexism, Sexual Prejudice, and Identification with U.S. Football and Men's Figure Skating." *New York*, vol. 74, no. 9–10, May 2016, pp. 464–71. *ProQuest*.

Longman, Jére. "Jealousy on Ice." *New York Times*, 6 Jan. 1994, archive.nytimes.com/www.nytimes.com/packages/html/sports/year_in_sports/01.06.html.

———. "Why Nathan Chen Shuns Sequins." *New York Times*, 15 Feb. 2018, www.nytimes.com/2018/02/15/sports/olympics/nathan-chen-figure-skating.html.

Meyers, Dvora. "Tumbling Ice: How the Differences Between Gymnastics and Figure Skating Explain the Winter Sport's Declining Popularity." *Slate*, 11 Feb. 2014, www.slate.com/articles/sports/fivering_circus/2014/02/gymnastics_and_figure_skating_how_the_differences_between_them_explain_skating.html.

O'Callaghan, Eoin. "Adam Rippon, John Curry and Figure Skating's Complex History with Gay Athletes." *The Guardian*, 17 Feb. 2018, www.theguardian.com/sport/2018/feb/17/adam-rippon-lgbt-figure-skaters-john-curry.

Ohlheiser, Andy. "Nobody Is Pleased with Johnny Weir's Support of the Sochi Olympics." *The Atlantic*, 21 Jan. 2014, www.theatlantic.com/international/archive/2014/01/nobody-pleased-johnny-weirs-support-sochi-olympics/357232/.

O'Malley, Margaret. "How to Stand Up to Bullies, According to Johnny Weir." NBC News,

11 Apr. 2018, www.nbcnews.com/better/pop-culture/johnny-weir-standing-bullying-being-comfortable-your-own-skin-ncna865151.
Reynolds, Daniel. "Johnny Weir Explains (Twice) Why He Didn't Come Out." *The Advocate*, 18 Jan. 2018, www.advocate.com/sports/2018/1/18/johnny-weir-explains-twice-why-he-didnt-come-out.
Root, Tik. "Tara Lipinski and Johnny Weir Aren't Mean, but 'Truth Can Be Hard to Hear.'" *Washington Post*, 13 Feb. 2018, www.washingtonpost.com/news/sports/wp/2018/02/13/tara-lipinski-and-johnny-weir-arent-mean-but-truth-can-be-hard-to-hear/?utm_term =.c5ad7d69a702.
Sandomir, Richard. "From Johnny Weir's Team, a Fresh Voice for NBC." *New York Times*, 21 Feb. 2014, www.nytimes.com/2014/02/22/sports/olympics/from-jonny-weirs-team-a-fresh-voice-for-nbc.html.
"Sass on Ice: Catching Up with Olympic Figure Skater Johnny Weir." *Lambda Legal*, 9 Feb. 2018, www.lambdalegal.org/blog/20180209_johnny-weir-interview.
Schwarz, Alan. "Figure Skating Rivalry Pits Athleticism Against Artistry." *New York Times*, 18 Mar. 2008, www.nytimes.com/2008/03/18/sports/othersports/18skate.html.
Schweigert, Ken. "5 Interesting Things We Learned from Johnny Weir's 'Ask Me Anything' on Reddit.com." *Lancaster Online*, 29 Oct. 2014, lancasteronline.com/features/entertainment/interesting-things-we-learned-from-johnny-weir-s-ask-me/article_a414eac0-5f74-11e4-95f7-001a4bcf6878.html.
Semerjian, Tamar Z., and Jodi H. Cohen. "'FTM' Means Female to Me": Transgender Athletes Performing Gender." *Women in Sport and Physical Activity Journal*, vol. 15, no. 2, Fall 2006, pp. 28–43. *ProQuest*.
Shipley, Amy. "Icebreaker and His Obstacles." *Washington Post*, 7 Feb. 2006, www.washingtonpost.co/wp-dyn/content/article/2006/02/06/AR2006020601832_2.html.
Sobel, Ariel. "As a Commentator, Johnny Weir Thrills, Infuriates, and Changes Minds." *The Advocate*, 12 Feb. 2018, www.advocate.com/sports/2018/2/12/commentator-johnny-weir-thrills-infuriates-and-changes-minds.
Stewart, Dodal. "Johnny Weir Steps Out of the Glass Closet." *Jezebel*, 7 Jan. 2011, jezebel.com/5727549/johnny-weir-steps-out-of-the-glass-closet.
Strauss, Amy. "Sports: Johnny Drama." *Philadelphia Magazine*, 20 Dec. 2007, www.phillymag.co/articles/2007/12/20/johnny-drama/print/.
"These 2 Aussie Commentators Made Fun of Johnny Weir. Here's What to Do About It." *Queerty*, 19 Feb. 2010, www.queerty.com/these-2-aussie-tv-commentators-made-fun-of-johnny-weir-heres-what-to-do-about-it-20100219.
"The 2 Canadian Sportscasters Who Think Johnny Weir's Faggyness Is Bad for Figure Skating." *Queerty*, 21 Feb. 2010, www.queerty.com/the-2-canadian-sportscasters-who-think-johnny-weirs-faggyness-is-bad-for-figure-skating-20100221.
U.S. Figure Skating Association. 2017, www.usfsa.org/.
"Vancouver 2010: Evan Lysacek's Flawless Routine." NBC Olympics, 6 Feb. 2018, www.nbcolympics.com/video/vancouver-2010-evan-lysaceks-flawless-routine.
Weaver, Hilary. "Johnny Weir and Tara Lipinski Once Again Brought Looks and the Sass to the Olympics." *Vanity Fair*, 9 Feb. 2018, www.vanityfair.com/style/2018/02/johnny-weir-and-tara-lipinski-sassy-2018-winter-olympics-commentators.
Weir, Johnny. *Welcome to My World*. Gallery Press, 2011.
Zeigler, Cyd. "ESPN Confirms: Johnny Weir Is a Real Man." *Outsports*, 15 Jan. 2010, www.outsports.com/2010/1/15/4049230/espen-confirms-johnny-weir-is-a-real-man.

John Daly
Golf's Enfant Terrible

Donna J. Barbie

Observing elite athletes compete, no matter the sport, is a pleasure and a privilege. I have attended many professional golf tournaments during the past twenty years, and I have witnessed some phenomenal play, including Bubba Watson's tee shot that nearly reached the green on Bay Hill's par-five lake hole. I saw Graham McDowell's come-from-behind victory at the U.S. Open at Pebble Beach and Tiger Woods's less surprising win at Royal Liverpool to capture his eleventh major championship. In the midst of such remarkable shot making, one of my most vivid memories is not about great golf at all, but of John Daly warming up on the Bay Hill practice range in 2002.

Daly was instantly recognizable because of his signature past-parallel swing. His ball striking was pure, and the irons and woods were long—really long. Even though everyone thought he was past his prime by the late 1990s, Daly's talent and power were still manifest. But those were not the images that lodged in my memory. Instead, I recall his bleary eyes. A giant belly hung far over his belt. He chain-smoked, a cigarette in his mouth even as he hit the ball. When his pre-teen daughter brought him a new basket of practice balls, he handed her the lit cigarette while he hitched up his pants and took a swig of something. This was the man I had read about and seen on television, the player with amazing raw talent but not a whit of discipline.

As this anecdote indicates, Daly is golf's enfant terrible. Quite literally the bad baby of the sport, he is unlike scores of professional athletes who structure every aspect of their lives, especially in training their bodies. Although Daly is a golfing genius of immense natural talent, he never tolerated limitations, nor has he even considered, much less led, a life of restraint or discipline. Daly's rejection of customary behaviors and mores, on and off the course, have made him a spectacle. As David L. Andrews and Steven J. Jackson note in *Sports Stars*, some athletes blossom into heroes while others become "notorious" (2). With the possible exception of Woods, whose infamy flared relatively briefly, Daly has been the most consistently notorious professional golfer of the past two decades.

Although he racked up some impressive wins on the tour, "Wild Thing," as Daly is often called, has not always adhered to on-course decorum, especially when he is angry or frustrated. More significantly, he is the consummate example of an athlete whose appetites for nearly every vice imaginable—food, tobacco, alcohol, women, gambling—have disrupted his personal life and derailed his professional career. Yet, throughout Daly's years of very public tribulations, many fans have remained mesmerized. Some identify with his foibles, and nearly everyone, fans and commentators alike, applaud his honesty. Such applause does not necessarily spawn success on the course, however. After losing his Professional Golf Association (PGA) Tour card in 2007 because he failed to earn sufficient money to rank among the top 125 golfers on the Tour, he has relied on sponsors' exemptions or played on less prestigious tours. Over the decades of his tumultuous career, Daly has often declared himself "mature," but his assertions never come to fruition. In essence, John Daly, golf's enfant terrible, committed the elite athlete's worst sin; he squandered his natural talent.

"Wild Thing's" Professional Accomplishments Despite His Lack of Discipline

Unlike the vast majority of professional golfers, Daly did not work his way up slowly through the PGA ranks; instead, he catapulted into celebrity as a rookie by winning the 1991 PGA Championship (one of the four most important tournaments of the year). Daly writes in his 2006 memoir, *My Life In and Out of the Rough*, that his was "not a household name" prior to that victory, but "word had been spreading a little about this redneck kid from Arkansas who could really let it fly but sometimes had to do some looking for it after it landed" (1). As the ninth alternate for the PGA Championship, Daly seemed to have little chance of gaining entry into the tournament until Nick Price dropped out at the last minute and the eight players ahead of Daly were unable to make it to the venue on time. He was the final player to make the field. Daly drove through the night to get to the course, and when he stepped up to the first tee, he began smashing the ball far past his competitors. The golfing world was enchanted. In a video of that winning performance, one commentator exclaims he has "never seen such an exhibition of strength and power." He then yells, "holy mackerel" when Daly hits a nine iron 172 yards. Several others note his remarkable balance, quite a feat because his powerful swing requires precise timing ("John Daly at the 1991"). After that incredible win, Daly became an overnight sensation, the embodiment of America's favorite narrative, the underdog prevailing with raw talent and grit. That was Daly at his best, the player golfing legend Jack Nicklaus claimed would be "great for the game of golf" ("John Daly at the 1991").

Unfortunately, all too often, Daly was not at his best because he lacked the discipline to sustain and build on the brilliance he showed in 1991. Most professional golfers embrace exacting discipline to succeed on the tour. Creating rigorous regimens, they "pound balls" for hours nearly every day. They have secret diets and employ specialists to devise workout programs. They go through lots of swing coaches and search for the perfect putting technique. They learn how to govern their breathing and emotions to regulate adrenaline in the hope of ensuring consistent shot distances. And more than anything else, they hit balls—over, and over, and over again. All of that translates to control. Professional golfers typically adopt this studied approach to gain the edge over their competition. Not John Daly. He acknowledges that golf "is truly an unbelievable challenge" that "tests your coordination, muscular strength, and athletic ability; it tests your mental toughness and your ability to manage both your game and your emotions" (*Grip It* 87). Nevertheless, Daly also admits, "I let my golf game slide" because of boredom during practice sessions and declares, "You can't do much on the PGA Tour if you spend too many Saturday mornings watching cartoons" (*My Life* 61, 163). Daly clearly had difficulty with focus and motivation.

Daly's "edge" over his competitors has always been natural talent. He reports that he had no teacher or coach when he first learned to play. At the age of six, he refused to let his father cut down full-sized clubs, and he taught himself that signature long swing out of necessity. When he was a bit older, he fished balls out of the water at a local club and practiced hitting in a field. As he claims, "At first, I'd just get up there and hit everything as hard as I could—that's how 'grip it and rip it' got started" (*My Life* 21). That phrase became Daly's trademark. In essence, he inadvertently mocked other players' dogged approach with his "grip it and rip it" style. It implies simplicity. It is not a bit nuanced, no deep thinking, no mental checklists, no long practice sessions, no need for a parade of coaches. As he reports, "I hit the ball as hard as I can. If I can find the ball, I hit it again" ("Sporting Mavericks"). How much simpler could it be? In the comments section of a video featuring Daly, Drinkingpoolwater writes, "imagine training for years, spending all your free time on the range to tighten up your game … then getting beat by this dude" ("John Daly—'Tee the Ball Up'"). As this comment implies, other players might have felt at least a bit disgruntled that Daly did not really have to work at it.

From 1991 to 2014, Daly accumulated eighteen professional wins on the PGA, European, and other lesser-known tours. His triumphs have been immensely compelling, especially the ones that ended in sudden-death play-offs. The most prestigious achievement came in 1995 at the Old Course at St. Andrews when he won the highly coveted Open Championship. He grabbed that win his way, with stunning drives and audacity. Refusing to play it safe or protect his lead, he almost never laid up or used an iron off the tee. Of his game, in general, Daly declares boldly, "[Y]ou gotta let the big dog eat [use the driver]." He claims that "fearless golf" has been key to his success (*My Life* 15). In the preface to Daly's golf-instruction book, Masters champion Fuzzy Zoeller remarks on Daly's "prodigious length off the tee" but also asserts he had "great touch on and around the greens" (*Grip It* ix). No one would deny Daly's amazing natural gifts, but he failed to live up to the prediction that he would be the next golf super star. More than three decades later, he still plays professional golf, in his inimitable style. As the 2016 YouTube montage of his first year on the Champion's Tour illustrates, the fifty-year-old Daly continued to astonish with his distance. A commentator notes that his drive was "hammered, hammered, hammered … tattooed right there" ("John Daly's Best"). His amazing shot making and innate genius have not been enough to propel him to true greatness, however, and Daly will likely never become a member of the World Golf Hall of Fame. Something has clearly been missing.

The Enfant Playing the Gentleman's Game

All professional golfers suffer terrible shots and high scores, but true practitioners of the "Gentleman's Game" must take adversity in stride and mask their emotions. Great Britain gave birth to golf during the same period that the ideal of gentlemanliness was concretized. Born of the landed gentry, a gentleman was blessed with sufficient wealth to protect him from the necessity of working. He socialized with people of equal, or higher, station and occupied himself with hunting and other suitable pastimes. Because only gentlemen belonged to links clubs, golfers and gentlemen were essentially an identity, bound by the same codes. Gentlemen, for example, spoke properly, dressed appropriately, and governed their behaviors rigorously. Even under the most stressful circumstance, they presented themselves with decorum and never revealed extreme emotion. Such displays would sully a gentleman's reputation.

Despite the passage of centuries, this code persists for professional golfers, at least for the most part. They must "respect" the game by being thoroughly courteous and, of course, never showing they are out of control.

Oliver Brown, commentator for the online newspaper *The Telegraph*, writes that Bobby Jones, founder of the Masters and the Augusta National Golf Course, prized gentlemanly behavior. The back of every Masters pairing sheet bears Jones' assertion that "In golf, customs of etiquette and decorum are just as important as rules governing play." The commentary continues with an admonition: "Excessive demonstration by a player is not proper." As Jones emphasizes, "proper" golfers are never "excessive."

And then there is Daly, who relishes excess, including in his on-course attire. Although Daly's clothing was not outlandish for the bulk of his PGA career, he began donning bizarre outfits in 2008 when he became the spokesperson for Loud Mouth Golf. The look is always colorful, with very bold prints. No matter how far away a spectator is from Daly on the course, no matter how tiny he is in the television shot, no one has to play "Where's Waldo" to find him in his group. He stands out. Invariably, spectators who spot him at a tournament say such things as "Get a load of those pants," and "Who dresses him, the resident clown?" Doubtlessly, the company's marketing goals include ensuring people notice the line as well as creating a buzz. They seem to have succeeded because after Daly started wearing their clothes, Loud Mouth Golf went from $88K to $2.6 million within a year ("John Daly—Obsessive").

Some folks must like the clothes, as evidenced by boosted sales, and many fans are obviously amused by Daly's audacity. However, more seem shocked by how far Daly strays from acceptable attire. Commenting on a YouTube video that featured a bizarrely outfitted Daly, Try-For-a-Change exclaimed, "he should be penalized for wearing [those pants] in public!!!" ("John Daly Worst Shots"). *Sportsbreak* journalists declare, "he's definitely the one guy on the tour that can give us a headache just by looking at his crazy pants." One outfit featured hot pink, blue, orange, yellow, and lime green pants that looked like "a rainbow threw up all over him." Another shirt/pants combo, of hot pink and orange camouflage, made Daly seem to be an aspirant "Pepto-Bismol mascot" (Goliath Team). Although golfer Ricky Fowler recently has been criticized for wearing flamboyant clothes on the course, he cannot even begin to compete with Daly.

Daly's attire, although considerably outside golfing norms, would not necessarily preclude him from being viewed as a gentleman, but his on-course temper tantrums have done just that. Various individuals have attempted to school him on golf etiquette, including his mother and college coach. Daly admits that his mom's advice never "sank in far enough" because he has always brooded over bad play and then gets "really, really mad" at himself. He continues, "Sometimes I'll just kind of explode inside while I'm on the course. Sometimes I'll lose it altogether, just go haywire" (*My Life* 25). Those explosions have taken place throughout his career, all around the globe. He has been disqualified from a considerable number of tournaments; at least once, he verbally accosted a tournament official after making a bad score; and he smashed a spectator's camera because he felt the guy was encroaching on his territory ("Daly snatches").

When Daly melts down, he loses control of his behavior and his game. As Johnette Howard of CBS writes, Daly has had "the most epic golf blowups" ever. By 2016, Daly had posted 17 double-digit scores on a single hole at PGA events. The next closest "competitor" for this distinction has only five. Golf.com additionally reports that Daly has two entries on the list of the top ten "Worst Holes in Golf History." His 11 on a par-4 at the 1999 U.S. Open pales in comparison to the 18 on a par-5 at Bay Hill when he hit six consecutive balls into the water. Daly still holds the record for the highest score on an official PGA Tour hole with that particular fiasco. Jeff Babineau, editor of *Golf Week*, was one of several journalists who claimed that the incident was "something straight out of *Tin Cup*" as Daly drowned ball after ball after ball. Calling the episode "another bizarre chapter in his [Daly's] career," *New York Times* sportswriter Clifton Brown claimed that Daly was prideful when the player said he "had the courage to do it." In another post-round interview, Daly asserted that "It wasn't that I didn't care.... I just lost my patience" (qtd. in Babineau).

In addition to melting down, Daly has engaged in some unusual antics on the course, much to the chagrin of the PGA Tour. In 2008, for example, he played a couple of holes during a live interview. That was not unusual except that he was shirtless and shoeless, with lots of belly fat hanging all over. Although the Tour merely chastised Daly for that ungentlemanly outing, they leveled significant fines for two other showboating episodes. A thirty-second video features Daly giving a "skills" demonstration at the Augusta National Golf Club after the Masters. He is barefoot, wearing Loud Mouth shorts, an untucked chartreuse shirt, and wrap-around sunglasses. Smoking a cigarette, he sets an open beer can in the grass, places the ball on the can, and then hits the ball. Of course, the can tips over and the beer spills out. With shocking speed, Daly jerks into motion to rescue the beer. He removes his cigarette just long enough to guzzle the rest of the beer while the crowd claps and cheers. A great many viewers posted comments, including john quackers, who writes, "What a legend. Would have been a perfect 10 if he crushed the can against his forehead" ("John Daly Smashes"). "Unbecoming" behavior is one thing, but risking lives is another. At a 1993 golf clinic, Daly teed up, waggled the club, took a sudden 180 turn, and hit the drive directly toward the fans in the bleachers. The ball trajectory was perfect, over everyone's head. In his memoir, Daly notes that a man in the back row of the bleachers egged him on by holding up his arms like a goalpost. He continues, "And so I stood up to the ball and let 'er rip. People went nuts. They loved it" (71).

All the Tours expect players to have impulse control, a quality that Daly seems to lack, and they have punished him for his outbursts. Australia's tournament director, for example, banned him from playing the Australian PGA and speculated that he would never be invited to another Australian PGA event after an on-course temper tantrum ("Daly walks off"). According to Howard, Daly has never been the U.S. PGA Tour's favorite child either, especially during major tournaments when he has melted down with great frequency. Although disciplinary actions are usually confidential, a lawsuit filed in 2010 opened Daly's lengthy personnel file to public scrutiny. Those documents verify that the PGA fined Daly approximately $100K, suspended him five times, placed him on probation six times, and cited him twenty-one times for not giving his best effort. *Golfweek* columnist Eamon Lynch declared that Daly is no longer entitled to "the benefit of the doubt" based on metrics like disqualifications, strokes gained because of "half-hearted effort," and the number of times he has withdrawn from tournaments. Lynch declared that 49 withdrawals marks Daly as "golf's most dependable no-show." In sum, Daly has never been the grown up on the golf course, much less a gentleman.

If It Feels Good: The Enfant Binging on All the Vices

In a series entitled "Sporting Mavericks," *Golf* correspondent Bill Elliott extols Daly's golfing gifts and his achievements but also expresses regret that such a talented player could not resist huge temptations off the course. Granted, Daly was young when he became a phenom, but Elliott also claims he was "outrageous" ("Sporting Mavericks"). During a video interview, Daly claims that athletes need obsessive behaviors to be great. He also says, "The problem is that it carries over into the other things we do" ("John Daly—Obsessive"). Like many elite athletes, Daly's excesses have been extreme and very public. Borrowing lyrics from a Tom Petty song, Daly aptly entitled the introduction to his memoir "Too Much Ain't Enough." He writes,

> You see, I haven't led what you'd call an ordinary life.... In my darker days, I had a few drinks, visited a few hospital ERs, and did time in a couple of rehab clinics. I've beat up hotel rooms, houses, and cars. I've gambled away a couple of fortunes.... I guess you could say I'm not exactly the poster boy for moderation [ix].

As Daly asserts, "Too Much Ain't Enough" is "not a half bad title for my life story" (ix). A binge eater, smoker, drinker, womanizer, and gambler, he is entirely right.

Although most elite athletes take care of their bodies through carefully controlled diet and exercise, Daly's weight has fluctuated wildly over the years, and his relationship with food has always been problematic. As he notes in his memoir, "I got teased a lot when I was a teenager because of my size. I was chunky. Not rally fat, but definitely chunky. Hell, I ate too much" (19). Despite that declaration, Daly's challenge was not only how much he ate, but also what he loved to eat: Mom's "chocolate gravy and hot biscuits," fried chicken, hamburgers and fries, chocolate shakes (*My Life* 19). When he enrolled at the University of Arkansas, his dream school, Daly wanted to be on the Hogs (Razorbacks) golf team, but the coach refused to let him play until he lost 60 pounds. Daly dropped the weight by using the most absurd methods imaginable. He switched to Diet Coke, ate almost no food except dry popcorn, drank a fifth of Jack Daniels every day, and began smoking. His coach told him smoking would kill his appetite, and Daly indulged in up to three packs a day. He notes in his memoir, "pounds were peeling away" (36-7). Within three months, he had lost 65 pounds and visited the emergency room twice after passing out from whiskey overdoses (37).

That period is emblematic of Daly's continuing food and smoking addictions. His eating binges were particularly extreme. When he tried antidepressants after one stint in rehab, he ate chocolate "like a madman," sometimes twenty packs of M&M peanuts a round (*My Life* 74). In a video, Daly reported that he also ate massive amounts of chocolate cookies, chocolate ice cream, chocolate muffins, and chocolate gravy (Bensinger, "John Daly on Diet"). In that same interview, conducted after his lap band surgery, Daly admitted that he eats fast food nearly every day, sometimes multiple times a day. One sitting at McDonalds, for example, involves two Big Macs, two or three cheeseburgers, a large fries, and a chocolate shake. After sharing that nugget, Daly smiles and says to the shocked host, "Some people are meant to be a little heavy to be healthy" (Bensinger, "John Daly on Diet"). For Daly, health would appear not to include any fitness training. He writes, "I try not to get within a pitching wedge of the fitness trailer.... And I'm sure as hell not going to some fucking health club, because they won't let you smoke" (*My Life* 155). The state of Daly's health revealed itself in a 2016 video interview with Anna Whitely of *Golfing World*, conducted while walking a course in Qatar. Overweight and clearly winded, he had to stop moving so he could talk without panting ("GW Walk").

Daly's affair with alcohol began before his college years. As he notes in his memoir, he and his brother hosted raucous parties when their parents were traveling (28). He also writes that he "got shit-faced drunk" the night before his last junior tournament. Vomiting and stinking of booze the next morning, he was disqualified when the officials found the JD, as Daly often calls his "best friend" Jack Daniels (25-6). He claims he played his best golf when he was drunk because his body would be "relaxed" and he could "play more aggressively" (Bensinger, "John Daly: I played"). With pride, he describes how he outwitted a waitress and bartender who refused to continue serving him the "usual," triple shots of Jack Daniels on the rocks, no water, three at a time (*My Life* 3). He simply ordered a triple-shot, drained it while the waitress stood there, and then ordered another (4). He apparently did not learn anything from previous trips to the emergency room because he passed out with his eyes open. As he writes, "the guys I was drinking with thought I'd had a stroke or something" (4), so they called an ambulance. That is probably the same incident when his blood alcohol concentration reached "3.7 or 3.6 or something" (Bensinger, "John Daly: I played"). Although the decimal point is incorrect, Daly is right when he said he could have died.

Daly drank excessively until the PGA Tour gave him an ultimatum to get professional help or be fined and indefinitely suspended (*My Life* 67). After rehab, he remained sober for four years but started drinking again when hotel personnel left alcohol in the mini-bar. Within six weeks, he "drank himself senseless" at the Players Championship, crashed through a glass door, and blacked out in the hotel suite. He quickly lost sponsors and eventually spent time at the Betty Ford Center (*My Life* 93–8). Although he no longer drinks whiskey because JD "will kill" him, Daly claims that even though he sometimes drinks too much beer, he is not an alcoholic (154). History probably indicates otherwise. Two years after that declaration, Daly spent hours drinking in a Hooters tent during a rain delay, and his new swing coach Butch Harmon dropped him because "the most important thing in his life is getting drunk" (qtd. in "Swing Coach Harmon"). Later that year, Daly passed out in front of a North Carolina Hooters and was held overnight in jail ("Golfer John Daly Detained"). Clinging to denial, Daly maintains a relationship with alcohol, but without his first love, JD.

Although Daly would probably not include women as a vice, he declares that he has always been "somewhat of a nympho" and that sex helps his golf game (Bensinger, "John Daly: Sex"). His sexual exploits might not compare in sheer numbers to Woods's conquests, but they are nonetheless noteworthy. Perhaps the most important difference between the two players' approach to women is Daly's penchant for marrying, often in haste. Perhaps not surprisingly, Daly's commentaries about his four marriages center on sex. Daly claims his first wife Dale became "cold" after the wedding (111). His marriage to second wife Bettye was a "case of sex at first sight" (113). When they first met, she lied to him about her age and neglected to mention her teenage son and that she was still married to her second husband. So, what was the draw? Bettye loved sex as much as he did. His story may be testosterone-driven bravado, but Daly claims that he and Bettye had sex ten times one rainy afternoon (Bensinger, "John Daly: Sex"). He argues that everything with Bettye went "downhill" after Sierra was born, citing that they would go for "like five or six days without having sex" (*My Life* 125). Daly married Paulette about a nanosecond after his divorce from Bettye, but then met "Leslie" who almost became wife number four (126). Giving her a pseudonym in his memoir, Daly was enticed because she was attracted to men and women. He notes that she was "really something when it came to sex" (130) and claims he would have married "Leslie" except that he met Sherrie.

Daly's fourth marriage became fodder for a media frenzy when Sherrie was charged with a felony because of her involvement in her parents' money-laundering operation; she pled guilty and served five months in jail (*My Life* 188). After her incarceration, Daly writes,

> Me and Sherrie have been through hell in this marriage, but she guards me, she protects me.... Granted, we're always at each other's throats. I think me and Sherrie fight more than any couple in the world. But it doesn't get in the way of the fact that I love Sherrie with all my heart and I always will [*My Life* 191–2].

Less than a year after publishing the book, Daly revealed that he and Sherrie had quite literally been "at each other's throats" when he showed up for the second round of the St. Jude with meaty gouges in his face. He claimed that Sherrie had tried to stab him with a steak knife ("Daly says wife attacked"), and they divorced shortly thereafter. Daly sums up his marriages, "When things were great, man, they were there, right by your side. But when things were bad [long pause] they were gone" (Bensinger, "John Daly: Dad"). He recounts with admiration that his beloved mother stayed in her marriage even though his father was an abusive alcoholic. Daly's perception of marriage and of loyalty would seem quite immature and unrealistic.

Among Daly's most damaging obsessions is gambling. He openly admits, for example, that he "could go out and lose everything" because gambling is "in my blood" ("Sporting Mavericks"). Prior to his first big tournament win, when he could ill afford such losses, he "pissed away something like $25K" at a Swaziland casino (*My Life* 57). Later that year, when he was "the hottest property in golf" and receiving big appearance money from sponsors, he dropped about $150K in South Africa (*My Life* 58). Thereafter, his addiction escalated. When he came out of rehab in 1993, for example, he promptly lost about $4 million (*My Life* 74). Daly claims that he was so deeply in debt that he "couldn't wait for quarterly payments [from his sponsor, Wilson]" ("Sporting Mavericks") and had to borrow money against future payments. Even the possibility of destitution did not stop him. He estimates that he lost $55 million or more at casinos in sixteen years, including $1.5 million in one sitting at a $5K slot machine at the Winn (Bensinger, "John Daly: I lost").

In addition to his "in my blood" justification, Daly asserts that he gambles "to enjoy myself.... I love the action" (Bensinger, "John Daly: I lost"). He offers more details in his memoir, asserting that gambling is "the only thing that gets my juices flowing like golf does—or whiskey used to" (194). He also says that gambling was a great way "to get away from everything" ("Sporting Mavericks"). Apparently, "everything" included nagging women. When Paulette sent him to get milk, Daly made a three-day detour to a casino where he was "looking for a little peace of mind" (*My Life* 125). Noteworthy is Daly's frequent use of the language of addiction: desire, stimulation, arousal, and escape. In other interviews, however, he recognizes the darker aspects of gambling. When asked about how it was possible to lose so much money, he answers very simply, "stupidity" (Bensinger, "John Daly: I lost"). He also declares that if he fails to "get control" of his gambling, the addiction will "flat-out ruin" him (*My Life* 197). Despite this acknowledgment, Daly sends a contradictory message in a recent video when he asserts of his gambling, "Hey, I had a great time doing it.... It wasn't a bad investment" ("Sporting Mavericks").

A quick scan of Daly's books and interviews reveals that he is a live-for-the-moment, pleasure-seeking being. One word crops up repeatedly: fun. When confronted with a long list of his obsessions—including food, smoking, alcohol, sex, and gambling—he blithely states, "You're only here for a short time. Might as well have a good time" ("John Daly—Obsessive"). Of life in general, he says, "I like to have fun, you know. [long pause] I like to have fun, and sometimes the tour gets mad at me. When you have fun, rumors start spreading.... What can you do? I like to have fun" ("John Daly Interview").

As these notations indicate, Daly has exuded a child-like hedonism. He wants what he wants, when he wants it, and he grabs all the pleasures he can without pondering the consequences. Sudden fame did not create Daly's appetites. They always existed. Success merely afforded him more opportunities to feed and grow his obsessions. Unlike so many around him, Daly has never blamed his addictions for his failure to fulfill his purported destiny; he simply accepts his gifts and his challenges without question.

Fans Celebrating the Enfant

Although the golfing world has typically disdained bad boys and applauded players who show discipline and restraint, the PGA struggles to engage more people in following and playing the sport. For golf aficionados, high quality shot-making and close competitions create suspense and excitement, but a great many people believe that watching golf, a game reliant on absolute physical control, is numbingly boring. No one has ever accused Daly of being boring. "Long John," another of Daly's nicknames, has wowed the galleries with distance, but he has also entertained them with volatility. His ball goes a long way, but no one, not even Daly himself, knows where. It could end up just about anywhere: the rough, the woods, out of bounds, or safely in the fairway. As former PGA professional and current commentator David Feherty states, Daly "has a bring-it-on nature," and the galleries love it ("Sporting Mavericks"). Whitley probes this issue when she asks him, "You always bring the crowds.... What do you think it is that people love to watch about you?" He answers, "They have no idea what I am going to do next. Throwing clubs, breaking clubs, or making nine birdies in a row. You just never know what I am going to do" ("GW Walk").

Daly's unpredictability is not the sole reason he draws huge galleries, however. Despite golf's lofty birth among wealthy gentlemen, or perhaps because of those origins, many fans have anti-elitism sentiments. Some of golf's most celebrated players have risen from modest circumstances. Zoeller, for example, asserts of Daly, "Not since Arnold Palmer captured the imagination of the golfing galleries has one player been so loved for a 'regular guy' personality" (*Grip It* ix). Daly collaborator John Andrisani concurs, "Daly captured the public's imagination.... His puff-a-cigarette pose and go-for-broke game were reminiscent of a young Arnold Palmer" (*Grip It* xi). Elliot concurs that Daly "represented the common working man ... opposite of the rather spoiled college kid." In a sport that suffers from elitism, Daly has served as a folk hero. Responding to a YouTube video, user Oldman with Abow writes, "Loved watching Daly play. [N]o one played with as much heart" (Bensinger, "John Daly on one of golf's"). Lynch sums it up when he declares that Daly was "an easy guy to root for among the khaki clones that populate the PGA Tour, a mullet-sporting, beer-bellied, working-class guy upending a country club world."

Perhaps ironically, part of Daly's folk-hero appeal arises from his lack of discipline. Daly affirms the connection between himself and his fans when he writes, "um, probably because [the fans] relate to the things I've gone through more than anything" ("The Bad Boy"). Here, Daly does not really accept responsibility for "things" he has "gone through," but he understands that fans identify with him. Some see him as an extension of themselves, like Daly fan David Larson, who writes, "He gives hope to fat guys everywhere" ("John Daly Smashes"). Not only does Daly look the part, but he also plays the "average" guy quite convincingly when he flails, swears, and throws clubs on the course. In response to a video of Daly's struggles, Mark Rubin writes, "Wow! John Daly doing an impression of me" ("John Daly Worst Scores"). Other fans apparently aspire to imitate Daly's brazenness—if circumstances allowed them sufficient freedom. For example, NemeanLion writes, "I swear, guys like this impress the hell out of me. He just devours life, completely unafraid of consequences," and Connor Laddy proclaims, "I love this man's style. Doesn't give a damn!" (Bensinger, "John Daly: A tour"). They applaud his boldness and forgive his foibles.

Daly's fans additionally approve his unabashed honesty, another lesson his mother preached. Although Feherty notes that honesty is "extremely rare" among touring professionals ("Sporting Mavericks"), Daly is adamant about truth-telling. As he notes in his memoir: "I don't have any skeletons in the closet. They're all out. I got all my skeletons out" (x). He adds, "My philosophy then, and my philosophy now, is that 'it is what it is.' You do what you do, and you accept responsibility for it" (96). Daly understands that speaking the truth, even his most difficult truths, has been essential in his relationship with fans. When asked to explain his fan appeal, Daly said, "I've been honest with a lot of the problems I've had in life. Everybody has problems. They can relate to that" (qtd. in Howard). He appreciates that fans have "rallied around me ... no matter how I'm playing at the time, no matter how much I've screwed up along the way" (*My Life* 15). And they do rally. Bamadeadhead, for example, exclaims, "John Daly is an absolute IDIOT but I love him" (Bensinger, "John Daly: I played my best"). As Lynch writes, "His many struggles with addiction—which he hid from no one—earned him tremendous support from fans and more than a few passes for conduct unbecoming."

Conclusion: *The Enfant's Squandered Talent*

I recently began accompanying a friend to the driving range to help him groove a swing. He topped the ball quite a bit at first, and hooks and slices came and went. He also made progress. After a couple of nice drives during our second session, he asked, "Which is better, long or straight?" That is a key question. Is golf about power, with its glorious adrenaline rush, or discipline? I said, "If you have to choose, go for straight." But discipline is so difficult to maintain, not to mention tedious. Eschewing discipline, probably because it is so dull, Daly has been an unorthodox and rebellious genius. To the delight of some and the chagrin of others, he has been that terrible child, devoid of impulse control or restraint.

For years, he has promised that maturity was imminent, and others have echoed his assertions. Zoeller, for example, claimed that Daly's marriage to Bettye showed that "he has settled down to a more mature life-style" (Daly, *Grip It* ix). Despite that declaration, the 26-year-old Daly had not settled down, not even close. In a 2001 interview, 35-year-old Daly acknowledged that his life "would be a hell of a movie" and the actor who plays him "better be a crazy you-know-what," but he also argued that he learned from his mistakes and had embraced "moderation" (qtd. in "The Bad Boy"). It is not entirely clear how Daly defines "moderation," but it seems to include obscenely excessive drinking and gambling. Five years later, Daly repeated his mantra, "Yeah, I'm more mature now" (*My Life* 15). A skeptical Lynch nonetheless writes, "He's 52 now, but maturity seems no nearer at hand." Although some may enjoy the "crazy you-know-what," other have lost patience with the eternal child.

As Rojek argues, talent is "a unique, ultimately inexplicable phenomenon" that can be "refined and polished through discipline" (29). He adds that celebrities often "collude in bringing about their own descent" (80). Daly might be the perfect exemplar for Rojek's claims. Many have abandoned hope for Daly to fulfill his supposed destiny because, as Zoeller notes, "to play winning golf, you have to have your personal life in order" (Daly, *Grip It* x). Instead of creating order, Daly created and lived in chaos and ultimately squandered his opportunities for golfing greatness. Of his intrinsic talent, Daly writes, "I'm lucky: I was born with a special talent for hitting a little white ball and making people happy" (*My Life* 199). A bit prideful in the telling, Daly often recounts a story about inviting Woods to have a drink. Instead of accepting, Woods headed to the gym. When Daly asked, "What are you doing, man?" Tiger purportedly responded, "If I had your talent, J.D., I would be doing just what you are doing" ("John Daly on relationship"). Therein lies the shame. If Woods, one of the greatest golfers in the history of the sport, recognizes Daly's in-born talent, what might he have become with even a modicum of discipline?

Scores of fans comment on Daly's "could-have-been" greatness. Tom Fisker notes that Daly was "Gifted with a wonderful talent which he threw away," and Bob Smith agrees that he had "Talent to burn but not an ounce of common sense to spare" ("John Daly Worst Scores"). James Purvis wistfully writes, "If only he knew how good he was and could have been" (Bensinger, "John Daly: A tour"). Lance Maryson is even more direct, declaring, "Wasted talent at its best" ("Beer?"). Although these fans do not indicate Daly robbed them, Lynch claims Daly "seldom" gave galleries what they "deserve: professionalism, courtesy, a simple bloody effort to justify their ticket price," adding that "the Daly Show has long since become tediously repetitive viewing."

Somewhat defiantly, Daly asserts that he will drink if he wants, gamble if he wishes, and play golf his own way because "That's just the way I am. That's the way I live" (*My Life* 106). Ever optimistic, he adds, "I think I'm going to do even better on the back nine" (*My Life* 199). In spite of his confidence, it would seem more likely that Daly will remain the enfant terrible, with no discipline on the course or in life. Of all the videos concerning Daly, one seems to encapsulate his past and possibly predict his future. It is a montage of his "blow ups" accompanied by the following narrated words:

> I've won and lost against the best.... There's rules I'd love to break and bend, mistakes I've made again and again, but I tell you this, my friends, I'm still around. I hit it hard, man, so far, man, no layin' up, no holdin' back ain't 'fraid of nothin'. It's a natural fact. Hit it long, man, 'til it's gone, man, keep taking chances, living large. I hit it, I hit it, I hit it hard ["John Daly Blow Ups 2"].

Those words sum up John Daly, the endearing and frustrating enfant terrible of golf, forever breaking rules and hitting life hard.

WORKS CITED

Andrews, David L., and Steven J. Jackson. *Sports Stars: The Cultural Politics of Sporting Celebrity*. Routledge, 2001.

Babineau Jeff. "It's A Comedy of Errors—Daly Gets Hole-in-18." *The Orlando Sentinel*, 23 March 1998, www.articles.orlandosentinel.com/1998-03-23/sports/9803230184_1_john-daly-tin-cup-hole.

"The Bad Boy of Golf John Daly/Full Uncut Interview." YouTube, uploaded by Trans World Sport, 8 Nov. 2018, www.youtube.com/watch?v=ywADJqYb5Sw.

"Beer? John Daly's Best Golf Shots 1991 PGA Championship." YouTube, uploaded by Jerry's Golf Gems, 19 Feb. 2018, www.youtube.com/watch?v=WXz1zZf2p6c.

Bensinger, Graham. *In Depth with Graham*. "John Daly: A tour of my home and RV." YouTube, uploaded by Graham Bensinger, 29 June 2016, www.youtube.com/watch?v=VHXfZTgcSFg.

——. *In Depth with Graham*. "John Daly: Dad put a gun to my eye, nearly killed me." YouTube, uploaded by Graham Bensinger, 29 June 2016, www.youtube.com/watch?v=4EcnB-ScaAand list.

——. *In Depth with Graham*. "John Daly: I lost $55 million gambling." YouTube, uploaded by Graham Bensinger, 20 June 2016, www.youtube.com/watch?v=PW8gDTY2b68.

——. *In Depth with Graham*. "John Daly: I played my best golf drunk." YouTube, uploaded by Graham Bensinger, 20 Jun. 2016, www.youtube.com/watch?v=ezr6myBTvDQ.

——. *In Depth with Graham*. "John Daly on Diet: Cigarettes, Candy, 15 Sodas." YouTube, uploaded by Graham Bensinger, 29 June 2016, www.youtube.com/watch?v=KKkwim3w8I0.

——. *In Depth with Graham*. "John Daly on one of golf's greatest underdog stories." YouTube, uploaded by Graham Bensinger, 29 June 2016, www.youtube.com/watch?v=xPwBm9H_ZQc.

——. *In Depth with Graham*. "John Daly: Sex helps my golf game." YouTube, uploaded by Graham Bensinger, 29 June 2016, www.youtube.com/watch?v=FZeK_OkE6ekandlist.

Brown, Clifton. "GOLF; Six in Lake Give Daly an 18." *The New York Times*, 23 March 1998, www.nytimes.com/1998/03/23/sports/golf-six-in-lake-give-daly-an-18.html.

Brown, Oliver. "Tiger Woods Should Be Spitting Mad Over His Latest Exhibition of Crassness in the Dubai Desert Classic." *The [UK] Telegraph*, 16 Feb. 2011, www.telegraph.co.uk/sport/golf/tigerwoods/8326610/Tiger-Woods-should-be-spitting-mad-over-his-latest-exhibition-of-crassness-in-the-Dubai-Desert-Classic.html.

Daly, John, with Glenn Waggoner. *My Life In and Out of the Rough: The Truth Behind All That Bull**** You Think You Know About Me*. HarperCollins, 2006.

Daly, John, with John Andrisani. *Grip It and Rip It! John Daly's Guide to Hitting the Ball Farther Than You Ever Have Before*. HarperCollins: 1992.

"Daly says wife attacked him with steak knife." Golf.com, 9 June 2007, www.golf.com/ap-news/daly-says-wife-attacked-him-steak-knife.

"Daly snatches camera, smashes it into a tree." Golf.com, 11 Dec. 2008, www.golf.com/ap-news/daly-snatches-camera-smashes-it-tree.

Ferguson, Doug. "Daly Might Not Be Welcomed Back After Meltdown." *The Ledger.com*, 10 Nov. 2011, www.theledger.com/news/20111110/daly-might-not-be-welcomed-back-after-meltdown.

"Golfer John Daly detained after passing out drunk at Hooters." Golf.com, 19 July 2010, www.golf.com/ap-news/golfer-john-daly-detained-after-passing-out-drunk-hooters.

Goliath Team. "9 of the Most Hideous John Daly Outfits." Sportsbreak.com, 27 Apr. 2017, www.sportsbreak.com/golf/9-of-the-most-hideous-john-daly-outfits/.

"GW Walk the Course: John Daly." YouTube, uploaded by Golfing World, 18 Feb. 2016, www.youtube.com/watch?v=08qkn1yGL5I.

Howard, Johnette. "Happy 50th birthday, John Daly, and thanks for these memories." *ABC-News*, 28 Apr. 2016, www.abcnews.go.com/Sports/happy-50th-birthday-john-daly-memories/story?id=38730436.

"John Daly at the 1991 PGA Championship." YouTube, uploaded by GolfDay, 23 Dec. 2016, www.youtube.com/watch?v=Dla7sdOTO8k.

"John Daly Blow Ups 2 (With Scorecard Montage at the End)." YouTube, uploaded by Chris C, 30 Aug. 2017, www.youtube.com/watch?v=VEWw1FiModA.

"John Daly Interview While Playing Golf-No Shirt or Shoes." YouTube, uploaded by Nate Allen, 28 Apr. 2008, www.youtube.com/watch?v=q6HXfA_e14.

"John Daly—Obsessive Behavior, Being Honest with Your Mistakes, Everyone Has Something to Offer." YouTube, uploaded by David Meltzer. 10 Apr. 2018, www.youtube.com/watch?v=PAssYDHzzOs.

"John Daly on relationship with Tiger Woods." YouTube, uploaded by Thuzio, 2 Aug. 2018. www.youtube.com/watch?v=laxho_4OWWA.

"John Daly Smashes Ball Off Beer Can at Monday After the Masters." YouTube, uploaded by Play Golf Myrtle Beach, 11 Apr. 2017, www.youtube.com/watch?v=pmJ2CspoFUw.

"John Daly—'Tee the Ball Up' by dj steve porter." YouTube, uploaded by Scratch, 28 Apr. 2016, www.youtube.com/watch?v=CUz5cMht6OE.

"John Daly Worst Scores and Blow Ups Compilation. YouTube, uploaded by Chris C, 9 Aug. 2017, www.youtube.com/watch?v=-ArNQiZ1PXk.

"John Daly's Best Golf Shots 2016." YouTube, uploaded by Short cut to a professional Golf Swing, 20 Jan. 2017, www.youtube.com/watch?v=AlaLl_jt-KI.

Lynch, Eamon. "19th hole: John Daly is at last beyond the benefit of the doubt." *Golf Week: Digital Edition*, 1 July 2018, www.golfweek.com/2018/07/01/john-daly-is-at-last-beyond-the-benefit-of-the-doubt/.

Rojek, Chris. *Celebrity*. London: Reaktion Books, 2001. "Sporting Mavericks—John Daly." YouTube, uploaded by BeagleBoy, 23 July 2018, www.youtube.com/watch?v=J6nET4Ga3Dw.

"Swing Coach Harmon Drops Daly." *The New York Times*, 12 March 2008, www.nytimes.com/2008/03/12/sports/golf/12daly.html.

"Worst Holes in Golf History: Tour and News." Golf.com, 5 Oct. 2011, www.golf.com/photos/worst-holes-golf-history.

Nothing but the Truth
The Rise and Fall of Marion Jones

Brock T. Adams

On October 26, 2000, in Sydney, Australia, two weeks after track and field phenom Marion Jones captivated the world and set records with five separate medals in the 27th official Olympic Games, the Spanish Paralympic Basketball squad became infamous in international competition. It was the second of three preliminary matches of the 2000 Paralympic Games, and up to that point, the team had been working on their internal chemistry, an effective strategy as evidenced by their victories in multiple regional competitions. They gelled to form what would be a dominant lineup. That afternoon, through a barrage of outside shooting and flawless execution of their defensive game plan, the Spaniards built an insurmountable lead early in the first half against the Japanese national team. A ten-point lead increased to fifteen, then twenty, then twenty-five. At one point, the Spanish coaches called a timeout with a thirty-point lead and brought the team to the sideline, advocating the use of cruise control for the remainder of the game. Former team member Carlos Ribagorda recounts the athletic trainer joking with them, "Lads, move down a gear or they'll figure out you're not disabled" (qtd. in Dunham).

As comedic as that comment sounds, the tragedy lies in the fact that it was true. The majority of the players did not have an intellectual disability; in fact, ten of the twelve athletes on their roster were not legally eligible to compete in the Paralympics. Ribagorda, then an undercover reporter, competed on the Spanish Paralympic team for two years and had never been given an intelligence test to assess if he had a disability. Prior to his involvement in Sydney, rumors were circulating that corruption was embedded in the Paralympic competition, with various other countries also using ineligible athletes.

The Spaniards went on to crush the Japanese team by 57 points that afternoon, one of four consecutive blowouts en route to a 24-point gold medal victory over the Russians on the final day of competition. It was one of 107 medals Spain tallied that year in the Paralympic Games, third behind Australia and Great Britain. However, the celebration was momentary as Ribagorda broke the news shortly after their return from Sydney in an article for the Spanish business magazine *Capital* that his home country had been cheating in the Paralympics for many years. He asserted, "Of the 200 Spanish athletes at Sydney at least 15 had no type of physical or mental handicap—they didn't even pass medical or psychological examinations" (qtd. in Dunham). Along with the ten members of the men's basketball team, Spanish athletes competing in track and field, swimming, and table tennis were also accused of cheating the system to compete because they had no disabilities.

This controversy stands as a historical blemish on the Spanish Paralympic program and is one of the greatest blunders in modern athletic history. It also raises ethical boundary questions that thousands of athletes in every possible sport consistently face: What violations are competitors willing to commit for the sake of standing as the lone victor? How far is too far? Also, how should athletes respond when the evidence tallies against them? Do they carry on with their delusional façade and blatantly lie to the media, fans, and peers of their respective sport? Or do they openly face accusations and accept full responsibility?

Like the Spanish Paralympic team, Jones demolished contenders on the way to the podium five separate times in Sydney, the most ever achieved by a woman in modern Olympic history. Unbeknownst to her at the time, Jones's legacy would be tarnished by arguably one of the greatest travesties ever to surface in track and field. She was among the many athletes caught up in a scandal that rocked the Olympic community, and in turn, raised questions regarding how far someone is willing to go in order to win. Jones reached beyond her biological limits by using a number of performance-enhancing drugs and supplements banned by the United States Track & Field Association (USATF) and the International Olympic Committee (IOC). She was also one of the marquee phonies of her time, dishonestly denying any connection to cheating. When confronted with accusatory testimonies and damning evidence, Jones took a position of aggressive rejection, which ultimately ended her potential legacy as an iconic American athlete.

Win at All Costs

Every sport has boundaries participants formally agree to abide by before they lace up their shoes or buckle their chinstraps. However, the question pulling at the moral seams of countless athletes begs how far they are willing to go in order to win. Some have posed as intellectually disabled individuals unable to achieve a score higher than 70 on a standard IQ test to win a basketball game at the Paralympics; others have used even more devious methods to stand on the highest platform. Rather than run all 26.2 miles of the Boston Marathon in 1980, Rosie Ruiz deviated from the original course and took shortcuts through back alleys and cross streets to gain a better time. This was similar to her actions in the New York Marathon, where she jumped on a passing subway and emerged from the crowd a few miles before the finish line.

Cheating in professional sports has a spectrum of controversies, from Olympic doping in Russia, to Spygate, to Blue Chips, to an ex-husband hiring a hitman to break the legs of a fellow competitor, to lies about an ace pitcher's age for the Little League World Series. One of the most bizarre "win at all costs" moments occurred in 2005 when Minnesota Vikings running back Onterrio Smith was apprehended at the Twin Cities airport for carrying a prosthetic penis known as "The Whizzinator," an apparatus that included an artificial bladder and athletic supporter. The complex device gave Smith the ability to submit clean urine whenever he was selected for a random drug test. Smith's way of beating the system might be viewed as brilliantly innovative, but the apprehension of his private privates features an all-too-familiar controversy surrounding professional athletes: the use of performance-enhancing drugs (PEDs).

Popular opinion contends that PEDs are a stain on the true spirit of sport. Prior to the advent of modern chemical concoctions, people viewed sports as opponents pitted against one another in a given competition, attempting to become victors through physical and mental dominance. The injection of PEDs into the sports landscape provided an alternative method to achieve success, and in turn raised the stakes on what athletes were willing to do in order to win. "The ideal of sport as a mutual quest for excellence brings out the crucial point that a sports contest is a competition between *persons*" argues Professor Robert Simon. He adds, "However, when [the] use of drugs leads to improved play, it is natural to say that it is not athletic ability that determines outcome but rather the efficiency with which the athlete's body reacts to the performance enhancer" (7). Many believe PEDs altered the arena of modern competitions, shifting from the field to the bloodstream. In his 2004 State of the Union Address, President George W. Bush offered words of caution, saying, "The use of performance-enhancing drugs like steroids in baseball, football, and other sports is dangerous, and it sends the wrong message: that there are shortcuts to accomplishment, and that performance is more important than character" (qtd. in Waldman).

The use of PEDs has nonetheless become more prevalent in professional sports, and the incentive to inject is attributed mainly to the perceived dominance it gives the athlete. One of the most notable PED users in modern sports, former baseball player Jose Canseco, discussed the prospective opportunities PEDs provide athletes willing to cross that ethical boundary. In an interview with Mike Wallace on *60 Minutes*, Canseco said, "I don't recommend steroids for everyone ... but for certain individuals, I truly believe, because I've experimented with it for so many years, that it can make an average athlete a super athlete. It can make a super athlete incredible" ("Juiced").

Jones was in fact that super athlete. She was a three-time Gatorade Player of the Year for track and field in high school, went on to win world championships in the 100m and 200m sprint, and helped the University of North Carolina women's basketball team win a national title her freshman year of college. Many athletes can contend against world-class competition in dual arenas, but only the elite emerge as the undisputed best in both sports. Jones was an elite athlete who left a catalog of competitors scrambling for second place.

Competition often prompts moral debates in athletes' minds regarding the boundaries they are willing to cross to claim greatness. It is difficult to identify what explicitly motivates someone to break the rules, but certainly at elite levels the pressures compound as the stakes grow higher with commercial endorsements, media coverage, and fan adulation, which in turn advances an athlete's competitive drive exponentially. In many situations, integrities are brushed aside as competitors dream of being that "incredible super athlete" or having that same success Jones achieved, emerging as the victor showered with praise. This type of aggrandized glorification could be the stimulus behind notorious rule-breakers such as Anderson Silva, Maria Sharapova, or Lance Armstrong. It also raises the question as to whether human beings are willing to put their mental, physical, and ethical health at risk in order to string together a streak of unbeaten fights in UFC, win yet another Grand Slam final, or don the yellow jersey of the Tour de France for seven consecutive years and be touted as the greatest human ever to ride a bicycle.

Jones faced these dilemmas while rising in popularity as a feminine icon on the track. She was a polarizing figure in spikes, earning accolades and first-place finishes well ahead of her time. At the age of 15, Jones was offered an alternate spot on the 1992 Olympic 4 × 100-meter relay team, which she respectfully declined, stating that coaches were less inclined to trust someone so young and with no Olympic experience. Five years later, Jones finished first in the 100m, 200m, and long jump events at the USA Outdoor Championships. Heading into the Olympic games in Sydney, she was heralded as the new queen of American Track and Field, anointed by the *Chicago Sun-Times* as "an American dream for the new millennium" (Mariotti). They later claimed 2000 as the "Year of Marion." The buzz surrounding her focused not only on her athletic potential, but also on her animated and audacious character. Prior to the Sydney Olympics, Jones forecasted in interviews that she would win an unprecedented five gold medals, something no other Olympic athlete had accomplished, let alone a young black woman in her first official Olympic competition. Statements such as these were unheard of, setting Jones apart in the eyes of the ever-fascinated American public. Jones appreciated the media attention and adoration from fans worldwide, calling it "intoxicating" (Wald).

Although she did not live up to her lofty expectations, her accomplishments in the Sydney Olympics were record-breaking. Jones won gold medals in the 100m dash, 200m dash, and the 4 × 400m relay, along with bronze medals in the long jump and 4 × 100m relay, becoming the first woman ever to win five medals at the modern Olympics. Her image transformed when media outlets such as *Sports Illustrated* and *Vogue* magazine touted her as being "Greater than Gold" (Reed). However, her celebration from the top of the podium in Sydney lasted for only an instant in comparison to what was developing on the other side of the globe. Just three years later, Jones's career and world were rocked by one of the worst doping controversies in the history of sports: the BALCO scandal.

BALCO

In 1984, Victor Conte established the Bay Area Laboratory Co-operative as a service business for the analysis of blood, urine, and food supplements. Conte's reputation and clientele grew while the knowledge and awareness of PEDs in professional sports remained in the dark. Heavy hitters such as Bill Romanowski and Chris Cooper became regular clients as the company evolved to provide athletes with the "extra edge" they needed on the field. Controversy erupted in 2003, however, when Jones's former coach Trevor Graham and fellow sprinter Tim Montgomery sent the U.S. Anti-Doping Agency a syringe filled with an anabolic designer steroid. Graham cited morality as the impetus for his whistle blowing, stating he was "just a coach doing the right thing" (qtd. in Fainaru-Wada and Williams). Some argued, nevertheless, that Graham's actions were a political tactic between athletes he represented and those represented by Conte. Regardless, his tip led to an investigation into BALCO and subpoenas of dozens of high-profile icons. At the time, the USADA announced a genuine doping "conspiracy" as they unearthed an overwhelming amount of evidence against eminent athletes.

BALCO was notorious for the simple format of their performance-enhancing supplements. THG, known as "the clear," was a transparent substance with a slight yellowish hue that could be administered by quickly placing a few drops underneath the tongue. "The clear" was also successful in that its half-life in the human body lasted only a few hours, not nearly as long as other PED supplements. This trait is similar to Trenbolone, a bovine steroid banned for human consumption in the United States. A key difference between THG and Trenbolone is that the latter is primarily used to bolster the weight of cattle for meat consumption, not to increase leg strength to decimate a world record time for the 100m dash. "The cream" was another recognized substance distributed by BALCO as a testosterone boost, applied by rubbing onto clients' muscles. It was also easily concealed by simply wiping it off, thus being undetectable by the majority of potential drug tests.

BALCO connected with figures in multiple sports, with athletes in the USATF being the most heavily influenced by the covert simplicity of using PEDs. In September 2003, federal agents raided both the BALCO offices in San Carlos and simultaneously Conte's home in San Mateo, seizing thousands of documents and materials related to business operations. Conte was taken to lead agent Jeff Novitsky, who informed Conte that there was an overwhelming amount of evidence against him and that the government would review his case more favorably if he came clean. Conte immediately confessed and unraveled his operations, including distributions of "the clear" and "the cream" to high-profile athletes. In his testimony, he incriminated 27 separate athletes, 15 from track and field, the most of any sport. Said Conte at the time of the investigation, "This is going to be very big…. The IOC, IAAF, USOC are all turned upside down now. This is huge" (qtd. in Vinton and O'Keeffe).

As a whole, track and field was no stranger to athletes veering off course to rely on prohibited supplements. One of the most tantalizing figures in its history, Canadian sprinter Ben Johnson, was stripped of the gold medal he won in the 1988 Seoul Olympics for testing positive for stanozolol, a banned anabolic steroid. In what is known as "The Dirtiest Race in History," Johnson broke the world record for the 100m dash in an unprecedented 9.79 seconds. This was the first time in modern sports history a sprinter had eclipsed the 10-second mark for the race; however, Johnson was not the only athlete to achieve this task. Four of the top five sprinters, including Americans Carl Lewis and Calvin Smith, as well as Great Britain's Linford Christie, would also best the 10-second time. Regrettably, four of the top five finishers, excluding Smith, would later test positive for banned substances, once again placing a glaring red flag on an incredible athletic accomplishment.

As the BALCO case unraveled, a number of high-profile athletes involved in the USATF program were identified as using PEDs. Sprinters Dwain Chambers, Tim Montgomery, Kelli White, middle-distance runner Regina Jacobs, as well as hammer thrower John McEwen, and shot putters Kevin Toth and C.J. Hunter were all found to have used multiple types of PEDs provided by

BALCO. Hunter, Jones's former college coach and husband at the time of the Sydney Olympic games, tested positive for Nandrolone and was disqualified from the Olympic competition that year.

Jones's involvement in the BALCO scandal was unknown at the time of the Sydney Olympics, but her secrets would be short-lived as investigations into the BALCO scandal linked her professional success to the use of PEDs such as "the clear." Initially, Jones denied the allegations and defended herself through threats to sue the United States Anti-Doping Agency (USADA) if they banned her from competing in the 2004 Olympics in Athens. At the time, Jones insisted she was drug-free, and to her credit, she did not have any positive drug tests on her official record. There were, however, levels of suspicion surrounding her as she had already been accused of using PEDs in high school. Back in 1993, Jones hired attorney Johnny Cochran (of OJ Simpson fame), who successfully defended her on charges of doping.

As the case against her then-husband Hunter, as well as her track teammate Tim Montgomery, began to build, Jones's defense tactics became much more aggressive. In 2004, Jones argued for a public hearing in which she demanded the USADA to document their accusations. She called the federal probe a "debacle" being handled in a "secret kangaroo court" saying, "I want this done today. I want this done yesterday. I want this done as soon as possible.... I'm hoping to send a message to USADA that I want this done and I want my name cleared. I want to move on. What are we waiting for?" (qtd. in Dubow). Jones heightened her hostility with a $25 million defamation lawsuit filed in 2004 against Conte, accusing the BALCO founder of attempting to "destroy her career and reputation." Jones adamantly denied using PEDs, declaring she had "never taken them" (qtd. in Jones and Sekules).

These remarks were not made in passing or in a few instances; rather her rhetoric was slanderous and antagonistic, repeatedly directed at those investigating her potential PED usage. The irony of her attacks came in 2006 when she tested positive for a banned substance in the U.S. Championships. Her positive test was later voided, however, when a supplemental sample (B) test came back negative. Jones was ecstatic at the time to return to competition, but after the BALCO scandal broke, her dominance on the track began to dwindle. Jones failed to medal in the 2004 Olympics in Athens, her best finish being fifth in the long jump. Before her positive drug test in 2006 at the World Championships, Jones withdrew from her heat in the 200m sprint only minutes before the race began, claiming leg fatigue. She was no longer a dominant athlete. While she struggled on the track, federal investigators were compiling evidence behind the scenes linking her with the PED-producing office in California. Further investigations into BALCO later proved she did in fact knowingly rely on PEDs throughout her athletic career and lied about it to federal agents. This evidence tarnished her professional reputation and negated her accomplishments in the 2000 Olympics. Once again, BALCO laid claim to the professional career and reputation of another exceptionally gifted track and field victor.

Cheating v. Lying

In November of 2003, federal investigators subpoenaed Jones to testify about her connection with the BALCO case. Ten days before her appearance before the grand jury, Jones's lawyers reached out to the investigators and requested a meeting to see what evidence the government had against her. The government agreed and issued Jones a "queen for a day letter," granting immunity from any prosecution for crimes Jones testified to during the interview. Such protections are contingent on telling the truth. If people lie under these circumstances, the government has the right to charge them with perjury, a federal offense (Jones, *On the Right Track* 7–8).

On the morning of her testimony, Jones met with Novitsky and other agents in a hotel conference room in San Jose. Novitsky questioned Jones about several documents, but Jones repeatedly denied having any connection with BALCO. Near the end of the interview, Novitsky pulled out two plastic bags containing the clear and the cream and asked if she recognized the substances. Jones lied and said she did not know what was in the bags. Novitsky asked her again, and Jones repeated her denial. The cycle of question and denial continued until Jones's attorneys broke up the dialogue and requested a short break. They counseled her to tell the truth, reminding her of the stipulations attached to the "queen for a day" letter, something the government rarely gave to public defendants. A few minutes later, Novitsky walked back into the conference room and asked her once again if she knew what was in the plastic bags. Jones said, "No sir, I do not know what it is." Novitsky and his agents then concluded their interview and walked out of the conference room (Jones, *On the Right Track* 11–13). The government gave Jones multiple attempts to come clean, and she repeatedly refused.

Following her testimony, federal investigations linked Jones to PED usage and receiving supplements from the BALCO offices. Overwhelming evidence mounted against her, and all she could do was face the harsh fact that she had indeed broken the rules by openly using performance-enhancing drugs to gain an edge over her competition. However, the larger dilemma looming over her camp did not concern her actions of repeatedly dropping "the clear" under her tongue; instead, it was facing the public outcry against Jones's continual and blatant dishonesty. On multiple occasions, she launched aggressive denials, and on a grander scale, Jones knowingly made false statements to federal agents about her involvement with BALCO, a felony offense.

Ultimately, her predicament centered around the moral question of which is the greater crime: cheating or lying about cheating?

Over the years, dozens of athletes have been linked to controversies arising from cheating, gambling, or blatant antagonistic behavior. Perhaps not surprisingly, very few of those athletes have been transparent and honest about their behavior. Many have played the denial card, only to have the truth come forth at a later date. However, that's not the case for all athletes. Charles Barkley, a former small forward of the National Basketball Association for 16 seasons and two-time member of the Naismith Memorial Basketball Hall of Fame, is a prime example. Barkley's career accolades are impressive: eleven-time NBA All-Star, two-time Olympic Gold Medalist (1992, 1996), a league MVP trophy (1993), and named one of the fifty greatest basketball players of all time (NBA). Currently, the basketball community adores him in his role as a co-host of the Emmy-winning show *Inside the NBA*. In addition to his accomplishments, Barkley also has stains on his record because of his involvement in a number of violent clashes with fans. In the winter of 1991, Barkley was jailed for three hours after a dispute with a fan in Milwaukee. Barkley broke the man's nose in a parking lot altercation. Seven more fans had confrontations with Barkley over the next few years, with the final clash occurring in 1997 as he threw a fan through the front window of a bar in Orlando, Florida. One consistent factor in all these interactions was that Barkley was direct and honest about what occurred, meaning he never hid behind a façade of dishonesty. Said Barkley following the arrest in Orlando, "I'm going to defend myself. Let there be no debate. If you bother me, I'm going to whip your ass. The guy threw ice in my face, and I slammed his ass into the window. I'm not denying that. I defended myself. He got what he deserved" (qtd. in Harris and Povtak).

Barkley was direct and honest, and because of this, he is still regarded as one of the greatest forwards ever to lace up a pair of sneakers. Jones, on the other hand, took the opposite course of action. Despite the accumulating evidence against her, despite sprinters all around her failing drug tests, despite being given opportunities to tell the truth about her involvement in BALCO to a federal prosecutor who asked her to gather her thoughts and even gave her a second chance to come clean about her PED usage, Jones unashamedly lied about her actions again and again. Because of this, her career imploded, and she paid the ultimate penalty of time in federal prison.

Jones, a mother of two sons, was sentenced to six months in prison on two counts of perjury for lying to federal prosecutors about taking PEDs, as well as for lying about knowledge of a bank-fraud case being prosecuted by the state of New York ("Six Month"). Said Judge Kenneth M. Karas of the United States District Court on the day of her sentencing, "The offences here are serious. They each involve lies made three years apart.... This is not a one-off mistake ... but a repetition in an attempt to break the law" (qtd. in "Six Month"). Karas went on to justify his sentencing with the chastisement that the actions enshrining her in the Hall of Shame were not the amount of PEDs she used; instead, it was the intensity of her blatant lies to law enforcement, the media, and the throngs of fans following her worldwide. Karas asserted, "I want people to think twice before lying." He added, "I want to make them realize no one is above the law" (qtd. in Zinser). A significant difference between Jones and others involved with the BALCO case, as well as many other athletes accused of lying, is that Jones not only prevaricated in press conferences and to the media but also to federal investigators in sworn testimony.

Over the years, dozens of athletes have come clean about previous fabrications they concocted and delivered to the press. American golfer Tiger Woods openly admitted to having extramarital affairs with over a dozen women, including a handful of prostitutes, while on the PGA Tour. Former NFL linebacker Lawrence Taylor declared to Mike Wallace on primetime television that he paid prostitutes to "do something strange for a li'l piece of change" and spent hundreds of thousands of dollars on illegal drugs and call girls, or what he termed as "coke and ho's" (qtd. in "L.T. Over"). Former professional basketball player Ron Artest knowingly jumped into the stands during the "Malice at the Palace" and beat up a Detroit Pistons fan. None of the above athletes were ever booked into a prison cell for committing these illegal acts, yet lying to a federal prosecutor about taking PEDs vilified Jones and cemented her legacy as yet another high-profile sports figure who fell from greatness.

Judge Karas went on to validate his verdict with the justification that athletes must live up to a higher standard, stating, "Athletes in society have an elevated status. They entertain, they inspire and perhaps most importantly, they serve as role models for kids around the world. When there is this widespread level of cheating, it sends all the wrong messages to those who follow these athletes' every move" (qtd. in Zinser). Judge Karas viewed the act of cheating as the definitive crime that ruined Jones's legacy. However, what class of cheating is he referring to: dishonesty to the American public, dishonesty to the divine nature of competition, or in Jones's case, both? Countless athletes who have engaged in all forms of competition have been dishonest in their actions and language. However, few athletes have cheated the sport and then adamantly lied about their fraudulence in a botched attempt of saving face. Those who were confronted about their dishonesty and came clean were more easily forgiven than those who vehemently denied the allegations until the evidence was too overwhelming.

Take, for instance, the case of retired basketball superstar Kobe Bryant. He was arrested in 2003, accused of sexually assaulting a hotel employee in

Edwards, Colorado. Two weeks following his arrest, Bryant held a press conference and openly apologized for the act of committing adultery. He did cheat on his spouse; however, he was candid about his actions and accepted the consequences. Bryant now has two numbers retired for the Los Angeles Lakers, a bronze statue standing outside the Staples Center, an Academy Award sitting on his shelf, and remains one of the most respected and revered athletes of his generation.

A more fitting example of an athlete committing both crimes is one of the greatest players in Major League Baseball history, Pete Rose. Rose ended his career amidst allegations that he placed bets on teams he was managing in the late 1980s. Rose denied the accusations, despite an overwhelming amount of evidence. He would continue his crusade while being banned from baseball and being placed on the permanently ineligible list. For decades, Rose denied he ever bet on his teams, claiming it would tarnish the sacred game of baseball, something he would never dare to do. However, in 2004, Rose came clean in an autobiography, finally admitting to his dishonest acts. His actions may have been in vain as Rose committed both the act of cheating his sport and cheating the fans. The combination will relegate him to signing books and memorabilia in a gift shop in Caesar's Palace rather than working in the front office of the Cincinnati Reds.

Jones is similar to Rose in the sense that she cheated the sport of track and field by using PEDs before regional, national, and Olympic competitions. Discovery of that act makes it difficult for any professional career to endure. However, her repeated denials and aggressive attacks on her accusers ultimately sealed her fate in the minds of both the members of the International Olympic Committee and the millions of fans who once supported her. One of the defining characteristics that set Jones apart from other dishonest athletes was the duration to which she extended her denigrations. Her denial was not one misspoken statement at a press conference; rather it was a repeated onslaught of fabrications, one specifically in a hotel in San Jose to federal investigators. Jones lied under oath to investigators about taking PEDs and then later lied about committing check fraud. Both the combination and lengthy duration of her dishonest actions could be the driving forces behind Karas' sentencing and may be why she is one of the only athletes ever to spend time behind bars for her involvement with PED usage.

The Aftermath

Following her sentencing, Jones served six months in a federal prison, released on September 5, 2008. Following her release, Jones spent two additional weeks in a halfway house before she was allowed to be reunited with her spouse and two children. It had been eight long years since her triumphs on the track in Sydney. Since having those medals honorably placed around her neck, her career had shockingly collapsed. In addition to her prison sentence, the International Olympic Committee banned her from participation in the 2008 Olympic Games in Beijing and additionally stated they had the power to bar her from participation in London in 2012 or any additional games. Her days as a track and field megastar were over, and she now faced the unenviable task of rebuilding her career, her brand, and her image. This act was set in motion following her initial admittance of guilt and a formal press conference where she wept over her crimes and begged forgiveness from the American public for openly shaming her network of supporters. As she said,

> It is with a great amount of shame that I stand before you and tell you I have betrayed your trust. I recognize that by saying I'm deeply sorry, it might not be enough and sufficient to address the pain and hurt that I've caused you. Therefore, I want to ask for your forgiveness for my actions, and I hope you can find it in your heart to forgive me [qtd. in Zinser and Schmidt].

Jones was broken and humiliated, and despite her delivery of what on paper is a sufficient confession, the American public did not forgive easily.

The content and delivery of formal acts of apology are debated by researchers, picked apart by public relations offices, and applied by many athletes in various situations. In contemporary communication, and with the emergence of technological advancements, more and more athletes are pushed to apologize for crimes they commit. Professor John Kleefeld suggests the "four Rs" are required to make an apology believable: responsibility, resolution, reparation, and remorse. Many athletes have broadcast formal apologies; nonetheless, in some cases, their nonverbal demeanor seemed to negate the sincerity of the words. Both Tiger Woods and Lance Armstrong included all of Kleefeld's Rs in detailed scripts read verbatim on televised events; however, for many observers, their remarks failed to relay genuine remorse for their actions. Woods' apology was criticized as being "fake" and "rehearsed to the point of insincerity" said Sally Jenkins of *The Washington Post*, declaring that his delivery of a "13½-minute speech before a controlled audience came off like an obligatory gated checkpoint that he clocked through on his way back to the golf course." Armstrong also received similar disapproval for his apologetic interview on *Oprah*, being called, "glib," "smug," "going through the motions," and not acting "like he cared what word would tumble out of his mouth next" (Brennan).

Jones, on the other hand, appeared to show true remorse for her actions. Rather than dispassionately reading a formal script constructed by her public relations firm, Jones stood before a small group of peers and friends following her sentencing and wept through her own words of guilt. She was broken and humiliated, displaying those feelings through tears on her face. Jones followed the same formula Kleefeld theorized; however, the distinct difference was that she seemed to do it as a genuinely broken individual, displaying true sorrow for both her connection to PEDs and her dishonesty to the American public. "It's hard not to feel sorry for her as she's crying on the steps of the courthouse, but for people who saw her lie so angrily and vehemently, for people in the sport, that was tough," said Jill Geer, USA Track and Field director of communication (Forde).

Some felt empathy because of Jones's courthouse apology; it was still difficult, nevertheless, for many to welcome her back as the iconic Olympic athlete she once was, primarily because she delayed coming clean for nearly four years after lying to federal investigators. Said journalist Christopher Clarey, "The truth and Jones have been separated for so long that you can't give her much credit for coming clean." Sean Gregory of *Time* magazine agreed, saying, "given all her lies of the past, it's not as if we have any reason to believe her." It had been four years since Jones lied to federal investigators; four years of denial, four years of deceit, four years of aggressively targeting innocent reporters who were looking for the truth, and for many, her apology appeared to be a political tactic rather than a genuine request for forgiveness.

Since her conviction and served jail time, Jones has attempted to rebuild her image. In 2012, she published an autobiography discussing the lessons she learned from her time as a professional athlete. She has also been the keynote speaker at many conferences and events worldwide. She advocates honesty, accountability, and hope in the modern era. However, she also understands that not everyone will whole-heartedly accept her messages and recognize her as a humanitarian activist, much of which is attributed to the appalling nature of her dishonesty. Says Jones,

> I know, particularly in the sports world, that there are a lot of people that will never ever forgive me—I understand that—or want to listen to me—and I understand all that. But if I really spend my time focusing on that small, small group of people then I really won't get anywhere. Generally, everyone that approaches me or contacts me sees the big picture here, that, hey, OK, you made a mistake and they were pretty bad, and I acknowledge that, but what you are trying to do now is extremely positive [qtd. in Vitti].

Another factor contributing to Jones's uphill battle with public relations is the arena in which she competes: the Olympics. Although other athletes committing crimes have had to go through the same process of brand repair, many of them were able to get back on the court or field immediately to reshape their images. Kobe Bryant committed adultery, admitted his wrongdoings, and 90 days later was standing on the court of the Staples Center as the local hero for the Los Angeles Lakers. Tiger Woods apologized for cheating on his wife, and three days later, he played in a nationally televised golf tournament. Both athletes had the benefit of being able nearly immediately to show the American public why we liked them so much in the first place. In Jones's case, the Olympics occur once every four years; therefore, her triumphs on the track are not current in the minds of the average sports fan. This dilemma made her mission to repair her image much more difficult because she could not show her fans why they loved her so much as a pure sprinter. Fans were forced to wait for the 2004 Olympics, and by that time, her athletic dominance was over.

Another dimension of sporting rhetoric is the idea that athletes are often remembered by their most recent or final performance. Kobe Bryant carries the shame of committing adultery in a hotel room in Colorado; however, the image people remember is not his weeping at a press conference, but instead dropping 60 points in his final game as a Laker in 2016. That image prevails because of its recency. Although Jones broke records and tallied medals in Sydney, that was not her final performance. Jones failed to reach the podium after the 2000 Olympics, and the freshest images are of her weeping in contrition on the steps of a New York courthouse. The stigma of the BALCO scandal is the last embedded image, the one that comes to mind when people discuss her career. The severity of Jones's villainy may stand as a blemish for many years to come. As discouraging as it may be, some people hold onto acts of iniquity much longer than the years of reparation and sincere remorse. Says former International Association of Athletics Federation President Lamine Diack, "Marion Jones will be remembered as one of the biggest frauds in sporting history" (qtd. in Knight).

The Finality of Infamy

We criticize athletes and hold them to an excruciatingly high standard of morality. However, cheating is something that some researchers argue is a natural reaction when humans enter the competitive arena. In 2016, Amos Schurr and Ilana Ritov wanted to understand how important winning is to the average competitor. To do this, they took a group of students and had them watch a computer screen flashing random symbols in order to estimate how many symbols appeared on the screen. Once they received the students' tallies, they randomly assigned "winners" to half of the group and awarded them a pair of earbuds, despite no true "winner" actually existing. Following this, they divided the students into pairs, one "winner" and one "loser," and had them play a game with a pair of dice and a small cup with a hole in the top. The instructions were simple: the winner of the previous competition placed the dice in the cup and shook it repeatedly. They then looked in the hole to see what the value of the dice read and reported the results to their partner. Whatever number the dice read, the winner exchanged for shekels, a monetary value, while the loser received the remaining value of shekels or the subtracted number from the dice.

The results were astonishing. Students who were declared "winners" in the previous competition lied about the true value of the dice in the cup. "Winners" claimed an average of 8.75 shekels more than the losers, while the control group participants earned seven shekels each, the average of two and twelve. This study reinforced the idea that in competitions, specifically in comparison with a socially equivalent opponent, people are more prone to lie, cheat, and swindle a path to victory, brushing aside any ethical standards that may have once existed.

As appalling and scandalous as these findings may be, this is not a new idea in the realm of competition, as this behavior has been enacted by numerous athletes, in a multitude of sports, over an extensive period. Essentially, this research demonstrates why ten men knew they were not eligible, but nonetheless participated in the 2000 Paralympics in Sydney. Yes, the scales are much higher when comparing shekel measuring and international Olympic competition; however, the principle remains the same. The natural competitor wants to win and will do anything and everything possible to emerge as the victor, even if that means openly lying about mental deficiencies on a rigged IQ test.

Jones followed that competitive pattern and cheated her way to the top, standing on a podium in Sydney with steroid-enhanced blood running through her veins and gold medals draped around her neck, something many track stars had done before her that day. Nevertheless, Jones compounded her error by repeatedly lying about her PED usage to the public, to her fans, and to the federal government in a sworn testimony. Dozens of athletes have cheated before; very few committed the crime of aggressively lying to the American public, hoping all of the evidence would be dismissed. That act of lying will forever blacklist Jones from ever being recognized as one of the greats and put her in the same discussion as Armstrong, Rose, and Barry Bonds.

On the day of her official sentencing, Jones's attorneys requested leniency, arguing in a memorandum that everything up to this point in her life had been tarnished and she would have the anti-hero stigma forever branded upon her name. As they wrote:

> She has been cast from American hero to national disgrace. This part of her story will forever be one of personal tragedy. To be clear, the public scorn, from a nation that once adored her, and her fall from grace have been severe punishments. She has suffered enormous personal shame, anguish and embarrassment. She has been

stripped of her gold medals, her accomplishments, her wealth and her public standing [qtd. in Vinton and O'Keeffe].

All of their words have emphatically been reinforced in the years following Jones's denial, confession, and apology, and it could take years of continued public service, charitable contributions, and humane work to reconstruct an image and a career that at one point was lauded to be the greatest dynasty in women's track and field history. That is the burden that Jones will live with for the remainder of her life and the cross she will bear as someone who did absolutely everything she could to win a race.

WORKS CITED

Brennan, Christine. "If possible, Armstrong less likeable after Oprah." *USA Today.* 17 Jan. 2013, www.usatoday.com/story/sports/columnist/brennan/2013/01/17/christine-brennan-lance-armstrong-interview-aftermath-oprah-winfrey/1843943/.

Clarey, Christopher. "Marion Jones Made Right Decision, but the Truth Comes Late." *The New York Times*, 9 Oct. 2007, www.nytimes.com/2007/10/09/sports/09iht-ARENA.1.78 11979.html.

Dubow, Josh. "Jones Wants a Public Hearing." *Associated Press.* 17 June 2004, www.rutlandherald.com/news/jones-wants-a-public-hearing/article_692a8a76-2e94-597f-9dee-501fe69547ce.html.

Dunham, Alex. "'Stop Playing Well, They'll Know You're Not Disabled.'" *The Local.* 11 Oct. 2013, www.thelocal.es/20131011/stop-playing-well-theyll-know-youre-not-disabled.

Fainaru-Wada, Mark, and Lance Williams. "Track coach Trevor Graham indicted." *San Francisco Chronicle*, 2 Nov. 2006, www.sfgate.com/bayarea/article/Track-coach-Trevor-Graham-indicted-2548113.php.

Forde, Pat. "Marion Jones's rise played out on the world's biggest stage; so did her fall." *Yahoo Sports.* 20 June 2012, www.yahoo.com/news/olympics—marion-jones—rise-played-out-on-the-world-s-biggest-stage—and-so-did-her-fall.html.

Gregory, Sean. "Feeling Betrayed by Marion Jones." *Time*, 5 Oct. 2007, content.time.com/time/nation/article/0,8599,1668849,00.html.

Harris, Kenneth, A., and Tim Povtak. "Barkley Throws Man Through Bar Window" *The South Florida Sun-Sentinel.* 27 Oct. 1997, www.sun-sentinel.com/news/fl-xpm-1997-10-27-9710270306-story.html.

Jenkins, Sally. "Tiger Woods's controlled apology leaves little room for sincerity." *The Washington Post*, 20 Feb. 2010, www.washingtonpost.com/wp-dyn/content/article/2010/02/19/AR2010021904960.html.

Jones, Marion. *On the Right Track: From Olympic Downfall to Finding Forgiveness and the Strength to Overcome and Succeed.* Howard Books, 2010.

Jones, Marion, and Kate Sekules. *Marion Jones: Life in the Fast Lane: An Illustrated Autobiography.* Warner Books, 2004.

"Juiced" *60 Minutes.* CBS. 13 Feb. 2005. www.imdb.com/title/tt0503007/?ref_=ttep_ep6.

Kepner, Tyler. "McGwire Admits That He Used Steroids." *The New York Times*, 12 Jan. 2010: B10.

Kleefeld, John C. "Thinking Like a Human: British Columbia's Apology Act." *UBC Law Review*, vol. 40, 2007, p. 769.

Knight, Tom. "Marion Jones Results Annulled." *The Telegraph*, 24 Nov. 2007, www.telegraph.co.uk/sport/othersports/athletics/2326511/Marion-Jones-results-annulled.html.

"L.T. Over the Edge" *60 Minutes.* CBS. 30 Nov. 2004, www.imdb.com/title/tt2591440/?ref_=ttep_ep35.

Mariotti, Jay. "Mere Hint of Tarnish Dulls Quest; Doubts Will Remain Even if Jones Wins." *Chicago Sun-Times*, 28 Sept. 2000, p. 130.

NBA.com Staff. "NBA at 50: Top 50 Players." *Indiana Pacers*, NBA.com/Bulls, 3 Nov. 2017, www.nba.com/history/nba-at-50/top-50-players.

Reed, Julia. "Marion Jones: Hail Marion." *Vogue*, vol. 191, 1 Jan. 2001, pp. 146–55.

Schurr, Amos, and Ilana Ritov. "Winning a Competition Predicts Dishonest Behavior." Proceedings of the *National Academy of Sciences,* vol. 113, no. 7, 2016, pp. 1754–59.

Simon, Robert L. "Good Competition and Drug-Enhanced Performance." *Journal of the Philosophy of Sport*, vol. 11, no. 1, 1984, pp. 6–13.

"Six Month Jail Sentence for Jones." *BBC News*. 11 Jan. 2008, news.bbc.co.uk/2/hi/americas/7182969.stm.

Vinton, Nathaniel, and Michael O'Keeffe. "U.S. track and field's dirty dozen affected by BALCO." *New York Daily News*, 12 Apr. 2008, www.nydailynews.com/sports/more-sports/u-s-track-field-dirty-dozen-affected-balco-article-1.283753.

Vitti, John "When Marion Jones speaks, she doesn't run from her past." *Boston Globe*. 8 Dec. 2011, www.bostonglobe.com/arts/2011/12/08/when-marion-jones-speaks-she-doesn-run-from-her-past/kz2p88FVqmkybqV9xegd8I/story.html#share-nav.

Wald, J. "Marion Jones on *Piers Morgan Tonight*." YouTube, uploaded by mailtruck, 28 May 2012, www.youtube.com/watch?v=UZw_e_a9jTw.

Waldman, Ed. "Bush Appeal to Set Examples for Youngsters Is Applauded." *Baltimore Sun*. 22 Jan. 2004, www.baltimoresun.com/news/bs-xpm-2004-01-22-0401220045-story.html.

Zinser, Lynn. "Judge Sentences Jones to 6 Months in Prison." *The New York Times*. 12 Jan. 2008. D3.

Zinser, Lynn, and Michael S. Schmidt. "Jones Admits to Doping and Enters Guilty Plea." *The New York Times*. 6 Oct. 2007. D1.

Lessons from #LochMess

Ryan Lochte in Our Rush-to-Judgment Culture

STEVE MASTER

For a split-second, it appeared Ryan Lochte's long but uncertain road to redemption had begun in earnest on September 12, 2016, in Los Angeles. To be sure, this was not the most graceful or efficient performance by Lochte, the swimming champion whose public image had sunk dramatically after his central role in a high-profile scandal at the Rio Olympics. But this day's performance wasn't expected to be so stellar. It was not, after all, an elite swimming competition, but *Dancing with the Stars*, the popular ABC dancing competition where "stars" are often selected to compete as much for their infamy as their fame. Lochte's debut performance with partner Cheryl Burke, a Foxtrot to aptly chosen "Call Me Irresponsible" by Michael Bublé, went well. There were no apparent glitches in the short routine, and host Tom Bergeron joked that it was the "most clothing Ryan Lochte has ever worn in competition." But as judges presented their scores and mostly positive critiques, this baby-step toward redemption was hamstrung in ways few would have imagined.

Protesters, wearing T-shirts containing a red circle with a slash through the word "Lochte," rushed the stage yelling anti–Lochte chants, creating a chaotic scene that ABC nimbly kept off camera during the live broadcast (Nededog). The protesters, who were arrested and charged with misdemeanors for interfering with a performance, later told ABC news they wanted to "get the message out that Lochte is a coward, a liar and, under Brazilian law, a criminal" ("Prosecutors"). The incident left Lochte shell-shocked and shaken—understandably so, considering his suspicion that much of the United States, and certainly many Brazilians, *already* considered him those

61

things, among others. And now, a night that was supposed to begin his long climb (or dance) from the abyss was instead a bizarre reminder of a regrettable, career-crushing incident. "My heart just sunk," he told CNN afterward. "It felt like somebody ripped it apart" (Park and Gonzalez).

Only five weeks earlier, Ryan Lochte was a mostly beloved Olympic mega-star. He was the second fastest swimmer in history behind Michael Phelps, and a six-time Olympic gold medalist, with Hollywood good looks and a playful, goofy, surfer-dude persona that set him apart from many of the more robotic, vanilla Olympic athletes. While Phelps was worshiped on his perch as the greatest swimmer ever, Lochte had a more colorful appeal—appreciated for his greatness, for sure, but also his light-heartedness, occasional recklessness, and quirky antics. Some joked, mostly good-naturedly, about his apparent empty-headedness reflected in media interviews and other public appearances, but as Lochte would say … whatever. It's a profile that served him exceptionally well financially and, for the most part, in the court of public opinion—until a misstep so consequential that not even an innocent appearance on a dancing show was safe from public ridicule. His fans, and even some of his detractors, might well wonder how it reached this point for Lochte. How one booze-infused night in Rio—when no one was harmed and no serious (if any) crimes were committed—could set aflame the public image of a guy who, until this point, had done nothing to elicit ill will of any kind except, perhaps, his starring role in what some have called the worst reality show of all time, E!'s short lived *What Would Ryan Lochte Do?*

While the "how we got here" is relatively straightforward, the "why we got here" is more nuanced. And the attempts to answer the "why" tell us as much about our culture as they do about Lochte, who made some regrettable decisions but has endured a stain on his reputation and faced a level of public outrage dramatically disproportionate to his misdeeds. A deep dive into the Lochte saga shows that the intellectual laziness and *Schadenfreude* exhibited by the public during the scandal was no less irresponsible than the swimmer's party night gone awry.

How We Got Here

From a swimming perspective, the 2016 Rio Olympics were not the best for Lochte. This was Lochte's fourth Olympics—a notable accomplishment in itself—and at the age of 32, it was evident he was past his prime. It is a testament to his skills, tenacity and durability that he still managed to add to his multitude of medals with a gold in the 4 × 200-meter freestyle relay, raising his career Olympic medal count to 12 (six gold). In so doing, he surpassed the career total of Mark Spitz (11) to become the second most decorated swimmer in Olympic history behind Phelps. Not bad for a kid who was not among the nation's most heavily recruited swimmers coming out of high school in Port Orange, Florida, in 2002. Most disappointing in Rio was Lochte's fifth-place finish in the 200-individual medley, one of his stronger events and a race billed as the final confrontation between the two best swimmers of their era—Phelps and Lochte. Phelps, the favorite, won the race, while Lochte finished a distant fifth in what many assumed was the final Olympic race of his career.

With his competition—and perhaps Olympic swimming career—behind him after the 200 IM disappointment, Lochte's primary responsibility for the remainder of the Olympics was to support his American teammates and, per tradition, have some fun. Although the Olympic Games represent the most serious of business for the swimmers, runners, archers and boxers, et al., worldwide the modern quadrennial competition has long transcended sport. Much has been studied and written about the political, cultural, economic, historic, even scientific elements of the Games. An understandably lower profile part of the event, however, is the unique, multicultural social experience (i.e., the party) it offers the athletes. If athletic performances are vigorous and epic on the fields of play, the socializing and partying among athletes has been described as equally so. In a 2012 *ESPN The Magazine* article, soccer gold medalist Julie Foudy described the social scene at the Olympics as a "frat party with a very nice gene pool" (qtd. in Alipour).

Lochte, whose chiseled frame has occupied the cover of numerous publications (*Men's Health, Men's Journal, Vogue*, to name a few), was a proverbial poster-child for that Olympic-quality gene pool and, according to many (including his own mother), an enthusiastic participant on the Olympic party circuit. But when he set out on the night of August 13, 2016, with Brazilian swimming rival Thiago Pereira and several U.S. teammates, he could never have imagined how this one night on the town would impact his career and reputation. According to multiple reports, Lochte spent part of the evening partying at the French team's hospitality house before catching a cab with three teammates to return to the Olympic Village, where most athletes reside during the Games. Trouble arose when the swimmers' cab stopped at a gas station, where armed security guards confronted Lochte and his teammates and demanded money as restitution after they witnessed vandalism that the swimmers had purportedly committed.

There is much dispute, even today, over what exactly transpired at the gas station, though it is commonly believed that the intoxicated swimmers, discovering the rest room locked, urinated behind the gas station and Lochte dislodged a framed advertising sign, which launched the gun-wielding security guards into action. But Lochte's false retelling of the story to the media ultimately turned this event from a drunken, albeit frightening for the swimmers, dust-up into an international scandal that, for a time, overshadowed the Olympics and ultimately decimated Lochte's public image.

The Echo Chamber

Of the many records set at the 2016 Rio Olympics, one belonged not to an athlete but an industry—the media. According to the International Olympic Committee's official web site, Olympic.org, it was the most extensively covered Olympics in history, setting a record of nearly 350,000 total digital and broadcast hours, up from 200,000 at the 2012 London Olympics. It was estimated that half of the world's population watched at least some coverage of the games. And for a 72-hour period, a disproportionate slice of that coverage involved Ryan Lochte's exploits on land, not water.

Amazingly, were it not for a chance encounter between strangers, the story might never have gone public. On a shuttle bus ride, Fox Sports Australia reporter Ben Way struck up a conversation with a woman he soon learned was Lochte's mother, Illeana, who appeared in some discomfort according to Way's account published in *Sports Illustrated* (Deitsch). "She proceeded to tell me how terrible her stay had been," Way told *SI*. "She'd broken her foot, and now her son had been held up at gunpoint." Way expressed sympathy and asked if her son was an athlete. She replied, "yes, and he is prone to big nights and that sort of stuff. He has bleached white hair, or grey hair, or blue hair, I don't really know what it is.' My camera man asked, 'Is your son Ryan Lochte?' To which she said, 'Yes, he is.'" Illeana went on to say Ryan had told her "he'd been held up at gunpoint and they stole his wallet" and that she was on her way to meet him. Way then asked if she would repeat what she had told them on camera, but she "politely declined." After checking in with his editors, Way filed a story detailing his exchange with Illeana Lochte at 10:20 a.m. Rio time and, a few minutes later, tweeted, "BREAKING: @USASwimming gold medalist Ryan Lochte has been held up at gunpoint at a party in Brazil. Details on @FOXSportsNews500."

This sequence of events triggered a predictable avalanche of media coverage led, of course, by NBC and two high-profile members of its coverage team who would soon be ensnared in scandals of their own—Billy Bush (the "co-star" of then Presidential candidate Donald Trump's infamous *Access Hollywood* tape) and Matt Lauer (multiple accusations of sexual misconduct in the workplace). About three hours after Way's initial Tweet, Lochte was approached by Bush on a Rio beach, agreed to be interviewed and responded to Bush's questions in a way he would ultimately regret.

> We got pulled over, in the taxi, and these guys came out with a badge, a police badge, no lights, no nothing, just a police badge and they pulled us over. They pulled out

their guns, they told the other swimmers to get down on the ground—they got down on the ground. I refused. I was like, "I'm not getting down on the ground." And then the guy pulled out his gun. He cocked it, put it to my forehead and said, "get down" and I put my hands up, I was like, "whatever." He took our money. He took my wallet. He left my cell phone. He left my credentials [qtd. in Jhaveri].

In the ensuing days, which included a formal apology to the swimmers from a Rio Olympics spokesperson and an Associated Press report indicating that Brazilian police had not found evidence supporting Lochte's claim, some details of Lochte's story began to unravel. He changed parts of his story in an interview with Lauer, and Brazilian authorities reported to ABC that the incident took place at a gas station the swimmers had vandalized while attempting to use the rest room, contradicting Lochte's tale of being "pulled over." On August 18, three days before the conclusion of the Olympic Games, ESPN's *SportsCenter* tweeted that Lochte's teammates, who were detained by police when trying to leave the country, told police he fabricated parts of the story about the robbery and that video had surfaced of the swimmers vandalizing the gas station. Later the same day, Rio police held a press conference and said the swimmers had lied and that "no robbery was committed against these athletes. They were not victims of the crimes they claimed." Some of the claims made by Rio police were later also proven to be untrue, but at this point, Lochte's fabrication and the optics of drunk American swimmers "trashing" a gas station became *the* story of the Olympics.

Lochte, who endured additional criticism for returning to the United States while his teammates were held behind for questioning, ultimately issued a *mea culpa* via Instagram and in an interview with Lauer. He apologized for his "immature behavior" and for "over-exaggerating" the story, explaining that his high level of intoxication had impaired his judgment (two years later, in October of 2018, Lochte's agent revealed the swimmer had entered treatment to address years of alcohol dependency). However, Lochte did not back down from the claim, supported by the investigation and video footage, that gun-wielding men, speaking a language the swimmers did not understand, demanded money from them, asserting "whether you call it a robbery, whether you call it extortion or us just paying for the damages—we don't know. All we know is there was a gun pointed in our direction, and we were demanded to give money" (Bowman). Still, he expressed deep regret for his "embarrassing" behavior and for creating, through his lack of candor, an international story that needlessly embarrassed the host country and took attention away from his fellow Olympic athletes. "I took away from their accomplishments.... I think that's what hurts me the most," he said.

Despite his apologies, Lochte took a predictable pounding in the news media and on social media, becoming the "object of his home nation's collective mortification and disgust" (Odell). He was America's "disgraced" swimmer, the bad boy of swimming, a "national embarrassment" (Reid) and "global symbol for the ugly American" ("Michael Phelps has") whose exaggeration unfairly played into Brazil's reputation for lawlessness. The *Daily Mail* noted that Lochte brought "hours and hours of shame for his nation" (Rahman), and the *New York Daily News* ran his smiling, strapping full-body image on its tabloid cover with the headline "The Lochte Mess Monster." On August 18, #LochteGate, #RyanLochte and #LochMess were among the top ten trends on Twitter. Social media commentary ranged from furious to snarky, labeling Lochte a fool, "dipshit" (@OldmanLogan2008), a "shitty white dude" (@nnabuck), and "douche canoe" (@FoxyJazzabelle). Memes emerged featuring Lochte as Pinocchio and on the movie poster for "Liar Liar 2" (Glover). One particularly biting tweet invoked Lochte's long-time role as bridesmaid to his rival, declaring that "Phelps would have trashed the gas station bathroom twice as fast" (qtd. in Bazzle).

The consequences of this growing stain on his image commenced quickly. Within days, he suffered a rapid loss of sponsorships, which represent the lifeblood of Olympic athletes like Lochte, who are part of the public's sports consciousness only once every four years. On August 21, 2016, swimwear giant Speedo USA, iconic clothing manufacturer Ralph Lauren and a skin care company, Syneron-Candela, announced they were cutting ties with Lochte. Gentle Hair Remover and mattress maker Airweave soon followed suit. Speedo, his sponsor for a decade, declared that his behavior was "counter to the values" of the brand, adding that it would donate $50,000 to Save the Children to benefit needy Brazilian children ("Speedo drops"). A *Forbes* article, headlined "Ryan Lochte sinks future Endorsement Potential with Actions Worthy of an Olympic Gold for Stupidity," estimated that the incident could cost Lochte from $5 to $10 million in future endorsements. "He will likely have extremely low odds of earning future endorsement deals due to his forever tarnished brand," wrote Patrick Rishe, who covers the economics of sports for *Forbes*. The USA Swimming establishment, meanwhile, doled out its own punishment for Lochte by suspending him from domestic and international competition for ten months. Months later, reflecting on the avalanche of public outrage and ridicule, loss of sponsors and his suspension, Lochte told ESPN he remembered feeling like "the most hated person in the world" (qtd. in Glock). One can only imagine how that must have felt, considering Lochte's career-long penchant for returning from world competitions as an American hero. But in today's culture, "haters" are always poised to pounce. No one is immune. Not our Olympic heroes, such as Lochte, nor the young men and women who risk their lives defending our country. Make one mistake, and watch out!

Submerged in Neverland?

In January 2012, six months before Ryan Loche would defeat Michael Phelps for a gold medal in the 400 individual medley in London, considered his signature Olympic triumph, a video emerged on the internet showing four United States Marines urinating on dead Taliban soldiers in Afghanistan. The incident drew swift condemnation from the highest rungs of the American government and predictable outrage from American citizens.

As fury grew and the talk of "war crimes" commenced, war journalist Sebastian Junger penned a column in the *Washington Post*, "We're all guilty of dehumanizing the enemy," asking Americans to take a step back from their near-instant condemnation and ask what conditions might have caused these young Marines to commit this seemingly cruel and dehumanizing act.

Although not explicitly defending the Marines, Junger invited readers to engage in a mental exercise that favored asking questions over pointing fingers. Junger, who embedded with Marines in his coverage of the war, noted that the "impulse to desecrate the enemy" comes from a "very dark and primal place in the human psyche" that is going to "break through" in a war zone, a setting only a minuscule percentage of the finger-pointing American public has endured. He explained that as these soldiers were growing up in post 9-11 America, they no doubt heard politicians and their friends and neighbors speak repeatedly about our enemies' use of dehumanizing terminology. They naturally would view the enemy the same way. Most poignantly, Junger wrote that dehumanizing the enemy might just be "a desperate attempt by confused young men to convince themselves they haven't just committed their first murder—that they have simply shot some coyotes on the back–40."

Although "Lochtegate" and the plight of these Marines could not differ more in their importance or gravity, the Lochte story does exemplify an underlying theme in Junger's article—Americans' overwhelming tendency toward knee-jerk demonization and vilification rather than reflection and clarification. Junger was practicing what author Lee Siegel calls "moral rigor," which Siegel explores in a July 2018, *New York Times* op-ed arguing that, in contemporary American society, the public would "rather condemn than understand." He writes that this "aversion to suspend moral judgment" is a relatively "new development in cultural life," noting that when Gore Vidal wrote sympathetically about domestic terrorist Timothy McVeigh and Norman Mailer wrote empathetically about double-murderer Gary Gilmore, they "were not trying to make excuses for their subjects.... Readers and critics understood them as efforts to expand and deepen our awareness of the forces, both inside and outside a person, that shape a human life." Siegel continued,

Today, however, our cultural style is very different. We thrill to a kind of pornography of exposing and shaming. We favor pre-determined verdicts that have been arrived at by collective sentiment—a cultural style that accuses first, presents evidence often without questioning it, then makes a judicial finding and then passes a sentence.

As Lochte, now married and raising his first child, continues to wrestle with the consequences of being exposed and shamed, it is useful to step back, as Junger did with the Marines, to contemplate and consider the mean-spirited hysteria and ill-conceived narratives as the scandal played out in front of the largest Olympic media audience in history. Only by applying moral rigor can we fairly and accurately assess what the events in Rio say about Lochte, the scandal, our culture and his ultimate legacy.

Any such discussion must start with the acknowledgment that Lochte messed up. Award-winning journalist Mike Lupica joked that a person's career should not be ruined because of a "piss and a poster," but that original sin, so to speak, was not what generated an international scandal. Had Lochte simply avoided Billy Bush, or told him the complete truth about the events of the night—something along the lines of "yep, I drank way too much, slapped down a poster (not sure why I did that), peed in the bushes, shouldn't have done those things, really sorry Brazil ... my bad"—the story would have been significantly less toxic, if at all. But toxic it was. And the level of toxicity says more about our culture—the "thrill of exposing and shaming" and the stubborn resistance to complicate our snap judgments by considering nuance and shades of gray—than it does about Ryan Lochte. The champion swimmer is a lot of things—a champion, immature, a devoted son and brother, now a husband and father, a flake, an incredibly disciplined athlete, *human*, but certainly not the "monster" he was made out to be in the immediate days following his "scandal."

One way to apply moral rigor to the Lochte scandal is to acknowledge the irrational expectations we place on our Olympic heroes, who are far more human and at times less mature than their corporate sponsors would have us believe. *In Living Out of Bounds—The Male Athlete's Everyday Life*, scholar Steven J. Overman writes about a "Peter Pan syndrome" common to men who play games for a living. From the time they begin showing promise in high school and throughout their college and professional careers, athletes are protected and sheltered in a way that stunts emotional maturity and suspends them in a Peter Pan–like "Neverland" (30). He notes that so much of a professional athlete's life is devoted to training and competing in a "paternalistic system cowered by authority and shielded from reality (38) ... with few responsibilities outside sports" (37) that many engage in "immature behaviors to a degree that appears extreme" (33). Overman cites numerous iconic professional athletes who fit this profile, from Dennis Rodman to Lance

Armstrong, Babe Ruth to Pete Rose, who once said "I was raised but never grew up" (qtd. in Overman 32).

So the idea that Lochte, even at age 32, would possess enough self-awareness to consider the possible consequences of a "big night" of partying doesn't square with what scholars know about athletes' off-the-field tendencies. Ironically, it was Phelps, not Lochte, who was the first of the rivals to stumble into scandal. In 2009, less than six months after winning eight gold medals at the Beijing Olympics, Phelps was photographed taking a bong hit at a University of South Carolina party. As public criticism toward Phelps ensued, award-winning *Washington Post* columnist Sally Jenkins reflected on the hypocrisy that Phelps had somehow crossed a line while 42 percent of Americans "have at one time or another gotten sweetly baked on hay"("Big Bong"). Jenkins went on to argue that criticism of Phelps was not only hypocritical, but that it represented a deep misunderstanding of the behavior the public should expect from its star athletes. While commercial interests may attempt to portray our sports icons as saintly, buttoned-up family men and women, this façade is inevitably toppled by scandal, contract dispute, or other public display of frailty akin to Lochte's in Rio. In a question-and-answer session with readers about her Phelps-marijuana article, Jenkins noted "Perfection in sports is a dangerous illusion. Don't ever confuse it with real virtue, or intellect ... the really marvelous thing about sports is that the most extraordinary things are accomplished by quite ordinary people, who are just as flawed personally as you and me." If Lochte's level of intoxication during his ill-fated night out seemed extreme, that, too, is typical of elite athletes. "Champions," Jenkins wrote, "tend to develop out of a state of emotional emergency. Their training methods are extreme, their goals are extreme and their rewards tend to be extreme." Hope Solo, the United States soccer goalie who has had her own share of public controversies, said "athletes are extremists. When they're training, it's laser-focused. When they go out for drinks, it's 20 drinks" (qtd. in Alipoud). Considering what we know about professional athletes' maturity and celebratory excesses, it is difficult to rationalize the surprise, let alone the level of outrage Lochte faced when his extreme night of partying ended in public urination, a downed poster, and a stretch of the truth.

Other narratives drawn during the scandal also generate skepticism—including the widely held perception that Lochte "made up" the story about being robbed. This much is clear: he stretched the truth, and his sensational exaggeration of having a gun placed to his temple certainly supports Overman's view of an athlete's life in "Neverland." Tall tales that depict the storyteller as heroic, not to mention fibbing to one's mother, are certainly examples of child-like behavior. However, a closer look at Lochte's actual story reveals one that was much closer to the truth than the public ever took the time to understand. A week after Lochtegate first made headlines, *USA Today* published its own investigation that supported the basic "framework" of Lochte's story. According to the *USA Today* report, which was supported by video evidence, eyewitness accounts, and an inspection of the gas station rest rooms, Lochte was drunk, tore down a "loosely attached" advertising sign and later exaggerated accounts of the event, including a "sensational allegation of a gun being held to his forehead" (Barnes and Meeks). But Lochte's basic account—that he thought the swimmers were being robbed when they were approached by armed men who "flashed badges, demanded money and pointed guns at them"—was true, according to the report. The *USA Today* report also refuted claims by Brazilian police that the swimmers had vandalized a bathroom. It also suggested, based on interviews with a Brazilian judge, that if anyone committed a crime during the incident, it was the security guards, who likely were not justified in pulling their weapons or determining independently the value of the damage allegedly caused by the swimmers. The judge also opined that if the amount of money taken from the swimmers was greater than the value of the damage, the guards' actions could be considered a robbery—just as Lochte contended. Lochte was ultimately charged with filing a false police report.

The Poynter Institute, the premiere United States journalism think tank, praised the persistent and dogged work of the *USA Today* reporters, who said they knew their reporting would "go directly against a huge tidal wave of media coverage that is condemning Lochte" (Hare). Unfortunately for Lochte, by the time *USA Today*'s investigative report was published on the day of the Closing Ceremony, fans' and the media's attention had shifted and opinions of Lochte had hardened. He was portrayed as an irresponsible, entitled frat boy and poster child for white male privilege, as being so self-absorbed that he never bothered to reflect (as though reflection and smart decisions are somehow unaffected by heavy alcohol consumption) on how his actions might impact Brazil, a country already battling stereotypes depicting it as crime-ridden. Nor did he consider, critics charged, how his actions would consume so much media oxygen that attention would be diverted from other athletes (as if Lochte was somehow making editorial decisions for the worldwide media). Although such charges may well contain slivers of truth—to varying levels—none of them are black and white, and all lack the nuanced thinking that can only emerge from moral rigor. Consider the criticism that Lochte brought unfair scrutiny on Brazil's ability to keep visitors safe. Security was a huge story (and, some said, a sensational one) leading up to the games, with headlines declaring this Olympics would be the most crime-ridden in history. Some derided this as "click-bait" unfairly depicting the city, mired in a depression, as "some kind of urban apocalypse" (Greenstein). The narrative was particularly painful for Brazilians, who possess a "cultural peculiarity" (Cuadros), according to the *New Yorker*, of obsessing over what the developed world thinks of them.

Yet, the fears of violence during the Olympics were largely validated, and not only by security guards allegedly overstepping their responsibilities by demanding money from the swimmers at gunpoint. According to the *Christian Science Monitor*, two Australian rowing coaches were robbed at gunpoint, and a stray bullet was fired into a media tent at the Olympic Equestrian Center (Kauffman). *Reuters* reported that "the two weeks of competition were overshadowed by armed robberies of foreign ministers, athletes and coaches" (Brooks and Flynn). It is perfectly fair to argue that Lochte touched a nerve with his exaggerations, unjustly magnifying a story that had already reflected poorly on Brazil. But as the *New Yorker* (Schwartz) and others note, it is a near certainty that he did so unwittingly. Said *Slate*'s Susan Matthews: "Lochte did not make up an elaborate lie and sell it to the press in an evil plan to paint Rio de Janeiro as a dangerous city. He told his mom something scary happened to him, which he believed."

This notion did not prevent some in the media from injecting race, white male privilege and perceived prejudice into the story. The *Chicago Tribune*'s Dahleen Glanton wrote that Lochte and his teammates "used one of the oldest, most proven techniques in the books for covering up their own misdeeds—they blamed it on brown people." In ESPN's *The Undefeated*, Kevin Van Valkenburg derided Lochte as a symbol of white male privilege, noting that he faced almost no initial skepticism for a "preposterous story where he cast himself as the Frat Bro version of Jason Bourne." "Try to imagine," he wrote, "what the world's reaction would be if a black athlete got drunk, urinated in public, destroyed some property, then concocted a story in which he bravely stood up to someone with a gun who was trying to rob him and his friends." A writer from *Nylon*, Kristin Iversen, introduced gender issues into the discussion, comparing the public reaction to Lochte's incident with the scrutiny faced by gymnast Gabby Douglas, an African American, for not putting her hand over her heart during the national anthem. Iverson wrote that people are "making jokes and laughing about" Lochtegate while "other people who aren't white and aren't men can be shamed, ostracized and harshly censored for not smiling enough while [T]he Star[-] Spangle[d] Banner plays."

These issues may or may not be worthy of exploration. But the way they were so often framed, it seemed, was not to generate a broader discussion, but to pile onto Lochte who, contrary to Iverson's claim, was indeed severely "ostracized and harshly censored." The outpouring of criticism—invoking race, white male privilege, gender, cultural prejudice—reflects the diversity of lenses through which the public addresses a scandal. Yet the tone and one-sided nature of the arguments exhibited not the moral rigor espoused by Siegel. Instead, the result was a relentless public shaming far disproportionate to Lochte's offenses and seemingly at odds with his dozen or so years in the public arena, as well as his middle-class upbringing in a family of mixed ethnicity (his mother is Cuban-American). As one observer posted on Twitter, "You people with the Ryan Lochte white privilege, get over it. Not everything is about race. Sometimes it's just about being stupid" (qtd. in Donnella). It is understandable, and often times admirable, that social justice advocates want to generate conversations about male white privilege when given the opportunity. But does it not water down the discussion when it seems so opportunistic? If Ryan Lochte is the epitome of white male privilege, what does that make the former Sanford University swimmer Brock Turner, who received a "slap on the wrist" six-month sentence after being convicted in June 2016 of sexually assaulting an unconscious woman behind a dumpster? Should Lochte, who assaulted a poster, be drawn into the same conversation because of his celebrity status? Ultimately, doing so creates an inaccurate picture of Lochte and does not serve the cause of raising awareness of white male privilege particularly well, either. This has become the new normal in society and explains, to some degree, the cultural backlash against political correctness.

The Lochte I Know

Ryan Lochte has always been a handful. For his coaches, parents, and even for me. As a sportswriter for the *Daytona Beach News-Journal* between 1988 and 2007, I had the privilege of covering Lochte's rise from high-strung tadpole to Olympic champion. It was quite a ride ... and challenge. Of the thousands of athletes whom I have written about in three decades as a journalist, I have never met one so great at his sport and seemingly so disinterested in talking about it. Interviews with Lochte were painful, something I was amused to see continue as his national and international profile blossomed and my colleagues grumbled, as I so often did, about the challenge of covering him. He was nice, polite and humble, but enticing him to reflect on even the slightest details of his achievements, race strategies, opponents, training—basically any of *normal* things reporters want to talk about—was maddeningly futile.

But as I observed Lochte's career, wrote about him, and spoke to people around him (his coaches, friends, teammates, family), I came to realize that this frustrating part of his makeup was integral to his success. In a sport where the difference between being a champion and an also-ran is a fraction of a second, those endeavoring to be Olympic champions must overcome two significant barriers unrelated to their physical skills and work ethic—burn-out (training too much) and psych-out (thinking too much). Lochte's persona represented an impenetrable wall against these threats, allowing him to blossom into one of the greatest in the history of his sport.

In essence, Lochte "Olympic champion" would not exist without Lochte "world class flake." His reckless, happy-go-lucky, non-reflective side seemed to immunize him from the pressure that can break swimmers at such a high level. More significantly, it served as a counter-weight to a lifetime commitment to a sport that, while ferociously challenging, can be more than a bit mind-numbing. There is a reason the world pays attention to swimming once every four years; every four years is plenty. Swimming is not particularly interesting to watch, or to do. There is little room for creativity—no Xs and Os or defensive strategies, curveballs or dunks, chip-ins or aces, jarring knockouts, gravity-defying vaults or goals scored from seemingly impossible angles. Training revolves around technique—much of it unrecognizable to the average spectator—and boring, painful repetition, often in a steamy indoor facility reeking of chlorine.

In his 1971 autobiography, *Deep Water*, American swimmer Don Schollander, who won five medals (four gold, one silver) in the 1964 and 1968 Olympics, describes his training, swimming laps three hours and eight miles per day, as "mechanical," "monotonous" and so "incredibly dull and boring" that "swimmers begin to feel like robots" (228–246). In her memoir, *Swimming Studies*, former Canadian Olympic hopeful Leanne Shapton describes vividly the toll swimming at such a high level has on the body and the psyche. She writes about how time "passes slowly" (8) in practices, which are spent "staring hard at the stripes at the bottom of the pool" (41) and immersed with "steady pain ... the mechanical cycle of breathe-pull, breathe-pull-pull, breathe-pull-pull and the dull gray noise of churning water" (41).

This has been a steady part of Ryan Lochte's life for as long as he can remember—but he has been careful not to make swimming his entire life. Say what you will about Lochte's intelligence, but he has managed his career as a swimmer with a strategic savvy those outside the sport cannot truly appreciate or understand. Those close to him have long marveled at his ability to compartmentalize and to embrace the part of his life that has absolutely nothing to do with swimming. Moreover, his coaches and family have been smart enough not to obstruct Lochte's "wild side"—as tempting as it may be at times. "I'm dealing with a 27-year-old man who lives on the edge a little bit," Lochte's longtime coach, Gregg Troy, said in a 2011 *New York Times* profile. He added, "If you do anything other than allow him to be himself, he's not going to be the same athlete" (qtd. in Crouse, "As Lochte Raises"). This unique ability to wall off his swimming life from his personal life began long before he became a household name in the sport. Inside the steel gates at the Port Orange YMCA, his training ground as a youth swimmer, he was all business (well, much of the time). The "outside the gates" Lochte has always been, well, interesting.

I first began chronicling Lochte's wild side during the run-up to the 2004 Athens Olympics, his first. In the lead to the cover story on him just days before his Olympic debut, I wrote "Many of the world's greatest athletes will relate stories the next two weeks about their long, arduous roads to the 2004 Olympics. They'll talk about the sacrifice, the painful workouts, the 24–7 obsession. Then there's Ryan Lochte. The Port Orange 20-year-old makes his quest for the Athens Olympics sound like something he managed to fit in between Sociology class and a run to the Laundromat." In the story, Lochte's friend and teammate, Kyle Deery, reflected on the time, when they were thirteen, they accidentally set fire to the neighborhood woods by lobbing paint cans into a bonfire, a stunt that attracted police and fire vehicles. The mischief, of course, began even earlier. Profiles of his earliest years as a youth swimmer depict a rambunctious, easily distracted prankster who would rather slide around in the showers at the YMCA and binge on candy than engage in serious training. Obviously, he matured physically during the progression from youth swimmer to high school state champion to college All-American to Olympic gold medalist. And, impressively, he ultimately embraced training in a way few outside the sport could ever imagine, as evidenced by his super-human accomplishments in the grueling sport.

And, yet, the playful, childish side of Lochte has long remained a staple of his public image—intentionally or not. He is known for attention-grabbing pranks, flashy wardrobe, injury-inducing recklessness and (earlier in his career) nutritional habits favoring Big Macs and Skittles. After winning a gold medal in London, his smile revealed a $25,000 custom-made, diamond-studded American Flag dental grill. At the U.S. Nationals in 2009, he sported a pair of oversized Clark Kent glasses even though he has 20-20 vision (Lewis). His own mother made fun of the "bleached white hair or grey hair or blue hair" he donned at the Rio Olympics and revealed her son's habits of "big nights" of partying and preference for "one-night stands" over committed relationships. Lochte is particularly notorious for his contribution to the Urban Dictionary with his trademark catch-phrase "Jeah," which he described as a "personalized" version of Young Jeezy's "Chea." Those wondering how Lochte developed his reputation as being, well, not so smart, need only to go to YouTube and listen to his explanation of the meaning of "Jeah." "It means almost like everything, like happy," he tells reporters in the video. "If you have a good swim you say 'JEAH' like it's good. So I guess … it means … good." Also maddening to his coaches have been his injuries, which have mostly stemmed from his recklessness and carefree lifestyle. He has suffered injuries breakdancing and skateboarding, and a motor scooter accident jeopardized his participation in a world championship meet. The *New York Times* described his vocabulary as "hip-hop infused" (Crouse "For the") and his infamous wardrobe, including a closet full of over 100 pairs of shoes, as "1970s consignment shop." "Though he could seldom match Phelps' results," wrote Karen Crouse of the *New York Times*, "Lochte nevertheless has enjoyed a long reign as the public's champion, providing the ballast with his fun-loving nature for Phelps' machine-like efficiency" ("For the").

That "fun-loving nature" was virtually the entire focus of the mercifully short-lived E! reality show *What Would Ryan Lochte Do?*, which follows Lochte on a drunken golf outing, tender moments with his family, and "his quest of seemingly dating every girl in Gainesville, Florida." *Hollywood Reporter* opines that the show depicts Lochte as an "empty-headed pretty boy" whose "true nature" is much like a "big, occasionally irritating Labrador puppy" with "truly deplorable grammar." "He's kind of a dope, but so loveable you can't really say a mean word against him" (Keene).

Life After Scandal

Lochte's "dopey" and "loveable" sides were evident in the months after the scandal. In May 2017, he posted a photo of himself on Instagram receiving an intravenous infusion of B-complex vitamins. Although the vitamins are not banned substances, the U.S. Anti-Doping Agency (USADA) prohibits IV infusions in a volume greater than 100 mL without a therapeutic use exemption. The idea that Lochte actually photographed and posted on social media his own Anti-doping violation played into the "dopey" stereotypes, and the incident had further consequences—a fourteen-month suspension from competition. Two months earlier, the *Orlando Sentinel* reported on Lochte's "loveable side," covering his appearance at a charity swim clinic for the Mac Crutchfield Foundation. According to the article, this was not part of some P.R.-orchestrated event to rehabilitate his image. Crutchfield drowned tragically in a drainage ditch in 2007, and Lochte has been attending the charity event since its inception. Mac's mother, Maggie Crutchfield, told the *Sentinel*, "Ryan is the most loving, giving man I've ever met. I've never met anybody more kind-hearted." Columnist Mike Bianchi, who authored the *Sentinel* article previewing the charity event and a writer not prone to candy-coating athletes' transgressions, wrote, "If you want to meet the real Ryan Lochte, not the one errantly portrayed amid an international scandal during the 2016 Olympics in Rio de Janeiro, now is your chance." His kindness and ability to connect with the public has been a consistent theme throughout his career. As a child, he was once snubbed when requesting a professional athlete's autograph and vowed he would never make a fan feel similar rejection if he ever reached his dream of swimming prominence. Sure enough, he spends hours patiently signing until the very last fan in line has his or her autograph. He is especially loyal—and generous—with family and friends. In college, he used money earned for winning his Olympic medals to purchase "tricked-out" (Glock) car stereos for his friends. Being a "compulsive people-pleaser," says teammate Cullen Jones, is Lochte's "Achilles heel." "He loves hard—to a fault," Jones told *ESPN the Magazine* (Glock). "When people get around him they never want to leave."

In *Living Out of Bounds*, Overman writes, "adversity has a way of accelerating the maturity process." Whether that will be the case with Lochte remains to be seen. Lochte's life post-scandal has included some significant setbacks, the suspension for the IV infusion and the revelation by his agent that he was seeking treatment for alcohol abuse, though the severity of his problem is unclear. Yet, according to numerous journalistic profiles and his constant social media presence, there is reason to believe that, despite his adversity, Lochte remains the happy-go-lucky, positive, quirky champion he has always been. Since the Olympics, he has married former *Playboy* model Kayla Rae Reed and become a father. The couple's first child, son Caiden Zane, was born in June 2016, and they announced in November 2018 that they were expecting their second child, Liv Rae, born in June 2019. Social media images project a beautiful, happy family. At the same time, Lochte has continued training in hopes of competing in the Tokyo Olympics. Merely making the team would be a remarkable accomplishment. He would be almost 37 years old, well past the prime of most American Olympic swimmers. Only two American swimmers have excelled internationally into their 30s—Jason Lezak and Anthony Ervin. And they swam sprint events (50- and 100-freestyle) whereas Lochte's premier events are longer and require more endurance and agility.

Beyond the questions regarding his age, one must also wonder whether his future performance might be affected by the developments in his life post–Rio. Will his determination to make amends for his scandal, coupled with his added responsibilities of being a father and husband, impede his legendary psychological strength to perform under pressure? Will maturity shatter the Lochte mojo? That, too, remains to be seen, as does the impact of the scandal on Lochte's legacy. It is worth noting that two years after Lochte's Rio scandal, golfer Tiger Woods re-emerged from a high-profile and embarrassing scandal of his own to play winning golf and become, remarkably, a beloved figure in his sport once again. Pro football player Michael Vick also overcame a scandal that sent him to jail for participating in a dog fighting ring. The difference is that these athletes were able to re-establish themselves in sports that are relevant year-round. They did so by exhibiting appropriate conduct and, most importantly, by having the opportunity to regain fans by winning their respective, high-profile sports.

Given Lochte's age and the sport of swimming's one-every-four-years relevance, it is far less likely Lochte will have the opportunity, despite the fact that his mistakes were arguably far less egregious than those of Woods and, more so, Vick. Although the passage of time will certainly ease the sting of Lochte's Rio misstep, the scandal will remain an irreversible and vastly overblown scar on his otherwise remarkable legacy, one that may never fully wash away. And that is unfortunate because for all his faults and missteps, Lochte's skills and accomplishments will long be underappreciated. According to Overman, sports fans may idolize and celebrate their champions, but even the most fervent sports fans "cannot appreciate the time and effort" (61) athletes dedicate to their sports. Nor will the average fan have the wherewithal, or exercise the moral rigor, to preclude his "scandal" from having a vastly outsized influence over his image of Lochte, the person. But this much is also true—Americans love a comeback story. Lochte has the opportunity to write one in Tokyo. And while the odds are stacked against him, what a comeback story it would be.

Works Cited

Alipour, Sam. "Will You Still Medal in the Morning." *ESPN The Magazine*. 8 July 2012, www.espn.com/olympics/summer/2012/story/_/id/8133052/athletes-spill-details-dirty-secrets-olympic-village-espn-magazine.

Barnes, Taylor, and Meeks, David. "USA TODAY Sports Investigation Raises Questions About Rio Cops, Lochte Incident." *USA Today*. 21 Aug. 2016, www.usatoday.com/story/sports/olympics/rio-2016/2016/08/21/investigation-ryan-lochte-rio-olympics-authorities/89082232/.

Bazzle, Kelly. "The Internet Responds to the Mess That Is #Lochtegate." ABC Action News. 19 Aug. 2016, www.abcactionnews.com/entertainment/the-internet-responds-to-the-mess-that-is-lochtegate.

Bianchi, Mike. "You Can Meet the 'Real' Ryan Lochte at Windemere Charity Swim Clinic Saturday." *Orlando Sentinel*. 13 Apr. 2016, www.orlandosentinel.com/sports/open-mike/os-sp-ryan-lochte-olympics-brazil-rio-dancing-with-the-stars-20180413-story.html.

Bowman, Emma. "Ryan Lochte to NBC's Matt Lauer on Rio Incident: 'I Was Immature.' NPR. 21 Aug. 2016, www.npr.org/sections/thetorch/2016/08/21/490790940/ryan-lochte-to-matt-lauer-on-rio-incident-i-was-immature.

"Brazilian Police Say Lochte, US Swimmers Were Not Robbed." *Associated Press*. 18 Aug. 2016, www.apnews.com/c29081e6ac6c4ed9b3eaaf400415b081.

Brooks, Brad, and Flynn, Daniel. "U.S. Swimmers Tall Tale Touches Raw Nerve in Brazil." *Reuters*. 19 Aug. 2016, uk.reuters.com/article/us-olympics-rio-lochte-brazil-idUKKCN10U28C.

Cauterucci, Christina, and Matthews, Susan. "Should We Feel Bad for Ryan Lochte?" *Slate*. 19 Aug. 2016, slate.com/culture/2016/08/should-we-feel-bad-for-ryan-lochte.html.

Crouse, Karen. "As Lochte Raises Profile, Image Makers Dive In." *New York Times*. 6 Aug. 2011, www.nytimes.com/2011/08/07/sports/as-lochte-raises-profile-image-makers-dive-in.html.

———. "For the Spotlight? Ryan Lochte Was Ready to Do Anything." *New York Times*. 18 Aug. 2016, www.nytimes.com/2016/08/19/sports/olympics/eccentric-everyman-ryan-lochte-profile.html.

Cuadros, Alex. "Why Brazilians Are So Obsessed with the Ryan Lochte Story." *The New Yorker*. 18 Aug. 2016, www.newyorker.com/news/news-desk/why-brazilians-are-so-obsessed-with-the-u-s-swimmers-story.

Deitsch, William. "The World Found Out About Ryan Lochte's Story ... By Accident." *Sports Illustrated*. 21 Aug. 2016, www.si.com/olympics/2016/08/21/ryan-lochte-robbery-story-rio-olympics-ben-way.

Donnella, Leah. "Roundup: Smart Thoughts on Ryan Lochte and White Privilege." NPR. 19 Aug. 2016, www.npr.org/sections/codeswitch/2016/08/19/490629815/roundup-smart-thoughts-on-ryan-lochte-and-white-privilege.

@FoxyJazzabelle. "Has that guy just … ALWAYS been a douche-canoe." Twitter, 18 Aug. 2016. 6:54 a.m. Twitter.com/Foxyjazzabelle/status/766272124600348672.

Glanton, Dahleen. "Ryan Lochte's Method of Covering Up Bad Behavior: Blame It on Rio." *Chicago Tribune*. 20 Aug. 2016, www.chicagotribune.com/news/columnists/ct-olympics-lochte-lie-glanton-20160819-column.html.

Glock, Allison. "Do You Really Still Hate Ryan Lochte." ESPN. 6 June 2017, www.espn.com/espn/feature/story/_/id/19506033/will-hate-ryan-lochte-end-story.

Glover, Sarah. "#LochMess: Ryan Lochte Memes Sprout Up on Social Media as Robbery Claim Unravels." NBC News. 18 Aug. 2016, www.nbcnewyork.com/news/national-international/LochMess-As-Ryan-Lochtes-Alleged-Lie-Unraveled-Memes-Sprouted-Up-on-Social-Media-390618001.html.

Gonzalez, Sandra, and Park, Madison. "Audience Members Crash Ryan Lochte's Debut on 'Dancing with the Stars.'" CNN. 13 Sept. 2016, www.cnn.com/2016/09/12/entertainment/ryan-lochte-dancing-with-the-stars/index.html.

Greenstein, Teddy. "When It Comes to Safety of Rio Games, Media Hysteria was the Real Crime." *Chicago Tribune*. 8 Aug. 2016, www.chicagotribune.com/sports/international/ct-navigating-rio-olympics-crime-safety-spt-0809-20160808-story.html.

Hare, Kristen. "How USA Today Unraveled Ryan Lochte's Rio Drama." Poynter Institute. 26 Aug. 2016, www.poynter.org/reporting-editing/2016/how-usa-today-unraveled-ryan-lochtes-rio-drama/.

Iversen, Kristin. "Ryan Lochte Shows the World What White Male Privilege Looks Like." *Nylon*. 18 Aug. 2016, nylon.com/articles/ryan-lochte-lies-white-privilege.

Jenkins, Sally. "Big Bong Theory." *The Washington Post*. 3 Feb. 2009, www.washingtonpost.com/wp-dyn/content/article/2009/02/02/AR2009020202973.html.

_____. "Michael Phelp's Tokin' Effort." *The Washington Post*. 3 Feb. 2009, www.washingtonpost.com/wp-dyn/content/discussion/2009/02/03/DI2009020300998.html.

Jhaveri, Hermal. "Ryan Lochte's Reaction to Getting Robbed at Gunpoint: Whatever." *USA Today*. 14 Aug. 2016, ftw.usatoday.com/2016/08/ryan-lochtes-reaction-to-getting-robbed-at-gun-point-whatever.

Junger, Sebastian. "We're All Guilty of Dehumanizing the Enemy." *The Washington Post*. 13 Jan. 2012, www.washingtonpost.com/opinions/were-all-guilty-of-dehumanizing-the-enemy/2012/01/13/gIQAtRduwP_story.html?utm_term=.192324f8c364.

Kauffman, Gretel. "Lochte Robbed at Gunpoint: Is Rio Crime Living up to the Hype?" *Christian Science Monitor*. 14 Aug. 2016, www.csmonitor.com/World/Olympics/2016/0814/Ryan-Lochte-robbed-at-gunpoint-Is-Rio-crime-living-up-to-the-hype.

Keene, Allison. "What Would Ryan Lochte Do?: TV Review." *Hollywood Reporter*. 21 April. 2013, www.hollywoodreporter.com/review/what-would-ryan-lochte-do-443085.

Lewis, Michael. "Renewed Focus." *Daytona Beach News-Journal*. 26 July 2009, *NewsBank*, infoweb-newsbank-com.ezproxy.libproxy.db.erau.edu/apps/news/document-view?p=AWNB&t=pubname%3ADBNC%21Daytona%2BBeach%2BNews-Journal%2B%2528FL%2529&sort=YMD_date%3AD&maxresults=20&f=advanced&b=results&val-base-0=renewed%20focus%20lochte&fld-base-0=alltext&docref=news/129C03914918CFC8.

Lupica, Mike. "Swim Shady: Lighten Up on Lochte." *Sports on Earth*. 23 Aug. 2016, http://www.sportsonearth.com/article/197196594/ryan-lochte-rio-tall-tale-overreaction.

Master, Steve. "High Water Mark—Lochte's Olympic Dream Reaches Surface Today." *Daytona Beach News-Journal*. 17 Aug. 2004, *NewsBank*, infoweb-newsbank-com.ezproxy.libproxy.db.erau.edu/apps/news/document-view?p=AWNB&t=pubname%3ADBNC%21Daytona%2BBeach%2BNews-Journal%2B%2528FL%2529&sort=YMD_date%3AD&maxresults=20&f=advanced&b=results&val-base-0=high%20water%20mark%20lochte&fld-base-0=alltext&docref=news/1048C5C7A6633128.

"Michael Phelps Has Done a Lot Worse Than Ryan Lochte, He Just Had Better Timing." *The Herd Now*. 23 Aug. 2016, www.theherdnow.com/michael-phelps-has-done-a-lot-worse-than-ryan-lochte-he-just-has-better-timing/.

Nededog, Jethro. "Anti-Ryan Lochte protesters stormed 'Dancing with the Stars' and left people shaken." *Business Insider.* 13 Sept. 2016.

@nnabuck. "Ryan Lochte epitomizes shitty white dude who thinks there's consequences for nothing ugh go away." Twitter, 20 Aug. 2016. 10:48 a.m. Twitter.com/nnabuck/status/767055665504276482.

Odell, Amy. "How Ryan Lochte Went from Disgraced Olympian to Engaged Man." *COSMOPOLITAN.* 5 Dec. 2016, www.cosmopolitan.com/entertainment/celebs/a8372733/ryan-lochte-kayla-rae-reid-internets-most-fascinating/.

@OldmanLogan2008. "Thought Lochte would be printing a tee. I went to Rio, won a gold medal and lost millions being a dipshit." Twitter, 19 Aug. 2016. 10:38 p.m. Twitter.com/OldmanLogab2008/status//766871896105246720.

Overman, Steven J. *Living Out of Bounds: The Male Athlete and Everyday Life.* Lincoln: University of Nebraska Press, 2010.

"Prosecutors Charge Men After Ryan Lochte Protest on 'Dancing with the Stars.'" ABC 13 Eyewitness News. 27 Sept. 2016, abc13.com/news/prosecutors-charge-men-after-ryan-lochte-protest/1528925/.

Rahman, Khaleda. "Ryan Lochte's Night of Shame." *The Daily Mail.* 18 Aug. 2016, www.dailymail.co.uk/news/article-3748228/Ryan-Lochte-s-night-shame.html.

Reid, Scott. "Disgraced U.S. Olympic Swimmer Ryan Lochte Welcomed Back at Masters Meet in Riverside." *Orange County Register.* 28 Apr. 2017, www.ocregister.com/2017/04/28/disgraced-u-s-olympic-swimmer-ryan-lochte-welcomed-back-at-masters-meet-in-riverside/.

"Rio 2016 Sets Records on the Field of Play and Online." Olympic.org. 22 Aug. 2016, www.olympic.org/news/rio-2016-sets-records-on-the-field-of-play-and-online-1.

Rishe, Patrick. "Ryan Lochte Sinks Future Endorsement Potential with Actions Worthy of an Olympic Gold for Stupidity." *Forbes.* 19 Aug. 2016, www.forbes.com/sites/prishe/2016/08/19/ryan-lochte-sinks-future-endorsement-potential-with-actions-worthy-of-an-olympic-gold-for-stupidity/#54f5e98c9fle.

Schollander, Don, and Duke Savage. *Deep Water.* New York: Crown Publishers, 1971.

Schwartz, Alexandra. "Ryan Lochte's Perfect Summer Scandal." *The New Yorker.* 19 Aug. 2016, www.newyorker.com/culture/cultural-comment/ryan-lochtes-perfect-summer-scandal.

Shapton, Leanne. *Swimming Studies.* New York: Blue Rider Press, 2012.

Siegel, Lee. "Whatever Happened to Moral Rigor." *New York Times.* 25 July 2018, www.nytimes.com/2018/07/25/opinion/james-baldwin-public-morality-empathy.html.

"Speedo Drops Ryan Lochte Sponsorship and Donates $50,000 Fee to Charity." *The Guardian.* 23 Aug. 2016, www.theguardian.com/sport/2016/aug/22/ryan-lochte-speedo-sponsorship-ended-rio-2016-olympics.

Van Valkenburg, Kevin. "Dear Fellow White People." *The Undefeated.* 23 Aug. 2016, theundefeated.com/features/dear-fellow-white-people/.

Diego Maradona
The Hand of God

Ismael Lopez Medel

For a sport that claims to be "the beautiful game," soccer has produced many players famous for their transgressions, rule breaking, and defiance. Zlatan Ibrahimovic, Eric Cantona, or Mario Balotelli, for example, have adopted a Machiavellian approach, emphasizing winning above everything else, through all means necessary. Disregarding the original values of the sport, these players view soccer (and usually life) as a constant battle against real and imaginary enemies. But above all those names stands one of the most talented players to take the field, a player who managed to embody all the negative values of the bad boys of soccer while also having a profound impact on the game: Argentinian soccer superstar Diego Argmando Maradona.

Maradona has been temperamental, aggressive, unethical, and impulsive. He also possessed perfect technical skills, displayed a never-seen-before ball-handling ability, and became the protagonist of a remarkable rags-to-riches story. Maradona's erratic behavior off the field has nonetheless overshadowed every accomplishment on the field as he has been engulfed by incidents, controversies, and polemics. Those have included tax evasion, violent behavior, Mafia connections, extramarital affairs, illegitimate children, obesity, alcohol abuse, radical political choices, and an ongoing feud with the media. As Mexican author Juan Villoro sarcastically notes, "[H]e's done everything possible to put an end to himself, but with no success" (127).

Maradona's legend was solidified during one game; in fact, a single five-minute stretch during the second half of that match can serve as a metaphor for his entire life. On June 22, Argentina faced England in the quarterfinals of the 1986 World Cup. The game took place in the midst of political tensions between the countries arising from the 1982 Falklands War. At halftime, the

Argentinians were down 1–0, but early in the second half, Maradona jumped to reach a loose ball in front of England's goalkeeper and surreptitiously used his hand to score a goal. Despite the illegal handball, the goal counted, and the match stood at 1–1. Four minutes after the first goal, he single-handedly dribbled past half of England's team to drive the ball to the back of the net in what the Fédération Internationale de Football Association (FIFA), the international governing body for soccer, considers the "Goal of the Century." That goal clinched the match. At the post-game press conference, far from apologizing for his illegal move, Maradona displayed bravado by claiming he scored the goal "a little with the head of Maradona and a little with the hand of God" (Williams). That, in a nutshell, is Maradona.

An unforgettable player, with an uncomfortable legacy of rebellion, scandals, and drug addiction. A player with a fanatic, cult-like fan base, especially in Argentina and Naples. A player who is known in Argentina as "D10S," a play-on-words coupling Maradona's iconic number 10 jersey with the Spanish word for God (Dios). In fact, the people love Maradona so intensely that they have created a religion, the Church of Maradona. Today, half a million people claim to belong to the religion that reveres the player as a deity. He is a public figure so famous that even kings and popes have interceded in his career and personal life. Maradona is both one of the greatest soccer players ever to step on a field and one of the most infamous bad boys ever to emerge from *the beautiful game*.

The Beautiful Game

Soccer is the world's favorite sport, played regularly by an estimated 265 million people (Kunz 10) and viewed by millions more throughout the globe. For example, soccer's championship tournament, the World Cup, is the most watched sporting competition in the world. Soccer is also the most followed sport on social media and has become profoundly engraved in culture, a real symbol of local and national identity. For instance, Real Madrid, the world's most valuable sports brand (Forbes), has 220 million social media followers, more than all NFL, MLB, NBA, and NHL teams *combined*. As might be expected, soccer comprises a sizable economic industry that dominates media markets in many countries, with thousands of digital media accounts, countless hours of radio time, and newspapers and television shows dedicated to building the larger-than-life narrative of the sport. Such accessibility has turned the sport into vehicle for political expression, nationalism, and patriotism.

Soccer has become so popular for a number of reasons. One of the keys is the game's simplicity and straightforward rules. It is flexible and adaptable:

it can be played in different formats and venues. It is also affordable, requiring practically no equipment beyond a ball, thus making the sport available to players of all statuses and social classes. Unlike other sports, soccer does not reward a particular physique, but it demands a variety of skills. It also requires a team effort, but a single player and a single goal can have a dramatic effect on the outcome of any match.

Most scholars date the birth of the modern sport to 19th century England although there is plenty of evidence of games similar to soccer played in China, America, and Europe before that point. In the 1820s, private schools in England tried to impose uniform rules to transform an old game of mob soccer that had turned excessively violent. Soon afterward, clubs emerged, each with its own set of rules. Boosted by soccer's popularity, the main eleven clubs in England agreed on a set of rules, leading to the creation of the Football Association in London in 1863. British soccer was imagined as a gentleman's sport, and players were expected to behave accordingly, showing deference and sportsmanship. In essence, the sport served as a cultural vehicle to transmit the values of the British Empire: tradition, honor, elegance, and style. Soccer supposedly built good character by teaching players the importance of team effort, sportsmanship, and fair play.

The English exported the game, and in 1904 seven countries founded FIFA ("Fifafacts"). Ironically, England would not join until 1906, after considering whether the game had lost its "Englishness." Soccer soon stretched beyond Europe and became the most popular sport in South America and Africa. It was also one of the first sports to recognize its international potential with the creation of the FIFA World Cup in 1930. Soccer proved to be an adaptable game, and although Europeans played it more physically, South Americans emphasized finesse and technical skills. Boosted by the successful World Cup tournaments and the expansion of national leagues, soccer became an industry, built on the backs of legendary players such as Stanley Mathews, Di Stefano, and Pelé. These players were creative and technically gifted, and they introduced new technical skills, as well as establishing the standard of greatness for younger generations of players.

Soccer's requirement of both technique and creativity has earned it the nickname "the beautiful game," an expression of disputed origins. Some attribute it to H.E. Bates' 1952 *Sunday Times* article "Brains in their Feet," that includes the lines: "Footballers think with their feet.... This would be as good a reason as any to think that football is the most beautiful game in the world." Radio Five commentator Stuart Hall used the phrase in 1958 to describe player Peter Doherty's style. In 1977, Brazilian superstar, Pelé popularized the expression in his biography *My Life in the Beautiful Game*, as a translation from the Portuguese *jogo bonito*. Nowadays, "the beautiful game" refers not only to the technical abilities of the players or the creativity associated with soccer, but also to the emotional connection between the fans and the sport. Soccer is a crucial element of the social fabric of many countries after decades of shared memories, experiences, and magical moments on the pitch.

Maradona's Beautiful Game

Soccer is a game rooted in tradition and symbolism. To those not familiar with the sport, the numbers on the players' jerseys may seem anecdotal. But in soccer terms, the first eleven numbers mean a position on the field, each with a particular responsibility to the team. For instance, number 2 represents a defensive right back, and a number 9 is the team's striker and main scorer. Number 10 is the most significant number of all. The player who wears number 10 is the team's leader: creative, intelligent, and technically skilled. Maradona was the perfect 10.

His professional career spanned more than twenty-two years, from his debut with Argentinos Juniors in 1976 to his retirement with Boca Juniors in 2001. He played in two of the most important leagues in Europe and accumulated eleven trophies: national championships in Argentina (1981), Spain (1983), and Italy (1987 and 1990), league cups in Spain and Italy (1983 and 1986), and international trophies (1989). Undoubtedly, the peak of his career occurred in 1986 when he led Argentina to the World Cup championship in Mexico.

Maradona's legacy extends beyond his record on the field, however. Other soccer giants have had more successful careers in terms of statistics (especially pertinent is the comparison between Maradona and fellow Argentinian Lionel Messi, who has won 32 titles). Maradona became legend because he had a profound impact on teams throughout his career, such as turning Argentinos Juniors and Napoli from bottom-of-the-league teams to title-winning squads. But he also failed in some of his most significant challenges: while playing for the Spanish giants FC Barcelona and in the 1990 World Cup in Italy.

Masterful ball handling and dribbling, which Argentinians call "gambeta," defined Maradona's style. His low center of gravity (he is only 5'5") allowed him to control the ball with precision at high speed. Maradona was quick, slippery, and technically gifted with both legs. In a sport with well-defined positions and roles, Maradona embodied the "total-player" ideal, a player who could cover the entire field. Maradona was not only more skilled than the rest, but he was also quick and shifty, changing positions continually, surprising rivals who could not find a way to stop him unless it was resorting to violence. The fact that he was left-footed played to his advantage, making defense against him more complicated. In the words of his 1986 World Cup squad teammate Jorge Valdano, "[N]ext to Maradona, teammates stopped being players and became spectators" (Brach 419).

Maradona's talent was innate. His skill was well beyond his years even at age fifteen when he became the youngest player to debut in Argentina's national tournament. His former teammate on the youth team *Cebollitas*, Daniel Delgado recalls, "Diego played the same way when he was ten as when he was thirty" (qtd. in Remoli). His style did not require maturation; he was the most technical player on every team he played. On the pitch, only his injuries were able to slow him down.

Maradona was also uncommonly driven. The first television interview he gave, at an early age, was telling. When asked about his dream, he said it was to play the World Cup and eventually win it (Campoamor 349). The coach who gave him his first opportunity with Argentinos Juniors quickly understood Maradona's attitude. He challenged him to beat the first defender that came his way with a tunnel, passing the ball between the defender's legs, a move that is as spectacular for the audience as it is humiliating for the rival. Maradona, age fifteen, did precisely as told (Murray, "FourFourTwo's"). In 1977, Maradona was a starter on the team, and he scored his first goals after dribbling past nine rivals (Robinson). In only two years, his skills allowed him to dominate the Argentinian league, and he became a national sensation and a familiar face on billboards and television commercials.

Although soccer is a worldwide phenomenon, the center of power is still in Europe, both in the five big leagues (England, Spain, Italy, Germany, and France) and in the Union of European Football Associations (UEFA) Champions League, an international competition involving the best teams in every European league. South American countries have a long tradition of exporting players to Europe as soon as they become noticed. That was Maradona's case. His agent and long-time friend Jorge Cyterspiller turned down the first international offer from Sunderland in England as early as 1977, but more international attention was to come.

During his time at Argentinos Juniors, Maradona's performance transformed a team that went from struggling to keep afloat in the first division (the relegation system automatically sends the worst teams to an inferior division) to achieving an unprecedented second place in the national tournament. Maradona scored a record 116 goals, finishing as the nation's top scorer for five consecutive years, something no one has yet matched. Argentinos Juniors became a real competitor to the country's two giants, Boca and River, and Maradona's popularity convinced the government to sponsor Argentinos Juniors through the nation's public airline. Maradona's fame reached Europe, and in 1979, his team embarked on a series of friendly games all over the world, including Maradona's first game in Barcelona.

The Spanish giants had already attempted to hire Maradona, but the Argentinian Military Junta had implemented legislation to prevent young players from leaving the country to join foreign teams. Maradona was no exception. In the midst of a violent military dictatorship (1976–1983), with a populace hungry for good news, Maradona became Argentina's hope. At the time, the government used soccer to distract the public from the political situation and seized the opportunity to claim the nation's soccer successes as their own, especially the 1978 World Cup and the 1979 Youth World Cup. As Valdano explained, "Maradona was more than just a great footballer. It was a special compensation factor for a country that in a few years lived through several dictatorships and social frustrations of all kinds" (qtd. in Burns, *Maradona* 115). Maradona managed to become both a poster boy for the government and an immensely popular figure, and his eventual retirement left "Argentina traumatized" (Burns, *Maradona* 115).

Nowadays, soccer has become extremely professionalized and commercialized, with players such as Neymar Júnior or Cristiano Ronaldo operating as multi-million-dollar brands. But Maradona played at a different time, when soccer was simpler and more direct. And although Argentinians love him and revere him because of his "Argentinan-ness that many Argentinians found difficult to express themselves" (Campoamor 359), the rest of the world sees a different side of Maradona: the bad boy.

"I made mistakes, and I paid for them"

Fast forward to November 10, 2001, Maradona's farewell game at a packed *Bombonera*, Boca Junior's legendary stadium. A visibly emotional Maradona summarized his career in one sentence: "I made mistakes, and I paid for them, but the ball is never soiled." In his goodbye, he admitted to his life of controversies while simultaneously declaring his love and reverence for a sport that he believes he did not despoil. Perhaps Maradona was being somewhat optimistic. Maybe he did not soil the game itself—maybe—but his legacy has certainly been sullied. When people ask who is the greatest soccer player of all time, Maradona's skills certainly make him part of the conversation, especially in Argentina, where he is still revered, but in the eyes of the rest of the world, he never surpasses the likes of Pelé, who was not only technically skilled but also a great ambassador for the game. In looking at Maradona's life, one cannot help but wonder: if not for all his personal baggage, would history regard Maradona as the greatest of all time? However, without these bad boy qualities, would Maradona still have been *Maradona*? These "what ifs" aside, Maradona's many issues are as much a part of his legacy as his unquestionable skills.

Unlike Pelé, Maradona was raucous and rebellious, with tendencies toward bad temper, aggressiveness, impulsivity, and entitlement. He struggled with addiction and seemed to embrace unethical behavior. Maradona sees himself as a modern-day Sisyphus, continually struggling to survive hostility and difficulties, whether real or invented. His tough upbringing provided him with a street-wary attitude toward the establishment and made him particularly unpredictable and rebellious. He was born in 1960 Villa Fiorito, a tough shantytown south of Buenos Aires, in a time where an economic depression stifled the country. The Maradonas lived in extreme poverty with no running water or even a floor in their humble home. In later years, he recalls having been stripped of his youth: success came at a very early age and turned a barely schooled kid into the spotlight without time to mature. Maradona's speedy rise to fame and fortune left him ill-prepared for the future, always surrounded by a troupe of friends and acquaintances, living a luxurious and extravagant lifestyle. As Jimmy Burns points out,

> [T]he more idiosyncratic characteristics, the mixture of indulgence, narcissism, and rebelliousness that would mark the later stages of Maradona's life, had begun to emerge unchecked around this time. The product of a family, society and a less readily identifiable enemy within [*Maradona* 25].

The inability to deal with fame was at the heart of Maradona's off-the-field issues. While at FC Barcelona, for example, Maradona was unable to cope with the intense pressure that he and the soccer club received, so he secluded himself in the castle the club had rented for him in the luxurious neighborhood of Pedralbes. His entourage surrounded him and offered protection from an outside world that seemed menacing and judgmental (Maradona, *México 86*). In Naples, Maradona secluded himself in his hotel room, always surrounded by admirers and stalked by strangers. His seclusion made him paranoid. Unable to leave his hotel room due to fan pressure, Maradona became undisciplined, missing practices, traveling on his own, disconnecting from his teammates and relying on his exceptional soccer skills to allow him to perform at a maximum level (Burns, *Barca* 155).

When not secluded, Maradona embraced a world of luxury, flattery, and excess, only finding relief in the city's intense nightlife. His lavish parties were legendary, with trays full of cocaine floating around, mobsters, and women brought in by the player's manager Guillermo Coppola (Campoamor 391). In a famous episode that summarizes Maradona's lifestyle, he had Ferrari hand-paint a black Testarossa just for him, but left the car in the garage and never used it. Maradona just wanted to be the one person in the world who owned such a rarity (Burns, *Maradona* 139).

Over the years, his cocaine addiction became serious, turning into an obsession that would haunt him for decades. As the player admitted in 1982, he started taking cocaine in Barcelona while he was enjoying the city's nightlife, a time he recalls as the unhappiest of his life (Burns, *Barca* 251). Later, while playing in Naples, his cocaine use was such an issue that the club's president had to remind Maradona that any substance taken after a Thursday would turn out positive in the drug test after the weekend game ("Diego Maradona Parte"). On Sunday, March 17, 1991, after a match against Bari, Maradona tested positive for cocaine. To this day, he claims it was the Italian Federation's *vendetta* for the 1990 World Cup elimination (Argentina, led by Maradona, defeated the host nation, Italy, in the semifinals) and explains the situation in his usual blunt and self-expiatory way: "I had a drug problem, yes, but for that very reason I tested myself" (Maradona et al. 101). He was suspended from the *Serie A* for fifteen months and would never play in Italy again. Instead, he returned to Buenos Aires, where his family and friends forced him to enter a "detoxification" program that included a diet, abstinence from alcohol, and psychological support (Burns, *Maradona* 201).

After a herculean effort to get back into shape, he was able to join the national team for the 1994 World Cup in the United States, but, in a well-publicized episode, he tested positive for ephedrine in what he calls his doctor's "honest mistake." Maradona was escorted off the field in Boston, after a game against Nigeria, and taken to a lab. When the results came back, he was expelled from the World Cup and suspended from all international competitions for another fifteen months (Burns, *Maradona* 201). At the press conference after the game, the Argentinian offered his conclusion: "they cut off my legs" (qtd. in Campoamor 396).

Maradona officially retired in 1997 and continued to lead an extravagant lifestyle, surrounded by controversies and scandals. The following years saw a significant decline in his health as he struggled with drug addictions and marital problems. Eager to show the world the quality of his country's public medicine, Cuban dictator Fidel Castro invited Maradona to travel to Cuba and enroll in a private clinic, La Pedrera, to immerse himself in an intense detoxification program. Argentinian media closely followed and published those events. In 2000, Maradona was rushed to an emergency room in Punta del Este, a luxurious resort in Uruguay, due to an overdose that kept him clinically dead for forty minutes (Nieto). His farewell game took place in 2001, and shortly after, he was admitted to a hospital in Buenos Aires after suffering a heart attack at age 51. Although his public image was declining, his support was still active: hundreds of fans camped outside the hospital in Buenos Aires, waiting for his release. Maradona later confessed to having been an addict until 2004, with a series of hospitalizations for hepatitis in Buenos Aires in 2007 that sparked rumors about his death.

Maradona's intense lifestyle, together with his fame and pressure, took a toll on his personal relationships. Although he enjoyed a long relationship with Claudia Villafañe, who was his companion since the early days, the marriage eventually dissolved in 2003. In Napoli, he had a scandalous extramarital relationship with an Italian high-society woman, Cristina Sinagra, resulting in the birth of Maradona's first son, whom he would not officially recognize even after a personal request from the Argentinian Pope Francis in 2015 (Parolo). Maradona had a reputation also of being a violent man, particularly aggressive toward women. He has been sued different times on accusations of sexual abuse and hitting women.

Maradona's relationship with money was as contentious as his relationship with fame, drugs, and women. At the peak of his career, he was the most highly paid soccer player in the world. He signed multi-million-dollar contracts but managed to lose his fortune and considered bankruptcy a number of times. Starting at an early age, Maradona became a widely recognized public figure, the center of what Nicolás Salazar-Sutil calls the "Maradona Inc. Corporation" in recognition of the immense value of the Maradona brand for merchandising and advertising. His relationship with his two managers, Jorge Cysterpiller and Coppola, ended abruptly after accusations of betrayal and threats of legal actions. Maradona's financial problems were profound, and suspicion surrounded his two former managers who might not have been entirely transparent when declaring his earnings in order to avoid taxes (Burns, *Maradona* 109). The lack of transparency in his finances was evident, for instance, in his arrival to Naples. The police suspected the local Mafia was involved because the small team had almost fallen into relegation the previous season but suddenly could afford the world's most expensive player (Burns, *Maradona* 122). Suspicion increased when the dangerous local Mafia, the *Camorra*, became his security guards, providing protection for him and his family (Maradona, *México 86*). His financial issues worsened in 2002 when an Italian court ruled Maradona guilty of tax evasion and ordered him to pay €18 million in local taxes. By 2009, the interest on the unpaid debt had compounded €37 million that he owed.

Controversy surrounding Maradona has also involved radical political discourse. Unlike the majority of soccer players, who tend to stay away from politics, Maradona has been blunt, provocative, and outspoken. While in Naples, Maradona started to engage in political discourse that would become more intense over the years. In his public appearances, he conquered the fans' *tifosi's* (hearts) by adopting a class warfare narrative, showing pride in the south, and presenting Napoli as the underdog before the powerful north. With a worldview rooted in Peronism (the populist ideology of former Argentinian president Juan Perón who had captivated blue-collar Argentinians in the 1940s with class warfare rhetoric), Maradona saw Napoli as the example of the struggle between the working-class, blue-collar society and the political and economic powerhouses of the Italian north. He notes, "We had truly become the club of the working class, of the poor. Even in the north, we could count on the support of the southern workers who lived there" (Maradona et al. 85).

Maradona's perception of racism originated in Barcelona, a city that he perceived to be filled with Spanish prejudice against South Americans. In Naples, Maradona became more and more outspoken about the discrimination suffered by the *Napolitani*, blaming the club for its passivity. Italy would host the 1990 FIFA World Cup and, as luck would have it, the semifinals matched Italy against Argentina in Naples. Before the match, Maradona caused a media storm when he requested that the local fans support Argentina instead of Italy. He claimed, "The Neapolitans must remember one thing: Italy makes it feel important one day of the year but forgets about it the other 364" (qtd. in Vecsey). In his autobiography, Maradona justified himself by writing, "I don't like the fact that now everyone is asking the Neapolitans to be Italian and to support their national team. The rest of Italy has always marginalized Naples. It is a city that suffers the most unfair racism" (Maradona et al. 201). The announcement created a ripple effect that had an impact on the team as half of the crowd cheered against Italy. Argentina won after a penalty shoot-out and moved on to Rome to play the final championship game against Germany. During that final game, Italian fans booed Argentina's national anthem, an event that Italy's goalkeeper Dino Zoff considered "a shameful moment for Italy" (qtd. in "Diego Maradona Parte"). When the television screen showed Maradona's face, he insulted the crowd with loud utterances of "sons of bitches."

Maradona's political rhetoric sometimes focused on particular people. When Maradona accepted Castro's invitation to join the detox program in Cuba, for example, he publicly praised Venezuela's Hugo Chávez and Nicolás Maduro and denigrated George Bush. Argentinian journalist Gregorio Tatián, organizer of *Diego Unchained*, a full-month festival dedicated to all things Maradona in Cordoba, Argentina, points out that Maradona is perhaps "one of the last outspoken political voices in a complicated time, when most of the political figures he praised are either dead (Chávez, Castro) or are in prison, and the right-wing extremism is on the rise in the region" (La Tinta). Again, Maradona becomes the folk hero, the countercultural figure deeply connected to the impoverished communities in Latin America. In stark contrast with the soccer universe, where players tend to shy away from politics, Maradona remains an exception.

If Maradona could have avoided off-the-field controversies, his legacy may have designated him the greatest player ever—while wearing cleats. But another critical feature of his career was his unethical behavior when playing soccer. His view of the game was profoundly impacted by the toughness of his upbringing in Villa Fiorito, where soccer was not just a sport, but more a matter of survival. Maradona carried with pride the flag of Carlos Bilardo's Estudiantes, a team that had been able to capture championships based on collective, extreme roughness and a street-smart attitude that Maradona considered very Argentinian. According to this philosophy, outsmarting rivals was the most important characteristic of the Argentinian player; winning by any means possible was the ultimate goal.

Cheating, according to Maradona, was quintessentially Argentinian. To this day, Maradona justifies his infamous 1986 "hand of God" as a legitimate strategy to win a game, even if it meant stealing. As he notes, "That's what I did to the English. I stole their wallet without them realizing. Argentinians are proud because no one saw me. They identify with that" (qtd. in Carlin).

As a player, Maradona could be extremely aggressive. One display of this was in the game against Brazil in the 1982 World Cup, where a frustrated Maradona lost his temper and launched himself cleats first into a Brazilian defender's knee, which earned him a red card and ejection from the game. Later on, while playing for FC Barcelona, Maradona was the antagonist during the infamous 1983 Spanish Cup's final title game against Athletic de Bilbao. The atmosphere around Maradona was strange because the player had lost the support of the Barcelona fans, who now openly criticized his performance and blamed it on his disorganized lifestyle. Before the game, Bilbao's manager Javier Clemente had called Maradona "stupid and castrated, with no human qualities" (qtd. in Murray, "The Joy") and asked his players to be aggressive. When FC Barcelona lost the game, a brawl of players from both teams, fans, and police officers ensued, including a frustrated Maradona, who threw fists and kicked rivals. The three-month suspension that followed the game effectively ended his time in Barcelona even though the nation's King Juan Carlos I ultimately lifted the suspension (Maradona et al. 183).

Maradona's impulsive personality played a major role in his lack of professional stability. He played for seven teams in eighteen years, which is unusual for players of his level, many of whom had long one-club careers: Pelé (nineteen years at Santos), Lionel Messi (fifteen years at FC Barcelona), George Best (ten years at Manchester United), or Di Stefano (twelve years at Real Madrid CF). This lack of continuity has also been the trademark of his post-soccer career as a manager; he had short runs at six smaller teams and a two-year term as national manager for Argentina.

One of the only consistent things about his playing career was his nearly constant disgruntlement with the soccer establishment, typically leading to a quick departure from his teams. Maradona sees himself as an Argentinian David fighting against many Goliaths of his time. In his mind, his problems always stem from others. First, he blamed Argentina's national team manager Cesar Menotti for not including him in the 1978 World Cup, a grudge Maradona holds to this day. While in Barcelona, he refused a blank renewal contract because he felt misunderstood by FC Barcelona's President José Luis Núñez Clemente (Bouchard 62), a man he called an "imbecile" in his 1996 biography. In Napoli, he became disenchanted with club owner Corriano Ferlaino, whom Maradona blamed for not fulfilling the promise of guaranteeing him a quiet life and who had refused to sell the Argentinian to Marseille FC, then Europe's wealthiest club (Maradona et al. 79). Above all, Maradona's disdain centered on Julio Grondona, president of the Argentinian Federation and FIFA vice-president, and Joao Havelange, FIFA's president and long-time friend of Maradona's rival, Pelé. Maradona sees them as the authors of a conspiracy to end his career and keep Argentina from ever winning another World Cup (Yallop 114). During his coaching career as the manager of Argentina's national team, Maradona famously quit after the 2010 World Cup in South Africa, publicly criticizing the Argentinian Federation and pointing fingers at Grondona, "He who will be in charge of the national football team (whoever he is) must know that treason is just around the corner" ("'Grondona Lied'").

Maradona's erratic behavior on and off the pitch has also been a product of a great sense of entitlement. Confident in his superior technical skills, Maradona admits to having misunderstood the demands of high competition, particularly in the 1982 World Cup. Maradona recalls the pre-tournament period as "a time of boredom, lack of physical preparation, and a sense of entitlement. By the time the tournament started, we believed we had already won the cup. We forgot one detail: To win you have to play first" (Maradona et al. 160). Such entitlement is probably the result of the fanatic adulation he has received throughout his life. Argentinian fans offer not only adulation, but forgiveness. They see Maradona as one of them, a fallible hero and have forgiven and forgotten Maradona's excesses. They have justified his anger, rebelliousness, and misbehavior. What Maradona did on the field for a country so desperate for a hero made everything else vanish. As Bartlomiej Brach explains, Maradona's erratic behavior makes him incomprehensible to Europeans but a hero in his own country because Maradona embodies the *pibe*, the blue-collar kid who plays in the rough street games Maradona grew up with.

Perhaps the most extreme case of fan adulation is the Church of Maradona, a group of soccer fans who claim to live in the year 60 AD ("After Diego," born in 1960) and recite their version of the Lord's Prayer entitled "Our Diego." The prayer begins, "Our Diego, who is on the pitches / Hallowed be thy left foot, bring us your magic" (Sehli). The religion, founded by three fans from Rosario in 1998, communicates through Facebook with over eighty thousand members, has a bible (Maradona's biography), apostles (people who helped the Argentinian), and meets twice a year: on Maradona's Christmas (birth) and on Easter (on the date of the game against England in the 1986 World Cup quarter-finals) (Sehli).

Life After Soccer

Life after soccer can be a difficult transition for professional players. Some enjoy successful managerial careers (Hendrik Cruijff, Zinedine Zidane), serve as club executives (Karl-Heinz Rummenigge, Roberto Carlos), or become part of the establishment (Pelé, Michel Platini). Maradona tried and failed at all of the above. His strong personality and constant rebelliousness have followed him in every endeavor, turning him into an uncomfortable presence for the soccer world, decades after storming the world at Argentinos Juniors.

After the 1994 suspension, Maradona started his managing career coaching a small club, Deportivo Mandiyu, lasting only a few months before insulting the club's owner in the locker room. The Argentinian returned to coaching in 2009 to manage the Argentinian national team in preparation for the 2010 World Cup, but after quitting that team, he has struggled to keep his coaching career alive, never making it to the top of the profession and only enjoying short-lived appointments in secondary markets. In 2011, he joined Al Was in Dubai as a manager but did not even finish the season. He returned to Argentina to manage Deportivo Riestra in 2013 and then joined Fujairah in the United Arab Emirates in 2017. In September 2018, he became the manager of the Dorados of Sinaloa, a Mexican second-division team located in the heart of Mexico's cocaine and marihuana industries, home to the infamous Sinaloa drug cartel (Parlow).

Despite his many transgressions, Maradona has managed to remain in the collective memory of the soccer universe as one of the greatest. Even FIFA, the organization he despises, named him FIFA's player of the 20th century, alongside Pelé. Perhaps Valdano was right when he said, "Maradona offered the Argentines a way out of their collective frustration, and that's why people love him. Over there, he is a divine figure" (qtd. in Mora y Araujo).

It has been three decades since the "hand of god" goal. Soccer is changing. New generations of soccer fans all over the world now enjoy a different game: more professionalized, structured, and business-oriented. Unlike Maradona, new superstars are athletes who follow carefully planned training regimens in top-quality facilities. Even as new stars emerge, the influence of Maradona refuses to vanish. Arguably, many players have surpassed Diego Maradona's accomplishments, yet the soccer family still holds onto Maradona as one of the greatest. Especially interesting is the case of fellow Argentinian Messi, arguably the best soccer player in the last decade, with a record-breaking career and undisputed ranking as one of the top five all-time players. In Argentina, the recurring and heated comparison between the two usually ends with the same result: there will be no one again like Maradona.

Long gone are the days of the dirt fields, the hunger to survive, and the need to play soccer. Those days and that soccer will most likely never come back. Still, when younger fans ask who was the best, they will probably hear about an unlikely hero, the most gifted player in history, who managed to be the hero and the villain at the same time: Diego Armando Maradona.

WORKS CITED

Bates, H.E. "Brains in their Feet." *The Sunday Times*, 16 Nov. 1952. p. 4, www.hebatescmpanion.com/sites/default/files/cx131.pdf.
Bouchard, Jean-Phillipe. *Los Bad Boys del Futbol*. T & B Editores, 2008.
Brach, Bartlomiej. "Who is Lionel Messi? A comparative study of Diego Maradona and Lionel Messi" *International Journal of Cultural Studies*. 22 Dec. 2011, doi.org/10.1177/1367877911422859.
Burns, Jimmy. *Barca: A People's Passion*. Bloomsbury, 2009.
―――. *Maradona. The Hand of God*. Bloomsbury, 2010.
Campoamor, Andreas. *Golazo! The Beautiful Game from the Aztecs to the World Cup: The Complete History of How Soccer Shaped Latin America*. Riverhead Books, 2014.
Carlin, John. "Maradona Opens Up on Life of Deception." *The Independent*, 18 Apr. 2009, www.independent.co.uk/sport/football/international/maradona-opens-up-on-life-of-deception-696671.html.
"Diego Maradona Parte 1,2,3,4." YouTube, uploaded by Eduardo Sakamoto, 18 Jul. 2013, www.youtube.com/watch?v=paKGuqK3iAY.
"Fifafacts." 2014, www.fifa.com/mm/document/fifafacts/bcoffsurv/emaga_9384_10704.pdf.
"'Grondona Lied to Me, Bilardo Betrayed Me,' Diego Maradona." *Ambito*, 28 July 2019, www.ambito.com/534648-grondona-lied-to-me-bilardo-betrayed-me-diego-maradona.
Kunz, Matthias. "265 million playing football." *FIF Magazine*, July 2007, 10–15, www.fifa.com/mm/document/fifafacts/bcoffsurv/emaga_9384_10704.pdf.
La Tinta. "El Diego es un héroe de TV entre héroes de redes sociales." 24 Oct. 2018, latinta.com.ar/2018/10/mes-del-diego-heroe-tv/.
Maradona, Diego Armando. *México 86. Mi Mundial, mi verdad: Así ganamos la Copa*. Suramericana, 2016.
Maradona, Diego Armando, Daniel Arcucci, and Ernesto Cherquis Bialo. *Maradona: The Autobiography of Soccer's Greatest and Most Controversial Star*. Buenos Aires, Suramericana, 2016.
Mora y Araujo, Marcela. "Does Diego still have the touch of a leader?" *The Guardian*. 18 Nov. 2008, www.theguardian.com/football/blog/2008/nov/18/diego-maradona-argentina.
Murray, Scott. "The Joy of Six: Hot Football Funks, from Diego Maradona to Graeme Souness." *The Guardian*, 5 Dec. 2008, www.theguardian.com/sport/blog/2008/dec/05/joy-of-six-scott-murray.
―――. "FourFourTwo's 100 Greatest Footballers EVER: No. 1, Diego Maradona." *FourFourTwo*, 28 July 2017, www.fourfourtwo.com/features/fourfourtwos-100-greatest-footballers-ever-no1-diego-maradona.
Nieto, Maite."Maradona, la vida de excesos de un mito." *El Pais*, 28 June 2018, elpais.com/elpais/2018/06/27/gente/1530112506_210609.html.
Parlow, Joshua."La grieta de Maradona: Sinaloa se debate entre los seguidores del Diez y los que no lo quieren." *La Nacion*, 20 Sept. 2018. www.lanacion.com.ar/deportes/futbol/la-grieta-maradona-sinaloa-se-debate-seguidores-nid2174107.
Parolo, Rogelio. "El papa Francisco le pidió a Maradona que reconozca su hijo." *Noticias Tucuman*, 24 Apr. 2015, noticiastucuman.com.ar/politica/6638-el-papa-francisco-le-pidio-a-maradona-que-reconozca-su-hijo/.
Remoli, Christian. "El Fútbol es Historia. Capítulo 5—El Sueño (1975–1986)." YouTube, uploaded by Koala Contenidos, 19 June 2016, www.youtube.com/watch?v=G0ABSNoemus.
Robinson, Michael. "Informe Robinson: Maradona, Los Años Felices." YouTube, uploaded by Movistar #0, 10 Apr. 2017, www.youtube.com/watch?v=cp-TUg_2mRY.

Salazar-Sutil, Nicolás. "Maradona Inc." *International Journal of Cultural Studies*, vol. 11, no. 4, 2008, pp. 441–458, doi:10.1177/1367877908096053.
Sehli, Myriam. "Church of Maradona: Worshipping a (Former) Demi-God with Unusual Athletic Abilities." *The Bubble*, 9 Nov. 2017, www.thebubble.com/church-of-maradona-worshipping-a-former-demi-god-with-unusual-athletic-abilities/.
Vecsey, George. "World Cup '90; Naples Loves Maradona, but Loves Italy More." *The New York Times*, 3 July 1990, p. 3, www.nytimes.com/1990/07/03/sports/world-cup-90-naples-loves-maradona-but-loves-italy-more.html.
Villoro, Juan. "'Diego Armando Maradona: Life, Death, Resurrection and a Little More Besides.'" In *God Is Round: Tackling the Giants, Villains, Triumphs, and Scandals of the World's Favorite Game*. Translated by Thomas Bunstead, pp. 169–199. Restless, 2016.
Williams, Bob. "Life and Crimes of Diego Armando Maradona." *The Telegraph*, 29 Oct. 2008, www.telegraph.co.uk/sport/football/international/3278819/ Life-and-crimes-of-Diego-Armando-Maradona-Football.html.
Yallop, David. *How They Stole the Game*. London, Constable & Robinson, 2011.

Barry Bonds v. Alex Rodriguez
Don't Hate the Player;
Hate the Steroid-Manufactured Game

Brock T. Adams

In 1989, Ray Kinsella stood on a baseball diamond in Iowa and had a conversation with a ghost. This memorable scene is from the motion picture *Field of Dreams*, one of the most iconic baseball films ever made. It tells the story of a small-town insurance salesman-turned-farmer receiving a divine command to construct a baseball diamond in his cornfield, a place former legends inhabit in their version of heaven. The film centers around the idea of relationships, many of which are created and nurtured on the baseball diamond. A subplot examines the very real scandal of "Shoeless" Joe Jackson when he and eight teammates of the Chicago White Sox were accused of throwing games in the 1919 World Series for $2,500 each. Throughout his real life, Jackson repeatedly denied the accusations, maintaining his honesty and integrity until his death in 1951. However, he and his teammates received lifetime bans from the sport and became part of baseball lore.

In one scene from *Field of Dreams*, Kinsella, played by Kevin Costner, sees two dozen men in his backyard warming up. He is greeted by the infamous baseball legend himself, Shoeless Joe Jackson, played by Ray Liotta. Jackson approaches Kinsella and asks permission for his teammates to use the field. Kinsella agrees and stares in awe at the legends on the diamond. One particular line during the scene could easily go unremarked, but it contains a fascinating juxtaposition that remains relevant even today. As a phantom fan from the bleachers remarks, "Hey, that's Mel Ott. And Carl Hubbell! Those are the New York Giants," Jackson responds: "With a couple of Cardinals and A's thrown in for good measure. Ty Cobb wanted to play, but none of us could stand the sonofabitch when we were alive, so we told him to stuff it" (*Field of Dreams*).

The scene is comical but also potent as one of the most beloved, yet possibly guilty players (Jackson) ridicules one of the most hated, yet innocent, players (Cobb) in Major League Baseball history. Jackson has the pedigree of one of the all-time greats, minus the glaring asterisk of throwing the 1919 World Series. He played left field for 13 seasons, amassing nearly 1,800 hits in his career with a .356 batting average, third-highest in Major League Baseball history. In 1911, he hit an astonishing .408 at the plate, the sixth-highest average in the modern era. Babe Ruth, one of the greatest players ever to play the game, praised his ability to hit the ball, referencing how Jackson influenced his own development. "I copied my swing after Joe Jackson's," Ruth told sportswriter Grantland Rice in 1919. "His is the perfectest" (qtd. in Golenbock).

Baseball historians peg Jackson as one of the greats; however, in comparison with Cobb, Jackson seems like just another left fielder. Cobb was a God among boys, compiling a resume of statistics that few, if any, have ever come close to emulating. He ranks first all-time in lifetime batting average at .367 as well as runs scored (2,245). He is second in hits (4,191), fourth in stolen bases (897), eighth in RBIs (1,944), and ninth in on-base percentage (.433). Cobb won the American League batting title a phenomenal twelve times, became one of fourteen players to ever hit for the Triple Crown in 1909 (league leader in batting average, home runs, and RBIs over the course of a season), recorded a .400 batting average three times, including a mind-boggling .401 over a four-year span ("MLB Stats"). His numbers speak for themselves, and he is regarded as one of the top three players all-time.

Off the field, Cobb was a dishonorable wreck, the center of many controversies damaging his reputation. For Jackson to call Cobb a sonofabitch is an understatement. He is notorious, one of the meanest, most disreputable individuals ever to play the game. In one instance, he lost his temper arguing a bad call at the plate and began choking the umpire before being pulled off by his teammates. In another situation, he jumped into the stands and began punching a heckler who also happened to be a double amputee after losing both hands in an industrial accident. Some baseball historians claim Cobb was a racist, citing his attack on a black groundskeeper for attempting to shake his hand. When confronted by the groundskeeper's spouse, Cobb began pummeling her as well. During the 1909 World Series, Cobb struck a black elevator operator for greeting him in his hotel and then stabbed the black hotel manager who tried to intervene.

Cobb and Jackson arose during the same era of baseball, yet baseball fans and critics place them at opposite ends of the likeability spectrum. Cobb is recognized as one of the best, but a bastard, an elite player nobody wanted to play with. Jackson, on the other hand, is regarded as foolish, but forgivable.

People are lenient about his dishonesty and even pay homage to him in Hollywood blockbusters.

The same comparison can be made of two modern-day superstars, Alex Rodriguez and Barry Bonds. Although they had nearly identical athletic skill, baseball intelligence, and competitive prowess, they have received entirely different receptions from fans, the media, and baseball critics across the country. Both were guilty participants in "the steroid era," arguably the greatest scandal in baseball history since the 1919 World Series. However, they differed in their handling of the criticism, possibly shifting the trajectory of their post-career accolades.

Bonds v. Rodriguez Career Comparison

On paper, Bonds and Rodriguez have ironically similar career paths. Both were first-round draft picks to small-market, mediocre ball clubs, with Bonds, drafted sixth overall in 1986 by the Pittsburgh Pirates, and Rodriguez, number one overall by the Seattle Mariners in 1993. Both led their teams to playoff berths in their first few seasons in the league and became the cornerstones of their respective franchises, only to abandon them a few years later and sign record-breaking contracts with dumpster-fire last place teams. Bonds signed a record $43 million, six-year deal with the San Francisco Giants in 1993. Rodriguez signed with the Texas Rangers in 2000, with one of the richest contracts in MLB history, $252 million over ten years. Both are on the short list of players who have won multiple Most Valuable Player awards and are on the even shorter list of players to win an MVP for their team and then to play for a different team the following season. Both made it to the World Series once in their storied careers, Rodriguez emerging as the victor in 2009 with the New York Yankees while Bonds finished as the runner-up in 2002 with the Giants.

Statistically, Bonds and Rodriguez also have interchangeable metrics. Both played twenty-two seasons in the big leagues, with fourteen All-Star appearances each. Both led the league in home runs for multiple seasons with Bonds winning twelve Silver Slugger awards and Rodriguez ten. Both were known for their defensive prowess on the left side of the diamond, receiving numerous gold glove awards; two for Rodriguez as a shortstop and seven for Bonds in left field. Their career numbers are again absurdly similar and are on levels few other players in baseball have ever glimpsed, including many who have been inducted into the Hall of Fame.

Stats	Bonds	Rodriguez
Batting Average	.298	.295
Hits	2,935	3,115
Home Runs	762	696

Stats	Bonds	Rodriguez
RBIs	1,996	2,086
Runs	2,227	2,021

("Baseball Almanac")

Although their statistics are astonishing, Bonds and Rodriguez are additionally known for coming up short during their most clutch moments, especially when the outcome of the game mattered most. Throughout history, few players are known for a single moment on the field that cements their story as fodder for sportswriters' debates; Derek Jeter is known for "The Flip," Kirk Gibson has "The Walk-off," Bill Buckner has "The Grounder." Arguably, the most iconic plays for Bonds and Rodriguez came on gaffes in post-season play. Interestingly enough, both occurred in the bottom of the eighth inning in Game 6 of a championship series.

For Bonds, the blunder came in the 2002 World Series. With the Giants leading three games to two, Anaheim Angels outfielder Garret Anderson hit a high fly ball to left field that would have been an easy out for any fielder. Bonds was surprisingly too deep in his coverage and let the ball drop in front of him. Rather than cleanly fielding it with his glove and thus preventing a mistake from becoming a disaster, he instead aggressively attempted to barehand the ball and throw out the advancing runner at second base. In the process, he bobbled the ball in the outfield and knocked it over the third-base line. As he attempted to correct his error, he slipped in the dirt, allowing the tying run, pinch-runner Chone Figgins, to advance to third base. The error ended up costing the Giants the game and eventually the series as they lost Game 7 to the Angels 4–1.

Rodriguez's gaffe was not nearly as atrocious; however, it came in one of the most pivotal series in the history of baseball. In what is heralded as one of the greatest comebacks in professional sports (Foss), the Boston Red Sox overcame a 3–0 deficit in the 2004 American League Championship Series to defeat the New York Yankees, four games to three. In the bottom of the eighth inning, with the Yankees trailing four to two, Rodriguez hit a blooper up the first base line. Red Sox pitcher Bronson Arroyo scooped the ball up and reached out to tag Rodriguez for an easy out. Just as Arroyo was about to make contact, Rodriguez swatted the ball out of his glove, knocking it loose. His swipe allowed Yankees captain Derek Jeter to score all the way from first base to cut the deficit to 4–3. Immediately following the play, however, the umpires briefly conferenced and ruled Rodriguez out for interference. The run was negated, and the Yankees would go on to lose Games 6 and 7.

Bonds and Rodriguez mirrored each other's careers on the field, from their statistical achievements to their career paths, even to their errors in high-profile post-season play. They also shared another commonality, involvement in the steroid era, one of the greatest scandals in professional sports. However, their demeanor and handling of public relations were distinctly different. Bonds lied to the public and was a jerk to the press, while Rodriguez admitted his wrongdoings and openly expressed regret for his actions. These behaviors made all the difference to fans, critics, and modern media.

The Steroid Era

The home run drives baseball. For a split-second, the ball captures fans' imaginations as it flies over the fence. In many instances, the home run is the deciding factor between wins and losses, between championships and heartache. Professor David Getz argues how the home run is one of the most instrumental moments in all of sport, writing, "In no other sport can one action so dramatically change the outcome of the game as the home run can in baseball" (5). The early years of baseball were known as the age of pitchers' duels, often showcasing the defensive nature of American ball clubs. Babe Ruth changed that in the 1920s. Ruth retired in 1935 with a then major-league-record 714 career home runs, a mark that would stand for nearly 40 years before Hank Aaron set the new precedent. Following Aaron's historic hit in 1975, baseball evolved to the point of offensive dominance. Over the next three decades, home run totals reached levels that Ruth, Cobb, and Jackson could never have imagined, obliterating major league home run records year after year. The numbers told baseball statisticians one story: players were getting better at hitting the ball, plain and simple. However, no one addressed the influence performance-enhancing drugs (PEDs) were having on those performances.

Following the players' strike in 1994 that wiped an entire season from the record books, baseball faced the uphill battle of luring its loyal crowd back to the ballparks. In 1998, two franchise cornerstones, Mark McGwire for the St. Louis Cardinals and Sammy Sosa for the Chicago Cubs, re-energized fans with a home-run race for the ages, knocking baseballs into the stands at a record-setting pace. McGwire finished with 70 home runs that year, Sosa with 66, in what was called "the greatest offensive performance in the history of the sport" (Fainaru-Wada and Williams xv). That season, both McGwire and Sosa toppled the previous single-season home run record set by Yankee slugger Roger Maris (Fainaru-Wada and Williams 61), a feat many baseball writers felt was as unattainable as Joe DiMaggio's 56-game hitting streak.

It was a brief moment of perfection for baseball, but disquiet arose about how two players in the same season could coincidentally best a 36-year-old home-run record. Was this pure, raw, unadulterated talent? Or was there an underlying issue yet to be discussed? Steve Wilstein, a reporter for the Associated Press, raised suspicions in his column by drawing attention to an unknown substance in the Cardinals' clubhouse.

> Sitting on the top shelf of Mark McGwire's locker, next to a can of Popeye spinach and packs of sugarless gum, is a brown bottle labeled Androstenedione. For more than a year, McGwire says, he has been using the testosterone-producing pill, which is perfectly legal in baseball but banned in the NFL, Olympics and the NCAA.

At first, the general public dismissed the article; the popularity of McGwire and Sosa's race to break the record overshadowed its significance. When asked about the medication in his locker, McGwire denied that the performance-enhancing drug had an effect on him. "Everything I've done is natural," he said. "Everybody that I know in the game of baseball uses the same stuff I use" (qtd. in Wilstein). Reporters believed McGwire, largely because there was no evidence to the contrary. Baseball, at the time, was the most lenient of the four major sports in terms of drug testing. In 1991, Major League Baseball had officially banned steroids. Commissioner Fay Vincent sent a memorandum to all teams stating, "There is no place for illegal drug use in Baseball," specifying that "This prohibition applies to all illegal drugs and controlled substances, including steroids or prescription drugs." The memorandum was a stern warning to all clubs; however, no provisions required players to be consistently tested for any illegal supplements. It was not until 2003 that baseball implemented random drug tests on its players.

McGwire's record lasted a meager three years before Bonds topped it in 2001, hitting his 73rd home run on the final day of the season, just inside the right-field wall of the San Francisco Giants' ballpark. Said former Giants manager Felipe Alou about Bonds's success, "Barry is the reincarnation of Ted Williams—with more power" (qtd. in Eliot and Robinson 23). By that point, however, sportswriters began questioning the array of genetically gifted baseball players. Bonds had never before come close to breaking the single-season home run record in his career, with his highest total being 49 home runs the prior year. For any player to hit 70 runs in a season was astonishing; however, for a 37-year-old, 16-year MLB veteran who had never before hit 50 home runs in a season to accomplish this feat was statistically and athletically inconceivable.

Performance-Enhancing Allegations

In 2002, a year following Bonds's record-breaking season, the federal government, as well as officials from the United States Anti-Doping Agency (USADA), began an investigation of the Bay Area Laboratory Co-operative

(BALCO), a San Francisco–area business supplying anabolic steroids to players in a variety of sports. BALCO was a three-man operation founded by businessman Victor Conte in 1984, who employed the intellectual genius of chemist Patrick Arnold to create undetectable drugs including tetrahydrogestrinone (THG, or "the clear"), testosterone cream (the "cream"), as well as human growth hormone (HGH). Greg Anderson, a close friend to Bonds and his personal trainer at the time, allegedly distributed the illegal substances to Bonds while he was a member of the Giants.

Bonds had never before failed a drug test. His name was nonetheless scattered throughout documents seized by federal agents from the BALCO headquarters. Frequently it appeared on a weekly schedule, with a corresponding code letter that suggested the use of an illegal substance. In 2003, Bonds appeared before a grand jury to testify about his involvement in BALCO. When questioned, Bonds said he used both "the clear" and "the cream" but that Anderson told him "the clear" was only a mixture of flaxseed oil, a legal nutritional substance, and that "the cream" was a simple rubbing balm used to treat patients with arthritis. Bonds played the hand of pure innocence, despite an overwhelming amount of evidence that he knowingly used steroids distributed by BALCO. Conte, Anderson, and then BALCO vice-president James Valente all struck plea deals, copping to lesser charges of distributing steroids and money laundering. However, their pleas were contingent on allowing them not to reveal the names of any athletes whom they knew had used illegal performance-enhancing drugs. Bonds was one of those athletes.

Two years following his testimony, many top baseball players, including McGwire and Sosa, testified before Congress about their knowledge and involvement in the use of performance-enhancing drugs. The summons came following the publication of a book by former big-leaguer Jose Canseco titled *Juiced: Wild Times, Rampant 'Roids, Smash Hits & How Baseball Got Big*. In that work, Conseco detailed the rampant steroid use in baseball and named players who previously denied ever using performance-enhancing drugs. Canseco was the only player to admit openly to Congress about his use of steroids while other players who testified denied relying on any supplements to boost their athletic performances. In one of the most quoted moments of the Congressional hearing, Baltimore Orioles slugger Rafael Palmeiro openly rejected any connection to performance-enhancing drugs, saying, "I have never used steroids. Period. I don't know how to say it any more clearly than that. Never" ("Performance-Enhancing Drug"). Five months following the hearing, evidence surfaced that Palmeiro had in fact tested positive for steroids and was aware of his test results on the day of his testimony.

At the time of the hearing, Rodriguez was also one of the players rumored to have a connection to PEDs, although he repeatedly denied any association with that lifestyle. In 2007, Canseco published his second book,

Vindicated: Big Names, Big Liars, and the Battle to Save Baseball. There, he identified Rodriguez by name, saying that Rodriguez sought him out in the late 1990s and expressed an interest in using steroids to boost his numbers. Rodriguez openly denied these allegations and in an interview on *60 Minutes* told Katie Couric he had never used any illegal supplements in his life. When asked if using steroids ever crossed his mind, Rodriguez said "No. I've never felt overmatched on the baseball field. And I felt that if I did my work as I've done since I was, you know, a rookie back in Seattle, I didn't have a problem competing at any level" ("A-Rod").

In 2009, evidence surfaced in a *Sports Illustrated* report stating Rodriguez tested positive for two separate anabolic steroids in 2003, the year he won his first Most Valuable Player award. One of the supplements was Primobolan, among the main PEDs linked to the BALCO investigation. Rodriguez later admitted his remorse to Peter Gammons on ESPN that he had taken steroids, saying,

> Back then, it was a different culture. It was very loose. I was young. I was stupid. I was naive. And I wanted to prove to everyone that, you know, I was worth being one of the greatest players of all time. And I did take a banned substance. You know, for that I'm very sorry and deeply regretful.

Bonds, meanwhile, was dealing with more complicated legal battles as he was being indicted on three counts of perjury and one count of obstruction of justice for his testimony in the 2003 BALCO case. Evidence arose that Bonds tested positive for anabolic steroids, as well as other performance-enhancing supplements in 2000 and 2001, and that he knowingly lied about it to investigators. Bonds's lawyers filed a motion to dismiss the charges, calling them "scattershot" and claiming the questions posed to him in the deposition were "imprecise, redundant, overlapping and frequently compound" ("Barry Bonds Files"). The motion was denied, and Bonds went to trial in March 2011. That fall, after nearly a month of testimony from federal agents, Bonds's personal assistants, former teammates Jason and Jeremy Giambi, and Kimberly Bell (Bonds's former mistress), Bonds was found guilty of obstruction of justice. However, the judge ordered a mistrial on the three charges of perjury after the jury did not come to a unanimous agreement. Bonds eventually was sentenced to 30 days house arrest, two years of probation, and 250 hours of community service.

At this point, Major League Baseball began cracking down on the steroid epidemic. Much of the criticism was fueled by political pressure from senators such as John McCain, as well as the publication in late 2007 of the Mitchell Report, a 20-month-long investigation into baseball players using anabolic steroids and human growth hormones. The report named 89 players who allegedly used steroids or other PEDs throughout their baseball careers, many of whom tested positive in previous drug tests. In 2013, baseball implemented more random, in-season testing for HGH and other testosterone boosters. During the 2013 season, twenty players tested positive, the highest number ever recorded. Despite his previous apology four years earlier for using steroids, Rodriguez was one of the players caught in 2013, resulting in a 211-game suspension, the largest ever given to an active player.

Rodriguez's suspension came at the hands of another doping conspiracy associated with Major League Baseball. Biogenesis of America, an anti-aging clinic in Coral Gables, Florida, had been accused of distributing performance-enhancing drugs banned by the league. Rodriguez was one of thirteen players whose names appeared in documents connected to Biogensisis. Twelve players linked to the company accepted their 50-game suspensions; however, Rodriguez and his attorneys took a more aggressive approach, arguing that efforts to suspend Rodriguez were a "crusade" against the three-time MVP, that baseball officials were engaging in a "shameful endeavor," and that baseball commissioner Bud Selig was participating in a "witch hunt" to get Rodriguez (Nightengale). Throughout the process, Rodriguez maintained his innocence, claiming he never used any performance-enhancing drugs associated with Biogenesis. In 2014, he dropped the lawsuit after arbitration lowered his suspension to 162 games, the entire 2014 season. It was later revealed that Rodriguez had admitted doping to Drug Enforcement Administration prosecutors.

The steroid era changed the landscape of baseball over a matter of two decades, with many statistical records and timeless moments of competition now including an asterisk, an addendum, or a question mark. For Bonds and Rodriguez, performance-enhancing drugs played a pivotal role in defining their legacies on the field and the remarkable numbers they delivered throughout their careers. Although both athletes share similar criticism for their roles in the inglorious two decades of cheating, their demeanor off the field was entirely different and steered the course of their legacies.

The Public Relations Gauntlet

On the field, Bonds and Rodriguez followed parallel career paths. Both put up Hall of Fame numbers only to have them tarnished by the shame of inflation from performance-enhancing drugs. Their careers on paper are equivalent; however, their statistical output and ties to performance-enhancing drugs are essentially where the comparisons stop. Bonds is branded an egotistical jerk, while Rodriguez is viewed as an all-around team player. Although they put up astonishingly similar numbers on the diamond, they blatantly differed in their treatment of teammates, the media, and the fans.

From the beginning of his career, Bonds rubbed people the wrong way. As a sophomore at Arizona State University, Bonds violated a team policy by breaking curfew. When asked about the violation, he mouthed off to then-coach Jim Brock, and Brock reacted in an emotional fever and kicked him off the team. After he calmed down, Brock approached his team and informed the players that Bonds had been suspended, asking if they would vote to bring Bonds back. Without question, he was the best player on their team, and Brock knew they needed him in the line-up. When the votes came in, nobody wanted him back. Brock lectured his team and asked them to consider a second vote. The team reluctantly did so, culminating in Bonds being reinstated; however, his lack of popularity continued to be a factor in the locker room at Arizona State.

During his career in Pittsburgh, Bonds won two MVP awards but was despised by both his teammates and the press. Bonds was disingenuous, rude, and insulting to the media, and in 1989, writers from the Pittsburgh media gave him the MDP award, or "Most Despised Pirate." While Bonds was with the Giants, sportswriter Rick Reilly spent six years blasting him, publishing multiple columns attacking his character as a teammate and as a human being. Reilly despised both dishonesty and the chaotic cluster of PED usage in baseball, and Bonds was always one of the names at the center of that controversy. In 2001, he discussed the in-house battle brewing in the San Francisco Giants' clubhouse between Bonds and the rest of his teammates.

> In the San Francisco Giants' clubhouse, everybody knows the score: 24–1. There are 24 teammates, and there's Barry Bonds. There are 24 teammates who show up to pose for the team picture, and there's Bonds, who has blown it off for the last two years.... When Bonds hit his 500th home run, in April, only one person came out of the dugout to greet him at the plate: the Giants' batgirl. Sitting in the stands, you could've caught a cold from the freeze he got. Teammates 24, Bonds 1 [Reilly, "He loves himself"].

One of the main teammates Bonds battled was Giants' second baseman Jeff Kent. Kent became teammates with Bonds in 1997, and over the next six years had multiple altercations with him on and off the field, much of which stemmed from the competitive nature of both players and the lack of respect shown from Bonds. Near the end of the 2000 season, voting for the National League MVP award was incredibly close between Bonds and Kent. One week before the award was to be announced, a representative from Bonds's camp called the commissioner's office to find out who was going to win the award. "We've got to know," they said, "Because if he's [Bonds] not going to win, he can get out of town" (qtd. in Reilly, "Back off"). The commissioner's office refused to comment on the standings. Kent went on to win the award in 2000, and Bonds was nowhere to congratulate him. Two years later, Bonds and Kent engaged in a shoving contest in the Giants locker room in what is known as "The Slugout in the Dugout." Both Bonds and Kent had to be restrained. Kent left San Francisco following the 2002 season, saying just before his departure, "On the field, we're fine, but off the field, I don't care about Barry, and Barry doesn't care about me. Or anybody" (Reilly, "Back off"). Three years later, Bonds incited another altercation with a Giants teammate in the clubhouse lunchroom. Witnesses alleged that Bonds repeatedly shoved pitcher Jayson Christiansen and punched him in the jaw over comments Christiansen made about Bonds's personal trainer (DiGiovanna).

Although Bonds alienated his teammates, the press, and virtually anyone who came in contact with him, Rodriguez took a different approach, often enacting the image of a "golden boy," someone everyone wanted to be around in a locker room. "Through all his preparation and work ethic, you saw how much he cared about this game and about helping this team win. I love him—as a friend and as a teammate. He was all you could ask for in both," said former Yankees reliever Mariano Rivera. Another of Rodriguez's teammates, Robinson Cano, reiterated Rivera's words, saying, "For me, he was one of the best teammates I've had and a guy who helped me when I first came up, and I appreciate all of the things he's done for me" (qtd. in Hatch). Teammates respected and appreciated him, mainly because they saw how he reciprocated respect and appreciation for them. When Rodriguez was traded to the Yankees in 2004, the national media began circulating speculations about potential conflict between Rodriguez and Yankees captain Derek Jeter. Rodriguez and Jeter played the same position, shortstop, and arguably Rodriguez was the better fielder, winning the previous two gold gloves while playing in Texas. However, Rodriguez sidestepped the controversy, agreeing to play third base for the Yankees. This was interpreted as an act of respect, with Rodriguez not letting his priorities take away from the potential team success.

Rodriguez's teammates loved him; however, the same could not be said at first from many baseball fans. He rejected the small-market team that drafted him and signed with one of the most notorious and hated teams in all of sport, the New York Yankees (Gonzalez). Both of these career moves angered many baseball fans. However, Rodriguez evaded some animosity due to his public-relations approach. Where Bonds was bitter, hostile, and blatantly rude with media members, fans, and the like, Rodriguez never lashed out while on camera or in the locker room, thus lessening the chances of being cast as the ultimate bad boy. Rodriguez did have legal battles with Major League Baseball's front office about the nature of his suspension in 2014; however, the majority, if not all, of the bitter dialogue came from his representing attorneys and not from Rodriguez himself. Whereas Bonds told reporters to "Back off or I'll snap!" (Reilly), Rodriguez embraced the criticism, never bursting out in emotional rants.

Another crucial difference between Bonds and Rodriguez was the nature of their public statements to the press. In *Effective Apology,* John Kador proposes essential steps to formulate an apology, whether public or private. They include the following: acknowledging fault, accepting responsibility and blame, expressing remorse, offering restitution, and assuring the offense will not occur again. Rodriguez appeared to follow the formula, which in turn may have had an impact on how the public received him. He acknowledged the acts were his fault, accepted responsibility for his actions, showed genuine remorse in multiple contexts, as well as assured that his mistakes would be left behind. Both Bonds and Rodriguez publicly denied ever having a connection with performance-enhancing drugs; however, only Rodriguez ever publicly apologized for his actions. When he was caught again in 2013 following the Biogenesis scandal, Rodriguez issued a handwritten apology to the fans, saying,

> I take full responsibility for the mistakes that led to my suspension for the 2014 season. I regret that my actions made the situation worse than it needed to be. To Major League Baseball, the Yankees, the Steinbrenner family, the Players Association and you, the fans, I can only say I'm sorry.... I accept the fact that many of you will not believe my apology or anything that I say at this point. I understand why and that's on me.... I'm ready to put this chapter behind me and play some ball ["Alex Rodriguez's Letter"].

Following his retirement, Rodriguez again admitted guilt in a 2017 interview with sportscaster Joe Buck on *Undeniable.* On the show, Rodriguez called himself a "jackass," referencing himself as the only fool with "pocket aces and figures out a way to lose the hand." He also admitted that his actions and deception cost him upwards of $40 million throughout his career and likely a spot in the Hall of Fame.

Bonds, on the other hand, never admitted guilt, shame, or remorse for any of his activities surrounding the BALCO controversy. Despite the overwhelming amount of evidence against him, as well as testimonies from former players, coaches, trainers, and girlfriends confirming his relationship with PEDs, Bonds never issued an apology to anyone, mainly because he was never formally convicted. The only apologetic response Bonds ever made came in 2016. Interestingly enough, that statement was not an admission of guilt. Instead it consisted of a hindsight confession of arrogance that ruined relationships. "I was just flat-out dumb," he said in an interview for the *LA Times.* Bonds added, "What can I say? I'm not going to try to justify the way I acted towards people" (qtd. in "Barry Bonds on His Playing Years"). The words indicated remorse, but Bonds never asked for forgiveness, expressed sorrow for his actions, offered any restitution, or asserted that his actions would never be repeated. These omissions call into question how genuine Bonds was that day. Were his statements motivated by true remorse or by political positioning?

Another element weakening the impact of Bonds's statement was timing. In his text, *On Apology*, Professor Robert Lazare suggests that an actual apology entails more than the steps Kador outlines. An additional element is the timing of the apology in relation to the heinous act itself. When Rodriguez was caught in the act of both using PEDs, as well as lying to the American public, he apologized quickly. Bonds, however, delivered his apology nearly ten years after his retirement, when many fans, critics, and baseball aficionados had moved on from his career. The words had little to no value because, in reality, no one was listening.

Since they have hung up their cleats, both Bonds and Rodriguez kept their affiliations with baseball. Their career paths are nevertheless dramatically different. After leaving the Giants as a player in 2009, Bonds completed a one-week stint as a guest spring-training instructor for the team in 2014. In December 2015, he was introduced as a hitting instructor for the Miami Marlins, but was fired after only one season, with rumors circulating that he was not committed to the franchise and that his work ethic was dwindling. Former player and current manager of the Marlins, Don Mattingly, commented on how Bonds's lack of commitment impacted his decision to be let go. "It just depends how good you want to be as a coach. If you want to be a really good coach, you've got to do the work" (qtd. in "Miami Marlins"). In 2017, Bonds rejoined the Giants as a special advisor to the CEO. While he remains tied to baseball, he has kept out of the limelight and is still largely remembered as a villain.

Rodriguez's post-retirement is very different from Bonds's in that Rodriguez is actively rebuilding a positive image. In 2015, he was hired as a commentator with Fox Sports 1 and immediately meshed with the on-air crew, former big leaguers Frank Thomas and Pete Rose, while covering the MLB playoffs. Thomas remarked that Rodriguez's commentator work has put him in a completely different light, noting, "What's been great about Alex so far is this is the first time I think the media has seen another side of him to just have fun and be one of the guys. Before he's always been serious, but now he's having fun" (qtd. in Best). In 2018, Rodriguez continued his success as a commentator by signing with ESPN to be a co-host for *Sunday Night Baseball*.

Rodriguez also flourished in other realms of public broadcasting. He has been a guest host for the hit TV show *Shark Tank* and has recently partnered with CNBC to host *Back in the Game*, a program designed to help former athletes get their lives back on track following their careers. Where many athletes struggle to rebuild their public image, Rodriguez has excelled beyond any expectations. Journalist Bill Simmons remarked that Rodriguez's rehabilitation is an outlier in comparison to other hated athletes' attempts,

He goes on TV, and he's really good. We've seen this with all kinds of athletes; they can reinvent the legacy of their career just by being on TV. It just doesn't feel like he has the baggage of some of the stuff that he did. You look at [Barry] Bonds, [Roger] Clemens, Sammy Sosa, Mark McGwire; these guys are synonymous with steroids. A-Rod is the only one who has come out of the abyss [qtd. in Guthrie].

The Hall of Shame

In a small town in upstate New York, there sits a large, red brick building housing plaques, statues, photographs, and memorabilia dedicated to America's pastime. The structure is the National Baseball Hall of Fame in Cooperstown and is the destination all players dream of ending up once their careers are over. The rules for getting into Cooperstown are simple; players must have played in the league for at least ten seasons and are eligible five years after they retire. From that point, their name will appear on ballots issued to sportswriters for a maximum of ten years. Players who receive at least 75 percent affirmative votes are elected to Cooperstown and receive a bronze plaque commemorating the career they had on the baseball diamond. If they fail to reach the 75 percent mark, their name returns to the pool of players good enough to play a professional sport but not elite enough to be recognized as one of the best.

Cobb was a Hall of Fame player, amassing a then-record 98.23 percent of votes cast in 1936, becoming one of the first five players elected as "first-ballot Hall of Famers." "Shoeless" Joe Jackson never had his name listed as a candidate, largely because baseball prohibits any player named on the ineligible list (those who are permanently banned) to appear on the ballot. Although Jackson's numbers make him Hall of Fame worthy, his alleged cheating in the 1919 World Series will forever keep him out of Cooperstown and limit his glory to big-screen depictions of baseball dreams in the Midwest.

The steroid era changed baseball altogether in that no longer were inflated numbers the primary variable deciding whether a player would get into Cooperstown. Instead, their association with PEDs played a more significant role in how critics viewed their careers. Palmeiro was one of four players to record 3,000 hits and 500 home runs, astonishing numbers on paper. However, he was listed on only four Hall of Fame ballots, his highest voting percentage just under 13 percent in 2012. The same can be said of Sosa and McGwire, the infamous figures in the 1998 home-run-title chase that recaptivated the imaginations of fans across the country. Sosa received his highest percentage in 2013 with 12.5 percent of the votes. However, his percentages decreased each year following his peak. The closest McGwire ever came to being enshrined in Cooperstown came in 2010, his fourth year on the ballot, when he amassed a whopping 23.7 percent of the votes ("MLB Stats"). McGwire's ten-year run expired in 2016, so his records, awards, and career will never be recognized with the greats.

The jury is still out as to whether Bonds will be elected to the Hall of Fame. Through 2019, Bonds has appeared on seven Hall of Fame ballots, and he has not yet been elected. However, an unusual trend shows Bonds's percentages increasing each year, unlike his fellow PED-accused counterparts. In 2019, Bonds received 59.1 percent of the votes, a significant jump from the 36.2 percent he received in 2013, his first year on the ballot. For a man recognized as the home-run king in the record books and one of the greatest players to walk the field, his reputation as a fraud could keep his legacy from being bronzed. However, voters may brush aside his arrogance, his disrespect, and his dishonesty simply because his name is at the top of the list for home runs hit in a season and in a career.

As for Rodriguez, his chance at the Hall of Fame will be up for debate in 2022, when he is eligible to appear on the ballots ("MLB Stats"). His career numbers, as well as post-season accolades and accomplishments should place him as a first-ballot Hall of Famer; however, baseball critics have not been so forgiving of players tied to the steroid era. While Rodriguez is connected to the most dishonest epoch in the history of baseball, he is one of the only players to openly admit his mistakes and ask for forgiveness. That action in itself could elevate him to receiving a plaque in Cooperstown. Rose, regarded as one of the greatest players of all time, received a lifetime ban for gambling and betting on the team he was managing in the 1980s. He will never be in the Hall of Fame. However, the media forgave Rose after his admission of guilt, and he is now on the sidelines of the baseball diamond as a commentator rather than sitting in a gift shop in Caesar's Palace signing autographs. If the media can be so forgiving of villains like Rose, they might be just as lenient of Rodriguez and allow him into Cooperstown.

Regardless of the outcome, Barry Lamar Bonds and Alexander Emmanuel Rodriguez are two of the greatest players ever to put on a uniform in the history of baseball. Only some hated Rodriguez while nearly everyone hated Bonds. Nonetheless, their involvement in the steroid era will forever place an asterisk next to their career accomplishments. In addition, the fact that they repeatedly lied about their actions distances their names from the rest of the Hall of Famers. Cobb may have been a sonofabitch, but at least he was an honest one. That in itself may be the reason he is viewed as one of the all-time greats. In the end, Bonds and Rodriguez may find themselves on the same field as "Shoeless" Joe Jackson, their legacies never immortalized in the white halls of Cooperstown, but rather in a posthumous exhibition match surrounded by the cornfields of Iowa.

WORKS CITED

"Alex Rodriguez's Letter of Apology to Fans." MLB.com, 17 Feb. 2017. www.mlb.com/news/alex-rodriguezs-letter-of-apology-to-fans/c-109501412.

"A-Rod." *60 Minutes.* CBS. 16 Dec. 2007. www.imdb.com/title/tt2268260/?ref_=ttep_ep48.

"Barry Bonds Files Motion to Dismiss Perjury Charges | CBC Sports." *CBCnews*, 23 Jan. 2008, www.cbc.ca/sports/baseball/barry-bonds-files-motion-to-dismiss-perjury-charges-1.753893.

"Barry Bonds on His Playing Years: 'I Was Straight Stupid.'" *Los Angeles Times*, 2 June 2016, www.latimes.com/sports/sportsnow/la-sp-barry-bonds-regrets-20160602-snap-html story.html.

"Baseball Almanac: Baseball History, Baseball Records and Baseball Research." *Baseball Almanac*, n.d., www.baseball-almanac.com/.

Best, Neil. "Best: A-Rod's Likability Comes across in Studio." *Newsday*, 25 Oct. 2016, www.newsday.com/sports/columnists/neil-best/a-rod-s-likability-comes-across-as-tv-studio-host-1.12501070.

Buck, Joe. "Alex Rodriguez." *Undeniable.* 18 Oct. 2017, www.imdb.com/title/tt7517176/?ref_=ttep_ep1.

DiGiovanna, Mike. "Christiansen Has Very Little to Say." *Los Angeles Times*, 7 Sept. 2005, www.latimes.com/archives/la-xpm-2005-sep-07-sp-angrep7-story.html.

Eliot, Tucker, and Zac Robinson. *San Francisco Giants: An Interactive Guide to the World of Sports.* Black Mesa Publishing, 2011.

Fainaru-Wada, Mark, and Lance Williams. *Game of Shadows: Barry Bonds, BALCO, and the Steroids Scandal that Rocked Professional Sports.* Penguin, 2006.

Field of Dreams. Directed by Phil Alden Robinson, performances by Kevin Costner, Amy Madigan, James Earl Jones, Ray Liotta, Burt Lancaster, Universal, 1999.

Foss, Mike. "The ten greatest comebacks in sports history." *For the Win-USA TODAY*, 13 Sept. 2013, ftw.usatoday.com/2013/09/the-10-greatest-comebacks-in-all-of-sports.

Gammons, Peter. "Rodriguez: Sorry and deeply regretful." *ESPN*, 9 Feb. 2009, www.espn.com/mlb/news/story?id=3895281.

Getz, David. "Going, Going, Gone!: How the Home Run Has Changed Major League Baseball." *Constructing the Past*, vol. 10. no. 1, 2009, pp. 1–5.

Golenbock, Peter. *Fenway: an Unexpurgated History of the Boston Red Sox.* Covered Bridge Press, 1997.

Gonzalez, Eduardo. "It's Official: The Yankees Are the Most-Hated Team in Baseball—and the Dodgers Aren't Far Behind." *Los Angeles Times*, 21 July 2017, www.latimes.com/sports/mlb/la-sp-baseball-hated-favorite-teams-20170721-story.html.

Guthrie, Marisa. "The Redemption of A-Rod Will Be Televised." *The Hollywood Reporter*, 4 Aug. 2017, www.hollywoodreporter.com/features/alex-rodriguez-rebooting-his-image-you-have-own-your-shit-1025983.

Hatch, Ryan, et al. "Former Teammates Shower Yankees' Alex Rodriguez with Praise." NJ.com, 12 Aug. 2016. www.nj.com/yankees/index.ssf/2016/08/former_teammates_shower_yankees_alex_rodriguez_wit.html.

Kador, John. *Effective Apology: Mending Fences, Building Bridges, and Restoring Trust.* Berrett-Koehler Publishers, 2009.

Lazare, Aaron. *On Apology.* Oxford University Press, 2005.

"Miami Marlins: Lack of Work Ethic Cost Barry Bonds His Job." *FOX Sports*, 6 Oct. 2016, www.foxsports.com/mlb/story/miami-marlins-lack-of-work-ethic-cost-barry-bonds-his-job-100616.

"MLB Stats, Scores, History, & Records." *SABR/Baseball Reference Encyclopedia*, Nd, www.baseball-reference.com/bullpen/.

Nightengale, Bob. "A-Rod attorney: Selig must explain 'witch hunt.'" *USA Today*. 5 Oct. 2013, www.usatoday.com/story/sports/mlb/2013/10/05/alex-rodrgiuez-mlb-lawsuit-joe-taco pina-statement-bud-selig/2928521/.

"Performance-Enhancing Drug Use in Baseball." *C-SPAN.org*, 13 Feb. 2008, www.c-span.org/video/?203998-1/performance-enhancing-drug-baseball.

Reilly, Rick. "Back off or I'll snap!" *Sports Illustrated*, 4 Nov. 2002, www.si.com/vault/2002/11/04/8118435/back-off-or-ill-snap.

———. "He loves himself so much, Barry Bonds has his own P.R. man, masseur and flex guy. He's an MTV diva, only with bigger earrings." *Sports Illustrated*, 27 Aug. 2001, www.si.com/vault/2001/08/27/309521/he-loves-himself-barry-much-bonds-has-his-own-pr-man-masseur-and-flex-guy-hes-an-mtv-diva-only-with-bigger-earrings.

Vincent, Fay, "Baseball's drug policy and prevention program." *Office of the Commissioner-Major League Baseball*. 7 June 1991, www.steroidsinbaseball.net/assets/memo.pdf.

Wilstein, Steve, "Drugs OK in Baseball, Not Olympics." *AP News*, 21 Aug. 1998, www.apnews.com/87e8d2a7928c8de874fdc3f43b53a33a.

No Coward

Hope Solo Battles Against the Status Quo, Injustices and, Sometimes, Her Own Poor Decisions

Joe Gisondi

As far as athletes' trash talk goes, calling someone a coward is mild. Yet, Hope Solo, the winningest American soccer goalkeeper of all time, was suspended for six months by the U.S. Soccer Federation after she offered that assessment of a Swedish team that had just defeated the U.S. women's National Team on penalty kicks in the 2016 Olympic Games (@GrantWahl).

It's not as if Solo had called a grown man a bitch in the NBA Finals, as Warriors forward Draymond Green once did to an exasperated Lebron James.

Or as if she had spewed vile comments about another player's dead mother, as NBA all-star Kevin Garnett purportedly did while playing Hall of Famer Tim Duncan.

Or even, say, calling opposing players "trash," "crappy," or "over-rated"— terms that Jacksonville Jaguars defensive back Jalen Ramsey uses to publicly lacerate opposing NFL quarterbacks, reserving "sucks" for Baltimore's Joe Flacco.

Former Florida State University football head coach Jimbo Fisher once called referees "cowardly, gutless and wrong" in a post-game press conference following his team's loss to Clemson in 2016.

None of these players faced suspensions. Fisher, meanwhile, was merely fined $20,000 for having violated the conference's sportsmanship policy, chump change for someone earning $5.25 million (Deen).

By any standard, Solo calling the Swedish team "a bunch of cowards" was lame, a laughable reason to deride her as a cretin. And, yet, Solo was not only penalized for her comments, but also harshly criticized by both sports media and soccer's governing bodies. This is just one of numerous examples where she broke from what is expected of a high-profile, female athlete, resulting in her being marked as a bad boy.

Almost everybody who plays sports understands that opponents frequently talk a blue streak inside the lines. Sometimes, that language spills into postgame interviews. Athletes invest a great deal of physical, emotional and psychological energy before and during major events, so it should not be surprising when these hyper-charged people react emotionally afterward, whether it is brooding, seething, or raging after a loss. As Tom Brady, arguably the greatest NFL quarterback of all-time, states: Losing sucks. "I'm a pretty good winner," Brady said. "I'm a terrible loser. And I rub it in pretty good when I win" (Kroft). Solo has tweeted essentially the same thing: "Losing sucks. I'm really bad at it" (@HopeSolo).

Brady is revered for this competitiveness; Solo is not.

Sports writers were aghast over her comments about the Swedes.

Washington Post soccer beat writer Steven Goff concluded "Solo has been a big inspiration between the goal posts but a small person off the field" ("Hope"). Another highly respected columnist, the *Washington Post*'s Sally Jenkins, essentially called Solo a loser when she wrote:

> It's called composure, and Hope Solo's never been overburdened with a lot of that, or grace either. The U.S. women's soccer team had their temperaments tested by a savvy, conservative Sweden in the Olympic quarterfinals and lost. Solo has spent years undermining their collective equilibrium, and this one's on her. She's a chronically rattled and rattling soul, the American goalkeeper. Let's face it: For every shiny marketing moment and big victory she's been a part of, she's given the U.S. a nasty unwanted drama. The victories usually smoothed over her behavior. Not this time. This time she went pure loser and lout.

USA Today columnist Nancy Armour called Solo a perennial problem child, concluding "Solo's comments were befitting of neither an American star nor an Olympian. She ought never wear the U.S. uniform again."

Keep in mind, these are excellent sports journalists. Yet, they and others claimed Solo had subverted the ideals of the Olympic Games that we see on display every few years—you know, like fixed badminton matches, rampant steroid usage, horses injected with stimulants, epees re-programmed to falsely record points, racial suppression, and marathoners who rode in carriages for several miles, to name just a few. Or this standard of purity: the International Olympic Committee ravages host countries economically, taking in billions of dollars at the expense of citizens who have been evicted from residences, whose schools have been plowed, and where ecologically delicate areas have been destroyed in order to make room for stadiums soon abandoned once the world departs. Brazil was left with a staggering $113 million in debt, unable to recover its $13 billion investment, according to the Council on Foreign

Relations (McBride). Sports writers sometimes prefer to create myths instead of focusing on the real bad boys because the truth is not always as sexy and rarely is as accessible. This all seems less than ideal. Leave a country writhing in debt. No worries. But call someone a coward after a competition. Boy, howdy. Take cover because the sky is falling.

Trash-talking is encoded in American sports' DNA, says Washington State Professor David J. Leonard, who regularly writes about media culture and sports. Every veteran sportswriter knows that. American patriotism, Leonard adds, is a form of national trash-talking that fits right into the Olympic spirit. "The Olympics is all about trash-talking; the medal count is the ultimate expression of bravado," he writes in his blog *The Undefeated*, "a public pronouncement that my country is better than yours." Adds sociologist Ben Carrington: "The Olympics is a jamboree of unabashed nationalism rather than a true celebration of our common humanity" (qtd. in Leonard).

Legendary college football coach Knute Rockne would have admired Solo's competitive fire, perhaps patting her on the back afterward and telling her: "Show me a gracious loser, and I'll show you a failure." Vince Lombardi, for whom the Super Bowl Trophy is named, might have tweeted her "Winning isn't everything, it's the only thing." Hall of Fame baseball manager Leo Durocher, no doubt, would have commended Solo's spirit. "I never did say that you can't be a nice guy and win," Durocher once said. "I said that if I was playing third base and my mother rounded third with the winning run, I'd trip her up" (qtd. in Kosner).

So save those enjoinders that we need to preserve the sanctity of any game. In America, we cannot help but get angry when we lose and gloat when we win—unless, of course, you're a woman, a strong-willed one at that.

Like Solo.

Fame Exacts a Heavy Toll

Hope Amelia Solo is one of the world's most recognizable athletes, having played in goal for U.S. Women's National Teams that won two Olympic Gold Medals and one World Cup—and, she might argue, would have won a second World Cup title had she not been yanked during a semifinal match against Brazil in 2007.

She has twice earned the Golden Glove Award that recognizes the best goalkeeper in a World Cup tournament. Plus, she holds numerous records for the U.S Women's National Team, having played in 202 games, started in 190, won 153, lost 11, and posted 102 shutouts. At one point, she won 55 consecutive games, a record that still stands. She allowed 117 goals in 202 total games, an average of about one-half goal per game. For more than a decade,

Solo was considered the best goalkeeper in the world—a fiercely competitive, talented player who regularly shut down the best players and teams that soccer had to offer.

Solo's fame expanded outside her field of play. She competed before millions of Americans in 2011 on ABC's reality show *Dancing with the Stars*, has been visible in ad campaigns for Nike and Gatorade, and has been featured on a cover of *ESPN The Magazine*'s popular "Body Issue." Solo also donates time and money to the Boys and Girls Club and appears in various charity events. In other words, she has the perfect resume to be considered a bad boy—someone who is famous and talented enough that we care about her personal life so much that it becomes fodder for tabloids and TMZ. God help anybody who gets to this level, where every decision is scrutinized and every action is judged. Fame exacts a heavy toll, especially when one breaks the law, strays from the status quo, and disregards decorum—as Solo has done several times.

Scorned More Than Men for Same Offense

On the same day that Solo was suspended for six months for the Swedish comment, a player for the United Soccer League's Orange County Blues was given a two-match suspension and fined an undisclosed amount for repeatedly calling an opposing player who is gay a "queer" during the match. Sure, Solo is arguably the most well-known female American athlete this side of Serena and Venus Williams—and had just performed on the world's biggest stage—but the comparison in penalties is still striking.

And how about this: UFC heavyweight champion Junior dos Santos called his opponent, Tui Tuivasa, a coward before their 2018 title bout. Did the governing agency suspend him? No, the two fighters instead settled it in the ring, where dos Santos recorded a second-round knockout. That same year, Carolina's Eric Reid called Philadelphia's Malcolm Jenkins a coward for not supporting the silent protests started by Colin Kaepernick. The NFL did not discipline either one.

Usually, calling someone a coward is no big deal.

A year after Solo's comment, NBA coach Gregg Popovich (Pop) called the President of the United States a coward (and a pathological liar) in response to Trump having falsely claimed that previous presidents had never contacted the families of fallen soldiers. "This man in the Oval Office is a soulless coward who thinks that he can only become large by belittling others," Popovich told *The Nation*. Popovich also called the President a "pathological liar" who is "unfit intellectually, emotionally, and psychologically" to hold office (qtd. in Zirin). Yet, the NBA did not suspend Popovich in what some might consider a far more egregious breach of conduct. Nor did it discipline NBA stars Lebron James for calling Trump a bum or Stephen Curry for saying POTUS was a racist. The commissioner, instead, permitted free speech to it players and coaches. To its men.

Think how U.S. Soccer Federation officials would have reacted had Solo uttered Popovich's assessment of the President. Pass the portable defibrillator. They would have definitely needed resuscitation.

Riling up the Media and Teammates

Hope Solo was furious after being benched for a 2007 World Cup semifinal game against Brazil. U.S. Women's National Team coach Greg Ryan told her that 36-year-old Brianna Scurry, who had relinquished the starting role several years earlier, had more experience facing Brazil, against whom she had posted a 12–0 lifetime mark. But Scurry, whose legendary block of a penalty kick had proved decisive in the 1999 World Cup final, was rustier and nearly a decade older than the 26-year-old Solo. Solo, meanwhile, had not allowed a goal in the previous three tournament matches, playing so well that she eventually was named the best goalkeeper in the World Cup. Brazil, subsequently, scored quickly and often in a 4–0 rout of the United States. Scurry reacted more slowly, even allowing a low shot by Brazilian star Marta that she might have stopped years earlier. After the defeat, Solo responded to reporters' questions before stepping onto the team bus: "It was the wrong decision, and I think anybody that knows anything about the game knows that. There's no doubt in my mind I would have made those saves." Plus, she added "The fact of the matter is, it's not 2004 anymore," a reference to the team's gold-medal performance at the Athens Olympics. "It's 2007, and I think you have to live in the present. And you can't live by big names. You can't live in the past. It doesn't matter what somebody did in an Olympic gold-medal game three years ago. Now is what matters, and that's what I think" (qtd. in Longman).

Afterward, Solo was gashed by both the media and her teammates, becoming the biggest female villain in sports for merely stating what any male athlete might. *New York Times* soccer writer Jere Longman characterized her response as caustic, and a *Washington Post* soccer beat writer said Solo had trashed her coach publicly—not knowing that this coach had shoved her and screamed curse words at her privately, according to Solo's memoir, *Solo: A Memoir of Hope*. In addition, Solo's teammates reacted angrily, calling her a traitor in a team meeting. Teammates requested that Solo not be allowed to play in the team's consolation game, which Ryan granted. Solo said that veteran Kate Markgraf told her "I can't even f—ing look at you. Who the f— do you think you are? I can't even be in the same room with you" (Solo).

Solo was vindicated when Ryan was fired a few days after the World Cup by United States Soccer Federation (USSF) president Sunil Gulati, who said Ryan was partially at fault for the players' reactions.

Ryan rationalized that Scurry had looked better in scrimmages even though Solo had recorded three clean sheets in a row. No team had ever changed goalkeepers at the semifinals of a World Cup for tactical reasons. It made no sense to expect Scurry, the Golden Glove Award winner as the best keeper in the 1999 World Cup, to perform at the same level against Brazil eight years later. It would be like asking an older quarterback to play in the Super Bowl because he had a great record against a team eight years earlier. Or imagine if San Francisco Giants manager Bruce Bochy had decided to replace eventual MVP Madison Bumgarner for his final start of the 2014 World Series with Tim Lincecum because the right-hander had won the Cy Young Award five years earlier. Or if New England Patriots coach Bill Belichick had replaced Tom Brady in the 2005 NFC playoffs for Doug Flutie because the former Boston College quarterback had a better career record against the Jacksonville Jaguars. Bumgarner and Brady would have said far worse, in far stronger terms, to a gaggle of nodding sports media.

Girls: Expected to Be Cheerleaders

Fog shrouds the upper elevations of the Smokies, preventing my daughter and me from seeing much more than the rosebay rhododendrons that grow thick along the dirt and gravel paths on a trail headed up Mount LeConte in the Smokies. We have navigated some tight walkways and slippery natural steps with no trouble. At 5,000-plus feet, Kristen and I can barely see the valleys and hollows below that are ostensibly filled with yellow buckeye, basswood, yellow poplar and several other trees I could never identify on my own. The fog hides the panoramic views that drew us to this trail. The fog also obscures almost everything else that might be lurking ahead—and there are definitely reasons to worry. Namely, black bears had recently killed one person and attacked two others in the region.

But Kristen doesn't care. She is determined to march on despite the challenges. She has seen far worse, both on and off the soccer field.

A few months before her senior season as goalkeeper for her high school soccer team, Kristen fractured her knee, required surgery to remove her gall bladder, and endured shin splints. Despite the pain, she worked hard on strengthening her body to endure a rigorous season. In order to do so, she worked with a trainer, lifted weights, and ran—doing so privately in order to focus. And that was my daughter's crime: she wasn't a cheerleader. Kristen did not hang out with her teammates during winter training, sitting along the sidelines and clapping a few times or lobbing a few "Keep up the good work" and "good jobs" to teammates running in the gym before the season started. Instead, she spent all day in class, all afternoon on her physical training, and most of the night on homework. She had the tenacity to fight through pain from the gall bladder surgery, which had created bands of scar-like tissue forcing some organs to stick together, and she had exercised her knee, sometimes to the point of tears, in order to prepare for the season. Some might call that dedication. Her coaches later considered this abdication. She was not a "team player."

Fast forward to March when the coaches named three captains for the team and did not include Kristen, the only senior not so honored. One captain sometimes tried to persuade teammates to cut runs and workouts when the coach was gone, but when the coach was present, this senior was Ms. Cheerleader.

Kristen nearly quit the team, but she ultimately decided her teammates meant too much. Good thing because Kristen allowed only six goals in 22 games, blocked shots in tight games and twice ran out, slid and blocked potentially game-winning shots in the final moments—the same kind of play that had led to her knee fracture. She was once again named to the all-sectional team, an all-state team, and received several scholarship offers. Yet, she did not receive any team awards at the end of the season for her role in helping the team go 19–1–3 because, mostly, she was not Little Miss Sunshine; rather, she barked orders at defenders on the field (but quietly praised them off it).

Had she been a guy, Kristen's demeanor would not have been an issue. Girls suffer when they are treated differently. Solo has learned this lesson time and again, but she refuses to be a proper cheerleader.

Solo's Arrest

And then there was the time that Solo got arrested for domestic violence. The night began with Solo upset, crying in a car outside her half-sister's house in Kirkland, Washington, about eight miles northeast of Seattle. It was evening, June 21, 2014. Solo had missed her flight for a USWNT game scheduled the next day. Her husband, former NFL tight end Jerramy Stevens, had left her for the night, refusing to provide a ride to the airport. So Teresa Obert poured a glass of wine, sat down, and chatted with her sister, according to police records.

The night soon devolved into name-calling and then fighting. Solo started punching her 17-year-old nephew, banging his head on the floor, and wrestling with her sister before her nephew hit Solo with a broom, the wooden handle breaking over her head. By the time police arrived, Solo was combative. She cursed at an officer when she was forced to the ground, screaming, "You're such a bitch. You're scared of me because you know that if the handcuffs were off, I'd kick your ass" (qtd. in Fainaru-Wada).

Bad girl fodder, to be sure. World Wrestling Entertainment worthy, too.

It is big news when the world's best goalie is arrested for domestic violence. It is even bigger news when a female is charged with this crime because women are usually the victims in such cases—three times more likely, according to the National Domestic Violence Hotline.

A few months earlier, a domestic abuse case involving Baltimore Ravens' star Ray Rice emerged. Rice punched his fiancée, Janay, in an Atlantic City elevator. Janay immediately slumped unconscious to the floor, and Rice awkwardly dragged her into a hotel hallway, nudging her with his foot until she finally regained consciousness.

This was not the first time that a professional athlete had battered a woman, but it might be the first time that it was captured on film. TMZ soon purchased and streamed the tape about a month before Solo's fight with her family. Like others across the country, I had watched Rice's brutal attack in horror. Soon thereafter, a few apologists leaped to the defense of the Ravens' prized athlete. America, though, was mostly aghast.

But many writers conflated the two incidents, saying Rice and Solo were guilty of the same charge—probably because they did not understand that domestic violence encompasses everything from a punch in the arm to vicious assaults that require hospitalization. More than anything, writers just did not think through their arguments. Rice, a muscular 200-pound running back, punched his shorter, slender fiancée, knocking her out cold behind a left hand that could bench press more than 400 pounds. Solo, meanwhile, is 5 feet, 9 inches. Her nephew is 6 feet, 8 inches and 270 pounds—nearly twice her weight and about a foot taller. She might as well have attacked Yankees outfielder Aaron Judge or NBA star Lebron James. Solo's sister, according to police reports, had a scratch on the right side of her neck, a sore jaw, and felt too weak to stand while her nephew bled from his ear—serious injuries, to be certain. None of this should excuse Solo's behavior, but it is important to keep perspective when making comparisons.

Radio talk-show hosts, beat writers, and columnists linked the two incidents. An *Orlando Sentinel* columnist wrote that Solo did not deserve to play in the women's 2015 World Cup, saying she should have been suspended the same as several NFL players, such as Greg Hardy, a 6-foot-4, 265-pound player for the Panthers who had flung his ex-girlfriend from her bed, into a bath tub, and onto a futon covered with rifles, slammed her arm under a toilet seat, and dragged her by the hair from room to room, according to court testimony (Gordon et al.). Like Solo's case, the charges against Hardy were dropped. The NFL player's cause was helped when the woman stopped talking with authorities after she had received a financial settlement. The league essentially suspended him for 19 games, whereas Solo did not miss any games—an egregious miscarriage of justice, according to arguments by sports writers. But look more deeply in the NFL's discipline patterns under commissioner Roger Goodell until that 2014 season, and you will find suspension to be the exception. In 56 previous allegations of domestic violence, players missed a total of 13 games, roughly one quarter of a game per infraction—or, as an *espnW* writer stated, roughly the accrued time it takes to stand in line to purchase a hot dog and soda at an NFL game (Fagan).

Solo justifiably received a great deal of criticism for brawling with her sister and nephew, the most damning evidence of Solo's badness.

Mother an Alcoholic, Father a Grifter

Solo writes in her autobiography that she is a survivor. Her mother was an alcoholic, and her father was a grifter. Her brother, Marcus, was frequently in trouble. Hope, meanwhile, put her energy into playing sports. She stated "all this bullshit was making me tougher" (61). She relied heavily on unconditional love and constant support from her grandparents, as well as the financial support of teammates' parents, who helped defray costs for travel soccer and supplied rides to games.

Instinctually, she fought back when others challenged her, family or friends. She punched a girl who had slept with her boyfriend in high school, battled against her mom's alcoholism and defended her father, even though he was sometimes living in a cardboard box in Seattle and had been accused of a murder that he did not commit. So it should be no surprise when she retaliates against those whom she perceives are trying to hurt her. She has complained about referees, game analysts, and fans on social media. In September 2010, she claimed refs favored the Washington Freedom in their playoff game. "It's official," Solo tweeted, "the refs are straight bad. It's clear the league wanted [DC] in [the] playoffs. I have truly never seen anything like this. It's sad. I am done playing in a league where the game is no longer in control of the players" (qtd. in Goff, "Goalkeeper"). The league slapped her with a $2,500 fine, a one-game suspension and, oddly, eight hours of community service.

Her words were less inflammatory than those spoken by Joel Embiid after his Philadelphia Sixers team lost in an NBA opening-round playoff game in spring 2019. At the end of the postgame press conference, Embiid took the mic and said: "These referees fucking sucked." He was fined, but not suspended. A writer even empathized with Embiid: "Understandably, the big man was a bit frustrated afterward" (Maloney and Siddiqi). Solo rarely gets such support, but that is probably because her indiscretions have built up like plaque.

It is difficult to say that Solo does not deserve criticism. On the other hand, she might not really have another choice. Solo is a battler on and off the field. She speaks her mind to address what she perceives to be injustices and inequalities. She fought the USSF for equal pay. In March 2019, the entire Women's National Team filed a lawsuit against the USSF on the same grounds, but this was years after Solo began clamoring for equality. Solo claims it was her fight for equality that ultimately caused her to get suspended, not her comments about cowardly Swedes.

Solo constantly battles the USSF over how soccer is supported and promoted in this country, saying youth programs for young women lack sufficient support. The current system, she told an audience at a sports conference in 2018, is alienating Hispanic, black, rural, and poorer communities because competing on travel teams has become too expensive, costing as much as much as $5,000–10,000 a year to train at higher-end programs. Solo likely would not have played beyond high school had it not been for the charity of other parents who covered expenses and provided transportation to games. Soccer, she said, has become "a rich, white-kid sport" (qtd. in McCarthy).

Solo the Role Model

Charles Barkley famously said that he was not a role model just because he played basketball well. That responsibility, he firmly believes, belongs to parents. He is mostly correct, except that many young boys did look up to Round Mound of Rebound back in 1993 when he wreaked havoc on and, sometimes, off the court. He was a Hall of Fame player who has become a reasonable voice in talking about basketball and non-sports. Some American kids spent more time watching him on TV than with their own absent parents. As parents try hard to model behavior, we are excited when athletes, business leaders, and politicians complement the ethical and moral lessons we offer. Sadly, finding such role models can be a challenge.

Like Barkley, Solo hates the term role model, although she feels honored whenever a girl looks up to her. "I think role model can mean a number of different things," she told *Deutsche Welle*'s Maximiliane Koschyk at a youth summit in 2015.

> What is a role model, who can really define that? Everybody has different personalities, different interests, but at the same time for me it is about inspiring the younger

generations, especially young girls. It is about changing the world, about showing young boys, that it is okay to look up to a strong female athlete. There are so many different ways to look at it, but ultimately we are in this together to show that athletes are more than just athletes.

My daughter Kristen counts Solo as a role model, along with Senator Elizabeth Warren, Supreme Court justice Ruth Bader Ginsburg, and former First Lady Michelle Obama—strong, smart, confident women who have accomplished a great deal. Young girls need female role models. Dads like me often coach young girls for years, but we need to find a way to step aside. I used to hire former soccer players from the Eastern Illinois University women's team to coach our travel teams. There is a seismic difference between a 38-year-old man yelling at ten-year-old girls on a soccer field and a 22-year-old young woman directing players to work harder and smarter.

Looking at my daughter's list, Solo might seem out of place, or, as they say in psychology, prompt a cognitive dissonant jolt. After all, how does a goalkeeper measure up to a United States senator or to a Supreme Court justice? On the other hand, RBG never dived into a scrum of muscular players, vulnerable to kicks to the head, scrapes across her exposed arms by cleats, and elbows tossed into the abdomen in order to catch or block a large soccer ball headed in her direction at high speeds (not that RBG can't do anything she wants, even in her 90s). And few women have fractured their leg by slamming knee against knee to prevent a breakaway goal by a much larger young girl running straight at them. Kristen has. As has Solo.

Kristen learned confidence from Solo's fierce actions and words. And I'm glad for that. But don't listen to me. Listen to a girl, now a young woman, if you want insights into Solo's character. "Hope Solo pretty much said 'I am a top athlete and this is how I act,'" Kristen says, "and don't apologize for it. That's inspiring for those who are quieter on the field. She showed it's OK. If you want to succeed, you can—and should—act that way."

Female Athletes, Double Standards

Serena Williams appreciates Solo's struggle to be treated equitably. Like the world's premier soccer goalkeeper, the foremost women's tennis player has been treated far differently by fans, media, and officials than male athletes in her sport. When umpire Carlos Ramos admonished Williams for receiving hand signals from her coach in the 2018 U.S. Open, Williams objected, saying she was not a cheater. Ramos agreed at first and appeared to shrug off the alleged infraction. That is a score of 15-love for common sense.

Williams soon became frustrated by Naomi Osaka, a talented, hard-serving 19-year-old, and double-faulted twice. Clearly frustrated at herself, she smashed her racquet into the Arthur Ashe Stadium surface, leaving it twisted and mangled on the court. For that, Williams received a one-point penalty. That's when she told Ramos: "You owe me an apology. You stole a point from me. You're a thief, too" (qtd. in Harwitt). The umpire awarded a game to Osaka, essentially ending the match. Like Solo, Williams was both angry and confused. After all, Roger Federer, the world's premier men's tennis player, was not penalized on this very court during the 2009 U.S. Open men's final: "Don't fucking tell me the rules," he had said (qtd. in Cambers). Federer later received a $1,500 fine, but the umpire did not assess any match point penalties.

And earlier in the same 2019 U.S. Open, Austrian player Dominic Thiem smashed his racquet to a nub, pounding it into the hardcourt four times in a row, without a point penalty. In fact, he was applauded for "delighting" the crowd after he handed the broken racquet to a young fan, whose beaming face was shown on TV and in several newspaper photos. The U.S. Tennis Federation double-faulted when it came to treating its female players the same as the men. But, really, should we be surprised?

Goalkeepers Need to Be Fierce

Soccer goalkeepers are the most vulnerable, and solitary, figures in all sport. That, in part, is what makes them different, a gentle word for weird, odd, crazy, off their rockers. It also makes them fiercer. They stand alone on the field, wearing a different jersey and seem useless while action takes place in the middle of the pitch. When teammates score, they get no credit. Yet, when the opposing team scores, blame often follows. On occasion, goalkeepers do make egregiously bad errors, such as fumbling a ball that rolls across the goal line, dribbling a ball back into the net or passing a ball directly to an opposing player camped near the goal. But those are the exceptions, especially at the higher levels. By and large, though, goalkeepers save teammates when they mess up.

Keepers are also physically vulnerable when they dive for loose balls amidst players who frequently step on their hands, scrape cleats across their legs, and shove them to the ground. Goalies rush in face-first in places where cleats fear to tread, regularly placing themselves in harmful situations when the action comes their way. Vladimir Nabokov, whose novel *Lolita* is considered one of the best written in the 20th century, understands the duality embedded in goalies—coiled yet analyzing, aloof yet loyal, impassive yet emotional, to strike at a moment's notice despite long periods of solitude. The great Russian novelist spent years goalkeeping in England and Germany, once getting knocked unconscious while playing for a Russian Sports Club in Berlin in the early 1930s. Keepers are the last line of defense. "He is the lone eagle," Nabokov writes in his memoir, "the man of mystery, the last defender." Solo proves women can be equally enigmatic and skilled.

Albert Camus, who won a Nobel Prize in literature at age 44, credits his time playing goal in Algiers for developing an absurdist philosophy that addresses the conflict in humans who seek to find an inherent value in life but who eschew meaning in a universe that appears chaotic. If anybody can understand dualities, it is a goalkeeper—whose absurd mission is to remain calm and coiled at the same time. Camus had a deep love for soccer and a deeper respect for goalkeepers—although the ensuing comment about soccer might be misinterpreted: "All that I know most surely about morality and obligations I owe to football" (qtd. in Humphreys). He knew what happened in scrums near the goal and how keepers were treated both on and off the field—and sometimes by teammates.

Few people understand how goalkeepers measure the world, wavering between peace and anger, action and tranquility.

Duality

We love to embrace our ideals in this country, even when they contradict one another. Winning is everything. But also be a good sport. In another incongruity, America is perhaps best defined by ancient Chinese philosophy, namely the principle of Yin and Yang that proclaims that all aspects of this world exist as antithetical, yet inseparable, opposites. Thus, the world includes men and women, old and young, dark and light (even the Red Sox and the Yankees). We cannot have one without the other. Thus, the desire that drives athletes to work hard and compete at all costs is exactly what hinders them after a competition in which they have lost. Certainly, we cannot appreciate victories without having suffered defeats. At the same time, we probably should not be so quick to dismiss antagonistic comments from athletes when they lose.

We also want athletes to be candid, only to vilify them when they comply. Grace requires cultivation; it is not a natural response to defeat—even more so among those who have to scrape and battle for success both inside and outside the lines. Drill into most athletes' psyches after they have lost a game, and you will likely hear that inner ego battling with the id, and at least a faint whisper of "I'm better than that fortunate bastard who won."

We also like to put women on proverbial pedestals and diminish their accomplishments when they challenge any aspect of maleness. Social media is filled with men who say nobody cares about the NCAA women's national basketball championship tournament, yet nearly five million people viewed it during a non-primetime slot on a Sunday afternoon.

In my journalism classes, I advise students to tread lightly before assessing athletes, especially if they have not regularly covered them. How much can we really get to know athletes whom we view mostly on a playing field—despite what social media tricks us into believing? Even on the beat, the best sports journalists are circumspect, realizing people are far too complex to define based upon a childish post-game interview, a few tweets, or even after an arrest.

Sadly, snark, hot takes, and bias have crept into sports media.

Those covering sports beats cannot reveal the essence of athletes any more than voters can discern the content of a politician's character from a few stump speeches. Remember: in fiction, as in life, the villain often thinks of herself as the hero of the story. It all depends on one's perspective. Ask any historian or screenwriter. Maybe the fault lies in us more than in a 30-something female athlete who has the audacity to just act like a man would. And maybe, just maybe, we're all bad boys once in a while ourselves.

Works Cited

Armour, Nancy. "Calling Sweden 'bunch of cowards' should be last straw for Hope Solo." *USA Today*, 12 Aug. 2016, www.usatoday.com/story/sports/columnist/nancy-armour/2016/08/12/armour-hope-solo-sweden-bunch-of-cowards/88639092/.

Cambers, Simon. "Juan Martín del Potro shocks Roger Federer to win US Open title." *The (London) Guardian*. 14 Sept. 2009, www.theguardian.com/sport/2009/sep/15/juan-martin-del-potro-us-open.

Deen, Safid. "FSU's Jimbo Fisher fined $20,000 for comments following Clemson loss." *Orlando Sentinel*, 30 Oct. 2016, www.orlandosentinel.com/sports/florida-state-seminoles/os-florida-state-fined-jimbo-fisher-comments-clemson-loss-20161030-story.html.

Fagan, Kate. "Why Hope Solo should be suspended from Team USA—immediately." *espnW*, 19 Sept. 2014, espn.com/espnw/news-commentary/article/11553070/why-hope-solo-suspended-team-usa-immediately.

Fainaru-Wada, Mark. "Documents reveal news details about Hope Solo's actions last June." ESPN.com, 2 Oct. 2015, abcnews.go.com/Sports/documents-reveal-details-hope-solos-actions-june/story?id=34207415.

Goff, Steven. "Goalkeeper Hope Solo vents again after women's soccer match, criticizes referee and league." *Washington Post*, 13 Sept. 2010, voices.washingtonpost.com/soccerinsider/2010/09/hope_solo_vents_again.html.

———. "Hope Solo never learned that words have consequences, so U.S. Soccer finally acted." *Washington Post*, 25 Aug. 2016, www.washingtonpost.com/hope-solo-never-learned-that-words-have-consequences.

Gordon, Michael, Joseph Person, and Jonathan Jones. "Panthers' Greg Hardy guilty of assaulting female, communicating threats." *Charlotte Observer*, 15 July 2014, www.charlotteobserver.com/news/local/crime/article9140591.html.

@GrantWahl. "Full Hope Solo quote on Sweden after US was eliminated from the Olympics today." *Twitter*, 12 Aug. 2016, 2:52 p.m., twitter.com/GrantWahl/status/764187928851582976.

Harwitt, Sandra. "Serena Williams loses US Open final in shocking, controversial match to Naomi Osaka." *USA Today*, 8 Sept. 2018, www.usatoday.com/story/sports/tennis/2018/09/08/serena-williams-loses-us-open-game-penalty/1240689002/.

@HopeSolo. "This was the full context of my comments today." *Twitter*, 12 Aug. 2016, 3:46 p.m., twitter.com/hopesolo/status/764201530475950080?lang=en.

Humphreys, Joe. "What does sport tell us about mortality?" *The Irish Times*, 23 May 2017, www.irishtimes.com/culture/what-does-sport-tell-us-about-morality-1.3085389.

Jenkins, Sally. "Hope Solo, talented and excused in victory, exposes herself in Olympics defeat." *Washington Post*, 12 Aug. 2016, www.washingtonpost.com.olympics/hope-solo-talented-and-excused-in-victory-exposes-herself-in-Olympics-defeat/.
Koschyk, Maximiliane. "Hope Solo: I hate the term role model." *Deutsche Welle*, 11 Nov. 2015, www.dw.com/en/hope-solo-i-hate-the-term-role-model/a-18867764.
Kosner, Edward. "The devil at Shortstop." *The Wall Street Journal*. 17 Mar. 2017, www.wsj.com/articles/the-devil-at-shortstop-1489778422.
Kroft, Steve. "Tom Brady: The Winner. Patriots Quarterback Discusses His Career and Other Aspects of His Life." *60 Minutes*. CBS News, 20 Dec. 2007, www.cbsnews.com/news/tom-brady-the-winner/.
Leonard, David. "The Olympic guide to trash-talking." *The Undefeated*, 18 Aug. 2016. theundefeated.com/features/the-olympic-guide-to-trash-talking/.
Longman, Jere. "After haunting loss, U.S. fires women's coach." *The New York Times*, 23 Oct. 2007, www.nytimes.com/2007/10/23/sports/soccer/23usa.html.
Maloney, James, and D.J. Siddiqi. "Sixers' Joel Embiid fined $25,000 for criticizing referees following close loss to Celtics." *CBS Sports*, 13 Feb. 2019, www.cbssports.com/nba/news/sixers-joel-embiid-fined-25000-for-criticizing-referees-following-close-loss-to-celtics/.
McBride, James. "The economics of hosting the Olympic Games." Council on Foreign Affairs. 18 Jan. 2018, www.cfr.org/backgrounder/economics-hosting-olympic-games.
McCarthy, Michael. "What's wrong with soccer in U.S.? It's a 'rich, white-kid sport,' says Hope Solo." *Sporting News*, 27 June 2018, www.sportingnews.com/us/soccer/news/world-cup-2018-hope-solo-rich-white-kid-sport/1xahd40xg3jn21t7zkvfr5hiyc.
Nabokov, Vladimir. *Speak, Memory: An Autobiography Revisited*. Vintage Books, 1989.
Solo, Hope. *Solo: A Memoir of Hope*. Harper, 2013.
Zirin, Dave. "'A Soulless Coward': Coach Gregg Popovich Responds to Trump." *The Nation*, 16 Oct. 2017, www.thenation.com/article/a-soulless-coward-coach-gregg-popovich-responds-to-trump/.

The Book of Dale Earnhardt
Beyond the Intimidator's Last Lap

Teresa Marie Kelly

Kirk Gibson limping around the bases after his heroic home run; Doug Flutie raising his arms after completing the last-second Hail Mary; commentator Al Michaels declaring "Do you believe in Miracles? Yes!" during the final seconds of the Miracle on Ice: every sport has moments that burn themselves into popular culture's collective psyche. Few sports bear the burden of having that most iconic moment also rank among the most tragic, but that is exactly the case for The National Association for Stock Car Auto Racing (NASCAR). The death of seven-time champion Ralph Dale Earnhardt, Sr., in his fatal wreck on the last lap of the 2001 Daytona 500, NASCAR's signature event, changed the sport and its associated culture, freezing that heartbreaking moment in fan memories forever.

At the time of his death, Earnhardt had ridden his win-at-all-costs "Intimidator" persona to the top of NASCAR's premier racing series, known as the Cup Series. His 74 Cup Series wins rank second, behind only Richard Petty's 200 Cup Series victories. His seven Cup Series championships tied him with Petty (a feat Jimmie Johnson matched in 2016). No one has yet eclipsed it.

Even today, Earnhardt influences the sport he brought to its zenith. In April 2018, his son and namesake, known in NASCAR as Dale Jr. (to distinguish him from his infamous father), celebrated Earnhardt's birthday and the Intimidator legacy on Twitter by calling him "the biggest badass ever to drive a racecar" (@DaleJr). Earnhardt's sudden death completed his transformation from an anti-hero to folk legend, and he remains the sport's most recognizable and beloved figure two decades after his last lap.

It was not always that way.

For most of Earnhardt's career, other drivers, crews, journalists, and fans loved him and hated him in equal measure, and he reveled in it. The strong, lasting reaction to his death speaks not just to his record-setting career, but also to his continued influence on the sport he made famous and the strength of the Intimidator legend.

NASCAR Gives Rise to the Intimidator

Today's NASCAR bears little resemblance to its roots. Called stock car racing because the modified racing chassis were street legal at one time before being massaged into racing cars, the sport began organically. According to NASCAR historian Neil Thompson, young men modified their cars to maximize speed and honed their driving skills to avoid the law and outrun each other while trafficking moonshine and other questionable cargo on the backroads of the early 20th century Deep South (8–10). The culture of the independent driver allowed for a cross-section of personalities to succeed in ad-hoc races with little or no sponsorship other than used parts or spaces to work. The drivers built fan bases across a rural South that no big-time sports team would call home until the Braves relocated to Atlanta in 1965 (9). The men Thompson calls "moonshining cousins and their four-letter-word-using friends" (10) provided the fertile ground and sowed the seeds to germinate modern stock car racing and the Earnhardt legend. A driver who raced harder than normal or wrecked others to take the lead could expect to be raced in the same way. Phrases like "checkers or wreckers" and "rubbin' is racing" made it clear that drivers did not have to worry about the fan base judging their aggressive actions.

In the early 21st century, contemporary NASCAR stars, such as former Cup Series champions Jeff Gordon and Jimmie Johnson, learned that classic all-American and likable does not a NASCAR icon make. Although both drivers have a solid fan base, they have never achieved an Intimidator-like cult following, despite the fact that they both have winning records as impressive as Earnhardt's.

Likewise, Kurt and Kyle Busch, Tony Stewart, Brad Keselowski, and others also learned that driving aggressively to the point of recklessness or letting their fists do the talking did not earn them the dominant image that the Intimidator enjoyed. Earnhardt had speed and aggressiveness, but he also possessed transcendent skills rarely seen in the sport. He could declare his car "junk" on lap 50 and win the race with an impossible pass and a smirk on lap 150, leaving drivers and observers alike asking, "Where did HE come from?" with an expletive or five thrown in. Earnhardt may not have always won cleanly, but he won unapologetically and sometimes inexplicably.

On the surface, Earnhardt's continued popularity reinforces the stereotype of NASCAR as a blue-collar sport, with him as a working-class hero who often bent—or broke—rules to win. However, although few extensive studies of NASCAR fan demographics exist, W.G. Spann debunks the idea that one social or income demographic dominates the fandom (353–4). The eclectic fan base likes what it likes, and some experts find that hard to predict. Rather than shared socioeconomics, fans often have personality traits that mirror what they want to see on the track, including a willingness to take risks, loyalty, faith, and a powerful sense of community and regional identity (357–8). In their star drivers, NASCAR fans appreciate personality, competitiveness, and spirit reminiscent of the moonshiners, coupled with respect for each other and the dangers of the sport.

NASCAR fans may defy specific stereotypes, but Spann notes that most popular drivers have a "type." NASCAR fans love their good-old-boy Southern driver with charisma (356), which partly explains the lukewarm acceptance of California natives Gordon and Johnson, as well as the reaction to the Las Vegas-born Busch brothers. Fans embrace the same type of character that Tom Wolfe depicts in his famous *Esquire* essay, "The Last American Hero," an homage to Junior Johnson, a driver-turned-car-owner and NASCAR Hall of Fame member. Wolfe called Johnson "a coon hunter, a rich man, an ex-whiskey runner, a good old boy who hard-charges stock cars 175 m.p.h. Mother dog! He is the lead-footed chicken farmer from Ronda, the true vision of the New South." Wolfe could have been describing Earnhardt. He never owned a chicken farm, but he had a lead foot, and no one was a harder charger.

Popular culture depicts multiple versions of the archetypal driver that Wolfe defined—many with traits that mirror Earnhardt's. A movie based on Wolfe's essay starred Jeff Bridges as the aggressive driver Elroy Jackson, Jr., as well as featuring Ned Beatty and a young Burt Reynolds. Reynolds would go on to personify the Southern rogue with heart and style as Bandit in the *Smokey and the Bandit* franchise. Other performances such as Kenny Rogers in *Six Pack* and Tom Cruise in *Days of Thunder* add to the pantheon. Will Ferrell parodied the archetype for a comic turn in *Talladega Nights: The Ballad of Ricky Bobby*, and Pixar depicted it in the character of Lightning McQueen, voiced by Owen Wilson, in the *Cars* franchise.

Television played a huge role in establishing the trope as well. CBS decided to air flag-to-flag coverage of the Daytona 500 for the first time on Sunday, February 18, 1979. Despite rain and trepidation, the network and NASCAR wanted to put on a show (Bechtel 96–8). It worked better than anyone could have imagined. All day, the racing was competitive, but the last lap is iconic. As Donnie Allison and Cale Yarborough—two of the sport's biggest names—raced side by side on the backstretch, they collided. Momentum took both cars into the wall, then down to the grass infield, allowing

Richard Petty to win the race. If that was not exciting enough, Allison's brother, Bobby, stopped in the infield to back up his brother, and a fight broke out between the Allisons and Yarborough (Bechtel 119–128). That fight changed everything.

After the 1979 race, an international audience finally saw beyond the "500 miles of left turns" to the personalities, passion, and barely controlled mayhem of a sport where a lanky driver in a cowboy hat and giant belt buckle could win a race while two brothers beat up the boy next door for wrecking one of them (Bechtel 129–38). Still, the sport needed a more relatable star. Earnhardt—who ran his first Daytona 500 at that 1979 race exactly 22 years to the day before he ran his last—became that touchstone for fans.

Enter the Intimidator

Earnhardt was from Kannapolis, North Carolina, and later lived in Mooresville. These two small towns (near the current NASCAR Hall of Fame) and others like them form the nexus of NASCAR country. His father Ralph had been a successful dirt track racer and NASCAR National Sportsman Division Champion. In a 1980 column commemorating Earnhardt's first Cup Championship, Tom Higgins, *The Charlotte Observer*'s long-time NASCAR reporter, put Ralph and Dale on par with the storied Petty clan. He wrote that Ralph Earnhardt "was a winner from the first time he climbed into a race car" ("A Real Father"). Legendary track owner Humpy Wheeler told Higgins, "Had Ralph lived, I have a feeling he'd still be the best dirt-tracker around … that's the kind of touch he had" (qtd. in "A Real Father"). Off the track, Ralph demanded a great deal from his son, something Earnhardt would later repeat with his son.

Whether as a reaction to the pressure from Ralph or because of his own personality, Earnhardt often let his immaturity spill into all aspects of his life—education, family, work, and racing. He had a willful, erratic nature, which may be one reason he climbed NASCAR's ranks slowly. Earnhardt cobbled together his "rides," NASCAR vernacular for an agreement to drive a car for a specific owner or organization. He drove aggressively, resulting in horrific wrecks, including one at a 1976 race in Atlanta that prompted Richard Petty to tell his #43 crew over the radio that "they just killed Ralph Earnhardt's boy" (Bechtel 163). Proving Petty wrong, Earnhardt walked away from that and other wrecks and continued to drive the way he lived—fast, without limits, and defying expectations. Eventually, his raw talent forced car owners and sponsors to see beyond potential downsides to working with the volatile young driver.

Eventually, Earnhardt would land a full-time ride with Richard Childress

Racing (RCR) who he would race for the rest of his life. The partnership resulted in 67 of Earnhardt's 74 Cup Series wins and six of his seven Cup Series Championships as well as giving rise to the Intimidator persona. Through his first decade with Childress, Earnhardt made more enemies than friends. According to reporter Ron Green of the *Charlotte Observer*, for most of his career, fellow drivers and fans called Earnhardt everything from "Knucklehead" to "the Man in Black," in addition to monikers that TV and radio had to censor. Green also noted "Dale Earnhardt's nickname around the NASCAR Winston Cup Circuit is 'Ironhead,' an obvious play on his last name.... To some, it is an affectionate sobriquet. Others feel the appellation should be 'Hardhead'" ("Other Drivers"). The name Intimidator would stick because that was what he was—intimidating. He could see or feel or hear the air around his car and do things other drivers only dreamt of being able to do. Although going to the back of the field or being a lap down would put most drivers out of contention, Earnhardt found the smallest openings to move around cars.

In stock car racing, being a bad driver differs from being a badass. A badass looks for the edge and takes it—some more aggressively than others. He pounces on little mistakes, like tiny skids or going too deep into a turn, and passes competitors through side drafting or moving them out of the way with a gentle tap on the bumper. *Sports Illustrated*'s Mark Bechtel contends Earnhardt's hard-charging style arose from the uncertain early days of his career and carried over to RCR. He writes

> Earnhardt's driving style had just as much to do with his situation as it did with his naturally aggressive personality. Stroking in a one-time deal was not going to do him any good. He needed to get noticed, and being conservative was not going to do that either. But if you put him in a situation where he didn't feel like he had to drive the wheels off the car, he could put his natural gifts on display [163].

Although other sports rely on trash talking or stare downs to gain a psychological advantage, drivers cannot look each other in the eye or hear each other during competition. They must gain an edge through consistent action like the bumper tap or soft turn into the wall on a cool-down lap—the stock car equivalent of a brush-back pitch in major league baseball. As Green wrote

> Nobody among the upper echelon of stock car racing drives harder, battles more fiercely, or takes more chances than Dale Earnhardt. He hurls his car around a track in a style that is often chilling to competitors and fans alike. He drives like a New York Cabbie with his throttle stuck ["Other Drivers"].

Earnhardt embraced the Intimidator moniker and persona because it helped him put drivers off their stride for a moment when he suddenly filled their rear-view mirror. That moment was all he needed to find an opening and pass a competitor. As Green notes, commentators and drivers alike would often ask him "How'd you do that?" ("Oh, So"). Higgins writes, "Ask other NASCAR competitors who they least like to see in their review mirror, the answer is Earnhardt" ("Ba-a-a-d"). When the black #3 suddenly appeared in drivers' mirrors, Earnhardt designed his persona to make sure they thought "Here comes trouble" and other, more profane things.

Trouble was sometimes putting it lightly. Some of those moves were reckless. At least one was bad enough to earn him death threats and long-term ill will from fans and competitors. In 1987, at the Winston All-Star Race exhibition at Charlotte Motor Speedway, Earnhardt was again racing hard against Bill Elliot, the sport's most popular driver at that time and one of Earnhardt's main competitors. As the race reached its final lap, Earnhardt dived below Elliot's car and slid off-track into the infield to execute the infamous and quasi-legal "Pass in the Grass" to beat the Georgia native. The Intimidator's "winner take all or wreck them trying" move in a non-point race that paid hard cash and bragging rights, but little else, struck many fans, especially Elliot's legions, as unsportsmanlike.

Elliot himself, normally mild-mannered, did not hold back his anger. According to *Deadspin* Editor Barry Petchesky, Elliot said, "I'm sick and tired of it.... If it takes that type of driving to be the Winston Cup champion, I don't want to be the champion." The incident still haunts the now retired driver. In a 2016 article, *Fox Sports* reported the older Elliot told NASCAR.com,

> I hadn't been so mad in ... I can't remember when. You have to remember; I worked on my race cars. My philosophy was to outrun someone fair and square rather than crash them up. It was just a turning point for me and Earnhardt. He had kinda been going at it with me here and there, but that was the end ["#TBT"].

According to Petchesky, Earnhardt later told the *San Diego Union-Tribune*, "We can't all be good guys. Some of us have to wear black hats. It's what makes the world go around." Those words became one of his most infamous quotes. Despite Elliot's residual anger, it speaks to Earnhardt's influence on the sport that after Earnhardt's death the other driver took himself out of the running for Most Popular Driver—an award he had won multiple times—and asked his fans to vote for Earnhardt. They did. Ten months after his death, the Intimidator earned his first and only most-popular-driver award.

Although Earnhardt rarely eased up on the track, he instinctively knew the other drivers had their limits and took their off-track actions in stride rather than chasing them through the garage area the way some contemporary drivers do. In 1995, following a brutal, wreck-filled race at Bristol, Tennessee, Rusty Wallace—whom Earnhardt always raced aggressively and who gave it right back—threw a water bottle at his friend/nemesis. Green began his account of the incident with a single sentence, "Dale Earnhardt can be so aggravating, he could make Mother Teresa want to slap his face" ("Take Aspirin"). Many drivers shared that sentiment.

Sometimes, problems did arise off the track, especially in the case of Darrell Waltrip, known as DW, the 1988 Cup Champion whom Earnhardt often tangled with on the track. DW's gregarious bravado (what some called a big mouth) rubbed many people the wrong way, but none more so than Earnhardt, who tended to be taciturn to the point of surly off the track and let his driving speak for him. DW wrote

> Our relationship had not always been cordial. We were rivals on the racetrack for years. Our rivalry had spilled into public view in the early 1980s after a flippant remark I'd made in an interview; I'd told a print reporter that I could say what I wanted about Dale and his team because "they wouldn't be able to read it anyway." Dale hadn't found the comment nearly as funny as I had [Waltrip and Larkin 4].

Although the two drivers battled on track and exchanged barbs off track, they had a grudging respect for each other. As they matured, that respect evolved. Later in both their careers, they would become friends. DW's wife Stevie regularly gave both drivers Bible verses to carry in their car. She continued the practice for one race after DW retired—the fateful 2001 Daytona 500. During that race weekend, DW and his younger brother Michael each played a pivotal part in the events leading to and following Earnhardt's death.

Earnhardt fit the uniquely American archetype of the anti-hero, a persona that sports has only recently embraced. A year before Earnhardt's death, Professors Rick Burton, Francis Farrelly, and Pascale Quester note, "it is only within the last three decades that athletes with negative or non-traditional reputations have emerged as viable product endorsers" (316). Statistics like Earnhardt's mean more to a fan base than likeability. Burton, Ferrelly, and Quester write, "In this sense, it may be more important for an athlete to appear 'true' to his or her values, regardless of public criticism or ongoing evaluations by the media" (319). As broader cultural changes in and outside of NASCAR shifted away from humble beginnings and rural Southern culture, fans appreciated that Earnhardt never lost sight of his origins. They identified more with him—a high school dropout who rose to the height of fame, yet insisted his own son and namesake stay in school and gave him a job sweeping—than they did with manicured all-American boys from California like Gordon, whom they booed mercilessly. According to motorsports writer David Poole, the displeasure of the fans caused Earnhardt to muse, "I wish they were booing me. If they boo you on Sunday, you go to the bank on Monday. I don't want to be the guy who's not the hero, but I want to be the winner" ("Will Someone"). Earnhardt's driving style and mannerisms never changed. That reality, along with his expressed appreciation for his roots and his continued connection to who he was and where he came from, contributed to his growing popularity.

Unlike other sports, stock car racing tends to forgive its villains and even canonize them—especially if they boast long careers and impressive records. In such a dangerous sport, it is often safer to embrace the hard-nosed veteran than the fresh-faced newcomer who might not pan out despite implicit promise. Over the years, fans slowly came to appreciate Earnhardt's bluster and bravado, not because they liked him, but because he won and made racing interesting. He did not have to dominate the race or lap the field to win. If he was running at the end, he was a threat to win—and drivers and fans alike knew it. Green wrote

> There was a time when they weren't sure he wasn't a devil, that ol' Dale Earnhardt, the way he drove that race car and knocked their favorites around. Gradually, though, they've come around, the people in the stands. More and more wear his color, black. It was inevitable ["The Man"].

Fan-conscious drivers followed suit and began using his mystique to their advantage. They learned that even when they wanted to kill him, joking about a run-in with Earnhardt got them airtime or in print, a crucial factor for a sport where drivers needed both success and media attention to lure sponsors. During the 1993 Pepsi 400 at Daytona, Kenny Schrader and Earnhardt were rubbing paint as they approached the finish line. Earnhardt won. Higgins notes, "I got my nose in there the last lap and Earnhardt kind of wiped it for me," Schrader reported ("Win No. 4"). Fans of the laid-back Schrader know two things: (1) That is about as mad as he gets and (2) He knew how to get publicity out of it. Even in races where Earnhardt dwarfed the competition and did not need to resort to wild antics and drama to win, fans tuned in. Like golfer Tiger Woods on a Sunday leaderboard, ratings went up when Earnhardt was in the mix. Although other drivers may have despised always seeing the #3 out front and the huge pack racing, they also knew what the fans wanted.

Despite honing his Intimidator persona, Earnhardt had a humorous side as fearsome and adept as his driving. According to the documentary *UnRivaled: Earnhardt vs. Gordon*, Earnhardt liked riling "the Kid," as he called the younger Gordon. During Gordon's 1995 Cup Series title run, Earnhardt mocked the younger driver for crying when he won and said Gordon's youth meant he would have to celebrate a championship with milk. But Earnhardt was always able to take what he gave. As shown in the documentary, Gordon toasted his first championship—and Earnhardt—with milk at the 1995 NASCAR awards banquet. Earnhardt stood with a smile and toasted Gordon back—with champagne.

Although Earnhardt continued to act and drive like a badass, he also believed that part of racing was respecting and honoring those who had come before him, as well as drivers who put everything into winning on the same track. The 1993 season, one of the most painful in NASCAR history, forced him into more of a public leadership role. In April, defending Winston Cup Champion Alan Kulwicki and several employees from his sponsor, Hooters, died when their plane crashed on approach to Bristol, Tennessee, for the spring race. In July, Davey Allison, the son of legendary driver Bobby Allison and a rising star, died of injuries from a helicopter crash at Talladega Motor Speedway. That July, Earnhardt won at Pocono after Allison's death—his first win since the death of Kulwicki. He pulled alongside the driver he had beaten, rival Rusty Wallace, and pointed to the #28 flag Wallace carried in memory of Allison (Higgins, "Davey Allison"). Earnhardt then picked up an even bigger Allison flag from his pits and did Kulwicki's famous "Polish victory lap," where the driver reverses direction on the track in order to be closer to the fans ("Win No. 5"). He made the tribute a habit for the rest of the season, something his peers would later do for him.

Daletona

Heroes and villains often find themselves equated with the places of their greatest triumphs and tragedies. King Arthur had Camelot. Brett Favre had Lambeau Field, and Derek Jeter had Yankee Stadium. By equal measure, Earnhardt had Daytona International Speedway.

Every February, NASCAR opens its season at Daytona with "Speed Weeks," a series of exhibition, dash, and qualifying events that culminate in the season openers for its top three series. On the second Sunday of Speed Weeks each year, NASCAR crowns a Cup Series race winner who forever carries the "x-time Daytona 500 champion" moniker. Between the Clash, non-points races, the twin Daytona 500 qualifiers, the July 400 mile race, and other non–Cup races, Earnhardt won more at Daytona than any other driver. However, the signature race—the Daytona 500—eluded him for over 20 years.

Earnhardt came close to winning the 500 many times, only to run out of gas or wreck. In a famous mini-rivalry that became known as the Dale and Dale show, he was beaten twice by second-generation driver Dale Jarrett by only a hair (Higgins, "Dale wins!"). That struggle marked the beginning of Earnhardt's shift from bad boy to a beloved icon, starting with the fans and the media and later including competitors and the rest of the racing community. His frustrations with the 500—and how much the win meant to him—showed that the Intimidator was not some devil or soulless evil. He was a man with both strengths and failings, one of which was his battle to win the 500.

Each February, the media would focus on the ways Earnhardt had lost the 500 and proclaim that year to be his year. With each checkered flag, something would get in the way. As Earnhardt fought to win the biggest race in the sport at a track he dominated, his battle touched something in the NASCAR community. His drive and determination let fans and media alike see the man under the persona—and that man wanted desperately to win the Daytona 500. For the first time, the Intimidator was the underdog. He was the hero on a quest, not the villain driving over the competition. Even his competitors rooted for him, but none of them would ever insult Earnhardt's talent and purpose by racing him any less aggressively down to the last lap.

Earnhardt's tenacity showed frequently during his quest to win the 500, even when the Universe appeared to conspire against him. At the 1991 Daytona 500, he was leading on lap 198 of 200 when his car became unstable, and he wrecked several contenders. According to Higgins, far from apologizing or acknowledging eventual winner Ernie Irvin, Earnhardt said, "The best car doesn't always win. We proved that last year" (qtd. in "This Can't"). During the 1997 race, Earnhardt crashed hard and flipped. Safety crews had to help him from the wreckage. Green recalls that when Earnhardt noticed his car had landed on its wheels and continued to run, he shook off the hands trying to steer him to an ambulance, grabbed his helmet, and climbed back into the car to finish the race ("Daytona"). In the face of such adversity and determination, many drivers adopted a simple approach to the 500. If they could not win in a given year, they hoped Earnhardt would.

In 1998, Earnhardt finally won his first and only Daytona 500. After the checkered flag, every member of every crew lined up on pit row to congratulate him, a scene often described as the most poignant in NASCAR history. "It was my time," he told Poole. "I have been passed on the last lap. I have run out of gas, and I have cut a tire. I knew we were coming back to the checkered" (qtd. in "Dale-tona 500"). The pure joy of the victory lane celebration, with Earnhardt crowing, "I just won the Daytona 500," appeared on broadcasts worldwide. For hours, he whirled around the speedway doing interviews on the back of a scooter—driven by someone else because he had imbibed a bit, was punch-drunk on his win, or both. His sense of fulfillment allowed him to push the Intimidator aside as he shared the story of a young girl from Make-A-Wish who had visited with him that week. She had given him a penny for luck in the 500, and he had epoxied it to his dash before the race started. He gave the little girl and the coin some credit, one of the rare times fans glimpsed a sentimental Earnhardt.

Ironically, three years later at the same track, joy would turn to tragedy. In 2002, a year after his death, Daytona immortalized the moment he hoisted the trophy in victory lane by erecting a statue that welcomes fans into the famed track. Had he not died, that iconic statue might never have existed, but that 500 win in 1998 changed many things for Earnhardt and NASCAR.

Shortly after his 1998 Daytona 500 victory, fans, drivers, and journalists alike began increasingly to see a softening in Dale Earnhardt. "From that moment on, he was right with the world it seemed," said Ty Norris, Former Executive Vice President at Earnhardt's Racing Team, Dale Earnhardt Incorporated (DEI), in *The Day: Remembering Dale Earnhardt*—a documentary made by NASCAR and SPEED TV (now FS1) for the tenth anniversary of Earnhardt's death.

On the personal side, Earnhardt was looking beyond driving. DEI thrived under third wife Teresa's business acumen, coupled with Earnhardt's racing know-how and eye for talent. His son, Dale Jr., already showed promise as a skilled racer, something that made Earnhardt practically glow with pride. Earnhardt always had his eye on the future with DEI. He wanted to give Dale Jr. a quality ride from the beginning of his career and to prove that, as an owner, he could find and develop talented drivers. As Speed Weeks 2001 approached, the Intimidator might have ruled on the track, but a happy, content Earnhardt was at peace off it.

After several injury-encumbered seasons, Earnhardt and Childress intended to win another cup championship in 2001, Childress said in *The Day*. During Speed Weeks, NASCAR also stood poised on the edge of a breakout season. A new television deal with Fox and NBC, a strong economy bringing sponsorship dollars to the sport, and a crop of "young gun" drivers including Dale Jr. promised finally to lift NASCAR to the level of the other major American sports.

During those Speed Weeks, Earnhardt's long-time nemesis turned dear friend, DW, debuted as a commentator for *Fox Sports* at Speed Weeks. Among his assignments, DW interviewed Earnhardt two days before the 500. Clips of the interview depict a man who found the keys to professional success and personal contentment. As *The Day* recounts, the Intimidator mask slid away as he told DW: "I'm the happiest I've been in my life.... I'm a lot better today than several years ago, because of family. Because of my wife. I'm a better person than I used to be. I've got it all, Darrell. I've got it all." A happy Earnhardt did not mean a complacent one. Leading up to the race, he had strategized with Dale Jr. and Waltrip how they could link up and win the race. Both were skeptical but also knew no one drove Daytona better than Earnhardt. When he spoke about what to do at that track, drivers had to listen. The race proved him correct, and everything came together perfectly until the last lap.

"We've Lost Dale Earnhardt"

For the first 499 miles, the 2001 Daytona 500 showed all that Speed Weeks had promised and more. At Daytona, like Talladega, NASCAR mandates restrictor plates to limit engine power and reduce speed on the notoriously difficult tracks. As a result, more evenly matched cars bunch up in packs and everyone waits for a wreck, "the big one," to decimate the field. Early on, a spectacular wreck took out many competitors and sent Tony Stewart flying. While under a red flag for the cleanup, Earnhardt commented on the radio to car owner Richard Childress that NASCAR needed to look at the new rules and car specifications on restrictor plate tracks before they killed someone.

As the race reached the last lap, it promised a "fairy tale" ending. Earnhardt, running third, appeared to be blocking for the two DEI cars in front of him, Dale Jr. in second and Waltrip in the lead, going for his first win in 462 Cup points races. Far from driving defensively, Earnhardt—Intimidator mode firmly in place—followed the plan he had developed with his team drivers: get to the front, hook up in a draft, keep the other cars behind them, and finish 1, 2, 3 with whoever happened to be first winning. In a segment of ESPN's *NASCAR Now* that paid tribute to Earnhardt before the 2011 Daytona 500, DW admitted expressing concern about the driver's aggressiveness to his broadcast partner Larry McReynolds, Earnhardt's crew chief for his only 1998 Daytona 500 win. DW said that if Earnhardt kept sticking his car in front of people, someone was going to wreck him.

On the track, cars began to stack up behind the top three. In the *NASCAR Now* episode, Kenny Schraeder recalled wondering what the drivers were thinking. "No way they were all getting under Dale," he said in *The Day*. The last lap proved both DW and Schraeder tragically correct. In turn four, driver Sterling Marlin tapped Earnhardt in the rear, destabilizing his car and sending it across Schraeder's path. Both cars slammed hard into the wall, with Earnhardt hitting head on and Schraeder riding along, the impact blunted for him by the #3 car. Waltrip and Dale Jr. crossed the finish line in first and second, just as planned.

In *The Day*, Schraeder recalls that the wreck did not feel bad. He quickly unbuckled and went to talk to Dale—or more likely the Intimidator. He figured Earnhardt would be angry, but not too unpleasant since his DEI cars had just finished one-two in the Daytona 500. As Schraeder reached the car and took down the window netting, he says, "I knew he was in trouble" (qtd. in *The Day*) and began gesturing to the safety crews. In an interview with Dan Coble for the tenth anniversary of the Intimidator's death, Schrader admitted "Here's the deal. When I went up to the car.... I knew. I knew he was dead." Schraeder also maintains he had no intention of being the first to say it. "I didn't want to be the one who said, 'Dale is dead,'" he told Coble. Schraeder has never publicly revealed exactly what he saw and likely never will.

In the Fox booth, DW expressed concerns immediately. He told broadcast partners Mike Joy and Larry McReynolds that "Those type of wrecks hurt you" (qtd. in *The Day*). The fledgling broadcast team did not want to be alarmist, yet Joy said that they could not pretend everything was okay (qtd. in *The Day*). When Fox returned from a commercial, the broadcast cut to Victory Lane then to an image of Dale Jr. exiting his second-place car and jogging toward the infield care center. After another commercial, the broadcast returned to the image of an ambulance slowly bypassing infield care and carrying Earnhardt to Halifax Medical Center. Higgins noted that knowledgeable observers knew the crawl of the ambulance meant either a serious head or neck injury or death (*The Day*). Rather than exiting or preparing to leave, uneasy fans, journalists, crews, and officials stood around, waiting.

For the TV audience, the reality set in more slowly, but anyone who saw Schraeder's FOX interview after his release from the infield care center knew something terrible had happened. As *The Day* shows, the ashen-faced, usually gregarious driver merely said he did not know Earnhardt's condition. Moments later camera footage shot off to the side in Victory Lane captured the moment but not the audio when Schraeder told race winner Mikey Waltrip his concerns. Later, a still photograph included in *The Day* showed a no-longer jubilant Waltrip sitting down with his head in his hands on the edges of the celebration. Fox ended its broadcast congratulating the Waltrips and praying for the Earnhardt family, as close as any of the broadcasters wanted to get to a confirmation that something terrible had taken place.

Fans watching on television anxiously waited for news. As local news programs began to air about two hours following the wreck, viewers saw brief video clips filmed outside the Halifax Trauma Center. Dale Jr. and Teresa were entering the trauma center and the ambulance arrived and quickly unloaded a stretcher as a paramedic appeared to perform CPR. Rumors began to circulate, but it was not until 7:00 p.m. ET—two and a half hours after the accident—that a shaken Mike Helton delivered the devastating news. His iconic words, although not unexpected, were heart-rending. "This is undoubtedly one of the toughest announcements that I've ever personally had to make. But after the accident in Turn 4 at the end of the Daytona 500, we've lost Dale Earnhardt." Helton also read a statement from then NASCAR Chairman Bill France, Jr., that described Earnhardt as the sport's "greatest driver ever." Years later DW aptly titled his autobiography *Sundays Will Never Be the Same*. He spoke for millions.

Horror and disbelief swept the NASCAR community and fan base. Earnhardt could not die. He was indestructible. One look at video of a sobbing Chocolate Meyers, Earnhardt's burly, long-time crew member, said it all. Fans, drivers, owners, sponsors, and track promoters had trickled out of the track between the last lap and Helton's announcement. Some would stay in the area to await word, while others would get on the private team planes and only find out the news when they landed in the Charlotte area. Statements filtered into the networks, but few of those big names associated with the sport spoke live to the media until the next morning. Others did not fully share their reactions for years. In his autobiography *In the Blink of an Eye*, published just before the tenth anniversary of his friend and mentor's death, Waltrip admitted struggling emotionally for many years with his guilt that what should have been the best moment of his life had become the worst with the loss of Earnhardt (4–5).

The shockwaves emanated beyond NASCAR as well. No analogy exists for that moment—a sport's biggest star dying at the climax of the sport's biggest event. His Speed Weeks' interviews with all the unrealized plans he had for his future in the sport added to the poignancy. The internet had just barely come into its own as a virtual water cooler, but it began to buzz with flashes and reactions. Cable news broke into programming and network nightly news led with the story. *The Daytona Beach News-Journal* ran a special edition with the headline "Black Sunday." In 2009, Bleacher Report called it "The Day the Engines Died" (Preston). *The Atlanta Journal Constitution*'s Pulitzer Prize–winning cartoonist Mike Luckovich captured the emotions of many with his depiction of Earnhardt arriving at the Pearly Gates; God wanted an autograph. In a reaction some compared to the throngs of mourners after the death of Diana, Princess of Wales, fans congregated at various tracks, at RCR, and at DEI. They left flowers, candles, and notes of all types. In typical resilient NASCAR fashion, Dale Jr. spoke briefly to a reporter when he returned to the track, thanking everyone for their prayers and making assurances that they—meaning everyone from the family to the fans—would get through it.

At a press conference two days after the accident, the three DEI drivers—Waltrip, Park, and Dale Jr.—showed the same strong determination to move forward that their boss had always demonstrated. Dale Jr. also made it clear that no one was to blame. He began to shoulder some of his father's leadership of the sport, flatly saying blaming anyone or worse, making threats, would not be tolerated. He urged everyone to focus on the next race and narrated a commercial where he consoled fans and encouraged everyone to do what his father would want, to go race. Park would go on to win the rain-delayed race the following Monday.

NASCAR and the Intimidator Today

In death, Earnhardt achieved an immortality seldom experienced by athletes, even those who die before their time. Unlike other sports deaths, fans experienced Earnhardt's loss in real time. They saw the wreck and the aftermath, they waited for word, and they got the news with everyone else.

In other cases of the loss of a major sports figure, the public hears the news after events have played out and the outcome is clear. With Earnhardt, fans had a window to what was happening. They saw Earnhardt's life end from one second to the next. That moment of trauma is what Scott Radford and Peter Bloc concluded contributed to the unique nature and longevity of the mourning for Earnhardt (48). History professor Richard Kimball says

> Dale Earnhardt's death was likely the most shocking and consequential death in American sports history. Never before had a sport's most popular athlete been killed participating in the sport's premier event in front of 150,000 people in the stands and thirty million more watching on television [100].

As sports psychologists Daniel Wann and Paula Waddill note, fans of drivers other than Earnhardt also felt sadness and loss (107). While the experience may account for the acute mourning, it does not explain why Earnhardt remains a constant presence at races. His image, memorabilia, and even cars detailed to look like his #3 appear at every track. Gear with his face or a facsimile of his signature—copyrighted long before his death—sells out every weekend. The sport has lost other drivers over the years on the track to accidents, to illness, or advancing years, but for every tattered Davey Allison shirt, there are fifty crisp, new Earnhardt shirts.

Part of his indelible memory doubtless arises from revisiting his death. For nearly two decades, Daytona has represented a strange mix of excitement and loss. Earnhardt still personifies NASCAR for many. Broadcasters and fans mention him easily as if he had just driven the week before. Nearly 20 years after his death, fans still report scanning the race field looking for him, but none can explain why.

Another facet of Earnhardt's immortality speaks not just to the timing for the sport when he died—at the zenith of the biggest race of the sport's breakout year—but to the timing in his life. He was 49 and would have been 50 that April. Injuries behind him, Earnhardt the driver prepared for one more title run. Earnhardt, the owner, prepared for the future, when he would step away from the car and let others like his son drive. Fans never saw Earnhardt slow down on the track to the point of being uncompetitive. Unlike DW, he did not experience a downward slide that forced him to hang up the helmet. He also did not get a goodbye—a moment, a tour, a final flag. Like Diana or even JFK, he is frozen in memory: young, vibrant, productive. NASCAR never had to deal with an aging Dale Earnhardt the way it did with Petty, Wallace, and DW. Fans expect to see him driving because that is what they last saw him doing. Nothing puts him back on the track, but commercials, references on live broadcasts, and the memorabilia keep him part of racing.

Despite this continued presence, one symbol of Earnhardt's career—the iconic #3 car—remained conspicuously absent. Because NASCAR does not retire numbers, Childress continued to pay for the #3 but did not field a #3 car in a Cup race until 2014. According to Lars Anderson, when Earnhardt's successor, Kevin Harvick, left RCR in 2014, a natural progression took place. Childress's grandsons, Austin and Ty Dillon, had been racing their way up the NASCAR ranks. Austin ran the #3 in the Xfinity series, and after checking with the Earnhardt family, Childress decided he would run the car with a familiar black paint scheme in the Cup Series.

At the 2018 Daytona 500—the first not to feature an Earnhardt since 1979—Dillon won his first Daytona 500 driving the #3 car owned by his grandfather. He emotionally recalled being a little boy watching Earnhardt win his only Daytona 500 in 1998. Drivers do not readily share their sport's biggest spotlight, but according to Peter Kerasotis, Dillon did just that by evoking the memory of Earnhardt. He honored his childhood idol by holding three fingers in the air, like the V for Victory with an added finger to replicate the signature "3" salute fans gave on the silent third lap of every 2001 race.

The response to Dillon's actions showed that Earnhardt's influence on the sport continues. Even after so many years, Earnhardt remains a powerful marketing tool, in no small part because of his Intimidator persona. His memory appears vital to the future of a sport in trouble due to declining attendance, TV ratings, and sponsorship dollars (Martin 56–58). During the early part of the 2018 season, Dillon also appeared in one of a series of NASCAR commercials called "The Book of Dale" where current drivers read quotes from the Intimidator. Dillon read Earnhardt's "We can't all be good guys" line from 1987. Designed to appeal to the old-school NASCAR fans who have begun to leave the sport, the spots attempted to shore up the sport's ratings and attendance that had steadily fallen in recent years (Birchfield). The quotes NASCAR selected reflected the Intimidator's anti-hero status to emphasize that, despite their polished appearances, this generation of drivers shared characteristics with the icon.

As part of the effort to help NASCAR reclaim its fans after his retirement, Dale Jr. filmed an emotional commercial for Goodyear, his father's primary sponsor. Released a week after the 2018 Daytona 500, the commercial features a car driving the pine-filled backroads of North Carolina and a series of vignettes—some staged and others from old footage of father and son—set to the Jim Croce song "I've Got a Name" performed by Croce's son (Dosh). The song speaks of traditions being passed from one generation to the next. While some industry pundits wondered if the looking backwards helped NASCAR, others believed reliance on tradition would help unite the fan base. Of the "Make a Name" commercial, Dale Jr. said

Goodyear has always been part of my family, and I'm proud to partner with them on this "Make a Name" spot, which is a reflection of one's legacy, values, and drive.... It tells a very personal story about me growing up, but it also hits home with where I am today, both personally and professionally [qtd. in Dosh].

Fans have made that journey of growth from rookie to retirement with Dale Jr., but for many, imagining his father growing old and retiring seems impossible because it never happened. He would be nearing 70 now and probably not driving in the Cup Series, yet it feels like he should be. Death froze Earnhardt in memory at 49. Today, they celebrate him with more appreciation than sadness. They and NASCAR recognize that as long as there is stock car racing, the Intimidator will remain a model for the typical NASCAR Racer for whom being bad is often good.

Earnhardt's tragic death temporarily blunted the reality that he inspired as much hate as love during his life, but his Intimidator persona—including rivalries with fellow drivers, complex personal relationships, and even death threats—has returned to the sport's collective psyche as something to be lauded. Early struggles and frustrations spawned a hunger for success that triggered an aggressive style on the track and left little room in his life outside of the car for two ex-wives and his three oldest children. As his success grew, so did the Intimidator legend and the polarized fan base that either loved or hated him. He relished both.

As his achievements as a driver and later a car owner cemented his legacy, and his personal life stabilized. Even with a third, successful marriage to wife Teresa and a renewed chance at fatherhood, Earnhardt worked to maintain the illusion that he was still a working-class journeyman and the bad boy Intimidator. He diligently kept his generosity and kindnesses quiet, but his tragic death sanitized his complexity as a driver, owner, husband, father, friend, and man. Earnhardt once told Kurt Busch, himself a perennial bad boy who appears to have grown up some, that it did not matter if the crowd cheered or booed, as long as they made noise. When they did not make a sound, then he would know to call it a career. Whichever Earnhardt they saw—the bad boy or the good man—fans have never stopped making noise.

Works Cited

Anderson, Lars. "Austin Dillon Steps In." *Sports Illustrated*, vol. 120, no. 8, Feb. 2014, p. 48.

Bechtel, Mark. *He Crashed Me So I Crashed Him Back: The True Story of the Year the King, Jaws, Earnhardt, and the Rest of NASCAR's Feudin', Fightin' Good Ol' Boys Put Stock Car Racing on the Map*. Little Brown, 2010.

Birchfield, Jeff. "Is the 'Book of Dale' good for NASCAR." *Johnson City Press* [Johnsonville, TN], 13 Mar. 2018, www.johnsoncitypress.com/Motorsports/2018/03/13/Why-the-Book-of-Dale-may-not-be-good-for-NASCAR.html.

Burton, Rick, Francis Farrelly, and Pascale Quester. "Exploring the Curious Demand for

Athletes with Controversial Images: A Review of Anti-Hero Product Endorsement Advertising." *International Journal of Sports Marketing & Sponsorship*, vol. 2, no. 4 Dec. 2000, pp. 315–20.

Coble, Don. "Ten after 3: Sterling Marlin's bump of Dale Earnhardt Changed Everything." *The Florida Times-Union*. 7 Feb. 2011, www.jacksonville.com/sports/racing/2011-02-07/story/ten-after-3-sterling-marlins-bump-dale-earnhardt-changed-everything.

@DaleJr. "Happy birthday to the biggest badass that ever drove a racecar." *Twitter*, 29 Apr. 2018, 4:32 a.m., twitter.com/dalejr/status/990554382713356288?lang=en.

The Day: Remembering Dale Earnhardt. YouTube, uploaded by SHEVYWOOD, 3 July 2017, www.youtube.com/watch?v=EO3Jazqvwrc.

Dosh, Kristi. "History Collides with Dale Earnhardt, Jr., Goodyear, A.J. Croce Collaboration Ahead of Daytona 500." *Forbes*, 14 Feb. 2018, www.forbes.com/sites/kristidosh/2018/02/14/history-collides-with-dale-earnhardt-jr-goodyear-a-j-croce-collaboration-ahead-of-daytona-500/#265198bd6207.

Gluck, Jeff. "Dillon Puts No. 3 on Pole for Return." *USA Today*, 2014, p. 03C. EBSCOhost.

Gordon, Jeff. *Unrivaled: Earnhardt vs. Gordon*. NASCAR Productions and Fox Sports Films, 2019.

Green, Ron. "Daytona Just Gets Weirder." *Dale Earnhardt: Review Mirror—Commemorating the Life of a Legend*, edited by Michael Persinger. Sports Publishing, 2001, p. 182.

———. "Oh, So He's a Magician…." *Dale Earnhardt: Review Mirror—Commemorating the Life of a Legend*, edited by Michael Persinger. Sports Publishing, 2001, p. 114.

———. "Other Drivers Notice When Earnhardt's Around." *Dale Earnhardt: Review Mirror—Commemorating the Life of a Legend*, edited by Michael Persinger. Sports Publishing, 2001, p. 168.

———. "Take Aspirin, Throw Perrier, and Call Me…." *Dale Earnhardt: Review Mirror—Commemorating the Life of a Legend*, edited by Michael Persinger. Sports Publishing, 2001, p. 66.

———. "The Man, the Fans…." *Dale Earnhardt: Review Mirror—Commemorating the Life of a Legend*, edited by Michael Persinger. Sports Publishing, 2001, p. 114.

Higgins, Tom. "A Real Father-Son Racing Success Story." *Dale Earnhardt: Review Mirror—Commemorating the Life of a Legend*, edited by Michael Persinger. Sports Publishing, 2001, p. 3.

———. "Ba-a-a-d in Black." *Dale Earnhardt: Review Mirror—Commemorating the Life of a Legend*, edited by Michael Persinger. Sports Publishing, 2001, p. 102.

———. "Davey Allison and Alan Kulwicki: A Tribute." *Dale Earnhardt: Review Mirror—Commemorating the Life of a Legend*, edited by Michael Persinger. Sports Publishing, 2001, p. 147.

———. "Dale Wins! No Not That Dale!" *Dale Earnhardt: Review Mirror—Commemorating the Life of a Legend*, edited by Michael Persinger. Sports Publishing, 2001, p. 173.

———. "This Can't Be Happening." *Dale Earnhardt: Review Mirror—Commemorating the Life of a Legend*, edited by Michael Persinger. Sports Publishing, 2001, p. 126.

Kerasotis, Peter. "Dillon's Daytona Victory in the No. 3 Car Resonates across History." *New York Times*, vol. 167, no. 57878, 19 Feb. 2018, p. D12.

Kimball, Richard Ian. *Legends Never Die: Athletes and Their Afterlives in Modern America*. Syracuse University Press, 2017.

Luckovich, Mike. "Dale Earnhardt: 1951–2001." *The Atlanta Journal-Constitution*, 19 Feb. 2001, p. 35.

Martin, Edward. "Speed Bump: NASCAR Chief Brian France Shakes up a Tradition Bound Sport, Hoping to Reverse a Slowdown." *Business North Carolina*, vol. 38, no. 5, May 2018, p. 54–61.

NASCAR Now: Dale Earnhardt Tribute. YouTube, uploaded by mriracing, 19 Feb. 2011, www.youtube.com/watch?v=SLBqEdaVUZE.

Petchesky, Barry, "'When I Get A Clear Shot…': 25 Years Ago, Dale Earnhardt Received This Death Threat for His Ornery Driving." *Deadspin*. 21 Aug. 2012, www.deadspin.com/5936579/when-i-get-a-clear-shot-25-years-ago-dale-earnhardt-received-this-death-threat-for-his-pass-in-the-grass.

Poole, David. "Dale-Tona 500." *Dale Earnhardt: Review Mirror—Commemorating the Life of a Legend*, edited by Michael Persinger. Sports Publishing, 2001, p. 196.

_____. "Will Someone Boo Me, Please?" *Dale Earnhardt: Review Mirror—Commemorating the Life of a Legend*, edited by Michael Persinger. Sports Publishing, 2001, p. 186.

Preston, Jan. "The Day the Engines Died: Remembering Dale Earnhardt, Sr." *Bleacher Report*. 3 Feb. 2009, www.bleacherreport.com/articles/119261-the-day-the-engines-died-remembering-dale-earnhardt.

Radford, Scott, and Peter Bloch. "Consumers' Online Responses to the Death of a Celebrity." *Marketing Letters*, vol. 24, no. 1, Mar. 2013, pp. 43–55. EBSCOhost, doi:10.1007/s11002-012-9202-5.

Spanu, M.Graham. "NASCAR Racing Fans: Cranking Up an Empirical Approach." *Journal of Popular Culture*, vol. 36, no. 2, Fall 2002, pp. 352–360. EBSCOhost, doi:10.1111/1540-5931.00010.

"#TBT: Dale Earnhardt's 'Pass in the Grass' still haunts Bill Elliott." *FoxSports*. 19 May 2016, www.foxsports.com/nascar/story/dale-earnhardt-pass-in-the-grass-bill-elliott-winston-all-star-race-051916.

Thompson, Neil. *Driving with the Devil: Southern Moonshine, Detroit Wheels, and the Birth of NASCAR*. New York, Broadway Books, 2009.

Waltrip, Darrell, and Nate Larkin. *Sundays Will Never Be the Same: Racing, Tragedy, and Redemption—My Life in America's Fastest Sport*. Free Press, 2013.

Waltrip, Michael, and Ellis Henican. *In the Blink of an Eye: Dale, Daytona, and the Day That Changed Everything*. Hyperion, 2011.

Wann, Daniel L., and Paula J. Waddill. "Examining Reactions to the Dale Earnhardt Crash: The Importance of Identification with NASCAR Drivers." *Journal of Sport Behavior*, vol. 30, no. 1, Mar. 2007, pp. 94–109. EBSCOhost.

Wolfe, Tom. "The Last American Hero Is Junior Johnson. Yes!" *Esquire*. Mar. 1965, www.classic.esquire.com/junior-johnson/.

"Often an Eyeful, Sometimes an Earful, but Always a Handful"[1]

Dennis Rodman, Quintessential NBA Bad Boy

SARAH D. FOGLE

Dennis Rodman is not the only bad boy in the NBA—Latrell Sprewell, Alan Iverson, Ron Artest, and Vernon Maxwell quickly come to mind—but he is the complete package of disruptive, distractive behavior. From 1986 to 2000, Rodman was a famous—frequently infamous—defensive and rebounding basketball whiz in the National Basketball Association (NBA). During his career, he played for five different teams: the Detroit Pistons (1986–1993), the San Antonio Spurs (1993–1995), the Chicago Bulls (1995–1998), the Los Angeles Lakers (1998–1999), and the Dallas Mavericks (1999–2000). In the midst of earning numerous awards for his on-court performance, Rodman also incurred frequent ejections for accumulating technical fouls and suspensions for missing practice or being late to games, many thousands of dollars in fines, and a ton of negative publicity and criticism. He famously kicked a courtside photographer in the groin after crashing into him on a defensive rebounding play, and he is well-known for head-butting, grappling, and shoving other players. He even danced with an opponent after a tussle and showed up in a televised wrestling match with Hulk Hogan when he was supposed to be at practice. Frequently the physical, rough play he inflicted could have injured opponents, perhaps even ended a career; Scottie Pippen, an NBA Hall of Famer and eventual teammate of Rodman, still has the scar from a fall after Rodman shoved him into a goal stanchion during a Pistons game.

Married and divorced three times, his personal life has been as erratic as his on-court antics, physical appearance, and penchant for unusual attire that frequently featured items of women's clothing. He was sometimes AWOL from practice or late to a game because of his impulsive wee-hours jaunts to Las Vegas to gamble away thousands of dollars. Headlines such as "Dennis the Menace," "Demolition Man," "Planet Dennis," and "The Worm Has Turned" described his persona and his play.

Some well-known, well-respected sportswriters had little patience with him. In *The Best of Frank Deford: I'm Just Getting Started*, Deford writes bluntly, "I'm sick and tired of Dennis Rodman" (57) for his antics and for what he perceived as Rodman's disrespect for his sport (58). Writing in *Esquire* early in Rodman's play with the Pistons, Mike Lupica presents "the Rodman Awards for outstanding achievements in sports obnoxiousness" and describes Rodman as "not just annoying [but] a punk for the ages" ("Dennis Anyone" 32). In the aftermath of criticism following the kick to the photographer, sports commentator Bob Costas said Rodman would "have to move up several notches to qualify as a fool" (qtd. in Futrelle 1) and later called him "a mindless exhibitionist degenerate" (qtd. in Miklasz 2). In a later *Esquire* article, Lupica expresses grudging respect for Rodman's on-court play, but he still uses derogatory language when describing him as "the Tattooed Mutant Ninja Forward"("Damn Bulls" 2). However, journalist after journalist, even those critical of his behavior, has expressed grudging respect for his work ethic during games, his conditioning, and his basketball IQ when defending and rebounding. As a subject of critical cultural analysis in professional sports, Rodman is second only to Michael Jordan, but the former's resume is dominated by his image as a bad boy. Rodman's name inevitably crops up during conversations about athletes who transgress, and if there were a Venn diagram titled "What Makes a Bad Boy in Sports," Rodman would be at the center of overlapping circles, making him an ideal case study of factors that contribute to an elite athlete being deemed a bad boy.

A Starting Point: The "Otherness" of Race

In many professional sports, black players substantially outnumber white players. Despite the advantage that a majority might imply, black players are often viewed as "other" and subject to stereotypes perpetuated over decades in American culture. During slavery, the "good" black man was the slave who worked in the house and who otherwise succumbed to the bidding of his master. The "bad" black man was the slave who resisted or fought back against, or tried to escape from, his oppressor. In his 2006 book about black athletes, *Forty Million Dollar Slaves: The Rise, Fall, and Redemption of the Black Athlete*, William C. Rhoden uses the plantation metaphor to explain the roles of black athletes in sports. In this construct, the team owners, predominately white men, are the plantation owners; the coaches are the overseers; and the players are, in sense, slaves to the system they have joined, perceiving that they have little or no control within this system. Players can even be traded, to extend the metaphor.

Adhering to meanings arising from America's slave past, images of potency and threat constitute the most significant elements of the "otherness" stereotype associated with black male athletes. According to Linda Tucker in "Blackballed: Basketball and Representations of the Black Male Athlete," "In a way that no other sport has, with the exception of boxing, professional basketball reflects histories of racist practices and racialized representations of Black men in the United States.... [Such images] are shaped by white lore of the Black man as a criminal and a figure of bestial sexual excess" (311). The locus of basketball competitions reinforces such stereotypes. Although NBA teams are comprised of predominantly black players, spectators are principally white, especially outside large cities. The court is a confined space that puts spectators into close proximity to big, strong players; no protective barrier, such as the Plexiglas wall in hockey, separates players and spectators. The shorts have recently lengthened and show less athletic leg than in the past, but basketball uniforms are still more revealing than football, hockey, or even soccer uniforms. Physicality is palpable during games as players' bodies are on full display: faces, muscles, and sweat. At times they hurl themselves into the crowd going after a ball. Such images play into the potency stereotype, but the threat is contained. As Tucker notes, sports arenas and commerce help "to confine and contain the... dangers this black body may bring.... [T]he black body relegates itself to the arena of sports rather than spilling far beyond its boundaries.... [It] is both a legitimate outlet for aggression and a viable means of encoding [it] as graceful" (41). Despite these impressions of containment, some players, particularly Rodman, have negated those "promises" through sheer physicality, aggression, and refusal to conform to team norms and rules of the game. In his own words, in *Bad as I Wanna Be*, Rodman puts it simply: "I'm nothing beyond a sports slave" (63). What Rodman wants is the freedom to be Rodman, to be his own man, to be himself, whoever that may be at any given time.

A Growing Reputation for Aggressiveness

When Rodman was drafted by the Detroit Pistons after he graduated from college, he had no reputation beyond his All-American play at Southeastern Oklahoma State and a few post-graduation all-star games. In joining the Pistons, however, he became a member of an entire team of bad boys, a moniker well earned by the likes of teammates Bill Laimbeer, Isaiah Thomas, Mark Aguirre, Ric Mahorn, and others. Although basketball is, to this day, not included in the definition of "contact sport," the Pistons' style of play belied its absence from that category. Rodman joined a team with a well-deserved reputation for an extremely physical and intimidating, often dirty, style of play. That team was nicknamed the "Bad Boys," a title derived from a video developed by N.B.A. Properties to document the Pistons' 1987–1988 season that led to the championship finals and the Pistons' loss to the Los Angeles Lakers. The video opened with George Thorogood's "Bad to the Bone," aptly setting the tone for the team; Thomas notably said, "If we're going to be the Bad Boys, we've got to act like Bad Boys" (qtd. in Araton). Sometimes the team referred to themselves as the "Oakland Raiders of basketball" (Boyd 107), apt perhaps, but nothing to be proud of. The Raider tag signaled the rough on-court treatment the Pistons' opponents could expect. Laimbeer was especially known as a dirty player, and lessons Thomas had learned from Chicago's West Side street gangs such as the Black Stone Rangers fed into developing the Pistons' physical, confrontational style of play (Boyd 107). Coach Chuck Daly, very much a gentleman himself, believed such tactics were the best way to defeat the Boston Celtics and Los Angeles Lakers, teams that had dominated the NBA playoffs year after year. When Michael Jordon emerged as the star of the neighboring state rival Chicago Bulls, Daly called his on-court tactics "The Jordan Rules" (Chirco 4); they were expressly designed and executed with the hope of dominating the Bulls on the court. Daly also "allowed his players to feel comfortable being their true selves on the floor because he knew it was the best way to get the most out of his teams" (Chirco 4).

The Pistons' aggressive style of play, particularly their defense, cannot be separated from race and the notion of black bad boys. Even Laimbeer, who came from a white, privileged background, became associated with this "black" style of play because he played as rough, or rougher, than his teammates; this style distinguished him from the public's perception of the play of white athletes (Boyd 108). Rodman reveled in what he could do to white players: "A black player knows he can go out on a court and kick a white player's ass.... The black player is conditioned to think he can take the white guy whenever he wants to" (Teitelbaum 117).

Athletic Ability Too Great to Ignore

After Daly voluntarily left his coaching job at Detroit, Rodman requested a trade, which landed him on the roster of the San Antonio Spurs. His time on the Spurs team, spearheaded by the likes of moral icon David Robinson, lasted only two years. His first coach, John Lucas, tolerated Rodman's nonconforming behavior, as his teammates generally did, in exchange for his tremendous defensive and rebounding skills and performance. Behaving badly, getting ejected, leaving the court, removing his jersey, and other outbursts earned him a summons from NBA Commissioner David Stern, who gave him an ultimatum to end this behavior—an ultimatum Rodman, in typical fashion, ignored. Writing about this incident for *Newsday*, Shaun Powell begins his account of Rodman's increasingly aberrant behavior with the following: "Too old for reform school, too outrageous for the military and surprisingly, not loony enough for the asylum. His behavior was getting odd, even by his own high standards." Lucas's successor in Rodman's second year, Brian Hill, was a more by-the-book coach who was much less tolerant than Lucas; during both years, team management remained frustrated with Rodman, and he was believed to have cost the Spurs their shot at a championship. He was traded to the Chicago Bulls after his second season on the Spurs.

It would have been no surprise if the new coach of the Bulls, Phil Jackson, had received a truckload of sympathy cards upon Rodman's signing with the team. But Jackson was sanguine about having Rodman play for the Bulls, hoping to find a path to successfully incorporating him into a team that featured standouts Jordan and Pippen along with a strong supporting cast of players. Although Jackson is commonly referred to as the "Zen master" or "basketball Buddha" (Marantz 1) of coaches, he acknowledges that he was not sure what to expect. After consulting with Daly and having a conversation with Rodman, Jackson determined he "just want[ed] Rodman to abide by the team rules and give his trademark dedicated effort on the court" (Ledbetter 2). Rodman was added to the Bulls team to help them win championships, and with him, win them they did: three in a row. For their part, Rodman's Bulls teammates generally did not make a public issue of his behavior as long as he remained a hardworking cog in the machine that made them successful on court. Jackson acknowledged that the team felt some disappointment at times, but as long as they performed as a team on court, they accepted Rodman's occasional outbursts. In a revealing comment to the media, teammate Ron Harper once said, "Dennis is Dennis.... He doesn't bother us. He bothers y'all" (qtd.in Schmitz 4).

Ultimately, athletic success can excuse a multitude of sins, and over the course of his career, teams decided Rodman was worth the baggage. Twice he made the NBA All Star team, seven times he was selected for the NBA All Defensive Team, and twice he was named the NBA Defensive Player of the Year. Although he never became a prolific scorer, nor did he care to, for seven years in a row he led the NBA in defensive rebounds, another record in itself; and he played on teams that won the NBA championship five times. In 2011, predictably dressed in an outfit worthy of the court of France's "Sun King,"

Louis XIV, Rodman was inducted into the Naismith Memorial Basketball Hall of Fame.

Influence of Hip Hop and "Gangsta" Counterculture

At the height of Rodman's playing career, hip-hop culture infiltrated the NBA, reinforcing the bad boy black man stereotype. Rodman's behavior, appearance, and style of play—along with that of Iverson and Sprewell, for example—were a part of this hip-hop image. In her article "The Modern Black Athlete, Hip-Hop, and Popular Perceptions of Black Masculinity," Thabiti Lewis argues that what was originally and centrally the "cool" vibe of the hip-hop cultural phenomenon became "gangsta" version, "shaped by media, professional sports leagues, and leading sports apparel companies to construct the negative stereotype of bad black men" and attributed to them the qualities of "narcissism, questionable values, poor sportsmanship, as well as a propensity for crime and violence" (1). Lewis adds that "The hyper-masculine representations in hip-hop narratives and athletes' playing performances and personas are also a direct response to a repressive culture; a response to, or attempted compensation for a perceived loss of power, potency, or manhood" (2). In essence, "Gangsta" brought to the NBA a constellation of assumed or expected black stereotypes: street gangs, ghettos, violent and other antisocial behavior, and criminality. As John Hoberman argues in *Darwin's Athletes: How Sport Has Damaged Black America and Preserved the Myth of Race*, "The black male style has become incarnated in the fusion of black athletes, rappers, and criminals into a single menacing figure who disgusts and offends many blacks as well as whites" (xxviii). One way this fusion is accomplished is through cultural artifacts of "otherness"—loose, baggy attire, prolific tattoos, hair styles such as corn rows and braids, and bling, lots of bling.

Rodman became an aficionado of some aspects of this "gangsta" spectacle shortly after he left the Detroit Pistons team. One of the most overt canvases for that activity was his body. When he reached the Bulls, he did not yet have the visible tattoos, body piercings, or multicolored hair, but he soon sported tattoos that nearly covered his body; had every possible body part pierced; cut his hair into patterns and variously dyed it red, fuchsia, the colors of the LGBTQ rainbow flag, among others—all of this before dye jobs, dreadlocks, and body modifications became commonplace in professional sports. His tattoos run the gamut from family to team affiliation, and the one that covers his back is virtually pornographic, certainly not suitable for public consumption. On the Bulls, Rodman was a stark visual contrast to Jordan, perhaps the only basketball player during this era that was more iconic than Rodman himself. A particularly good analysis of their bodies as text is explained in Roger Gilbert's article "Air, Worm, Pip, Zen: The Chicago Bulls as Sacred Book," in which he discusses their "contrasting versions of American selfhood so vividly that they've taken on a genuinely iconic status" (246). He likens their celebrity to that of a rock group and notes that these three dominant players express the team's "profoundly suggestive differences in style, stance and image… that produce drama and beauty while leaving the team's shared identity intact…. They are like three organs of a single being" (Gilbert 247). Headline phrases mentioned earlier in this essay depicted Rodman as a monster, a destroyer; his nickname "Worm" associates him with the Earth. In stark contrast, Jordan was, and still is, "Air Jordan," "His Airness," or simply "Air": "If Jordan is essentially ethereal, a creature belonging to the upper regions of the atmosphere, Rodman is a denizen of the dank depths" (Gilbert 260). Jordan is "classically beautiful in his proportions and features," even "archetypal" (Gilbert 250). His head is shaved clean, his skin is blueblack, lacking in visible body art. By contrast, Rodman is physically unattractive, his large ears projecting from his head and his body colored with tattoos. Jordan is almost ballet-like in his play; he is not rough, he soars, his shots swish through the net. Rodman is all knees, elbows, shoving, taunting, flopping. According to Gilbert, "With the addition of Rodman the Bulls became something larger even than Jordan; they became a text" (254). One can argue that both the angel and the devil are characters in this text.

Nonconforming Appearance and Attire

Rodman also used attire as spectacle, appearing on late-night talk shows and out on the town clad in flamboyant, florid outfits featuring large velvet hats, satins and sequins, and feathered boas and wearing make-up and nail polish. His attire has certainly been characterized as feminine, and some have likened his style, particularly his hats, to that of a pimp. In his own words, in *Bad as I Wanna Be,* Rodman says, "I like bringing out the feminine side of Dennis Rodman. I like to shock people, to have them wonder where in the hell I'm coming from" (166). He once showed up for a book signing wearing a wig and a wedding dress, declaring himself bisexual and announcing that he intended to marry himself. His behavior is designed to shock, to gain attention, and to make others uneasy about his nonconforming behavior and what it may actually mean (which may be nothing more than pleasing himself and shocking others).

His commitment to "activism" for the LGBTQ community is less clear. Rodman's penchant for cross dressing and frequenting gay clubs has been interpreted as signaling his support of the LGBTQ community and its causes. He touts his popularity with gay men and talks about how comfortable he is among patrons at gay bars, even when he is with a female date; he claims he has "done more to recognize them than any pro athlete" (*Bad* 170). That point alone is debatable in the broader world of professional sports, but his questionable rationale follows:

> When I put the AIDS ribbon on my head during the playoffs against the Lakers in 1995, I think that opened a lot of eyes. These people were finally seeing somebody openly recognize them. For the first time they saw someone openly show some support.... It let them know there's someone ... who understands and isn't going to pretend they don't exist [*Bad* 170].

Dyeing his hair was a good gesture, although the AIDS ribbon depicted in his hair could easily have been dismissed as just another wacky Rodman hair color among many others; but the question is what else has he done? In their analysis of what they term "excursions into otherness," Melisse Lafrance and Genevieve Rail, while acknowledging that Rodman may have, through his outspoken affinity for gays, "'queered' mainstream audiences" (37), note that his hyperheterosexuality and related behaviors allow him to "benefit from the publicity and popular exoticization of queer chic while successfully courting a primarily heterosexual male reader/viewership" (37). Gary Whannel's assessment is somewhat more negative, describing Rodman as a "postmodern bad boy" whose appearance and actions are not consequential because he can do anything and it does not matter because it is a façade. Whannel asks, "has he broken through boundaries, or merely been boxed inside the category of 'flash but crazy nigger?'" (179). Essentially, Rodman has little or no skin in the game when it comes to advocating for the LGBTQ community.

None of this is to say that Rodman has not made some valid points about the homosocial elements of sport and the lack of tolerance for nonconforming sexual orientations in professional sports. He asks, "Why are athletes treated differently than people in everyday society?" (*Bad* 173). He describes the physical touching that occurs in sports—pats on the behind, men kissing cheeks, men hugging men, men grappling with men in play—behavior that he believes is never acknowledged as on the spectrum of homosexual behavior (*Bad* 169). Point well taken. Unfortunately, it is difficult to accept that Rodman's visual displays and comments about homosocial behavior are anything more than self-motivated. He knows that with his reputation for flamboyant dress, if he engages in this behavior on the court, his fingernails painted, his trash talk referring to dates, he could, and did, throw opponents off their games. Additionally, his image as a sexual, social, sartorial rebel is part and parcel of his commodification and celebrity, which translate ultimately into money. In "Dennis Rodman—Do You Feel Feminine Yet?"

Michelle D. Dunbar offers an excellent analysis of Rodman's portrayal of black masculinity:

> Although Rodman actively takes part in the construction of his own visual image ... the monetary rewards that [he] receives for his transgressions shed light on the possibility that Rodman is appropriating resistance discourse that does not necessarily resist oppressive structures of society, such as race and gender relations [269].

Dunbar argues further that Rodman can get away with his nonconformity precisely *because* he is a man: "a man's physical and social dominance give him the power to play with codes of female sexuality; he is 'so much a man' that he is even a man while wearing women's clothing" and that he "may be invoking such a meaning rather than employing resistant agency against rigid gender rules" (271). Ultimately, Rodman is trumpeting his heterosexuality, studliness, and objectification of women.

Commercial Success and Overindulgence

The question about Rodman's financial motivations is an important one. The huge paychecks that elite professional athletes earn allow them to indulge in human vice in ways that the rest of us can only imagine, and in Rodman's case (as well as the case of many other bad boy athletes), the image he cultivated as a bad boy only increased his access to endorsement deals. Interestingly, throughout his playing career, Rodman complained about being underpaid and under-recognized, and it is very true that he did not earn the top salary that iconic stars such as Jordan commanded. When Rodman began to garner commercial endorsements, however, his income rose. His agent, Dwight Manley, a millionaire rare coin dealer, was the engine that fueled his fortunes through his first book deal and product endorsements for Kodak, Converse, Carl's Jr., hamburger restaurants, Comfort Inn, Oakley sunglasses, Victoria's Secret, and the California Milk Producers' *Got Milk?* ad campaign, to name just a few. Rodman met Manley while both were gambling in Las Vegas; Manley began to manage the newly formed Rodman Group, and the two became good friends. The Rodman Group made the basketball player a "hot media commodity that flaunts his wild man image to the hilt for a fast-growing roster of product endorsements, interviews, film and TV appearances and commercial deals" (Hesketh 3). In addition, Manley secured for Rodman "cameo movie appearances, a cartoon series, and a set of collector cards" (Hesketh 3). Converse hired Rodman to hawk their athletic shoes because "they needed a big, fat jolt of electricity, some star power" (Tierney 2).

Eventually, the combination of Rodman's salary and commercial activity "made him the ninth highest paid athlete in the world in 1996" (Burton et al. 6). For the maker or seller of the product, the selection of a controversial athlete for endorsement can be a case of high risk, high reward. Victoria's Secret learned this lesson quickly when their lingerie ad with Rodman went far over the line. Writing for the *New York Daily News*, George Rush and fellow writers wryly observed that "Victoria's Secret will need to invent some asbestos lingerie for [model] Helena Christensen, judging from the way she flirted with Dennis Rodman in the company's latest assault on TV's standards and practices" (1). In the commercial, when Christensen asked Rodman what he would like for her to wear her black bra and briefs under, "he dead-panned, 'Me'" (Rush et al. 1). NBC and CBS refused to air the ad, ABC would air it only very late at night, and only VH1 and MTV aired it with any regularity (Rush et al. 1). According to Mike Tierney, only a felony or premeditated harm to someone would render Rodman persona non grata in the advertising world (2).

Tierney's comments were possibly accurate since Rodman gained endorsements despite well-publicized overindulgences. He has had, throughout his adult life, problems with alcohol that have led him to rehab multiple times. He is also an inveterate gambler. But Rodman's money and celebrity especially enabled him to indulge in his favorite activity: sex. In his autobiography, Rodman openly discusses that he questioned his sexuality when he was a boy but claimed he "decided" he did not want that sexual orientation (166). The very notion that he believes he can decide his sexual orientation reveals his lack of understanding, deliberate or otherwise, of what sexual orientation means or derives from. He also says he fantasizes about being with men and writes that "Mentally, I probably am bisexual" (172)—whatever he thinks that means. Regardless of his stated sexual orientation, in his mind, Rodman is a virtual sex machine, fueled much of the time by the well-known easy availability of enthusiastically willing women. Overman notes that "A standing joke circulated among players in the NBA is that the hardest thing about going on the road is wiping the smile off your face before you kiss your wife goodbye" (105). Lakers star Wilt Chamberlin once claimed he had slept with over a thousand women while playing in the NBA. Although such behaviors are an open secret for most NBA wives and girlfriends, Anicka Bakes, Rodman's live-in girlfriend of two years, apparently was not privy to that knowledge. She had assumed they were monogamous. In an interview with *People Magazine* (while pregnant), she acknowledged, "I would find as many as fifty women's names and telephone numbers written on scraps of paper in Dennis's clothes ... *in a month*" (qtd. in Overman).

Rodman had flings with celebrities Madonna and Carmen Electra, and he published nude or near nude, often sexually suggestive, photos of himself in magazine articles. On the cover of his book *Walk on the Wild Side*, Rodman is pictured naked, except for a black thong, crouched on all fours, his upper body painted with black stripes all over, his face colored with black eye shadow and lipstick, his face contorted in a snarl. The dust jacket blurb features Rodman's own words:

> I have this fantasy that I can live my life like a tiger in the jungle—eating whatever I want, having sex whenever I want, and roaming around butt naked, wild and free.... It sounds difficult and complicated, but it doesn't have to be. Everything you need to set yourself free is right there inside of you. If you close your eyes and concentrate, you feel it in the blood rushing through your veins and the thumping of your heart.

Throughout the book, Rodman plays into the stereotype of the black male as an overly endowed, sexual predator. He prefers the word "fucking" to the term "making love": "You really can't make love as much as you can fuck. Fucking is so much better because you let all the aggression out" (*Walk* 75). Rodman is also a fan of masturbation and catalogs his array of sexual aids at home, all dedicated to his, not a partner's, enjoyment (*Walk* 83). In his version of the Ten Commandments, all but one have to do with having sex (*Walk* 205). Contemplating his ultimate demise, he muses whether "DEATH IS LIKE THE ETERNAL ORGASM [sic]" (*Walk* 193). Learning that Rodman had said he might change his name from Dennis to "Orgasm," the *Chicago Tribune*'s Bernie Lincicome drily commented, "If Dennis Rodman wants to change his name to a convulsive body function, vomit isn't taken" (1). Rodman gives a vivid, graphic account of his sexploits during his relationship with Madonna in *Bad as I Wanna Be* (196). He often brags about the size of his penis and also boasts that he has broken it several times during sex. Even in something as wholesome as a *Got Milk?* ad, Rodman was the only male depicted in a sexually suggestive manner (Cuneen and Spencer 148): naked from the waist up, his arms raised akimbo and clasped behind his head in a "hunk model" pose, gazing directly into the camera. In Rodman's world, sex and money are integrally connected.

Attainment of Celebrity Status

Almost universal among sports bad boys are the dual characteristics of athletic ability and celebrity. Following his NBA career, Rodman pursued celebrity status with as much zeal and ferocity as he had demonstrated on the hardwood. In addition to the MTV reality series *The Rodman World Tour*, he appeared on *Celebrity Mole* on ABC and twice on Donald Trump's *Celebrity Apprentice* on NBC, as well as on the UK series *Celebrity Big Brother* and *Love Island*. Note the frequency of the word *celebrity* in these endeavors. He has also appeared in films, playing alongside Jean-Claude Van Damme, Mickey Rourke, and Tom Berenger. His film *Double Team* earned three

Golden Raspberries, and Rodman won three "worst" awards for his acting. In 2005, he served as the Commissioner of the Lingerie Football League and flirted with the idea of starting a women's topless basketball league, a venture that, unsurprisingly, never gained traction. He also had a stint as a professional wrestler whose ring name was Imposter Sting. In this entertainment endeavor, he had a few successes, wrestling alongside Karl Malone and Hulk Hogan. In 2008, as a contestant on *Hulk Hogan's Championship Wrestling* on the CMT television network, Rodman won, triumphing over such luminaries as Butter Bean and Dustin Diamond. His agent Manley secured most of these media opportunities, as well as his book deals. All were lucrative ventures, and they fueled his ongoing pursuit of celebrity. Historian Daniel Boorstin, known for his work on the distinction between heroes and celebrities, claims, "*The celebrity is a person who is known for his well-knownness....* The hero ... by his achievement; the celebrity by his image or trademark. The hero created himself; the celebrity is created by the media. The hero is a big man; the celebrity is a big name" (qtd. in Andrews and Jackson 2). Rodman is unquestionably known for his "knownness," and he certainly is a big name. But even this reality did not prepare the public, and U.S. government, for Rodman's role as accidental ambassador to the hermit kingdom to conduct "basketball diplomacy."

Unlikely Emissary to North Korea

The intersection of sports and politics is not a new phenomenon; one has only to consider the roles that the Olympics and the FIFA World Cup play on the world stage. President Richard Nixon famously used ping-pong diplomacy in his efforts to forge a way into China. The idea that sports might be involved in making connections with North Korea is not farfetched; however, that Rodman became the person to do it was certainly unexpected. Chairman Kim Jong-un is known to have developed a fondness for basketball when he was a young student in Switzerland; from the standpoint of physique and rumored health issues, he is an unlikely candidate for action on the hardwood, beyond perhaps a slow game of HORSE. Perhaps because Secretary of State Madeline Albright had given Jong-un a gift of a basketball autographed by Jordan, "His Airness" had received Jong-un's first invitation. Jordan declined. Through the efforts of Vice Media, in preparation for a series on HBO, however, Rodman became a candidate for the visit.

When star athletes wade into political waters, their actions are frequently not widely met with the approval of fans, owners, political pundits, and others. Years ago, when sports luminaries such as Muhammad Ali, Billie Jean King, Jim Brown, and others took vocal, principled stands on issues of civil rights or gender equity, "many in the stands responded with a grumble: shut up and play" (Crouch 3), as if playing a sport was their singular ability and purpose on the planet. Today, not much has changed. Consider the case of Colin Kaepernick and, more recently, LeBron James, who was admonished by Fox News pundit Laura Ingram, of all people, to just shut up and dribble. Her demeaning jab implies that a star athlete is neither entitled to freedom of expression nor has the intelligence to engage in such discourse. Rodman's trip to North Korea, however, was seen as amusing and frivolous (Crouch 3). Worse to contemplate is that "in the popular imagination ... there is something simply funny about North Korea itself.... There was a sense that North Korea and Rodman, two versions of strange and damaging excess, somehow deserved each other" (Crouch 4–5).

Beginning in 2013, Rodman made a total of five visits to North Korea. He traveled to Pyongyang three times in 2013, played an exhibition game with several Harlem Globetrotters in early 2014, and made his last trip in 2017. Whatever one thinks about Rodman, he achieved something neither President Barack Obama nor former Governor Bill Richardson, an eight-time visitor to North Korea, had achieved: face time with the newest Kim dictator (Sang-Hun and Sanger 1). Richardson's opinion was that any information Rodman could glean would be welcome, even helpful—for example, mannerisms, English language skills, whatever he could observe. However, when the Sunday political shows hosted Rodman, he revealed himself woefully uninformed about, even uninterested in, North Korea's human-rights transgressions. Further, he did not seem to have any interest in a deeper understanding of the country in any respect, instead praising Jong-un as his new friend. When newswoman Andrea Mitchell asked then Secretary of State John Kerry what he thought about Rodman going to North Korea, he replied, "Dennis Rodman was a great basketball player.... And as a diplomat, he is a great basketball player" (Johnson 1). In regard to Rodman's rant on CNN in defense of his January 2014 trip, President Obama's Press Secretary Jay Carney responded, "I'm not going to dignify that outburst with a response" (qtd. in Nakamura 1).

Unsurprisingly, Rodman's behavior and ignorant comments landed him in trouble. The exhibition game, during which he serenaded Jong-un with "Happy Birthday," was followed by a drunken party that continued nonstop long after the birthday celebration. When CNN interviewed Rodman in North Korea, he went on a drunken, profane diatribe, for which he later apologized (Boren 1). Finally, in a CNN interview with Chris Cuomo during the Singapore Summit with North Korea, Rodman distinguished himself in yet one last drunken, crying rant, where he wore his Make America Great Again hat and praised President Trump and Jong-un to the skies ("Dennis Rodman"). One hopes that Rodman is not holding his breath to be named a Nobel Peace Prize finalist, as he expected after his first trip.

If it had been possible, Obama's administration would have kept Rodman from going to North Korea, but they did not have the power. The NBA remained silently at a distance; the most vocal critics were "politicians and human rights advocates for giving friendly publicity to one of the world's most repressive states" (Ramzy 4). And as it happened, Governor Richardson perhaps had a point because Rodman did learn two details previously unknown in the United States: Jong-un's birth date and the name of his child, Sol Ju (Soong 1). *The Guardian* provides a succinct summary of the events detailed here: "It says a lot about the world that the only man on good terms with both Donald Trump and Kim Jong-un is a former basketball player" (Felt 1). And of all the basketball players in the world, past and present, it was Rodman.

The Total Rodman

To paraphrase a partial quote attributed to Winston Churchill in 1939, Rodman is a riddle, wrapped in a mystery, inside an enigma. His life could be described as a Horatio Alger rags to riches story, but he does not embrace his past, his roots, or his family. He is inherently generous and prone to random acts of kindness, such as when he paid the funeral expenses for James Byrd, the black man dragged to his death by three white supremacists in Texas in 1998. He was a professional basketball player of unsurpassed defensive talent, aggressive play notwithstanding. He is flamboyant in appearance and behavior and cares not a whit about public approval. He has contemplated suicide more than once, and he has never restrained himself from overindulgence. He is a sought-after, celebrated celebrity—a goal he always desired to reach. His personal life is often in turmoil, but he loves his children without measure. In delving into his life and career, however, one cannot but view him as a conflicted, often troubled person who has not dealt successfully with the demons he needs to tame. One also wonders what result or outcome his intelligence and energies might have achieved after basketball if he had pursued goals other than celebrity. That will remain the riddle, the mystery, the enigma that is Dennis Rodman.

NOTE

1. Quote taken from Ira Berkow's article, "Sports of the Times: As Expected, Rodman Does What's Unexpected."

WORKS CITED

Andrews, David L., and Steven J. Jackson, editors. *Sport Stars: The Cultural Politics of Sporting Celebrity*. Routledge, 2001.

Araton, Harvey. "PRO BASKETBALL; N.B.A. Dilemma: Boys Will Be Bad." *New York Times*, 11 Apr. 1993, www.nytimes.com/1993/04/11/sports/pro-basketball-nba-dilemma-boys-will-be-bad.html.

Boren, Cindy. "Dennis Rodman says, 'I had been drinking' in apology for comments." *The Washington Post*, 9 Jan. 2014, www.washingtonpost.com/news/early-lead/wp/2014/01/09/dennis-rodman-i-had-been-drinking-in-apology-for-comments/?utm_term=.ce7137b75148.

Boyd, Todd. *Young, Black, Rich, and Famous: The Rise of the NBA, the Hip Hop Invasion, and the Transformation of American Culture*. University of Nebraska Press, 2003.

Berkow, Ira. "Sports of the Times; As Expected, Rodman Does What's Unexpected." *The New York Times*, 30 May 1998, www.nytimes.com/1998/05/30/sports/sports-of-the-times-as-expected-rodman-does-what-s-unexpected.html.

Burton, Rick, Francis John Farrelly, and Pasquale G. Quester. "Exploring the Curious Demand for Athletes with Controversial Images: A Review of Anti-Hero Product Endorsement Advertising." *International Journal of Sports Marketing and Sponsorship*, vol. 2, no. 4, 2001, pp. 44–59, doi.org/10.1108/IJSMS-02-04-2001-B005.

Chirco, Vito. "Daly Was the Right Man to Lead the Bad Boys to Greatness." *Detroit Athletic Co.*, 24 Aug. 2017, Detroitathletic.com/blog/2017/08/24/daly-right-man-lead-bad-boys-Greatness/.

Crouch, Ian. "Dennis Rodman and Diplomatic Dystopia." *The New Yorker*, 4 Mar. 2013, www.newyorker.com/sports/sporting-scene/dennis-rodman-and-diplomatic-dystopia.

Cuneen, Jacquelyn, and Nancy Spencer. "Gender Representation Related to Sport Celebrity Portrayals in the Milk Mustache Advertising Campaign." *Sport Marketing Quarterly*, vol. 12, no. 3, 2003, pp. 140–150.

Deford, Frank. *The Best of Frank Deford: I'm Just Getting Started*. Triumph Books, 2000.

"Dennis Rodman gets emotional after Trump-Kim summit." YouTube, uploaded by CNN, 11 June 2018, www.youtube.com/watch?v=dAJLJRRJY3E.

Dunbar, Michelle D. "Dennis Rodman—Do You Feel Feminine Yet? Black Masculinity, Gender Transgression, and Reproductive Rebellion on MTV." *Masculinities, Gender Relations, and Sport*. Edited by Jim McKay, Michael A. Messner, and Don Sabo, SAGE, 2000, pp. 263–285.

Felt, Hunter. "How NBA Star Dennis Rodman Came to Stand Between the World and Nuclear War." *The Guardian*, 14 Sept. 2017. www.theguardian.com/sport/2017/sep/14/dennis-rodman-north-korea-kim-jong-un-basketball.

Futrelle, David. "Media Circus: Who's bad?" *Salon*, 22 Jan. 1997, www.salon.com/1997/01/21/media_161/.

Gilbert, Roger. "Air, Worm, Pip, Zen: The Chicago Bulls as Sacred Text." *Salmagundi*, no. 118-9, Spr. 1998, pp. 246–272.

Hesketh, Peggy. "Dennis Rodman, Incorporated." *Orange County Business Journal*, vol. 19, no. 24, 15 July 1996, p. 1.

Hoberman, John. *Darwin's Athletes: How Sport Has Damaged Black America and Preserved the Myth of Race*. Houghton Mifflin, 1996.

Johnson, Luke. "John Kerry Weighs in on Dennis Rodman's Trip to North Korea." *Huffington Post*, 5 Mar. 2013, www.huffpost.com/entry/john-kerry-weighs-in-on-dennis-rodmans-trip-to-north-korea_n_5b573d97e4b0cf38668fa214.

Lafrance, Melisse, and Genevieve Rail. "'As Bad as He Says He Is?' Interrogating Dennis Rodman's Subversive Potential." *Reading Sport: Critical Essays in Power and Representation*, editors Susan Birrell and Mary G. McDonald, Northeaster UP, 2000, pp. 74–107.

Ledbetter, D. Orlando. "Jackson Won't Invade Rodman's Special Space." *Milwaukee Journal Sentinel*, 8 Oct. 1995, p. 10.

Lewis, Thabiti L. "The Modern Athlete, Hip-Hop, and Popular Perceptions of Black Masculinity." *Ameriquest*, vol. 6, no. 1, 2008, ameriquest.org/index.php/Ameriquest.artile/view/146.

Lincicome, Bernie. "PUNISHMENT AND ADVICE FOR RODMAN, AMONG OTHER THINGS." *Chicago Tribune*, 5 May 1997, www.chicagotribune.com/news/ct-xpm-1997-05-05-9705050016-story.html.

Lupica, Mike. "Damn Bulls." *Esquire*, vol. 127, no. 5, May 1997, pp. 44–46, classic.esquire.com/article/1997/5/1/damn-bulls.

———. "Dennis Anyone?" *Esquire*, vol. 128, no. 1, July 1997, pp. 32–34, classic.esquire.com/article/1997/7/1/dennis-anyone.

Marantz, Steve. "The Basketball Buddha." *The Sporting News; St. Louis*, vol. 220, iss. 23, 3 June 1996, p. 46.

Miklasz, Bernie. "MVP Rodman? That Would Cap Wild Ride." *St. Louis Post-Dispatch*, 12 June 1998, p. D8, www.newspapers.com/newspage/141882025/.

Nakamura, David. "White House: No Response to Dennis Rodman 'Outburst' on North Korea." *The Washington Post*, 7 Jan. 2014, www.washingtonpost.com/white-house-no-response-to-dennis-rodman-outburst-on-North-Korea.html.

Overman, Steven J. *Living Out of Bounds: The Male Athlete in Everyday Life*. University of Nebraska Press, 2010.

Powell, Shaun. "Bulls Don't Take Worm Seriously." *Newsday [Long Island]*, 10 June 1998, p. A79.

Ramzy, Austin. "Dennis Rodman, Frequent Visitor to North Korea, Is Back." *The New York Times*, 13 June 2017, www.nytimes.com/2017/06/13/world/asia/dennis-rodman-north-korea.html.

Rhoden, William C. *Forty Million Dollar Slaves: The Rise, Fall, and Redemption of the Black Athlete*. Three Rivers P, 2006.

Rodman, Dennis, with Michael Silver. *Walk on the Wild Side*. Delacorte, 1999.

Rodman, Dennis, with Tim Keown. *Bad As I Wanna Be*. Delacorte, 1996.

Rush, George, Joanna Mallow, and Baird Jones. "Rodman and Christiansen in a Hot Spot." *New York Daily News*, 19 Aug. 1996, www.nydailynews.com/archives/gossip/rodman-christensen-hot-spot-article-1.745326.

Sang-Hun, Choe, and David E. Sanger. "Way to Reach Kim Jong-un? Follow the Ball." *The New York Times*, 1 Mar 2013, www.nytimes.com/2013/03/02/world/asia/way-to-reach-kim-jong-un-follow-the-ball.html.

Schmitz, Brian. "Bulls Tolerate Freak Show That Is Dennis Rodman." *Orlando Sentinel*, 11 June 1998, www.orlandosentinel.com/news/os-xpm-1998-06-11-9806110358-story.html.

Soong, Kelyn. "Former NBA-star Dennis Rodman plans to train North Korea Olympic basketball team." *The Washington Post*, 9 Sept. 2013, www.washingtonpost.com/sports/former-nba-star-dennis-rodman-plans-to-train-north-korean-olympic-basketball-team/2013/09/09/14d840d4-1964-11e3-a628-7e6dde8f889d_story.html?noredirect=on&utm_term=.da85abafa4da.

Teitelbaum, Stanley H. *Sport Heroes, Fallen Idols*. University of Nebraska Press, 2005.

Tierney, Mike. "For Sale: Rebel Without a Pause: $9M and Growing, Controversy Pays If You're Rodman." *The Atlanta Constitution*, 13 Feb. 1997, www.ajc.com/for-sale-rebel-without-a-pause.

Tucker, Linda. "Blackballed: Basketball and Representations of the Black Male Athlete." SAGE, vol. 47, no. 3, 2003, journals.sagepub.com/doi/abs/10.1177/0002764203256189.

Whannel, Gary. *Media Sport Stars: Masculinities and Moralities*. Routledge, 2002.

Reframing Jameis Winston
Fan Response When Players Go "Bad"

JOHN C. LAMOTHE

This essay is not just about Jameis Winston; it is also about sports fans. Specifically, it is about how fans react when their sports heroes do something stupid, or immature, or potentially illegal ... or all three, as in Winston's case. Although the essay will highlight Winston, he is merely a case study to analyze fan response.

Sports fanatics are an interesting breed. I should know because I am one. When I think of myself, descriptors like *husband*, *father*, *teacher* certainly come to mind, but right behind those is *fan*, and on Saturdays in the fall, *fan* probably jumps to the top of the list. We fans are passionate creatures, devoting enormous amounts of time, energy, and money to follow our teams. True sports fanatics are loyal, cheering on our teams no matter how badly we are playing or how long it has been since we made a championship run. And yes, I use "we" intentionally because sports fans like me wholeheartedly believe that we are an integral part of the team. When asked how the game is going, it is not uncommon to hear me say, "We're winning/losing," "We can't tackle," or "We made a nice play," and the inclusive pronoun never seems forced or illogical. I justify such language because, although I may never slap on a helmet and step onto the turf, the elation and despair I feel when we win or lose is as palpable for me as it is for anyone in the locker room ... at least that's what I tell myself.

In addition to passionate and loyal, many other adjectives epitomize sports fanatics: loud, emotional, superstitious, intense, fiery, fervent. And those occur before the game even begins. However, beyond all else, beyond all the terms that sports fans would lovingly and knowingly embrace, fanatics are biased—incredibly, unrepentantly, and perhaps ignorantly biased. The referees, when they make a call against our team, are out to get us (or are blind or incompetent). The other team is a bunch of jerks. The other team's fans are obnoxious (because they are loud, fervent, and clearly biased). And our players? Our players are Mother Teresas with pads. Or if not quite that virtuous, we can justify or excuse their flagrant misdeeds or off-the-field antics.

A great deal of research has focused on sports fans in recent years. And why not? We are fascinating. Whether it is describing the impact of mirror neurons on team association, investigating the psychological or sociological pros and cons of fan passion, or analyzing the ritualistic nature of pre-game tailgating, researchers have put sports fans under a microscope. One useful project centered on sports fans' biased perceptions while they watched a game. However, very little scholarship has focused on how fans perceive their sports heroes when those athletes cross a line, when they are labeled bad boys.

Which brings us to Winston, the starting quarterback for the Florida State University (FSU) football team between 2013 and 2014. Winston was a hugely popular and successful figure at FSU during his tenure, winning the Heisman trophy during his freshman year and leading the Seminoles to the College Football National Championship win in 2014. Even today, in Tallahassee, his legend persists. Five years after Winston stepped off the FSU football field for the last time, his name still served as a benchmark for the current quarterback, as evidenced by the headline in an article for the *Tallahassee Democrat*, the local newspaper, claiming, "Florida State quarterback James Blackman a 'Jameis Winston' type of leader" (McGahee).

Unfortunately, at the same time he was enjoying so much success on the field and forging his legend, Winston was embroiled in numerous controversies off the field, all making national headlines because of his prominence in college football. The incidents ranged from moments of "youthful ignorance" (Winston qtd. in Axon), such as stealing from a local grocery store, to much more serious accusations of sexual assault. Even the most conservative commentator would agree that Winston's actions not only impacted his reputation, but also became a smear against Florida State specifically and college football in general. At least, that was the case on the national level. On the local level, Winston maintained strong fan support throughout all the controversies. The key question is why Florida State fans viewed the situation differently from the larger culture, and why sports fans in general often continue to support their favorite athletes even after they cross a line.

Winston the Winner

Even rival fans who support the University of Florida Gators or the Clemson University Tigers have to admit grudgingly that Winston was a college athlete with rare talent. Coming out of high school, Winston was rated the number one football player in Alabama and the number one quarterback prospect nationally by most recruit trackers. Rivals.com, arguably the most prominent recruit-evaluation service, ranked Winston tenth overall nationally for the entire 2012 recruiting class. His natural athletic talent allowed him to excel in multiple sports, and in 2012, while still in high school, he was selected in the 15th round of the Major League Baseball draft by the Texas Rangers. He played both sports throughout his two years at FSU. As the starting quarterback for the FSU football team, Winston had a stellar 26–1 record, finishing both regular seasons with perfect 13–0 records and only suffering one loss during the semifinal game of the 2015 College Football Playoff. In addition to winning the National Championship and the Heisman trophy as a redshirt freshman, he collected numerous Atlantic Coast Conference (ACC) Championships, as well as player-of-the-year and athlete-of-the-year awards, during his college career. In 2015, Winston was selected first overall by the Tampa Bay Buccaneers in the National Football League draft, earning himself a four-year $23 million contract and a $16 million signing bonus.

In addition to his superior athletic talent, Winston has often been credited for his vocal leadership in the huddle and locker room. He has a boisterous, type–A personality with an often jocular, "goofy" demeanor that other players were drawn to. Even when Winston was a freshman, his coaches praised him as "a natural leader" (Winegardner). During games, he was a dominant presence, whether he was barking orders in the huddle, pumping up his teammates on the sidelines, or exerting his will on the other team's defense. Much to the dismay of his competitors, the Winston-led Seminoles could never be counted out. Even when it looked like the other team had a win in hand, Winston rallied his teammates and marched down the field for a score. The 2014 National Championship is a perfect example. With just 1:19 remaining in the game, Auburn University scored and took a 31–27 lead over FSU. The Seminoles needed 80 yards for a touchdown. On the ensuing drive, Winston completed five of six passes, and with 13 seconds left, threw a 2-yard touchdown pass to win the game, 34–31.

Winston the Bad Boy

During his years at FSU, Winston was involved in scandals, ranging from fairly minor to quite serious. He was accused of "stealing" soda from Burger King (i.e., using a water cup to get soda from the fountain without ordering any food) ("Jameis Winston: 'HE'S STEALING'"), and he was involved with a BB-gun "battle" at his apartment complex that resulted in property damage and Winston nearly being evicted (Ellis). Both of these incidents could be characterized as fairly normal teenage impulsiveness, and the only reason they made headlines was Winston's celebrity status.

More serious were two incidents that occurred in 2014. In April, Winston was charged with stealing crab legs from a Publix grocery store (Elliot, "Jameis Winston cited"), and in September, the University punished him when several students tweeted that Winston stood on a table in the middle of the student union and shouted, "Fuck her right in the pussy" (Trahan). The seafood theft grabbed national headlines and generated countless internet memes. Photoshopped images included Winston holding crab legs instead of his Heisman trophy. A grocery store in Alabama even created a "Jameis Winston King Crab Legs" label for their product and posted the image on Facebook (Khan). The FHRITP incident, which stemmed from a viral video that some people—including Winston—were mimicking at the time, earned Winston a full-game suspension against rival Clemson, arguably the most important game of FSU's regular season that year. Again, all of these could be viewed as indiscretions committed by a very immature teenager, but, as the incidents and headlines mounted, they pointed to a possible flaw in his character. As the face of the FSU football program and as a nationally known sports figure, he had been coached in media relations and knew the level of scrutiny he would receive. The University also provided him every resource for success, including a chaperone to monitor his behavior (Carson). Despite all of that, he consistently demonstrated poor decision making, irresponsibility, and a complete disregard for the potential consequences of his actions.

Overshadowing all of these less damaging incidents were allegations of sexual assault. In late 2012, Erica Kinsman, a student at FSU, filed a report with the Tallahassee Police Department (TPD) accusing Winston of raping her while she was intoxicated and while some of his friends and fellow teammates watched. Winston initially denied any involvement with Kinsman; however, after Winston's DNA was found on Kinsman's clothing, he claimed that the sex was consensual. The case played out in the courts over the next three years. Eventually, the State Attorney, citing a lack of evidence, declined to bring criminal charges against Winston. Court documents from the Kinsman case indicate that Winston was also accused of sexually assaulting another student at FSU at about the same time (Dick and Ziering), and many college-football fans and commentators have speculated that the TPD and FSU colluded to cover up the incidents. Whether siding with Kinsman (whose credibility was called into question throughout the legal battle) or with Winston, most of those familiar with the case—even FSU fans—agree that the TPD botched the initial investigation and that FSU struggled mightily to follow Title IX procedures for reporting, investigating, and processing the rape claim. Eventually, Winston and FSU settled with Kinsman in separate civil lawsuits for significant sums of money.

After leaving FSU, Winston became the starting quarterback for the Tampa Bay Buccaneers; however, his legal problems did not end when he left Tallahassee. In 2016, a female Uber driver, known as "Kate P," accused Winston of groping her while he was in her car, and the case concluded in 2018 when Winston settled out of court with Kate P; he was also suspended for the first three games of the 2018 season. After a lengthy investigation, the NFL asserted that "Winston engaged in detrimental conduct that night by 'touching the driver in an inappropriate and sexual manner without her consent and that disciplinary action was necessary and appropriate'" (qtd. in Laine, "Jameis Winston, Uber"). In a written statement released to the media, Winston said, "First and foremost, I would like to say I'm sorry to the Uber driver for the position I put you in. It is **uncharacteristic** of me and I genuinely apologize" (emphasis added) (qtd. in Laine, "Buccaneers' Winston").

Fan Response to Winston

Which brings us back to sports fans. According to Pulitzer Prize–winning reporter George Dohrmann in *Superfans*, "Among sports fans, *bias* is the harshest of the four-letter words, yet they are quick to use it. Talk to enough fans and you'll quickly discover that everyone is biased ... except the fan you are speaking with at that moment" (151). Spend enough time in the sports world, and Dohrmann's claim will start to ring true. As far back as the 1950s, researchers began studying sporting bias. In a foundational article titled "They Saw a Game: A Case Study," Albert Hastorf and Hadley Cantril surveyed college football fans after they watched a Dartmouth/Princeton game. The researchers found that one team's fans were "'seeing' an entirely different version of the game" from the other team's fans (129). For example, when asked how many infractions they witnessed during the game, one fan base would report seeing twice as many fouls perpetrated by the other team as their own; the other fan base saw the exact opposite. Hastorf and Cantril concluded that "It seems clear that the 'game' actually was many different games and that each version ... was just as 'real' to a particular person as other versions were to other people" (132). In other words, spectators may all watch the same game, but depending on how they identify as fans, they will perceive actions and remember events very differently from others.

Psychologist Daniel Wann, arguably the most prominent figure in fan research, has extended the work of Hastorf and Cantril over the past 40 years. In the 1970s, Wann developed the Sport Spectator Identification Scale (SSIS), an instrument that establishes how intensely a fan's identity revolves around a particular sports team. The tool poses such questions as "How important (on a scale from 1–8) is it to *YOU* that the team listed above wins?," "How much do you dislike the biggest rivals of the team listed above?," and "How often do you display the team's name or insignia at your place of work, where you live, or on your clothing?" Individuals who constantly wear team apparel and raise their children to despise the rival team will find themselves ranked in the top category, "Extreme Identification."

Wann and other researchers have used SSIS to explore a variety of issues relating to sports fanatics. When it comes to a discussion of Winston and sports bad boys, one important finding is that sports fanatics more often attribute a loss to external factors (i.e., poor officiating, bad luck, or dirty play by the other team) and attribute a win to internal factors (i.e., skill or effort) (Wann and Dolan 784). Wann and Dolan have demonstrated that the level of fan identification matters as well. For example, highly identified fans are more likely to attribute a loss to external factors than fans who are lowly identified (789). Another important finding is that the depth of emotion we feel as sports fans also correlates to our level of identification with the team, with highly identified fans responding more passionately to games. Wann and others have demonstrated that "those high in team identification are more likely to attempt to influence the outcome of a sporting event, experience greater levels of anxiety and arousal watching their team compete, feel that sport spectating is a more enjoyable activity, and possess a greater level of knowledge about their team and about sport in general" (Wann et al. 4).

Underlying both of these points is the connection between fandom and personal identity. SSIS illustrates that identifying ourselves as fans can be paramount to how we view ourselves. As Dohrmann notes,

> Almost all of the behavior, good and bad, we associate with passionate fans takes on new meaning when framed as acts in support of or defense of one's identity. When you defend your team against insults from fans of a rival team, you are actually defending yourself. When you are justifying your team signing a player who has a long rap sheet, you are making yourself feel better about supporting that team. When you downplay your team's chances before a big game, you are bracing your identity, your self-esteem, for a potential blow [44].

This research helps to explain why sports fans, especially fans of team sports, might be more willing to defend athletes who have been labeled bad boys because, as Wann argues, "the team becomes an extension of the individual. The team's success becomes the fan's success and the team's failures become the fan's failures" (Wann et al. 4). In the case of Winston, we see this play out in fan comments and opinions. Whereas much of the rest of college football viewed Winston as immature and irresponsible at best and a criminal at worst, FSU fans often defended the quarterback vigorously.

Take, for example, an article titled "Report blasts Jameis Winston rape investigation" published in the *Washington Post*. Nearly every comment added to the discussion board bashed Winston, FSU, and the investigation. Reader tojo45 summed up the general consensus, "It's just crazy how some universities push back against assault victims, spin their wheels on investigations, and on and on. He won't just be 'Famous Jameis' now. It will become 'Famous Rapin' Jameis'" (Boren). Similarly, in the nearly 500 comments posted on the *New York Times* article titled "A Star Player Accused, and a Flawed Rape Investigation," a significant majority condemned Winston and FSU, with contributors often expressing the underlying assumption of Winston's guilt. Many of the comments were rather lengthy and scathing, but user Mike H from San Diego, California, succinctly encapsulated the general feeling when writing, "Lovely, Tallahassee and Seminoles. Every time you see Jameis' Heisman and that BCS championship crystal ball in your trophy room, you can take great pride on the foundation of rape they were built on" (Bogdanich).

Mixed into the comments stemming from the same *New York Times* article are supportive posts of him and the university, often from readers who identify themselves as FSU fans and past/present students. For example, Chelsey from Tallahassee declares, "[I]t is difficult for this student body to listen to an accuser who has lied about so many pieces of this story, when Jameis' side has always remained the same. I hope the rest of the country will realize that FSU does not support rapists, because that is not what Jameis Winston is" (Bogdanich). Noteworthy here is the focus on Kinsman's lack of credibility, a dominant characteristic of Winston supporters' arguments. Among highly identified FSU fans, Kinsman is almost universally viewed as dishonest, a gold digger, a slut, and an opportunist. A survey of Tallahassee voters, commissioned by Kinsman's legal team, found that 51 percent of respondents did not feel Kinsman was telling the truth. Two-thirds of those polled did not believe Jameis Winston raped her, and even more argued that her suit against Florida State was motivated by desire for financial gain ("Poll: Tallahassee-area"). In their posts, highly identified fans often refer to Kinsman as a "cleat chaser," a woman who methodically attempts to have sex with college athletes. They often paint Winston as the victim of a predator and Kinsman as a woman attempting to cash in on Winston's celebrity and future earnings as a top-tier NFL quarterback. Their logic is problematic, at best. The alleged rape happened in 2012, and the initial investigation concluded in early 2013. Although Winston was a high-level recruit and athlete, he was far from the number-one NFL draft pick that he would become by 2015. Yet, defenders routinely cited money as her main motivation for leveling accusations. Additionally, the fact that Kinsman's recollection of events varies throughout the investigation is also cited as proof that there was no rape, but recent research shows that shifting recollections are common among assault victims (Stelloh).

After the *New York Times* published an article about the faulty TPD investigation, FSU fans also targeted the *NYT*. Seminole fan sites like *Toma-*

hawk Nation included lengthy discussion threads in response to the article, with the vast majority of comments noting that the original story was misleading. Many users even went so far as to accuse the *NYT* of deliberately leaving out important details in order to paint a narrative that would be damaging to FSU and Winston. For example, user madridbend sums up the general sentiment with "This is yellow journalism, intended to grab attention by slanting the story" (Elliot, "NYT").

As these examples illustrate, Winston fans often used external factors (i.e., Kinsman is a cleat chaser attempting to cash in; the *NYT* is attacking Winston because a sensational article sells more papers) to defend their star athlete and their team. This rhetorical approach is similar to fans blaming the officials or the other team after their own team suffers a loss. The strategy also extended to other infractions. Take, for example, user keno213's comments on an article concerning Winston's counterclaim to Kinsman's civil suit. When another contributor to the discussion thread jokingly mentions the crab-leg theft incident, keno213 proclaims,

> He didn't steal crab legs. They were given to him by an employee. Actually the employee should have been fired. Probably was. But, all folks talk about is Winston being a "clepto." LOL.... Jameis was just picking up a "perk" from some diehard FSU fan. I think it's a big difference. I love him taking photograph eating crab legs on draft day. Talking about funny [Payne].

Here, keno213 places the blame on the employee, freeing Winston from any wrongdoing despite the fact that any 20-year-old, regardless of his status as an elite athlete, should know that an employee cannot just give free perks and that taking the crab legs would be stealing. Keno213 even appreciates Winston mocking the entire incident.

Dohrmann argues that fans very often demonstrate this kind of cognitive bias, a tendency to favor information that confirms previously held beliefs (153). In *The Science of Underdogs, The Value of Rivalry, and What We Can Learn from the T-Shirt Cannon*, co-authors L. Jon Wertheim and Sam Sommers discuss how sports fanatics are influenced by the halo effect, whereby "The formation of positive overall impressions of people projects a perceptual halo around them, casting other characteristics in a similarly positive light" (20). FSU fans in general and keno213 in particular appear to bestow a halo on this talented quarterback, and the halo effect seems to help them to look more favorably on his other characteristics. In other words, since he is a talented athlete, fans are more likely to believe he also is intelligent, handsome, and honest. At the same time, cognitive bias causes them to downplay any information that tends to contradict their previously held opinion about that player (i.e., Winston was just getting a free "perk"; no harm done). Because of this, according to Dohrmann,

> If the best player on your favorite team gets arrested for a DUI, you might say it was a one-time mistake and that severe punishment is unwarranted. But if the best player on a rival team gets arrested for the same offense, he is a horrible person and his team is full of renegades and no punishment is severe enough [153].

If we start to pull these pieces of fan research together, we begin to see a revealing process when athletes cross a line and become bad boys. First, fans view the details differently from non-fans, unconsciously focusing on information that supports previous beliefs (i.e., fans focus on how Kinsman's story changed, but ignore the fact that Winston's story also changed after DNA evidence proved the two had had sex). Next, fans tend to externalize bad behavior (i.e., the accuser is after money; the media is out to get him), and downplay negative characteristics that run counter to the other positive characteristics they feel that player possesses (i.e., it is just a free perk for a star athlete). All of this occurs because highly identified fans' personal identities are so wrapped up with the team that defending the team or its players is tantamount to defending themselves. When athletes cross a line, fans have a vested interest in defending or dismissing those actions. In an effort to help ourselves feel better, we create what psychologists would call false narratives—the autobiographical stories we tell ourselves about the world we inhabit and that are "replete with revision, fabrication, and an unrealistically egocentric perspective. We twist the past (and the present) into narratives that make us look better to others and feel better about ourselves" (Wertheim and Sommers 35–36).

These false narratives can lead some highly identified fans down paths they probably would not consider in other contexts. For example, while Winston was dealing with his legal issues, a persistent rumor circulating around Seminole fan circles was that ESPN deliberately attempted to undermine FSU and Winston because of ESPN's investment in the Southeastern Conference (SEC). The rather convoluted line of reasoning was that ESPN, heavily invested in creating the SEC Television Network, wanted to see more SEC teams in the College Football Playoff. FSU, which plays in the ACC, was one of the premier non–SEC programs at the time, so hurting the school and Winston was a deliberate attempt to assure they ranked outside those who would make the playoff. One of the main sources for this conspiracy theory was an FSU graduate's opinion piece published in *Rolling Stone* magazine that argues ESPN treated Winston unfairly compared to other college football players who got themselves into trouble. Jordan Buchette mentions how, after Winston had been suspended for a half game because of the FHRITP incident, an ESPN writer asked in his blog, "How many strikes does Winston get before he goes from being a foolish, immature college student to a complete knucklehead who can't be trusted?" Shortly thereafter, the suspension was increased to a full game. True believers see a direct correlation between the writer's words—words that many college-football fans were thinking at the time—and the increased suspension. This conspiracy theory, like so many others, is flawed on so many levels that it is akin to believing in the "Curse of the Bambino" or that Big Foot is a Washington State fan (just ask head coach Mike Leach). Despite its ridiculousness, even FSU's head coach at the time, Jimbo Fisher, when asked why his team was in the news so often for the wrong reasons, said, "ESPN has money in the SEC" ("Jimbo Fisher").

Conclusions and Confessions

Sports and heroes go hand in hand. It is common, even for non-sports fans, to take exceptional athletes, put them on a pedestal, and revel in their greatness. Researcher R.K. Barney offers criteria for a true sports hero (Wann et al. 70). In addition to having exceptional skill, Barney argues that a true hero must display "moral excellence in all aspects of his or her life, acting with honesty, humility, generosity, sportsmanship, and self-control" (71). He also believes a true hero gives unselfishly to aid those less fortunate and demonstrates practical wisdom.

Perhaps that is what we *should* label a hero; reality can be very different.

Despite all of Winston's reprehensible actions, he still has a strong following among FSU fans, and any unbiased observer would have to say that Winston only demonstrates the first of those hero characteristics—exceptional skill. Winston brought the team—and by extension the fans—wins, and wins have the power to overcome almost any obstacle. One area of fan research that has not been explored enough is at what point players become important enough to be part of team/fan identity. In other words, if a fourth-string quarterback were accused of the same infractions as Winston, would FSU fans defend him as vehemently as they do Winston, or would he be excised like an unwanted skin growth? Along the same lines, if the starting quarterback were not securing wins, would the fanatics be more likely to view him in the same way as non-fans? Or would they view him more harshly? Lastly, at what point does a bad boy cross such a significant boundary that even the most highly identified fans stop defending the player? From my own experience as a fan and sports researcher, my hypothesis would be that players seen as less impactful on achieving wins are much more likely to be cast aside by fans when they cross social boundaries. And if players are successful on the field, it takes a lot of serious transgressions before they become unforgiveable.

To be fair, not all FSU fans were Winston fans in the midst of his controversies. I have talked with numerous FSU fans who were glad to see

Winston go, despite all the success he brought. Not long after the crab-leg theft, the *Tallahassee Democrat* ran an article that asked residents to respond, asking them what they would say to Winston if given the chance. Two days later they ran a follow-up article and published numerous responses. As the author says, "Most people had a more parental reaction, expressing concern about what life lessons are being sent and what incidents like this latest one say about the rest of Jameis' life" (Gabordi). For example, one fan, Judy Watson, writes

> With your latest episode, Jameis, I am inclined to believe ANYThing untoward about you.... You are old enough to know right from wrong and NOT need a babysitter watching your every move to make sure you don't do stupid things.... As far as I am concerned, you are an embarrassment to yourself, FSU and Tallahassee.

Such people might have been low-identified fans or more highly-identified with the university than the football team. Or perhaps they are simply parents themselves, and that part of their identity is stronger than being a fan.

At this point, I must reveal an important aspect of my identity. I have already acknowledged that I am a sports fan, and much of this chapter has discussed fan bias, so it is only fair that I acknowledge my own bias—and it is a doozy. I graduated from the University of Florida, and when it comes to Saturdays in the Fall, I am 100 percent a Florida Gator. By extension that means I *must* despise the Florida State Seminoles. What can I say? It is in my blood (which bleeds orange and blue). When it comes to bad boys in college football, Winston certainly is not the only player who has committed grievous transgressions. Any of them could have served as the centerpiece of a case study. Placing a magnifying lens on my own team would generate any number of examples. Aaron Hernandez immediately comes to mind. He played for the Gators and then the New England Patriots (who I am also a fan of) before being convicted of murder. Numerous other Gator athletes could be examined to highlight fan response; however, I chose Winston. This easily could be interpreted as a form of *blasting*, a term for fans who enhance "their psychological state by drawing attention to something negative about a rival team or its fans" (Dohrmann 141). Maybe it is. I consider myself a self-aware fan, but that does not mean I am above protecting my own self-identity through cognitive bias, externalization, or blasting. It is not really something that fanatics have much control over. And in the end, it simply is much more enjoyable to air FSU's dirty laundry than my own.

Works Cited

Axon, Rachel. "Dad: Family, Florida State failed Jameis Winston." *Tallahassee Democrat*, 12 May 2014, www.tallahassee.com/story/sports/college/fsu/football/2014/05/11/jameis-winston-heisman-winner-florida-state/8970279/.

Bogdanich, Walt. "A Star Player Accused, and a Flawed Rape Investigation." *The New York*

Times, 16 Apr. 2014, www.NYTimes.com/interactive/2014/04/16/sports/errors-in-inquiry-on-rape-allegations-against-fsu-jameis-winston.html.

Boren, Cindy. "Report Blasts Jameis Winston Rape Investigation." *The Washington Post*, 16 Apr. 2014, www.washingtonpost.com/news/early-lead/wp/2014/04/16/report-blasts-jameis-winston-rape-investigation/?utm_term=.445e4c243eb7.

Burchette, Jordan. "The Worldwide Cheerleader: ESPN and the College Football Playoff." *Rolling Stone*, 28 Oct. 2014, www.rollingstone.com/culture/culture-sports/the-worldwide-cheerleader-espn-and-the-college-football-playoff-80005/.

Carson, Dan. "Jameis Winston Now Shopping for Crab Legs with Chaperone?" *Bleacher Report*, 7 Oct. 2014, bleacherreport.com/articles/2223827-jameis-winston-now-shopping-for-crab-legs-with-chaperone?m=1.

Dick, Kirby, and Amy Ziering. "How Florida State Covered Up Two Rape Reports Against Jameis Winston." *Huffington Post*, 11 Mar. 2016, www.huffpost.com/entry/how-florida-state-covered_b_9421824.

Dohrmann, George. *Superfans: Into the Heart of Obsessive Sports Fandom*. Ballantine Books, 2018.

Elliot, Bud. "Jameis Winston cited for shoplifting crab legs at Publix." *Tomahawk Nation*, 30 Apr. 2014, www.tomahawknation.com/2014/4/30/5668004/jameis-winston-arrested-shoplifting-crab-legs-publix.

———. "NYT on Jameis Winston, FSU, TPD Investigation." *Tomahawk Nation*, 16 Apr. 2014, www.tomahawknation.com/2014/4/16/5619946/NYT-jameis-winston-fsu-investigation-florida-state#comments.

Ellis, Zac. "Report: Jameis Winston stopped by police in pellet gun incident in 2012." *Sports Illustrated*, 30 July 2014, www.si.com/college-football/2014/07/30/florida-state-jameis-winston-pellet-gun.

Gabordi, Bob. "Community has a lot to say to Jameis Winston." *Tallahassee Democrat*, 14 May 2014, www.tallahassee.com/story/gabordi/2014/05/14/jameis-winston/9071915/.

Hastorf, Albert H., and Hadley Cantril. "They Saw a Game: A Case Study." *Journal of Abnormal and Social Psychology*, vol. 49, 1954. pp. 129–34.

"Jameis Winston: 'HE'S STEALING SODA' Burger King Employee Told Cops in 2013 Call." *TMZ*, 21 May 2014, www.tmz.com/2014/05/21/jameis-winston-stealing-soda-burger-king-employee-stealing-soda-911/.

"Jimbo Fisher blames ESPN and SEC for FSU's negative attention." *Fanbuzz*, 28 Oct. 2014, fanbuzz.com/college-football/acc/florida-state/jimbo-fisher-blames-espn-and-sec-for-fsus-negative-attention/.

Khan, Sam, Jr. "Alabama Supermarket advertises Winston crab legs." *ESPN*, 1 May 2014, www.espn.com/blog/sec/post/_/id/82701/alabama-supermarket-advertises-jameis-winston-crab-legs.

Laine, Jenna. "Buccaneers' Jameis Winston suspended first three games of 2018." *ESPN*, 29 June 2018, www.espn.com/nfl/story/_/id/23936785/tampa-bay-buccaneers-quarterback-jameis-winston-suspended.

———. "Jameis Winston, Uber driver reach settlement in 2016 groping case." *ESPN*, 27 Nov. 2018, www.espn.com/nfl/story/_/id/25391534/jameis-winston-tampa-bay-buccaneers-reaches-settlement-uber-groping-case.

McGahee, Wayne III. "Florida State quarterback James Blackman a 'Jameis Winston' type of leader." *Tallahassee Democrat*, 18 Feb. 2019, www.tallahassee.com/story/sports/college/fsu/football/2019/02/18/florida-state-qb-james-blackman-jameis-winston-fsu-leader-quarterback-kendal-briles-willie-taggart/2909151002/

Payne, Marissa. "Jameis Winston files counterclaim in response to rape accuser's civil suit." *The Washington Post*, 9 May 2015, www.washingtonpost.com/news/early-lead/wp/2015/05/09/jameis-winston-files-counterclaim-in-response-to-rape-accusers-civil-lawsuit/?utm_term=.6a56f73ab326#comments.

"Poll: Tallahassee-area residents don't believe Winston's accuser." *Tallahassee Democrat*, 10 Mar. 2015, www.tallahassee.com/story/news/local/2015/03/11/poll-tallahasse-area-residents-believe-winstons-accuser/24717015/.

Rivals. "Jameis Winston," n.d., n.rivals.com/content/prospects/2012/jameis-winston-12172.

Stelloh, Tim. "Science around trauma and memory shifting how police respond to victims." *NBC News*, 8 Oct. 2018, www.nbcnews.com/news/us-news/science-around-trauma-memory-shifting-how-police-respond-victims-n917211.

Trahan, Kevin. "Jameis Winston suspended for first half vs. Clemson after obscene comment" *SB Nation*, 17 Sept. 2014, www.sbnation.com/college-football/2014/9/17/6337857/jameis-winston-suspended-for-first-half-vs-clemson-due-to-obscene.

Wann, Daniel L., Merrill J. Melnick, Gordon W. Russell, and Dale G. Pease. *Sports Fans: The Psychology and Social Impact of Spectators*. Routledge, 2001.

Wann, Daniel L., and Thomas Dolan. "Attributions of Highly Identified Sports Spectators." *The Journal of Social Psychology*, vol. 134, no. 6, 2001, pp. 783–92.

Wertheim, L. John, and Sam Sommers. *This Is Your Brain on Sports: The Science of Underdogs, The Value of Rivalry, and What We Can Learn from the T-Shirt Cannon*, eBook, Crown Archetype, 2016.

Winegardner, Mark. "Is this kid serious?" *ESPN*, 12 Nov. 2013, www.espn.com/college-football/story/_/id/9961573/florida-state-quarterback-jameis-winston-stellar-rise-fame-espn-magazine.

When "Bad Boys" Resist, "Good Ol' Boys" Revolt
Colin Kaepernick's NFL Protest

Taylor Joy Mitchell *and* Jessica McKee

A backup quarterback sat during the national anthem before the kickoff of an NFL 2016 pre-season game; two weeks later, on August 26, that same man, now wearing his San Francisco 49ers uniform, again sat silently on the sidelines as the song played (Sandritter). The following week he knelt beside his teammate, Eric Reid, to "stand with the people being oppressed" (qtd. in Biderman). Their kneeling ignited a firestorm of controversy. The following season, neither player was signed, and, by May 2018, the players filed a collusion lawsuit against the NFL (which the NFL settled in February 2019 for an undisclosed amount). Late into the 2018–2019 season, the Carolina Panthers picked up Reid for a safety position; however, multiple franchises continue to pass over the kneeling quarterback. Now declared "one of the most polarizing figures in sports," Colin Kaepernick has become a living monument to the way cultural anxieties about power and privilege play out on the field (Taylor, "Nike Releases"). And even if some fans, players, and commentators acknowledge *why* Kaepernick protested, many can't get beyond *how* he protested: rather than stand proudly, hand on heart, as the national anthem played, he took a knee.

Kaepernick's bended knee "catalyzed a level of public hostility that the NFL had never experienced" (Belson and Leibovich). Hours after Niners Nation's Jennifer Lee Chan tweeted a photo of Kaepernick sitting as the anthem played, the 49ers were facing a public relations nightmare. Forced to issue a statement detailing the patriotic importance of the flag as "pre-game ceremony," the 49ers insisted that "in respecting such American principles as freedom of religion and freedom of expression, we recognize the right of an individual to choose to participate, or not, in our celebration of the national anthem" (Weinsein). The 49ers' statement clearly expresses support for Kaepernick's first amendment rights, and two days later, he gave an 18-minute post-game interview explicitly stating he would continue to protest police brutality (Weinsein). Calling for more officer training, Kaepernick argued, "Cops are getting paid leave for killing people." "That's not right," he continued; "that's not right by anyone's standards" (qtd. in Weinsein). By August 31, NFL front offices were burning with "hatred" for Kaepernick. *Bleacher Report*'s Mike Freeman interviewed seven NFL executives, each of whom registered disdain: "one [executive] even compared the 'collective dislike' to that of Rae Carruth, a former player who remains jailed on charges in the murder of his pregnant girlfriend." For this executive, kneeling for social equality was akin to murder.

Critics echoed this disdain. Former NFL quarterback and current ESPN commentator Trent Dilfer blasted Kaepernick for "disrupting the [NFL] organization" and becoming "the center of attention." His role as a backup quarterback, Dilfer reasons, is to "be quiet and sit in the shadows" (qtd. in Inman). Fox News' Sean Hannity referred to him as "spoiled brat, out-of-touch, super-rich athlete" (qtd.in Preza). Another former player and NBC pundit, Rodney Harrison claimed that "[Kaepernick's] not black" and thus "cannot understand what ... young black men and black people face, or people of color face" (qtd. in Heck). Harrison's comment was not only false (Kaepernick is a person of color), but it also suggested that blackness is a prerequisite for protesting racial oppression. These comments posit that Kaepernick's singular role is to entertain fans and pad the pockets of franchise owners. Perhaps the greatest insult to Kaepernick's activism, however, came from the self-declared conservative Michael Savage. On his nationally syndicated radio show, Savage insisted, "that boy needs to stick to throwing a ball" (qtd. in Marks). Savage's use of the word "boy" is especially telling—not only because of its emasculating implications, but also because of the word's history as part white supremacists' efforts to deny the humanity of enslaved men, a tradition that continues even after the Jim Crow era. Thus, "boy" is a problematic term when referring to a black man. We use bad boy, however, because it emphasizes the racialized responses to Kaepernick's activism. Critics clearly want Kaepernick to be a good boy: to shut up and play ball, literally and figuratively.

Kaepernick became Public Enemy No.1 for multiple reasons: his sport, his method of protest, and his position. In comparison to other professional sports, football is steeped in overt military symbolism; its fan base tends to be conservative, and those in leadership positions are typically white (Gabler). Moreover, *CBS Sports* journalist Tony Barnhart defines football as a Southern tradition—one that would allow Southerners to nurse old Civil War wounds.

In *Southern Fried Football: The History, Passion, and Glory of the Great Southern Game,* Barnhart reasons, "We may not be able to beat the North in the war or economically, but by God we can beat them on the football field" (qtd. in Hall). Barnhart's observations show that football is more than a just a game; it is a cultural battlefield. Much like those earlier Civil War wounds that Barnhart mentions, football is a means for licking old wounds and winning lost battles. We locate Kapernick protest, and the reactions to it, within this context. Thus, we interpret his critics as operating within a "good ol' boy" network, a network that has previously denied the agency, intellect, and patriotism of black athletes—especially at moments of cultural crisis.

"Combatants on the Field": Patriotism vs. the Patriot

Negative responses to Kaepernick illustrate how reverence for football has come to stand in for American patriotism. As Duke Professor of Cultural Anthropology and History David Orin claims, "There's kind of a sacred bundle between football, war, and American identity.... In football, you see patriotism on steroids" (qtd. in Roos). Warfare and football even share a lexicon—formation, zone, ground attack, flanks, bombs, trenches, blitzing. Two opposite teams line up to "battle" each other on a specified yard (front) and try to invade each other's zones, earning points for the victor. According to Paul Vasquez's "How the U.S. Armed Forces Shaped College Football," the structure of the game provided military academies in the 1890s with an effective method to train cadets in the ways of war. Schools like West Point and the Naval Academy democratized and popularized football, bringing the sport beyond the gates of elite colleges. Military academies continue to use football as a recruitment technique because it would keep students away from the front lines (Vasquez); ironically, then, the sport that most resembled warfare could be used as a way to avoid it. During the cultural wars of the Vietnam era, football franchises presented themselves as pro-war, sending players on goodwill tours, introducing flyovers, and "expressing patriotic fervor" (Levin). This practice peaked in the years following 9/11 and continues today. As Shaun Scott argues in *Sports Illustrated*'s "How the NFL Sells (and profits from) the Inextricable Link between Football and War," football has been "the medium to relay America's military response to the trauma of terrorism."

After 9/11, the NFL used funds from the Department of Defense for "paid patriotism" (Theobald). Senators McCain's and Flake's investigative report found that the Pentagon spent over $6 million on national-anthem singers, aircraft flyovers, enlistment services, recognition ceremonies, and emotional surprise reunions with returning service members (Theobald). McCain and Flake observed that "Unsuspecting audience members became the subjects of paid-marketing campaigns rather than simply bearing witness to teams' authentic, voluntary shows of support for the brave men and women who wear our nation's uniform" (3). While it is difficult to discern legitimate from illegitimate recruitment techniques, some commentators note that these practices were at least somewhat successful. Not coincidentally, the Atlanta Falcons were the highest beneficiaries of these funds (Theobald), and Georgia had the highest average of military enlistees between 2010 and 2015 (Clark). Such data point to the reciprocal relationship between the armed forces and the NFL—in essence, a collusion that ended with the NFL returning $723,734 that had been used for "recruitment" purposes (Theobald). Hence, it is hardly a stretch to conclude that these "paid for patriotism" activities, coupled with the collusive relationship between the military and the NFL, provided some of the fuel that set flame to Kaepernick's jerseys.

Due to this long-term connection between sports and the military, some fans easily conflated Kaepernick's protest with contempt for the military—and by extension the nation. Days after his protest went viral, NFL executives called him a "traitor," claiming he "had no respect for our country … [so] fuck that guy" (Freeman). This limited understanding of patriotism, what veteran sportscaster Bob Costas referred to as "bumper sticker style kind of flag waving," contributed to internet rumors alleging that Kaepernick had converted to Islam (qtd. in Harris). Entrepreneurial fans even created "Wanted" t-shirts with a direct gun sight hovering over Kaepernick's chest (Rossi). Superimposing Kaepernick's face on an image of Osama bin Laden, critics fed into a narrative that cast this bad boy as more than an unpatriotic player; he had become an enemy of the state (Beydoun). Furthermore, President Trump stoked the flames when he called out Kaepernick for "disrespect[ing] the flag" at a Republican rally and again on Twitter (Tatum).

'Tis "The Star-Spangled Banner": Battle Song as Battleground

When fans denounced Kaepernick as unpatriotic, they often pointed to his method of protest—refusing to stand for the national anthem. This particular criticism connects to the song's militaristic history. As Luke Cyphers and Ethan Trex detail in ESPN's "The Song Remains the Same," "The Star-Spangled Banner" was "hatched during one war, institutionalized during another.... The most memorable lines involve rockets and bombs, and the lesser-known verses conjure 'the havoc of war' and 'the gloom of the grave.'" Although Cyphers and Trex decry the song's glorification of war, the U.S.

military was the first to honor and use the song in ceremony and on the battlefield before it became an intrinsic element of sporting ritual.

The song's significance at sporting events reflects the ebbs and flows of America's wartime involvement. For instance, in the midst of a bloody World War, the U.S. Navy band played the anthem in an attempt to cheer up a World Series crowd (Little). It worked. An infielder, given furlough from the Navy to play in the series, gave the American flag an official salute (Little). With a swell of patriotism, the standing crowd began to sing and players decapped, hands over hearts (Little). Next-day reports claimed that "the mind of the baseball fan was on war" and the "thunderous applause" was not for Babe Ruth, but for the patriotism the song stirred ("Red Sox"). Franchise owners played the song for the rest of the series and began to peddle cheap tickets to veterans and service members (Troy), beginning a custom that Senators McCain and Flake would come to criticize. By the end of World War II, NFL Commissioner Elmer Layden ordered the anthem to be played at every football game, wanting it to be "as much a part of every game as the kickoff" because fans during peace times should not forget what the national anthem stands for (qtd. in Willingham, "The national"). During the upheavals of the Vietnam War, the NFL commissioner played the song to "put their sports on record in support of the Vietnam War, while laboring to silence those in the game who disagreed" (Levin). Post-9/11 patriotism solidified the song's place in rituals of American sport, and even though Kaepernick protested more than a decade after the tragic tumbling of the Twin Towers, America is still waging that war.

Unable to excise Kaepernick's protest from his patriotism, critics claimed that Kaepernick was violating codes of conduct like Title 36, section 301 "Patriotic and National Observances and Ceremonies" ("36"). However, as privately-owned franchises, the NFL maintains no strict regulations on how athletes behave during the song. In the 1960s, NFL Commissioner Pete Rozelle first started "policing" players' behaviors to ensure the league "unambiguously demonstrated" its support for the Vietnam War (Levin). Such behaviors excluded "talking, nervous footwork, gum chewing and shoulder-pad slamming" (Reed). Oilers coach Bill Peterson later defined expected behaviors: lecturing players, he said, "I want you out there at attention, standing on the sideline, with your helmets under your arms!" (qtd. in Reed). In subsequent decades, the Game Operations Manual tried to relay these rules; it stipulates how players should act, but it uses the word "may" in regards to compliance—a phrasing without much teeth. Even though current Commissioner Roger Goodell thinks Kaepernick should stand, no disciplinary action was levied against him or other players ("Goodell"). In May 2018, all NFL owners approved a policy requiring players to stand during the anthem, if they are on the field. This policy prevented NFL players from protesting and attempted to appease offended fans. Less than two months after announcing the new policy, the players' union successfully argued against the rule (Stites). For many fans, Kaepernick's protest during the national anthem violated a norm, but no actual rule exists. Still, his bended knee was interpreted as a call to arms.

"When Freemen Shall Stand": Comparing How Players Have Protested

Because of the connections among sports, military action, and patriotic sentiment, those athletes—Kaepernick included—whose protests involve the national anthem have always gotten special attention, but not all have been met with the same vitriol. Consider, for example, Jackie Robinson's silent protest of the national anthem. Robinson's refusal to honor the flag and the song could be considered particularly disrespectful given his two years of service in the Army's all-black battalion. In *I Never Had It Made*, Robinson claims that he "cannot" salute the flag or sing the anthem because he "know[s] that [he is] a Black man in a white world" (qtd. in Joseph). As a soldier and a baseball player in the Jim Crow era, Robinson knew he had to behave within the constraints of a "good ol' boy" network. In 1947, poised to sign Robinson to his first contract, Brooklyn Dodgers Baseball Club sports executive Branch Rickey questioned Robinson's temperament, not his skills. Rickey told him he was "looking for a ballplayer with guts enough not to fight back," and for at least two years Robinson did just that in the face of terrible bigotry (qtd. in Klein). During his baseball career, Robison ignored racial slurs, focusing instead on his batting average (Long). And yet, sports commentators later characterized Robinson as a "trouble maker" and a "rabble rouser" because he dared to argue with referees.

Perhaps the most telling label, however, was the insistence that Robinson was "uppity"—a word that is "almost exclusively used to describe black people who did not show the appropriate level of deference to whites" (Mason). As C. Nicole Mason explains, the "uppity Negro" trope is the African American caveat to the American dream: "Don't outshine, out earn or outperform whites. If and when we do achieve outsized success, we should be appreciative and deferential. If we're not, we are considered 'uppity.'" Kaepernick's white, biological mother reiterated this advice when she tweeted: "There's ways to make change w/o disrespecting & bringing shame to the very country & family who afforded you so many blessings" (@Heidirn1). The word "uppity" was used to remind Robinson that he should "just shut up and play ball," just as the word "boy" was used to put Kaepernick "in his place." As quarterback, Kaepernick was already outperforming, out earning, and outshining white

white players. Therefore, when players like Robinson and Kaepernick take a stand, they are often met with disdain for not appreciating their professional opportunities or paychecks. For critics, Robinson and Kaepernick should play ball as a *good boy* would: submissively and with gratitude.

Even though Robinson refused to salute the flag, his patriotism was never called into question, most likely due to differences in sports and statistics. Robinson racked up impressive statistics during his eight-year career while Kaepernick's are often considered middling (Jaffe). Some commentators like Kevin Seifert of NFL Nation cite his poor performance on the field—not his politics or protest—as the reason he is still unsigned. However, while his record is not as impressive as Robinson's, Kaepernick did lead the 49ers into Super Bowl XLVII in 2013, passed for 72 touchdowns, threw for 12,271 yards, rushed for 2,300 more ("Colin"), and maintained the sixth lowest interception rate in 2016 (Liotta). After posting his worst statistics in 2015, the 49ers put him on injury reserve, ending his season ("San Francisco"). Kaepernick returned in 2016 as a second-string quarterback. ESPN's NFL Total Quarterback calculations ranked him 23rd for that season.

Beyond sports and statistics, Kaepernick and Robinson's differing attitudes about equality influence their legacies. Robinson acknowledged that it is a "white man's world," and he merely wanted to have a dignified life within it. As he penned to Malcolm X in 1963, "America is not perfect by a long shot, but I happen to like it here and will do all I can to help make it the kind of place where my children and theirs can live in dignity" (qtd. in Long). Robinson's dream, like Dr. Martin Luther King, Jr.'s, was still radical to many Americans, but his goal of living in dignity is similar to the American dream—one that many fans would encourage. On the other hand, Kaepernick does not often mention a love for his country, and his protest reminds people that for some the dream is a nightmare. Although Robinson did not salute the flag because he knew "he never had it made" as a black man in a white world, Kaepernick refused to stand "because [t]here are bodies in the street and people getting paid and getting away with murder" (qtd. in Wyche). Both athletes challenge the systemic power afforded to whites, but Robinson's protest was more abstract, calling for general dignity and respect for blacks; Kaepernick, however, specifically blames police and prosecutors for perpetuating racial injustices. Therefore, even though sports commentators like Bill Baer claim that Robinson would have supported Kaepernick's protest "without question," many fans do not.

In order to compare reactions to Robinson and Kaepernick's national-anthem protests more fully, we would be remiss if we did not include John Carlos and Tommie Smith's iconic and incendiary 1968 Olympic protest. The image of Carlos and Smith standing on the Olympic podium, waiting for the medal with raised, clenched fists has become a cultural touchstone of civil rights activism. This action, like Kaepernick's kneeling, is passive, but it was interpreted as an act of aggression. Carlos and Smith were called "black-skinned stormtroopers" and received untold death threats (Buehrer). Comparing two Olympians to the paramilitary wing of the Nazi party goes beyond vilifying them, and, similar to Kaepernick, they were labeled as enemies of the State. Unlike the "human tanks" of World War II, Carlos and Smith were armed with beads and scarves to protest continued lynching, unzipped jackets to support the Harlem working class, and shoeless feet to represent those in poverty. The majority of media coverage depicted Carlos and Smith's action as militant, and they were cast as disrespectful even though—as Smith recounts—"There was no hate, no hostility shown or intended" (qtd. in Barra). Because they protested at the Olympics during the national anthem, Carlos and Smith were seen as unpatriotic at the pinnacle of patriotic games. While Robinson is labeled a "True American Hero," memorialized in the naming of parks, stadiums, streets, and even highways, Carlos and Smith are still waiting for their medals and, Kaepernick is currently out of an NFL job.

A possible explanation for this disparity is that unlike Robinson, Carlos, Smith, and Kaepernick are more closely aligned with the Black Power Movement. This movement is often associated with violent upheaval, as activists called for self-determination that existed outside of the "good ol' boy" network. As James Baldwin wondered, and many Black Power activists asked, "Do [we] really want to be integrated into a burning house?" (94). This Black Power association relegates Kaepernick to being a bad boy. When reporters discovered that Kaepernick had been wearing socks that depict cops as pigs, they surmised that "He isn't asking for peace—he's asking for justice. He's not interested in hearing both sides; he's choosing one, and he's not interested in propriety" (Gentille). Note the insistence on justice, as if justice is a bad thing, and the emphasis on propriety, both of which testify to Kaepernick's refusal to abide by "good ol' boy" expectations. In other words, he is not supposed to care about justice; he is supposed to sit quietly in the shadows. Here, Kaepernick is boxed in as a radical, similar to Carlos and Smith. These three examples of athletic activism help explain why Kaepernick is a bad boy for snubbing "The Star-Spangled Banner."

"As It Fitfully Blows": Sports as Cultural Battlefield

Robinson, Carlos and Smith—and now Kaepernick—reveal the intricate relationship between sports and cultural values. In many cases, that relationship is racialized and gendered. Consider the so-called Fight of the Century between James Jeffries and Jack Johnson in 1910. Johnson's heavyweight victory, and his perceived immorality, challenged claims to white racial superiority: "Indeed, white fans deemed him a brute and felt that he represented all that was wrong with the black race" ("A Question"). As Jeffries himself admits, he staged his comeback "for the sole purpose of proving that a white man is better than a negro" ("A Question"). Just as Jeffries was fighting as the representative for white men, Joe Louis' successful boxing career made him a "credit to his race" ("A Question"). These examples suggest a testing of white male dominance, just as "each matchup of a woman and man in direct competition is understood as the test of all women against all men" (Crawley et al. 125). For example, the 1973 tennis match between Billie Jean King and retired professional Bobby Riggs was famously dubbed the Battle of the Sexes. In these instances and others, sports can be seen as a way to exert dominance—be it whites over blacks or men over women. It is no accident that the Battle of the Sexes occurred when women were gaining political, social, and economic advances, just as the Fight of the Century happened when black intellectuals and professionals began to gain political prominence and social recognition. Bad boys or, in the case of King, bad girls must be returned to "appropriate" positions.

One way to return victorious athletes to their appropriate position is to emphasize their physical, rather than mental, attributes. We hear this echoed in coded biological phrases that draw attention to the so-called natural, genetic differences between black and white players. For example, the same year Doug Williams, the first African American quarterback, led the Washington Redskins to Super Bowl victory, Jimmy the Greek famously stated, "The black is a better athlete to begin with because he's been bred to be that way, because of his high thighs and big thighs that goes up into his back, and they can jump higher and run faster because of their bigger thighs and he's bred to be the better athlete because." Jimmy continues, "this goes back all the way to the Civil War when during the slave trade ... the slave owner would breed his big black to his big woman so that he could have a big black kid" (qtd. in Shapiro). Jimmy's overt bigotry cost him his broadcasting position with CBS, but the sports industry—football in particular—continues to emphasize the physicality of black athletes over their mental capabilities.

Studies show this attitude is reinforced when recruiters and coaches subconsciously rely on racial stereotypes to determine player placement. Stereotypically, if given a choice, "football men seek to repeat the past. Empirically, (white) executives hire (white) coaches who come from a background of historical (white) success, who then draft quarterbacks that pass the 'eyeball test' (and are thereby white)" (Schalter). The tradition of football, and the experience of its players, reveals a long-seated tradition of denying black athletes the role of team leader and decision maker—precisely because of the pervasive belief that black athletes lack the mental acumen to be leaders on the field (Bigler and Judson). For example, Andrew Billings' 2004 study of 162 hours of transcripts of televised college and NFL games revealed a tendency to characterize black athletes as "naturally" athletically superior. J.R. Woodward's research on racial stacking shows that "African American players are more likely to be described in physical terms (rather than mental terms) than are White players in the same positions," and that white players are more likely to be given positions that are associated with intelligence and decision-making abilities. These studies help to explain why there are so few black quarterbacks and why there seems to be a racial divide in quarterback styles (Schlater). The focus on physicality reveals how racism operates in football. White dominance cannot be guaranteed in every circumstance, but it can be confirmed on the field—if the athletes are willing to play along. Kaepernick obviously is not.

When Kaepernick secured a quarterback position, he automatically disrupted the dominant narrative that black athletes do not have the intellectual capabilities to make the calls—whether on the field or in the streets. Considered the most important player on the contemporary NFL team, the quarterback position requires the most intelligence, and it has drastically changed in the decades since Rutgers and Princeton squared off in 1869. At the line of scrimmage, the quarterback's duties involve communicating with coaching staff, relaying that information to the offense, assessing the defense, changing the play if necessary, knowing the responsibilities and routes of all of the offensive players, and managing all of these responsibilities before the play clock runs out. The quarterback also needs to make snap decisions of where to throw the football while trying to avoid being pummeled by the defensive pass rushers. Beyond the field, the quarterback must speak to reporters, represent the team as spokesperson, and generally serve as the team leader.

As the "smartest" players on the field, professional quarterbacks and other team leaders still tend to be white. Warren Moon, the only black quarterback inducted into the Hall of Fame as of 2019, describes that black college quarterbacks anticipated being moved to other non-"thinking," more physical positions when drafted to the pros (Powell). Even though Moon was referring to the NFL of the 1980s, the subconscious, structural racism remains, as only a handful of starting quarterbacks are black (five out of 32 in the 2017 season). A noteworthy comparison is the number of starting quarterbacks in 2017 to the number of black generals or admirals serving in the military. Sixty years after desegregation, only one of the 38 four-star generals or admirals serving was black, and according to a list of active duty, four-star generals or admirals, only two are black ("After"). Thus, positions of leadership, be it on the battlefield, the playing field, or the White House, are not often afforded to black people. Each leadership position is presumed to be for "thinkers," and when blacks rightfully earn this position, as Kaepernick has done, they are seen as a threat to the "good ol' boy" network.

Perhaps this helps explain why critics are so quick to diminish Kaepernick's protest as imprudent even if they are sympathetic to his cause. For example, sports journalist Jason Whitlock characterizes Kaepernick as wrong-headed: "And I don't think what Kaepernick understands—and some other people don't understand—is the 1960s were about changing fixing laws [sic]," Whitlock continued; "you can address laws; you can't legislate feelings—and it's stupid!" (qtd. in Ruiz). Even Supreme Court Justice Ruth Ginsberg described Kaepernick's actions as "dumb and disrespectful," but reasoned that "being stupid" was not cause for arrest. Ginsburg's critique, while harsh, pales in comparison to sports journalist and television analyst Clay Travis' declaration that Kaepernick is a "fucking idiot." Travis reasons that Kaepernick's gesture is an "absurd attention-seeking statement with no substance behind it." Although less overt than claims of black athletes' physical superiority, characterizing his actions as "stupid" reflects and reinforces negative stereotypes about black intellect.

And yet, Kaepernick has demonstrated academic excellence. He earned a 4.0 GPA at the University of Nevada–Reno, where he studied Business Management (Beydoun). He boasted an impressive 37 (4 points higher than Tom Brady) on the NFL's Wonderlic test, and he is a member of Kappa Alpha Psi, "a black fraternity built upon academic excellence, political leadership and community empowerment" (Beydoun). Sports commentators, who would rather dismiss his actions as stupid, often ignore these accolades.

"The Havoc of War and the Battle's Confusion": Golden Boy vs. the Bad Boy

Critics not only perceive Kaepernick as "a fucking idiot," but he also undermines the ideal image of the quarterback—an image that remains "firm in our minds" (Schalter). As NFL analyst Ty Schalter points out, this ideal quarterback is "tall, lean, cannon arm. Handsome, clean-cut, dates the cheer captain. Stays in the pocket, stays cool under pressure. Confident, outgoing, looks you right in the eye and shakes your hand. Well spoken. Makes good decisions. Smart. White." Schalter is, of course, describing Paul Hornung, the original "Golden Boy" player who is still remembered as an "all–American triple-threat from Notre Dame"—even after being suspended for a season because he bet on games. This "glamour boy" with golden locks and youthful athleticism won the Heisman Trophy in 1956. In his biography of Hornung, Ron Flatter describes the Notre Dame star and Hall of Fame inductee as having "a charisma [that] he continues to carry well into his seventh decade of life and fourth decade of retirement." Hornung's charisma seems to outshine his actual performance as a ball player, however. He is the only player to win a Heisman with a losing record (he only won 20 percent of their games), and, as Scott Kacsmar notes, Hornung was not even the best player on his team. Yet, he remains the ideal *image* of a football player—one who plays pro-style, staying deep in the pocket, and romancing the cheer captain. He is an All-American "good ol' boy," so good he is golden.

The contemporary Golden Boy is Tom Brady, whose good looks and strong arm make him a favorite on and off the field. In the words of Tricia Romano, he suffers from "too much winning." Romano characterizes this century's Golden Boy as a "metaphor for rich white men who get the girl, the gig, the fame, the money without anything or anyone standing in their way.... Deflategate and other scandals ... bounce off him like a deflected pass." Even though Brady was suspended for four games, he can do no wrong, like his Golden Boy predecessor. His image is merely "tarnished," but he continues to lead the Patriots to the Super Bowl (Chase). He married the model he left his pregnant girlfriend to date; he destroyed evidence against charges of cheating, and yet he continues to have the backing of political figures. Senator Ted Cruz suggested that Brady had been framed by Hillary Clinton (Campbell). The biggest political heavyweight to comment on the ruling was President Trump, who tweeted his praise for Brady: "He's a very honorable guy and an honest guy and a truly great athlete. He is really a very good friend of mine, and I just spoke to him a little while ago" (qtd. in Campbell). Once again, our Commander in Chief has elevated a matter of sport to a matter of State. President Trump's praise for Brady's violation of the NFL law strongly contrasts with his condemnation of Kaepernick's non-violent, legal protest. Despite his tarnished image, Brady, like Hornung, will remain in popular lore as a good boy with a golden arm.

Enter Kaepernick, whose "unapologetic blackness," epitomized by his hair, challenges the Golden Boy image of the so-called All-American football player and quarterback (Crockett). The longer he protested, the bigger his hair got: "As the spotlight on his activism grew, so too did his locks, first into a mass of short curls, then cornrows, then a bigger crown of still-defined curls and, finally, a billowing, uncontrolled, woolly, seemingly semi-sentient mass that doubled as a silent trigger of white fragility" (McDonald). His hair generated its own hashtag (#Kapsoblack), cartoons, memes, and Halloween costumes (Steele). A Google search on Kaepernick and his hair results in a Yahoo Answers entry on how he can fit his helmet over his afro, and Twitter has a "stupid hair" feed dedicated to Kaepernick's hairstyle (Steele). Unlike Troy Polamalu and other NFL players with notably different hairstyles, Kaepernick's afro was viewed as an act of aggression, more threatening than charming and less likely to secure him a Head and Shoulders commercial.

His hairstyle has also functioned to prompt another layer of critique: the afro's affiliation with the Black Power Movement and the Natural Hair Movement of the 1990s attests to its ability "to fight the status quo without saying a word" (Gabbara). In short, his hair has been as silent and powerful as taking a knee, and it has produced just as much vitriol. Michael Vick suggested that it was the reason the NFL refused to pick up Kaepernick: "The first thing we got to get Colin to do is cut his hair," Vick said. "I don't think he should represent himself in that way in terms of the hairstyle. Just go clean cut. Why not?" Vick queried (qtd. in Mather). Although Vick supports Kaepernick's activism, he seems to buy into the logic of "respectability politics," which is predicated on the notion that "if you talk 'right' or act 'right' that white people will treat you 'better'" (qtd. in Tynes). As Vicks suggested, those bad boy locks are keeping him out of the locker room. Kaepernick's afro and its ties with radicalism, specifically that of the Black Power Movement, becomes an easy target and exacerbates the simple divide between the enemy and the good guy.

"And the Flag Was Still There": Conclusion

When Kaepernick uses his position to advocate for social justice, critics ignore the depths of his analysis and continue to insist that he must "be quiet and sit in the shadows." Nevertheless, he persists. By the end of 2018, Kaepernick kept his pledge to donate $1 million to his #10for10 program (Willingham, "While"). The range of donations reflects his intersectional approach to dealing with complex social issues, from Meals on Wheels to the Standing Rock Sioux Reservation to Somalia ("Million"). His Twitter feed is filled with civil rights messages. His "Know your Rights" campaign for youth raises awareness on self-empowerment in a way that echoes the civil rights mantra that "Black is Beautiful" and James Brown's refrain "I'm black and I'm proud." Modeled after the original Black Panthers' 10-point plan, Kaepernick's youth campaign teaches adolescents that they have the fundamental rights to be free, safe, educated, courageous, loved, and more (Zirin). The camp's first session invited kids from all over the San Francisco Bay area—including a number of homeless children living in a halfway house (Spears). Speakers discussed organic nutrition, holistic healing, financial knowledge, higher education, the history of policing, and more (Spears). Not a single workshop discussed sports, which seems to challenge the dominant idea that, for some, sports can be the sole method of achieving economic stability (King). For these efforts and others, *Sports Illustrated* named Kaepernick the recipient of its 2017 Muhammad Ali Legacy Award, *GQ* designated Kaepernick "Citizen of the Year" for 2017, and the ACLU followed suit by awarding Kaepernick its Eason Monroe Courageous Advocate Award. The following year, Amnesty International declared Kaepernick its 2018 Ambassador of Conscience, the organization's highest human rights honor (Gamble).

On Monday, September 3, 2018, Nike reignited the social media firestorm by making Kaepernick the face of its "Just Do It" campaign. By aligning itself with Kaepernick two years after his protest, Nike took a calculated risk. Shares initially went down, but by late September 2018, the company had earned six million dollars and ignited multiple bases: "black Americans, Democrats and younger generations were much more receptive to Kaepernick's involvement and message than white Americans and Republicans" (qtd. in Pasquarelli). These bases reflect the initial divided responses to Kaepernick's protest, with the "good ol' boy" network remaining staunch in its opposition. Instead of burning Kaepernick jerseys, critics organized a boycott, setting their Nike shirts and shoes aflame—sometimes while still wearing them—and President Trump tweeted, "what is Nike thinking" (Pasquarelli). The day after Nike launched the campaign, New Jersey State Policemen's Benevolent Association tweeted a photo of Army Ranger Pat Tillman, who was killed by friendly fire in Afghanistan. The following statement framed the image: "We just want everyone to know what it really means to.... 'Believe in something, even if it means sacrificing everything'" (Cohen). Politicians like GOP Rep. Doug Collins of Georgia jumped on the bandwagon, sharing their own images of Tillman as the ultimate, patriotic sacrifice (Taylor, "People"). Circulation of these images continued even after Tillman's widow requested that her husband's image not be exploited, particularly because Tillman's sacrifice was in the service of "self expression and the freedom to speak from one's heart—no matter those views" (qtd. in Taylor, "People"). The Police Union's false analogy between Kaepernick's activism and Tillman's service epitomizes how convoluted the conversation has become.

Casting a bird's eye view over the history of football—from its militaristic origins to Golden Boy quarterbacks—helps explain why Kaepernick created so much ire. Due to the deep-rooted associations among football, the anthem, and patriotic sentiment, many cast Kaepernick as anti–American, or in some extreme cases, a terrorist responsible for 9/11. These military associations, however, fail to explain fully why other athletes can protest with little fanfare. Several athletes have taken a knee since Kaepernick, but he alone has had the honor of being called a "son of a bitch" by the President of the United States (Tatum). What is unique about Kaepernick is the fact that he plays a position usually reserved for "Golden Boy" quarterbacks. As a dual-threat quarterback, Kaepernick is "uppity" because he refuses play safely in the pocket or remain quietly in the shadows. Therefore, reactions to Kaepernick illustrate how American society—and one of its loudest mouthpieces, the NFL—continues to struggle with racial inequality. As Francis

Maxwell astutely observes, "American society still can't handle a prominent black person questioning whether this country lives up to its purported ideals of freedom, equality and justice for all. Seriously, only in America can a white man cost his company $13 million in settlement fees, yet remain employed, while a black man peacefully protests in a corner, and is blackballed." Kaepernick's "unapologetic blackness" is especially egregious to the "good ol' boy" network that would prefer this bad boy to patriotically stand, with hand on heart, and honor a "flag that's still there."

Works Cited

"After 60 Years, Black Military Officers Rare." *Associated Press*, 23 July 2008, www.nbcnews.com/id/25809737/ns/us_news-life/t/after-years-black-military-officers-rare/#.XCjyfFxKh1s.

Baer, Bill. "Here's What Jackie Robinson Had to Say About the National Anthem." *NBCSports*, 24 Sept. 2017, www.mlb.nbcsports.com/2017/09/24/heres-what-jackie-robinson-had-to-say-about-the-national-anthem/.

Baldwin, James. *The Fire Next Time*. Vintage International, 1993.

Barra, Allen. "Fists Raised, but Not in Anger." *The New York Times*, 22 Aug. 2008, www.nytimes.com/2008/08/23/opinion/23barra.html.

Belson, Ken, and Mark Leibovich. "Inside the Confidential N.F.L. Meeting to Discuss National Anthem Protests." *The New York Times*, 25 Apr. 2018, www.nytimes.com/2018/04/25/sports/nfl-owners-kaepernick.html.

Beydoun, Khaled A. "Colin Kaepernick: Mix of Racism Anti-Islamic Rhetoric are Increasingly Toxic." *The Undefeated*, 2 Sept. 2016, www.theundefeated.com/features/colin-kaepernick-mix-of-racism-anti-islam-rhetoric-are-increasingly-toxic/.

Biderman, Chris. "Transcript: Colin Kaepernick Addresses Sitting During the National Anthem." *Ninerswire*, 28 Aug. 2016, www.ninerswire.usatoday.com/2016/08/28/transcript-colin-kaepernick-addresses-sitting-during-national-anthem/.

Bigler, Matthew, and Jeffries Judson. "'An Amazing Specimen'; NFL Draft Experts' Evaluations of Black Quarterbacks." *Journal of African American Studies*, vol. 12, no. 2, pp. 120–141.

Billings, A.C. "Depicting the Quarterback in Black and White: A Content Analysis of College and Professional Football Broadcast Commentary." *Howard Journal of Communications*, vol. 15, pp. 201–210, 2004.

Buehrer, Jack. "Olympics Black Power Heroes Are Still Waiting for an Apology." *The Daily Beast*, 4 Aug. 2016, www.thedailybeast.com/olympics-black-power-heroes-are-still-waiting-for-an-apology.

Campbell, Colin. "Donald Trump: I just spoke to Tom Brady—'he is so thrilled and so happy.'" *Business Insider*, 3 Sept. 2015, www.businessinsider.com/donald-trump-tom-brady-suspension-deflategate-2015-9.

Chase, Chris. "Tom Brady Tarnished His Legacy Forever." *USA Today Sports*, 28 July 2018, www.usatoday.com/2015/07/tom-brady-suspension-appeal-upheld-tarnished-legacy-roger-goodell-deflategate.

Clark, James. "These States Have the Highest (And Lowest) Enlistment Rates in America." *Task and Purpose*, 27 June 2017, taskandpurpose.com/states-highest-lowest-enlistment-rates/.

Cohen, Noah. "Police Union Uses Fallen NFL Player Pat Tillman to Troll Colin Kaepernick Over Nike Ad." *NJ.Com*, 5 Sept. 2018, www.nj.com/middlesex/index.ssf/2018/09/colin_kaepernick_nike_ad_nfl_pat_tillman_kneeling_national_anthem_nfl.html.

"Colin Kaepernick: Career Stats." *NFL*, 2017, www.nfl.com/player/colinkaepernick/2495186/careerstats.

Crawley, Sarah, et al. *Gendering Bodies*, Rowman and Littlefield, 2008.

Crockett, Stephen. "Police Union Is Big Mad After Colin Kaepernick and His Protest Afro

Visited Rikers Island Prisoners." *The Root*, 13 Dec. 2017, www.theroot.com/police-union-is-big-mad-after-colin-kaepernick-and-his-1821255009.

Cyphers, Luke, and Ethan Treks. "The Song Remains the Same." *ESPN*, 19 Sept. 2011, www.espn.com/espn/story/_/id/6957582/the-history-national-anthem-sports-espn-magazine.

Flatter, Ron. "Hornung Excelled on the Field and had Fun Off It." *ESPN Classic*, Nd. www.espn.com/classic/biography/s/Hornung_Paul.html.

Freeman, Mike. "Mike Freeman's 10-Point Stance: Kaepernick Anger Intense in NFL Front Offices." *Bleacher Report*, n.d., bleacherreport.com/articles/2651681-mike-freemans-10-point-stance-kaepernick-anger-intense-in-nfl-front-offices.

Gabbara, Princess. "The History of the Afro." *Ebony*, 2 Mar. 2017, www.ebony.com/style/the-history-of-the-afro.

Gabler, Neil. "NFL: Last sports bastion of white, male conservatives." *Reuters*, 30 May 2014, blogs.reuters.com/great-debate/2014/05/30/nfl-last-sports-bastion-of-white-male-conservatives/.

Gamble, J.R. "Kap Continues to Receive Awards from the People, Hate from the NFL." *The Shadow League*, 9 July 2018, theshadowleague.com/kap-continues-to-receive-awards-from-the-people-hate-from-the-nfl/.

Gentille, Sean. "Why Colin Kaepernick's Pig Socks Proved a Point." *Sporting News*, 1 Sept. 2016, www.sportingnews.com/nfl/news/colin-kaepernick-pig-socks-national-anthem-san-francisco-49ers/p2z50yslsqsy1ba71dlurxblf.

Ginsburg, Ruth. Interview by Katie Couric. *Yahoo News*, 10 Oct. 2016, www.yahoo.com/katiecouric/ruth-bader-ginsburg-on-trump-kaepernick-and-her-lifelong-love-of-the-law-132236633.html.

"Goodell: NFL Believes Players Should Stand for Anthem." *Around the NFL*, 18 Oct. 2017, www.nfl.com/news/story/0ap3000000863544/article/goodell-nfl-believes-players-should-stand-for-anthem.

Hall, Tony. "College Football: The Pride and Joy of the South." *Bleacher Report*, 6 Dec. 2013, bleacherreport.com/articles/1875948-college-football-the-pride-and-joy-of-the-south.

Harris, Sara Jane. "Bob Costas delivers powerful message on NFL protests and patriotism." *Sporting News*, 25 Sept. 2017, www.sportingnews.com/nfl/news/nfl-national-anthem-trump-players-kneeling-protest-bob-costas-colin-kaepernick-nbc-video/1ed2cql9zqukc1nctrsscvtgbl.

Heck, Jordan. "Rodney Harrison on Colin Kaepernick: 'He's not black.'" *Sporting News*, 30 Aug. 2016, www.sportingnews.com/nfl/news/rodney-harrison-colin-kaepernick-not-black/172krqvl6ji66153ho89cy75i5.

@Heidirn1. "There's Ways to Make Change." *Twitter*, 27 Aug. 2016, 4:38 p.m., twitter.com/Heidirn1/status/769680524994449408.

Inman, Cam. "Colin Kaepernick told by ESPN's Trent Dilfer to 'be quiet, sit in the shadows.'" *The Mercury News*, 11 Sept. 2016, www.mercurynews.com/2016/09/11/colin-kaepernick-told-by-espns-trent-dilfer-to-be-quiet-sit-in-the-shadows/.

Jaffe, Jay. "On Jackie Robinson Day, appreciating his extraordinary numbers." *Sports Illustrated*, 15 Apr. 2016, www.si.com/mlb/2016/04/15/jackie-robinson-statistics-hall-of-fame.

Joseph, Andrew. "Kaepernick shares Jackie Robinson anthem quote." *USAToday*, 15 Apr. 2018, www.usatoday.com/story/sports/ftw/2018/04/15/colin-kaepernick-shares-powerful-reminder-of-jackie-robinsons-stance-on-the-anthem/111150556/.

Kacsmar, Scott. "And the Least Deserving Player in the Pro Football Hall of Fame Is…" *Bleacher Report*, n.d., bleacherreport.com/articles/1213659-nfl-and-the-least-deserving-player-in-the-pro-football-hall-of-fame-is.

King, Shaun. "Colin Kaepernick's 'I Know My Rights Camp' Cements His Status as a Cultural Superhero in the Black Community." *NY Daily News*, 29 Oct. 2016, www.nydailynews.com/news/national/king-kaepernick-camp-cements-status-black-community-article-1.2850326.

Klein, Christopher. "Silent No Longer: The Outspoken Jackie Robinson." *History.com*, 2017, www.history.com/news/silent-no-longer-the-outspoken-jackie-robinson/print.

Levin, Justin. "National Anthem Protests aren't Politicizing the NFL—it was Already Political."

The Washington Post, 26 Sept. 2017, www.washingtonpost.com/news/made-by-history/wp/2017/09/26/national-anthem-protests-arent-politicizing-the-nfl-it-was-already-political/?utm_term=.6c559cf4ef4d.

Liotta, Colin. "A Look at Colin Kaepernick's 2016 Stats May Make Your Head Spin." *USA Today*, 24 May 2017, touchdownwire.usatoday.com/2017/05/24/a-look-at-colin-kaepernicks-2016-stats-may-make-your-head-spin/.

Little, Becky. "Why the Star-Spangled Banner Is Played at Sporting Events." *History Channel*, 25 Sept. 2017, www.history.com/news/why-the-star-spangled-banner-is-played-at-sporting-events.

Long, Michael G. "Jackie Robinson on the 4th: The Prophet and the Flag." *Huffington Post*, 3 July 2013, www.huffingtonpost.com/michael-g-long/jackie-robinson-on-the-fourth-prophet-and-the-flag_b_1644831.html.

Marks, Terry. "Savage Calls Kaepernick 'Boy,' Says He Should Stick to Football." *The Business Standard News*, 30 Aug. 2018, www.bizstandardnews.com/2016/08/30/savage-calls-kaepernick-boy-says-he-should-stick-to-football/.

Mason, C. Nicole. "I Am Your Uppity Negro." *The Root*, 1 July 2017, www.theroot.com/i-am-your-uppity-negro-1796522107.

Mather, Victor. "Michael Vick's Advice for Unemployed Colin Kaepernick: Cut Your Hair." *The New York Times*, 18 July 2018, www.nytimes.com/2017/07/18/sports/football/michael-vick-colin-kaepernick-hair-nfl.htm.

Maxwell, Francis. "Kaepernick Situation Proves America Still Seeks to Punish Black Protesters." *Huffington Post*, 7 Apr. 2017, www.huffingtonpost.com/entry/kaepernick-situation-proves-america-still-seeks-to_us_58e53f32e4b02c1f72345999.

McCain, John, and Jeff Flake. "Tackling Paid Patriotism: A Joint Oversight Report." www.fff.org/explore-freedom/freedom-on-the-web-link/tackling-paid-patriotism-a-joint-oversight-report-pdf/.

McDonald, Soraya Nadia. "Kaepernick's Afro and the Visual Shorthand of Radicalism." *Undefeated*, 17 Oct. 2018, www.theundefeated.com/features/kaepernick-trademark-afro-kneeling-protest-and-the-visual-shorthand-of-radicalism/.

McLellan, Ilya. "Football and War: The Warlike Origins of The Game." *The Bleacher Report*, n.d., bleacherreport.com/articles/76052-football-and-war-the-warlike-origins-of-the-game.

"Million Dollar Pledge." *Kaepernick7*, kaepernick7.com/million-dollar-pledge/. Accessed 12 May 2018.

"NFL Total QBR—2016 Season Leaders." *ESPN*, 2017, www.espn.com/nfl/qbr/_/year/2016.

Pasquarelli, Adrianne. "Real-Time Reaction: Watch Nike's Kaepernick Ad Expose a Generational Divide." *AdAge*, 7 Sept. 2018, adage.com/article/cmo-strategy/watch-nike-s-kaepernick-ad-expose-a-generational-divide/314874/.

Powell, Michael. "Warren Moon, Who Helped Clear Way for Black Quarterbacks, Recalls His Struggles." *New York Times*, 6 Feb. 2016, www.nytimes.com/2016/02/06/sports/football/warren-moon-clearing-way-for-black-quarterbacks-recalls-his-struggles.html.

Preza, Elizabeth. "Self-Fulfilling Prophecy: Racism Goes Mainstream with Conservative Reactions to Colin Kaepernick." *The National Memo*, 31 Aug. 2016, www.nationalmemo.com/self-fulfilling-prophecy-racism-goes-mainstream-conservative-reactions-colin-kaepernick/.

"A Question of Racial Supremacy: Jack Johnson vs. Jim Jeffries, 1910." *Sports in Black and White*, 2 Nov. 2012, www.sportsinblackandwhite.com/2012/11/02/a-question-of-racial-supremacy-jack-johnson-vs-jim-jeffries-1910/.

"Red Sox Beat Cubs in Initial Battle of World Series." *New York Times*, 6 Sept. 1918, timesmachine.nytimes.com/timesmachine/1918/09/06/97025138.pdf.

Reed, J.D. "Gallantly Screaming." *Sports Illustrated Vault*, 3 Jan. 1977, www.si.com/vault/1977/01/03/617338/gallantly-screaming.

Reid, Jason, and Jane McManus. "The NFL's Racial Divide." *Undefeated*, 2017, theundefeated.com/features/the-nfls-racial-divide/.

Romano, Tricia. "Why We Love to Hate Tom Brady." *Long Reads*, 31 Jan. 2018, longreads.com/2018/01/31/why-we-love-to-hate-tom-brady/.

Roos, David. "How Patriotism and American Pro Sports Became Allied." *HowStuffWorks*, 27 Sept. 2017, entertainment.howstuffworks.com/american-patriotism-and-pro-sports-allied.htm.

Rossi, Rosemary. "T-Shirts with Colin Kaepernick in Rifle Crosshairs Sell Out at Bills Game." *The Wrap*, 16 Oct. 2016, www.thewrap.com/t-shirts-with-colin-kaepernick-in-rifle-crosshairs-sell-out-at-bills-game/.

Ruiz, Steven. "Jason Whitlock Says Fighting Against Racism Is 'Stupid' During Bizarre Anti-Kaepernick Rant." *USAToday*, 12 July 2017, ftw.usatoday.com/2017/07/jason-whitlock-colin-kaepernick-rant-racism-joe-montana.

"San Francisco 49ers: Colin Kaepernick Placed on Injured Reserve." *SI Wire*, 21 Nov. 2015, www.si.com/nfl/2015/11/21/san-francisco-49ers-colin-kaepernick-injured-reserve.

Sandritter, Mark. "A Timeline of Colin Kaepernick's National Anthem Protest and the Athletes Who Joined Him." *SBNation*, 25 Sept. 2017, www.sbnation.com/2016/9/11/12869726/colin-kaepernick-national-anthem-protest-seahawks-brandon-marshall-n.

Schalter, Ty. "Why African-American QBs Are Systematically Trained to Abandon Mechanics." *The Bleacher Report*, n.d., bleacherreport.com/articles/1089785.

Scott, Shaun. "How the NFL Sells (and Profits from) the Inextricable Link Between Football and War." *Sports Illustrated*, 9 Sept. 2016, www.si.com/thecauldron/2016/09/09/remembering-september-11-nfl-football-warfare.

Seifert, Kevin. "Colin Kaepernick's biggest problem? Performance, not politics." *ESPN*, 20 Mar. 2017, www.espn.com/blog/nflnation/post/_/id/234081/colin-kaepernicks-biggest-problem-performance-not-politics.

Shapiro, Leonard. "'Jimmy the Greek's Says Blacks Are 'Bred 'for Sport." *The Washington Post*, 16 Jan. 1988. www.washingtonpost.com/archive/politics/1988/01/16/jimmy-the-greek-says-blacks-are-bred-for-sports/128a889e-83e2-44a3-b911-851d5281ade4/?utm_term=.f94fc1bbf554.

Spears, Marc. "Colin Kaepernick: 'There's Nothing That Anybody Is Going to Say that's Going to Change How I Feel About These Issues." *Undefeated*, 29 Oct. 2016, theundefeated.com/features/colin-kaepernick-know-your-rights-camp-san-franscico/.

Steele, David. "Colin Kaepernick's Afro is drawing out racists like no hairdo since Allen Iverson." *Sporting News*, 21 Oct. 2016, www.sportingnews.com/us/nfl/news/colin-kaepernick-afro-hairdo-message-critics-supporters-push-buttons-protest-national-anthem/nlth0cwvam3n1regnl4oxfm72.

Stites, Adam. "What the NFL's halted anthem policy means for the players, teams, and league." *SB Nation*, 9 Sept. 2018, www.sbnation.com/2018/7/23/17596078/nfl-national-anthem-policy-ramifications.

Tatum, Sophie. "Trump: NFL Owners Should Fire Players Who Protest the National Anthem." *CNN*, 23 Sept. 2017, www.cnn.com/2017/09/22/politics/donald-trump-alabama-nfl/index.html.

Taylor, Kate. "People Are Saying Nike Should Have Featured Pat Tillman in Its New Ad About 'Sacrificing Everything' Starring Colin Kaepernick." *Business Insider*, 4 Sept. 2018, www.businessinsider.com/nike-colin-kaepernick-ad-brings-pat-tillman-into-spotlight-2018-9.

_____. "Nike Releases Colin Kaepernick Commercial." *Business Insider*, 5 Sept. 2018, www.businessinsider.com/nike-releases-colin-kaepernick-commercial-2018-9.

Theobald, Bill. "Pentagon paid sports teams millions for patriotic events." *USAToday*, 4 Apr. 2015, www.usatoday.com/story/news/2015/11/04/millions-paid-pro-teams-patriotic-events-sens-flake-mccain-say/75141688/.

"36 U.S.C. 301-National Anthem." *Government Publishing Office*, 3 Jan. 2012, www.uscode.house.gov/view.xhtml?path=/prelim@title36/subtitle1/partA/chapter3&edition=prelim.

Travis, Clay. "Colin Kaepernick Is an Idiot." *Outkick the Coverage*, 27 Aug. 2016, www.outkickthecoverage.com/colin-kaepernick-is-an-idiot-082716/.

Troy, Travis. "How the National Anthem Got Tangled Up with American Sports." *Politico Magazine*, 26 Sept. 2017, www.politico.com/magazine/story/2017/09/26/how-the-national-anthem-got-tangled-up-with-american-sports-215646.

Tynes, Tyler. "Colin Kaepernick, Michael Vick, and the Fallacy of Respectability Politics." *SB*

Nation, 19 July 2017, www.sbnation.com/2017/7/19/15990134/colin-kaepernick-michael-vick-and-the-fallacy-of-respectability-politics.

Weinsein, Arthur. "Colin Kaepernick Timeline: Looking Back at Year of National Anthem Controversy." *Sporting News*, 23 Aug. 2017, www.sportingnews.com/nfl/list/colin-kaepernick-national-anthem-protest-timeline-one-year-anniversary-nfl-quarterback-job-sign/t56iyqmc463n1b7ukuby2f02n/slide/1.

Willingham, AJ. "The national anthem in sports (spoiler: it wasn't always this way)." *CNN*, 25 Sept. 2017, www.cnn.com/2017/09/25/us/nfl-national-anthem-trump-kaepernick-history-trnd/index.html.

―――. "While You Were Arguing About the Anthem, Colin Kaepernick Just Finished Donating $1 million." *CNN*, 31 Jan. 2018, www.cnn.com/2018/01/31/sport/colin-kaepernick-million-dollar-donation-pledge-anthem-nfl-trnd/index.html.

Woodward, J.R. "Professional Football Scouts: An Investigation of Racial Stacking." *Sociology of Sport Journal*, vol. 21, 2004.

Wyche, Steve. "Colin Kaepernick Explains Why He Sat During National Anthem." *NFL*, 27 Aug. 2016, www.nfl.com/news/story/0ap3000000691077/article/colin-kaepernick-explains-why-he-sat-during-national-anthem.

Vasquez, Paul. "America and the Garrison Stadium: How the U.S. Armed Forces Shaped College Football." *Armed Forces & Society*, vol. 38, no. 3, 2012, pp. 353–372.

Zirin, David. "Colin Kaepernick's Message to Chicago Youth: 'Know Your Rights'" *The Nation*, 10 May 2017, www.thenation.com/article/colin-kaepernicks-message-to-chicago-youth-know-your-rights/.

Ronda Rousey from Badgirl to "Femininely Badass"

Joseph M.M. Aldinger

> I believe that a girl should not do what she thinks she should do, but should find out through experience WHAT SHE WANTS TO DO.[1]
>
> —Amelia Earhart

A groundbreaker and precedent setter, Ronda Rousey was the first American woman to earn an Olympic medal in judo; she won Bronze at the 2008 Summer Olympics in Beijing. It was also in judo that Rousey began to establish herself as a badgirl—a role she later relished and embraced. For instance, in her memoir *My Fight/Your Fight*: *Rousey*, she tells an anecdote of how she, even at a relatively early age, strove to control her natural badgirl inclinations. Recounting the World Judo Championship, Rousey describes an incident in which Team USA's scale was misaligned and weighed athletes as lighter than they weighed on the official tournament scale (268). Rushing to check her weight at the last minute on the unofficial scale, Rousey, then twenty years old, was so close to weight that she had to jog to lose water weight. She also knew that she needed to weigh in naked. After her run, Rousey took her sweat-soaked clothes off to check her weight on the unofficial scale that was across the hotel lobby from the official scale. Frustrated at team USA's scale, at having to cut weight by running at the last minute, and at the prospect of having to put her sweat-soaked clothes back on, she writes: "I held my towel with one hand [naked underneath] and looked straight ahead [as she walked back across the hotel lobby to the official scale]. If I could have walked through there with my middle finger up in the air and not have risked getting in trouble for violating some tournament rules of conduct, I would have" (132).

As this anecdote illustrates, even young Rousey was already "rowdy"—a nickname she has acquired from former professional wrestling superstar Rowdy Roddy Piper, a bad boy himself (Kurchak 269). Rousey began her career as a judoko, but she later transitioned into Mixed Martial Arts (MMA) where she actively built her badgirl persona, even catching the eye of Hollywood and starring as a "tough girl" in several movies. After retiring from the MMA cage, badgirl Rousey stepped into the wrestling ring where she is the current World Wrestling Entertainment's (WWE) women's Raw Champion. Unlike many athletes who are labeled as badgirls/boys by the media or other outside forces, Rousey carefully crafted her badgirl image and understood its cultural function. Pam R. Sailors and Charlene Weaving argue in "Foucault and the Glamazon: The Autonomy of Ronda Rousey" that cultural representations of Rousey position her as a Glamazon, a term that, "describe(s) women who are different from other women, but who also fit societal ideals and gender norms. They are feminine and heterosexual" (432).

Rousey fits this designation quite well for a variety of reasons. Rigorous training has sharpened her muscle tone, and the nature of her sport arguably may have heightened her aggression. Although musculature and aggression reveal her kinship with the fabled Amazon women, Rousey is able to counter potential gender "transgressions" by presenting a hypersexualized self outside of the ring. Rousey posed, for example, in nothing but a painted-on swimsuit in the Swimsuit Edition of *Sports Illustrated*, and she appeared naked in a photo spread in The Body issue of *ESPN The Magazine*. In short, Sailors and Weaving claim that Rousey and Glamazons "simultaneously overturn and recuperate gender-norms" (431). They conclude that Rousey can maintain autonomy by being self-reflective and taking part in the process (438). This essay extends their research by considering how Rousey enhances her autonomy by cultivating a badgirl persona.

In such active creation, Rousey engages with what French philosopher, Michel Foucault, describes as "the techniques of self" (87). For Foucault, these techniques are the ways people navigate and use culture to fulfill their life projects. Or said a bit differently, "the techniques of the self" are all of the things individuals do to construct an identity. Rousey not only constructs her badgirl persona as an identity, but she also simultaneously creates new cultural possibilities. Her self-work thus constitutes a cultural project that Foucault describes as a struggle and creative process that resists current power structures. He defines resistance as, "not simply a negation but a creative process; to create and recreate, to change the situation, actually to be an active member of that process" (168). For instance, Rousey leveraged her badgirl persona to persuade the stalwart owner of the Ultimate Fighting Championship, Dana White, who previously had stated there would never be a women's division in his league, to change his mind and create one.

In the conclusion, Rosemarie Thomson-Garland's *Extraordinary Bodies* serves as a lens to examine Rousey's portrayal of the "DNB" (Do Nothin' Bitches) and "the femininely badass," terms she uses to describe two different types of females. In essence, Rousey's notion of the "femininely badass" woman emerges from her understanding of autonomy. By creating such clearly delineated categories, she also metaphorically relegates DNBs to the classification of disabled figure/body. Garland-Thomson's concept of "absolute able-bodiness" relates directly to Rousey's dichotomous females. As Garland-Thomson notes, absolute abled-bodiness is based on two fantasies: (1) that an autonomous individual's success can be attributed to the athlete's ability to discipline his/her body and (2) that an athlete's body does not require care (46). Although Rousey may have been able to leverage her badgirl persona to raise questions about gender norms, this does not mean all women can ultimately become femininely badass in a similar rhetorical fashion. Rousey's self-work and development of the badgirl creates a space of possibility and, within that space, new cultural forms can emerge. However, we need to be cautious in making Rousey and the figure of the badgirl the only model for resistance.

The Badgirl: Becoming Femininely Badass One Transgressive Act at a Time

In 2013, Rousey became the first female fighter to sign with the Ultimate Fighting Championship (UFC). Created in 1992, the UFC has been the biggest stage for Mixed Martial Arts (MMA) practitioners, broadcasting in 149 countries to nearly a billion homes world-wide and generating 6 million pay-per-view purchases in 2012 alone (Weaving 129–30).[2] Describing her time in the UFC and other competitions, Rousey and Ortiz write

> I have been booed in thirty countries. I have been booed following UFC victories. I'm more used to being booed by a crowd than I am being cheered. I have never been a fan favorite. Pretty much my entire competitive career has been defined by people hoping to see me lose. In the UFC, I've embraced the role of the villain. I don't shy away from controversy. I don't hold back when it comes to speaking my mind. That doesn't always endear me to the masses. In a world that loves to root for the underdog, I'm always the favorite—and I always win [129].

More noteworthy than Rousey's "embrac[ing] the role" of a badgirl or villain, as she defines it, is her understanding of the badgirl persona. For her, being a badgirl means, at least in part, pushing back against prevailing sports narratives such as the story of the underdog. Although sports are dominated by narrative structures of the underdog who overcomes great adversity and hardship to win, Rousey enjoys disrupting stories that offer hope by normalizing hardship and adversity. Badgirls, for Rousey, do not allow their language or words to be censored; they "speak their minds." In short, Rousey characterizes the badgirl as an individual who resists and disrupts dominant cultural norms.

Rousey's commentary before and after fights emphasizes her awareness that language and representation play an important role in contributing to and developing her badgirl image. In one post-fight interview inside the octagon, the announcer steps in to congratulate Rousey and asks her, "What did you think of your fight?" Rousey's joking, yet taunting, response is that in the thirty-nine seconds (that is how long the fight lasted), "She got tagged [hit] a bit more than she would've liked. [And] She is glad you guys [i.e., the fans] are cheering for her this time" (Florettarowan). Underscoring the fact that she was barely touched and that the fight did not even last a minute, Rousey mocked other competitors in her division. Following her taunts, Rousey used her post-fight interview to challenge or "callout" the top contender, Sarah Kaufman. This was after winning just two fights in Strikeforce (a fighting organization that is tantamount to the minor leagues for the UFC), and her callout was a first for women's MMA.

True to badgirl form, Rousey turned the traditional Q and A post-fight into an audacious demand to be given a shot at a top contender—Sarah Kaufman. Beating Kaufman would put Rousey next in line for a title fight against Miesha Tate—the Strikeforce champion and woman who would eventually become Rousey's nemesis. Beating a top contender was the traditional path to a shot at the title, but Rousey's challenge was also a subtle insult aimed at Tate. Why did she challenge Kaufman? Rousey "didn't want to take a chance of her [Tate] losing" to Kaufman, who would then take the belt (Florettarowan). In other words, Rousey not only wants a shot at the 135-pound belt, but she wants to take the belt specifically from Tate and no one else.

What makes this move daring is the fact that Rousey, in true Rowdy fashion, not only had just four professional victories, but also because she had not fought in the octagon in any single fight for longer than a minute. Her combined total time inside the cage as a Strikeforce competitor was fifty-four seconds, and here she was demanding a shot at the title and insulting the current champion—the person she wanted to take it from. Rousey's callout was also controversial because both victories came via armbar submissions, her signature move. At the time, fighting community critics viewed her callout as a naïve act of poor sportsmanship and perceived that her reliance on an armbar branded her as an inexperienced, one-dimensional fighter. Rousey, for some, was becoming a one-trick pony. She countered these naysayers by promising that she would make the fight exciting for the spectators. Rousey uses the uncensored language of the badgirl not only to speak her mind but also to create enough hype and demand during her title run that Strikeforce officials let Rousey overstep Kaufman (an unprecedented event) and move straight to a title fight against Tate. In effect, Rousey's badgirl image and behaviors allowed her to create a non-traditional path to the Strikeforce title—one that would not have been available to her had she been a "good girl."

What may appear to have been audacious antics following a victory was actually a cool and calculated plan. Early in her career, Tate changed her nickname from "Takedown" (an homage to her wrestling background) to "Cupcake"—a perfect contrast to Rousey's "Rowdy." Tate made the change to signal an alteration in her wrestling-heavy fight style and to indicate her new focus on staying positive and having fun (Holden). From the onset, Rousey understood that the fight against Tate was more than simply a title fight; it provided Rousey with the necessary material for transforming her badgirl image into a public persona.[3] Of equal importance, others in the fight community, including UFC owner White, also understood that Rousey was prompting social change. Commenting on the Tate vs. Rousey fight, White explains that, while "there have been great fighters before Ronda Rousey," what changed for him, "and what I think changed a lot of people's [minds] about women's MMA was Tate vs Rousey. That was a fight worthy of a men's fight: two incredibly talented women who are very well-rounded, and it doesn't hurt when they're beautiful too" (MMA Junkie, "'All Access'"). In a rather crass and misogynistic way, White acknowledges what Rousey seems to have already understood: it was not just about who could do the most damage to an opponent through striking, joint locks, and submissions; it was also about the spectacle. Rousey had a broader sense of the fight game and understood that her badgirl image was matched perfectly against Tate's wholesome "cupcake" persona.

In *My Fight/Your Fight*, Rousey concedes that she only knew two things about Tate prior to challenging her: she was the champion, and "there were people who thought she was reasonably good-looking" (218).[4] Rousey's strategy was to create insults that downplayed Tate's skills in favor of shifting the focus to Tate's appearance. She understood that part of what makes a "good fight" is selling it. However, she was not going to be a "good sport" in her promotional efforts. Instead, she continued to utilize her badgirl ways to insult Tate to draw attention to the fight. In *My Fight/Your Fight*, Rousey asserts that

> The fight game is not just about the fight. It's about the show. The athleticism is an integral part of the show, but that alone is not enough to keep people coming back. People watch fighters, but they remember characters. You have to keep them excited. You have to make them intrigued. You have to captivate them [218].

Rousey's conflation of the "fight game" with "the show" or theater is a comparison made famous by Roland Barthes in his essay "The World of Wrestling," where he compares wrestling to "ancient theatres" (15). He writes that both were "spectacles of excess" because the audiences understand "obviousness of the roles" played by the fighters/actors (15–17). Rousey's understanding that fight game is not purely an athletic competition reflects arguments found in Barthes's analysis. Rousey's piling up of excess (e.g., "keep them excited," "make them intrigued," and "captivate them") prevents viewers from reducing the fight game to merely a display of fighting and athleticism; it becomes a show. Furthermore, Rousey draws a rigid dichotomy between "fighters" and "characters." She applies a metaphorical understanding of the "fight game" in order to position herself as character—something far more memorable than just a fighter. Rousey's notations about her fight against Tate demonstrate her ability to transform her public image into a carefully crafted persona.

It is perhaps no coincidence that comments in Rousey's memoir mirror Barthes's discussion of wrestling, as she is a die-hard wrestling fan who left the UFC to become part of the World Wrestling Entertainment's (WWE) roster and is now the current female Champion. Her love for wrestling emerged in very formative years. In fact, her earliest childhood memory is centered around wrestling and language acquisition, a fitting combination, given her astute awareness of the relationship between language and representation. Rousey's description of that memory in *My Fight/Your Fight,* moreover, possibly identifies the foundation for her badgirl persona.

When Rousey was born, the umbilical cord was wrapped around her neck, cutting oxygen off from her brain. Although she survived, the part of her brain that controls speech had been irreparably damaged. Rousey's brain, however, rewired itself so "the part that controls speech is located in a different part of [her] brain than it is in most people" (12). Her brain's struggle to rewire itself manifested as a speech impediment that made it difficult for family and others to understand her. On her fourth birthday, wrestling became a means of translating her birthday wish. Rousey, a true millennial, grew up watching *WWF Super-Stars of Wrestling* on Saturday mornings. She and her sisters used to "launch [themselves] off the brown upholstered couch, attempting to submit one another [i.e., force the other to give up] on the itchy tan polyester carpet" (12). It should come as no surprise that three-year-old Rousey wanted "one of the greatest toys to come out of the 1980s," a Wrestling Buddy—"a two-foot-tall pillow version of Hulk [Hogan, the most famous wrestler of the day]" (12).

Rousey's speech impediment, however, made it difficult for her to communicate her desire for the toy. She writes, "Each time I tried to explain what I wanted, sounds spilled out in a jumbled mess that no one understood" (12). When her mother asked her what she wanted for her birthday, Rousey answered "Balgrin" (12). Going to toy store after toy store in search of "Balgrin" led to confused parents and clerks and a frustrated child. Eventually, a clerk asked what the Balgrin does, and when young Rousey threw herself on the ground several times mimicking wrestling moves, one clerk eventually realized she wanted a Wrestling Buddy. This event in Rousey's life demonstrates not simply her affinity with wrestling, but also the formative role that wrestling played in her understanding of what defines a fighter. A fighter, for Rousey, is someone who never gives up, and even baby Rousey embodied this fighting spirit. As Rousey and Ortiz describe the doctor's assessment of her difficult birth, "Babies are unbelievably resilient and this one is certainly a fighter" (9). In this account, Rousey uses metaphor to compare her birth to a fight, perhaps marking her destiny to become a fighter who never gives in and is tenaciously resilient. Rousey thus creates an origin story that portrays her as a fighter both when she was an infant and again as a young child learning to speak.

Rousey's connection with wrestling never severed. Even while fighting in the UFC, Rousey and fellow female athletes (Shayna Baszler, Jessmyn Dukes, and Marina Shafir) dubbed themselves the "Four Horsewomen" a play on the "Four Horsemen"—a professional wrestling group led by hall of famer Ric Flair, an infamous bad boy of wrestling. When taken in concert with her decision to adopt her "Rowdy" nickname, Rousey's connection to wrestling demonstrates the self work that Foucault describes as techniques that "determine ... identity, maintain it, or transform it ... [for a] certain number of ends" (87). However, Rousey's moniker was not the only technique of the self she practiced. Prior to her fight with Miesha "Cupcake" Tate, she carefully paired her "self" (including her Rowdy Ronda Rousey image) with Joan Jett's "I don't give a damn 'bout my bad reputation" to create a fully formed badgirl identity. As Rousey's fight song, it plays in the stadium as she walks from the locker room to the octagon. By coupling herself with Jett, Rousey solidified the transition from passively using her badgirl image to actively embracing it and shaping it to her advantage. Rousey was rowdy, she was bad, and she did not give a damn. Becoming "Rowdy" Ronda Rousey demonstrates the kind of careful attention she gave to creating and cultivating her badgirl persona.

Rousey's UFC career ended with two total knockout (TKO) losses: one to Holly Holmes at UFC 193 and another, a first round TKO, to Amanda Nunes at UFC 207. A badgirl to the core, Rousey accentuated these losses and subsequent retirement from the UFC with badgirl flair. Fighters typically bump or touch gloves prior to the fight as a sign of respect for their competitor. Prior to being knocked out by Holly Holmes, Rousey refused to touch gloves with Holmes. In addition, since leaving the UFC, she has refused to respond or has taken a hostile tone when asked about anything pertaining to her MMA career. She seemed to be attempting to make a clean break from the world of MMA as she entered the professional wrestling ring. Why would

Rowdy Ronda Rousey leave the UFC where fights are not scripted for scripted fights of the WWE? Her explanation of the value of wrestling can help unpack her intentions and offer information about this transitional period in her career.

In Google's new "Ask and Answer" feature—where celebrities and athletes provide answers to commonly asked questions by Googlers—Rousey is asked bluntly: "Is the WWE scripted?" Her answer can help to uncover the possible endgame of her self work and her assessment of the WWE's cultural value. She responds

> Yes, WWE is scripted, but I like to sum it up as being a social commentary for whatever is going on in the world; umm, there is some sort of parallel in the WWE for it. And umm, that is where I think it is a great venue to effect social change and that is why I'm getting involved [Google "Ask"].

Rousey's answer draws a sharp contrast between her conceptualization of herself as a fighter and Barthes' understanding of wrestling. For Barthes, wrestling "is nothing but the popular and age-old image of the perfect intelligibility of reality"; that is to say, signs and symbols such as a wrestler's entrance song and outfit offer "pure and full signification" (25). The audience immediately understands who the villains and heroes are inside the ring, based on cultural symbols. For Rousey, though, wrestling makes possible "social commentary."

The difference in these positions is rooted in each one's explanation of why individuals go to wrestling matches. Barthes perceives that people watch wrestling because they face complexity in their day-to-day lives. The enjoyment in wrestling derives from the pleasure of reduction and simplification; "it is the euphoria of men raised for a while above the constitutive ambiguity of everyday situations" (25). A key element of being a modern subject, for Barthes, is complexity and ambiguity; that is to say, in everyday life, meaning is not as simple as it may appear in a wrestling match. For instance, consider his discussion of justice. Watching a goodguy punish a badguy, as fans see in a wrestling match, reduces justice to a simple balancing of scales—a common symbol for justice.

However, in everyday life, the goodguys and the badguys are not always readily identifiable, nor does the judicial system render the meaning of justice so nicely and neatly. In this way, wrestling is a kind of cathartic pleasure— one that is nonetheless necessary, Barthes argues. For Rousey, however, wrestling is more akin to the genre of satire. Wrestling holds a mirror up to the audience and asks them to reflect on socially constructed problems/issues that perhaps cause social unrest, limit equality amongst individuals, or address current political topics. Or as she puts it, wrestling provides a "social commentary for whatever is going on in the world, [that].... makes it a great venue to effect social change." As she believes, individuals go to wrestling matches in order to see a "parallel" between the social issues/problems of their world acted out in the wrestling match. The key difference between these perspectives lies in Rousey's implicit belief that individuals who watch wrestling actually reflect on what they see and are motivated to "effect … change."

An example of this kind of social commentary occurred amidst rumors in early 2019 that Rousey would cut her WWE contract short and retire after WrestleMania 35 in order to start a family with her husband, UFC Heavyweight Travis Browne. Under contract until 2021, Rousey vehemently denied the rumors in inimitable badgirl style. She said, "I honestly don't know why [anyone] feels like [they're] an authority to speak on the plans for my uterus.… I really don't feel like I should have to respond to that kind of thing. It's my vagina, my life; keep the speculations to yourself. Leave me and my reproductive organs alone" ("UFC legend"). In one brusque interview, Rousey draws a line of what she will accept as reasonable inquiry into her personal life, and she used the platform that wrestling afforded to remind the world that she is in control of her own body.

Instances of Rousey believing she can influence popular culture to promote social change are not unique to her wrestling career, though. In UFC's "Embedded Vlog," the off-camera interviewer asks Rousey about being a role model. The scene opens with Rousey saying, "being put in the position of role model.… I don't think that I'm infallible enough for that" (Cepeda). Her rejection of the concept calls into question both the tradition that athletes are automatically role models and the notion that athletes want to be role models. Not wanting to imply that she does not have some influence, Rousey offers a different set of terms for explaining her impact. Rousey explains

> I have this one term for the kind of woman my mother raised me to not be … a do nothin' bitch or DNB. This kind of chick who just tries to be pretty and be taken care of by someone else. That's why I think it is hilarious when people say that my body looks masculine.… Listen just because my body wasn't developed for fucking millionaires doesn't mean it is masculine. I think it is femininely badass as fuck because there is not a single muscle on my body that isn't for a purpose because I'm not a do nothin' bitch. It is not very eloquently said, but it is to the point and maybe that is just what I am not very eloquent but to the point [Cepeda].

Rousey's critique is largely based on a broad generalization of other females and an able-bodied person's assumptions about the body and autonomy. For instance, a DNB's body is not only dependent on others, but its creative capacity also serves others. As Rousey snarkily implies, DNBs "try" to build aesthetically pleasing bodies that are built for "fucking millionaires." The DNB, for Rousey, turns her body into a subject in need of care and thus foregoes the ability to develop an independent and autonomous agency.

Rousey's negative view of the DNB is rooted in her belief that an individual should be autonomous and that there are appropriate and inappropriate ways to use one's body to contribute to society. For Rousey, "just try[ing] to be pretty," or more explicitly, being pretty is an inappropriate use of one's body because choosing to be just pretty creates a dependency on others' caretaking. Rousey's animosity toward DNBs is rooted in what she sees as an unproductive dependency. For Rousey, DNBs limit themselves.

In juxtaposition with the DNB, her definition of being "femininely badass" is grounded in the idea of developing a body for a productive purpose. Rousey additionally views that the payoff for being femininely badass is freedom, gained through autonomy, as well as the ability to win or be successful in competition. She perceives that her purpose-built body is not dependent on others, and her autonomy moreover allows her to cross (i.e., defeat) both gender and body norms. For instance, Rousey rejects the idea that being muscular or "ripped" is masculine. Instead, she suggests that it is sexy. For Rousey, the femininely badass's creative capacities step over the pitfalls of dependency. Moreover, being femininely badass results in success, where payment is twofold: winning and the ability to influence popular culture by promoting social change.

The connection between Rousey's impetus to "effect social change" and her definition of the femininely badass is unified by the creative capacities found in both. Foucault provides a vocabulary to help define the contours of this creative capacity. In an interview in *Ethics: Subjectivity and Truth*, Foucault defines a resistant subject. Summarizing Foucault's position during their discussion, the interviewer states, "to resist is not simply a negation but a creative process; to create and recreate, to change the situation, actually to be an active member of that process" (Foucault 168). Key to Foucault's resistant subject is not just resistance, but the capacity to create new possibilities. Clearly, Foucault's resistant subject shares the ability to create with Rousey's femininely badass. Being femininely badass offers Rousey avenues for creating cultural discourse that does not simply negate or oppose cultural norms (i.e., being muscular is not masculine), but instead creates new possibilities in popular culture (i.e., being muscular is sexy and feminine, not just masculine). The difference, here, is in the shift from simply opposing a position to modifying cultural attitudes, values, and beliefs to change the way we think about a subject. And to be clear, Rousey is a creator of the new in many ways; for instance, she created a women's division in the UFC, and she created a space for outspoken women's voices to be heard.

Measuring the creative capacities of the femininely badass offers a more comprehensive understanding of the badgirl figure in sports. In *My Fight/Your Fight*, Rousey and Ortiz write that her "life turned into something much bigger than [she] thought." She not only "created the job [she wanted]," but she "inadvertently created something not just for myself, but for *all* the *other women too* [my emphasis]" (296). It is Rousey's last claim that raises questions concerning the limitations of the femininely badass. Could "all ... other women," no matter race, ethnicity, religion, sexual orientation, abled bodiness, etc., really be a badgirl in the same way she is? Can any woman be femininely badass? Although it is tempting to wholeheartedly embrace Rousey's notion of the femininely badass, doing so leaves the constitutive fantasy that enables it unexamined and unquestioned.

In *My Fight/Your Fight*, Rousey's most salient badgirl characteristic is that she is a strong, independent woman, and as she understands it, her strength and independence lead to her success. This is a familiar narrative for an American audience, and it is made even more familiar in sports where discipline becomes almost synonymous with success. And Rousey ties her badgirl image, and hence the femininely badass, to elements of the "American Dream." For instance, *My Fight/Your Fight* provides multiple iterations of how her discipline allows her to overcome adversity. Rousey overcomes her speech impediment, grows up in a single-income household, loses her father at a young age, protests socio-economic disadvantages of USA Judo (as exemplified by their failure to provide world class athletes with proper scales), hits the glass ceiling of MMA, and ultimately riles against gender biases in American culture. As a result, Rousey becomes an influencer and creator of popular culture.

The problem with Rousey's conception of the femininely badass is that it fails to recognize that this rugged individualism—often stereotyped in bad-boy/girl figures as the "lone wolf" mentality—is a myth. Sports, especially in America, perpetuate the overarching mythological equation of the American Dream—hard work equals success. Rousey's sharp focus in her discussion of the femininely badass as independent, in addition to her relegation of the DNB as being a dependent individual, presents these two figures as metaphorical symbols for the abled bodied and ability, in juxtaposition with the disabled body and disability. Whereas the femininely badass can govern her destiny and life through the discipline of her abled body (i.e., work), the DNB is dependent upon others, "millionaires," to care for her disabled body. The femininely badasses are productive members of society who contribute while the DNBs take from society through the care they receive from others.

The specter that haunts her pronouncement of being femininely badass arises in the ephemeral moments of *My Fight/Your Fight* where Rousey discusses her need of a boxing coach, a strength coach, a corner person, a manager, a jujitsu/wrestling coach, a nutritionist, and a sports doctor. These moments are also mirrored by instances directly following a fight when Rousey and other fighters thank all of their coaches, trainers, sponsors, etc., for all of the sacrifices (i.e., care) that they have given them. This band of individuals (a.k.a., the fighter's "crew") is nothing less than a group of caregivers, and Rousey is no more the autonomous, independent self, free of needing help/assistance, than any other human. Athletes' bodies are constantly in need of care, but their idealized muscular bodies are often represented as absolute and perpetually abled. Such is the case in Rousey's conceptualization of the femininely badass.

Helping to sustain the fantasy of autonomy and perpetual ability is the connection between the figure of the badgirl and the mythology of the "lone wolf"—the competitor who steps outside normal social bonds/structures in order to achieve greatness. In the chapter "Find Fulfillment in the Sacrifices," Ortiz and Rousey portray her lone wolf qualities, citing a number of sacrifices that position her outside of normal social structures. Whereas normal teenagers would perhaps choose their friends first and be interested in hanging out and eating junk food, Rousey chose no friends and maintained a strict training and dieting regimen. The sacrifices that marked sixteen-year-old Rousey as a lone wolf included moving away from family to live with Big Jim (Jim Pedro, Sr., a USA Judo coaching legend, who "lived in a small house on a lake in the middle of nowhere New Hampshire"); dieting to cut weight, foregoing traditional schooling and the usual sixteen-year-old's activities to train judo all-day, every day; and eliminating all social relationships except with fifty-eight-year-old Big Jim, her only roommate.

This tale of sacrifice is grounded in the mythology of the lone wolf, which in Rousey's story additionally props up the troubling narrative of the American Dream found in sports. Her hard work with Big Jim resulted in her becoming the World Junior Judo Champion and being the youngest female to qualify for the 2004 Olympics. Moreover, it also supports the femininely badass's claims to perpetual ability; that is to say, Rousey's body seems capable of keeping up with this grueling regimen without consequence. However, this is not reality. Rousey's body is constantly breaking down (she injured herself during Worlds), and she admits that her dieting also led to an eating disorder. Years later, she realized she needed a nutritionist to care for her body in ways that she could not because she does not understand the science of weight loss.

Scholars who study the relationship between disability and ability often look at how cultural narratives inform understandings of the body and its care. For instance, Garland-Thomson demonstrates how the "liberal self" presents "the illusion of autonomy, self government and self-determination ... [that] underpins the fantasy of absolute able-bodiness" (42–6). Ultimately, Rousey's portrayal of the femininely badass as being capable of disciplining her body is based on the same fantasy of American exceptionalism found in Garland-Thomson's reading of the invalid. The problem is that "the life of a well-governed, self-determined man [in Rousey's case, woman] is imagined as a narrative of progress on which ... the doctrine of success, and the concept of self-improvement all depend" (46). Her analysis complicates how we measure Rousey's cultural impact, the badgirl turned femininely badass, because ultimately the fantasy of the limitless autonomous subject is just that—a fantasy.[5]

On the one hand, Rousey played an active role in creating new cultural possibilities. Her influence, especially during her nascent UFC career, was ubiquitous. A popular Halloween costume in 2015 for females of all ages was dressing in Rousey's UFC fight gear (MMA Junkie, "So, Ronda Rousey"). Beyoncé Knowles, a cultural force in her own right, opened her "Diva" performance in Philadelphia with audio of Rousey's DNB monologue. Rousey's badgirl persona became an emblem for feminine strength that united women and offered them a voice. Although young badgirl Rousey may have clenched her fist, Rousey's femininely badass united women in sticking their middle fingers up at gender inequality, stereotypes, and the glass ceiling. On the other hand, Rousey's conception of the femininely badass is accompanied by a very problematic metaphor for disability that represents disabled individuals as unproductive and in need of care.

These narratives and representations influence the way people think about individuals who are differently abled. Rousey's scathing critique of the DNB is rooted in a cultural paradigm of self and other. The femininely badass posits the DNB as a dependent, disabled body in order to reassure us and Rousey herself that she is not that,[6] much like the "disabled figure in cultural discourse assures the rest of citizenry of who they are not while arousing their suspicions about who they could become" (Garland-Thomson 41). The palpable hatred evident in Rousey's discussion of the DNB is the expression of the fear that one day the fantasy of her unlimited absolute abled-bodiedness will be popped. After all, every athlete suffers injuries, and every athlete must eventually retire.

From badgirl to femininely badass, Rousey's impact on the figure of the badgirl in sports and popular culture is undeniable. Her biography points to moments that blend her natural inclination to be bad with her deliberate choices to construct a badgirl image for herself. Looking at her understanding of the femininely badass, Rousey constructs the badgirl that allowed her to create new possibilities for females. Yet her understanding of the femininely badass is not without its problems, as she also bases it largely on a problematic narrative that is often found in sports, that of overcoming obstacles through autonomous grit. Such narratives perpetuate cultural understandings of disabled individuals through metaphorical representations of the disabled body as needy, helpless, and unproductive.

Notes

1. Ronda Rousey posted this quote to her Instagram feed on August 8, 2018. She presumably found this material at www.goalcast.com/2017/05/24/top-amelia-earhart-quotes-inspire-soar/.
2. For a sense of industry growth, the recent UFC event 229 generated 2.4 million pay-per-view buys.
3. Dana White has credited Rousey's 2012 fight with Tate as being one of the deciding factors for changing his mind and starting a women's division and offering Rousey the first UFC contract for a woman.
4. Throughout *My Fight/Your Fight*, Rousey uses sarcasm and portrays her verbal exchanges as a battle of wits in order to sharpen her badgirl persona.
5. Perhaps even more telling are the connections between Garland-Thomson's argument that the invalid must be cast as effeminate while the liberal autonomous self is characterized as masculine—a move that Rousey makes by simultaneously representing the DNB as an unsexy frail form of femininity while also portraying the femininely badass as an acceptable form of sexy "masculinity."
6. As of October 16, 2018, Rousey has reinvented her DNB figure in a WWE feud with the Bella twins. On Instagram under her handle (rondarousey), she used the hashtag #Do NothingBellas to describe the twins.

Works Cited

Barthes, Roland. "The World of Wrestling." *Mythologies*. The Noonday Press, 1957, pp. 7–25.
Cepeda, Elias. "Ronda Rousey: 'I'm not a do-nothing b****.'" *Fox Sports*, 29 July 2015, www.foxsports.com/ufc/story/ronda-rousey-i-m-not-a-do-nothing-bitch-072915.
Florettarowan, "Ronda Rousey vs Julia Budd." *Dailymotion*. Dec. 26, 2016, www.dailymotion.com/video/x2ocx2d.
Foucault, Michel. *Ethics: Subjectivity and Truth*. The New Press, 1994.
Garland-Thomson, Rosemarie. *Extraordinary Bodies: Figuring Physical Disability in American Culture and Literature*. Columbia UP, 1997.
Google. "Ask and Answer: Ronda Rousey." www.google.com//ask.fm/askfm.
Holden, Eric. "Miesha 'Cupcake' Tate Explains Her New Nickname." *Prefix*, 21 Aug. 2012, www.prefixmag.com/news/miesha-cupcake-tate-explains-her-new-nickname/68196/.
Kurchak, Sarah. "'Rowdy' Roddy Piper Talks About Handing His Nickname Over to Ronda Rousey." *Fightland Blog*, 3 Jan. 2014, www.fightland.vice.com/blog/rowdy-roddy-piper-talks-about-handing-his-nickname-over-to-ronda-rousey.
MMA Junkie staff. "So, Ronda Rousey Was a Pretty Popular Halloween Costume." *MMA Junkie*. 1 Nov. 2015, www.mmajunkie.com/2015/11/so-ronda-rousey-was-a-pretty-popular-halloween-costume.
———. "'All Access Video': White Says Rousey Would Likely Be First Female UFC Fighter." *MMA Junkie*. 9 Aug. 2012, mmajunkie.com/2012/08/all-access-video-white-says-rousey-would-likely-be-first-female-ufc-fighter.
Rousey, Ronda, and Maria Burns Ortiz. *My Fight/Your Fight: Rousey*. Regan Arts, 2015.
Sailors, Pam, and Charlene Weaving. "Foucault and the Glamazon: The Autonomy of Ronda Rousey." *Sport, Ethics and Philosophy*, vol. 11, no. 4, 2017, pp. 428–39.
"UFC legend Ronda Rousey has hit back at WWE retirement reports after WrestleMania 35." *SportsHeadlines.News*. 28 Jan. 2019, sportsheadlines.news/2019/01/ufc-legend-ronda-rousey-has-hit-back-at-wwe-retirement-reports-after-wrestlemania-35/.
Weaving, Charlene. "Cage Fighting Like a Girl: Exploring Gender Construction in the Ultimate Fighting Championship (UFC)." *Journal of Sport Philosophy*, vol. 41, no. 1, 2013, pp. 129–42.
———, and Jessica Samson. "The Naked Truth: Disability, Sexual Objectification, and the ESPN Body Issue." *Journal of the Philosophy of Sport*, vol. 45, no. 1, 2018, pp. 83–100, doi:10.1080/00948705.2018.1427592.

The Rise, Fall and Rebirth of "The Baddest Man on the Planet"

Bad Boy Mike Tyson

BRANDY MMBAGA *and* NICK MMBAGA

"Kid Dynamite." "Iron Mike." "The baddest man on the planet." The average non-boxing fan today may know Mike Tyson from his cameos in *The Hangover* movies, but long before he ever stepped into Hollywood films, he had undergone a meteoric rise and notorious fall that seems more like a movie script than real life. Simply put, Tyson had a tumultuous career of dominant performances and vicious knockouts in the ring, as well as controversial activities outside of the sport. Tyson's quick rise to fame and high visibility created the perfect recipe for the ultimate bad boy. Being labeled a bad boy can, in some cases, work in one's favor, especially in aggressive or violent sports. A fast life, throngs of women, and a tough image, for example, often enhance notoriety. However, when athletes cross certain boundaries, as some bad boys do, they can be seen as villains or as a public threat to society. Tyson has been viewed as being a bit of both.

Although a short piece cannot capture Tyson's entire life nor every quote that points to his bad boy identity, highlights of some events and processes help to illustrate what led to Tyson's bad boy persona. His life's trajectory has included a rise, fall, and rebirth as he ascended early in his career, descended after serious personal and professional mistakes, and reemerged over time through a different medium. Because this last phase happens infrequently among fallen athletes, Tyson's story is particularly compelling.

Professional Rise

Tyson was born on June 30, 1966, in Brooklyn, New York, to a single mother and an absent father. One might argue that Tyson was destined to be a menace to society based on his upbringing of minimal parental guidance and impoverished conditions. By age 13, he had already been arrested 38 times (Tannenbaum). His way out of these circumstances was through the ring, and Tyson exploded on the boxing scene as a force to be reckoned with. Almost all of his bouts were more akin to one-sided assaults than competitive matches. He began garnering his bad boy reputation in the ring as an amateur by knocking out many competitors, an uncommon occurrence in such ranks. As a teen, he added to his reputation during his run through the New York boxing circuit and punching his way to gold medals in the 1981 and 1982 Junior Olympic Games. When he turned pro at age 18, he was already being celebrated and described as a living legend.

Tyson carried his raw talent as an amateur to his professional career. His 1986 match up against Marvis Frasier, son of boxing legend Joe Frasier, became one of his most noteworthy fights because of Frasier's record and family legacy. Tyson knocked out the younger Frasier in less than 20 seconds. This event was not an anomaly as during his first year as a professional he knocked out 26 of 28 opponents, often in three minutes or less. At age 20, with his victory over Trevor Berbick, Tyson fulfilled his late trainer's prediction of one day being a heavyweight champion. In this fight, Tyson won in the second round with a technical knock-out (TKO). This was no small feat as Berbick arrived at the fight as the reigning champion and possessed more years of experience than Tyson. Making history as the youngest heavyweight champion (a record he still holds) was a pivotal event that afforded Tyson tremendous recognition, but with relentless drive, Tyson solidified his undisputed reputation in 1987 when he became the first ever heavyweight boxer to hold all three titles—the World Boxing Council (WBC), World Boxing Association (WBA), and International Boxing Federation (IBF)—at the same time. In essence, Tyson's fame rivaled other great fighters from New York who rose out of poverty, including Carmen Basillo, Ray Robinson, and Rocky Graziano. During this ascension, several reports described Tyson as the next great New York heavyweight (Berger). He had built a fierce reputation and a strong fan base in a very short span of time.

Professional and Personal Fall

Despite his successes in the ring, Tyson's willingness to fight dirty, break rules, and harm others precipitated his fall and placed him at the top of the list of bad boys. He became a predator during several infamous fights. For example, during a boxing bout with Lou Savarese, Tyson attacked his opponent even after the referee stopped the action during the bout. Also, in a match against Francois Botha, Tyson used illegal tactics that resulted in a brawl between cornermen, the people who give fighters instructions during a bout. One of the most notable altercations in the ring was his rematch against Evander Holyfield in June 1997. In that bout, Tyson bit Holyfield's ear—twice. Even after the fight was stopped because of Tyson's unsteadiness and antics, he continued to lunge toward Holyfield with the intention of getting in some off-the-record punches. Commentators watched in sheer disbelief, stating they have never witnessed anything like that before and asserting that his actions showed desperation and instability. During interviews following the fight, Tyson did not appear to be remorseful but instead continued to show total disregard for his opponent. After the Holyfield fight, more was written about Tyson's bad boy tactics than ever before, and the boxing commission withheld the $30 million purse pending an official review. As a result, Tyson's life was in disarray, culminating in bankruptcy and an arrest for possessing cocaine.

Throughout his career, Tyson's life outside of boxing did not always match his professional ascension. In particular, Tyson has a troubling and often violent record with women. The roots of this very well may have stemmed from the fact that his mother ran a brothel out of his childhood home. Although these living conditions arose from financial necessity in a neighborhood that did not have many monetary resources to offer, it is fair to say that it contributed in no small part to the contentious relationships with women he has had for much of his life. For instance, he married actress Robin Givens in 1988, but within a year, Givens reported that Tyson had physically and sexually abused her. In a highly publicized interview with Barbara Walters, Givens, with Tyson sitting right beside her, alleged that her relationship with Tyson was life threatening. The two divorced in 1989. Tyson was vilified as a result of the divorce from Givens, and he was subsequently more widely known as an abusive husband than as a great boxer. This event added to his bad boy moniker (Gross).

Another situation that largely cemented his negative reputation was a felony conviction for raping Desiree Washington. Washington, who was a contestant in the Miss Black America pageant, accused Tyson of raping her in 1991. A college student at Rhode Island at the time, Washington agreed to be Tyson's date at a concert. Washington claimed that Tyson forced himself on her when they returned to his room to retrieve something that he forgot. She stated that Tyson told her to relax and proceeded to carry out the rape, and doctors confirmed that sexual activity had taken place. Tyson refuted her story, saying that she lied, suggesting that the sexual encounter was consensual and that she was accusing him for personal gain. Other women participating in the beauty pageant nonetheless supported Washington's testimony and stated that Tyson had been inappropriate in conversations with them (Berkow, "Sports of The Times"). During the lead-up to the trial, Tyson was depicted as a "crude, sexual brute" (Sharpley-Whiting 52). Ultimately, he was convicted of rape and two counts of sexual deviancy and sentenced to three years in prison. This episode constituted the top story of 1992 (Sharpley-Whiting 47).

The Givens and Washington cases were widely broadcasted, but two other women also sued Tyson for sexual abuse and defamation. The cumulative effects of these cases resulted in a reoccurring narrative of Tyson as a convicted rapist, noted for crossing moral and legal boundaries and for not taking responsibility for his actions. Such narratives led to his stigmatization.

The Media

Make no mistake, Tyson was a bad boy, with or without anyone watching. The media, however, played a role in crafting his persona by dehumanizing him and dramatizing his narrative. They painted a picture of his aggression and his supposedly animalistic nature, exaggerating stereotypes that spectators held about him. This ultimately gave him even more visibility and coverage because Tyson was considered "must see tv." Media coverage adhered to the pattern noted in a study that suggests being a black, male celebrity was a liability. Biased coverage depicted Tyson as primitive, echoing similar narratives written in the early 1900s about Jack Johnson, the first black heavyweight champion who generated significant controversy in his defeats of white opponents, his fast and famous lifestyle, and his interracial relations with white women (Eligon and Thorp).

Tyson made it very easy for reporters to sensationalize his story by giving them material that begged to become leading articles. In fact, many of Tyson's quotes still possess shock value, twenty plus years later. He would sometimes express homophobia, biases and aggression—all engulfed in profanity, such as "I'll put your mother in a straitjacket, you punk ass white boy.... I'll fuck you in the ass until you love me, faggot.... You're such a little white pussy, scared of a real man. You wouldn't last a day in my world, bitch!" (qtd. in Michell). Tyson thrust these words at a sportswriter after one of his fights. Such outlandish and offensive rhetoric made him an easy target and actually incentivized the media to write more sensational stories.

A review of *New York Times* articles from 1980 to 2009 helps to illustrate the coverage that featured Tyson. The media certainly did not make up the information, nor were they the sole or overarching cause for Tyson's bad boy status. However, media coverage did indeed play a central role in the process of creating what many know as Tyson, the bad boy, because they controlled both how much information was disseminated about him, as well as the content provided to the public. Tyson was an alluring figure for the media to follow and sensationalize due to his extreme success and provocative actions.

Two primary types of portrayals emerged from the media review. One type presented Tyson as an object of fascination who scintillated audiences with his pugilistic ability and prowess in the ring. His shrewd and raw comments before fights made him irresistible to the press and allowed him to draw large numbers to the box office (Berkow, "BOXING") and a significant amount of press coverage around the world. Such stories provided facts about Tyson and portrayed him as one of the most talented heavyweights in the sport since the great George Foreman. In essence, these articles were largely unbiased and neutral in tone and most importantly did not conflate Tyson's antics outside the ring with his performance inside the squared circle.

The second type of portrayal "depicted him as a savage and decidedly inhumane beast" (Lule 182). Many writers described Tyson as a helpless and confused person who had little control or empathy for women (Lipsyte; Berger; Lule; Berkow, "BOXING"). Tyson was characterized as a man who lacked agency and instead relied purely on his animal instincts. Some of these articles referred to him as "psycho pup," a fragile, yet violent creature that was a "public health menace" (Lipsyte). The boxer was also largely portrayed as "a criminal" (Berkow, "BOXING") who lashed out at the world and media. Very different from articles that celebrated Tyson's accomplishments, these stories grabbed audience attention by drawing connections between Tyson's violent actions inside the ring and his eruptions outside the ring. Together, the two types of portrayals created an image of Tyson as both an astonishing fighter and menacing figure whose life seemed to be heading toward an abrupt, dramatic, and potentially violent ending, similar to the fate of his foes in the ring.

Other reports celebrated Tyson's failures in and out of the ring (Eskenazi). For example, Dave Anderson's 1992 article relegated Tyson to a prison number (922335) and described him as a "jail house celebrity" who was humiliated and fell into a violent pattern of boxing's bright stars. Others described the fighter as a firecracker and suggested that he had never learned how to control his self-destructive instincts (Anderson; Scott). Even after Tyson served his time in prison for the rape of Washington, some writers denied that he had become a redeemed man. These reports suggested that celebrating his release would send a "dangerous message to all people" but especially women of color (Nelson). Upon his release from prison, Tyson lamented how a documentary portrayed various aspects of his life, including his rape conviction. He stated, "[W]hen I went to prison, I lost my humanity, I lost my reputation, I lost everything I had worked for" (Garnham). To many in the media, Tyson was beyond redemption, likely because animals cannot be redeemed, only controlled or contained.

Categorization, Reputation, Identity, and Stigma

Media generated some clear generalizations about Tyson that they relayed to the public. He was considered violent because of his malicious acts inside the ring, such as biting Holyfield's ear. He was also viewed as violent because of his actions outside the ring. For example, Tyson physically assaulted one of his opponents, Mitch Green, in a street fight prior to their boxing bout, giving Mitch a black eye and fracturing his right hand. Tyson was charged with simple assault and received negative press coverage. He was also considered uncontrollable because of his flagrant disregard for the law, particularly for lewd acts committed against others, especially young women. In the broadest sense, Tyson departed from social norms (Hogg and Reid) and acted in socially unacceptable ways. As a result, he was labeled and vilified. A theory from social psychology, termed *categorization theory*, can help to highlight why negative attention followed Tyson despite his best efforts to change this characterization.

According to categorization theory, people cast others into buckets or clusters using general characteristics associated with certain groups (Tajfel). For example, it is common to categorize people based on gender, age, nationality, race, and moral character because such characteristics are fairly easy to discern. Categories are used to make an assessment about a person and allow people to process information or situations about a person more easily. One consequence of being categorized is that once a person has been associated with a category, it may be difficult for others to remove generalizations held about that person, or a person's actions can be overstated. Categories, in turn, elicit stereotypes that can be a pretext for discrimination, mischaracterization, and even abuse.

Another consequence of being categorized is that it can result in a person becoming an outgroup member. Tyson was considered an outgroup member because he was a convicted black felon who grew up in poverty and participated in a violent sport. Because of his outgroup status, many, including the media, discounted his past accomplishments. For example, in multiple publications, Tyson was not included in a roster of top heavyweights despite having similar accolades as those who appeared on the list. In another example, renowned boxing commentator and trainer Teddy Atlas, who served as one of Tyson's trainers in the 1990s, stated that Tyson was "only in five fights in his life and he lost all five fights" (qtd. in Blair), and Atlas made his comments despite the fact that Tyson's final boxing record at retirement was 50 wins and only 6 losses (44 wins coming by knock out). In short, Tyson's actions led others to classify him as one of the bad guys in sports. People who opposed Tyson viewed him in a particularly negative light, leading to increased scrutiny and dramatic narratives that were disproportionately critical. Ultimately, this tainted his reputation, transforming him from a celebrated sport figure into an infamous and notorious character.

Reputation Matters

A reputation is established by a collection of interconnected impressions shared by a large consensus of individuals. In essence, a reputation is a shared social impression (Bromley 36). Future predictions of an individual's behavior are largely assumed based upon behaviors associated with the subscribed reputation of that person. It is widely acknowledged that many of Tyson's foes were defeated before they ever stepped into the ring because his reputation as a bad boy created an aura that made them afraid of Tyson. His reputation conveyed information that was not readily available nor tangible. Another point of importance is reputational spillover, which is when an individual's reputation is transferred to other individuals who share similar characteristics or with whom they are closely associated. Tyson became a contentious figure based on his own actions, but his bad boy label was also enhanced when he befriended other controversial celebrities who were also associated with violence, sexual misconduct, corruption, and divisive or controversial ideologies and identities. Other celebrity bad boys Tyson has been paired with include Bobby Brown, Robert Downey, Jr., Spike Lee, Rick James, Donald Trump, Tupac, Suge Knight, and Paul Hogan, to name a few. Like Tyson, many of his celebrity associates have been involved in activities such as tax fraud, drug addiction, gun violence, and more. These individuals' reputations spilled over to Tyson, and vice-versa, further solidifying his persona.

Reputations are not solely comprised of a person's actions, but also are behaviors anticipated or embedded within a person's identity. Therefore, Tyson's perceived behaviors were largely a part of how audiences viewed his reputation as a bad boy and how they assumed he would behave. For instance, a 2005 experimental study tested perceptions of who would more likely be viewed as a rapist. Participants in the study read a fictitious news story recounting a rape; the race of the accused perpetrator was varied (either black or white), as well as the celebrity status (either a celebrity or not). The study found that race was a liability for a black male celebrity in comparison to a white male celebrity, whose race was an asset (Knight et al.). Tyson's identity as a black male celebrity played a role in dramatizing his actions.

Other scholarly work has noted that historical representations of black male athletes have identified them as "hypersexual criminals," an association that still influences contemporary perceptions (Tucker 307). In this same vein, other scholars have noted that American perceptions of black male and female sexual politics brand them as animalistic and vulgar and that black males are seen as "natural rapists" (Sharpley-Whiting 48; Worden and Carlson). As some experts have recognized, Tyson's actions did not solely lead to his infamous reputation. Other factors, such as his role as a professional fighter and his brutal efficiency, his race, and his celebrity status, catalyzed a "spoiled" identity (Goffman). In other words, multiple stigmata attached to Tyson that resulted in negative stereotypes.

Religious Stigma

Tyson has been quite vocal on his religious viewpoints. In his commentary regarding religion, he has discussed his opinion of Christian hypocrisy. He notes that Christians do not accept him or try to reach out to him and that they would rather throw him in jail. Tyson gained no Christian approbation when he alluded to his willingness to fight Jesus if they were ever to be physically in the same room. Furthermore, Tyson has openly identified as a Muslim, a religion that is highly marginalized and met with disdain by many in the United States. The practice of Islam has been conflated with extremist ideology and Islamophobia and at times has become synonymous with terms such as terrorism and violence (Gottschalk and Greenberg 42). For instance, a recent poll found that just under half of Americans have positive or "warm" feelings toward Islam. Hence, public sentiment in the U.S. held toward those who practice Islam, such as Tyson, are generally more negative than positive.

Allowing no ambiguity about his religion, Tyson regularly and openly praised Allah after most of his bouts. He uttered one of the most infamous quotes in an interview with Jim Gray immediately after his fight against Lennox Lewis in 2002: "I'm the best ever. I'm the most brutal and vicious, and most ruthless champion there's ever been.... My style is impetuous, my defense is impregnable, and I'm just ferocious. I want your heart! I want to eat his children! Praise be to Allah!" (qtd. in Linneweber). Instead of answering the reporter's questions, he verbally attacked his opponent and touted himself and his prowess in a gruesome, intimidating way. In the midst of that tirade, he also calls to Allah. By acknowledging and praising Allah, in addition to exhibiting extreme behaviors within the ring, Tyson used rhetoric that fostered and nurtured negative stereotypes that often envelop Islam and radicalism.

Though one of the bedrock principles of the United States is freedom of religion, the Islamic faith has been slow to receive acceptance in the U.S. In essence, this is another example of how Tyson distinguished himself from the general American public, thus attaching himself to a less accepted group, or outgroup, based on his religious beliefs. Being Muslim was taboo because he operated outside the social norms of religion in the U.S. His association with Islam, pre- and post-9/11 attacks, helped classify him as a bad boy.

The Rebirth: Modern Day Mike Tyson

It is not often that people, in general, especially black male celebrities, are granted a second chance at acceptance. Yet, Tyson has managed to work his way back into the mainstream and is now regarded in a more positive light. Over time, media narratives about Tyson changed. His recognition of his own menacing actions led to his rebirth, and this captivated a new generation of audiences. His role in popular movies such as *The Hangover* series and his critically acclaimed documentary *Tyson* catapulted him into a place of recognition. It has been in media such as these that narratives about him moved from negative to positive.

Tyson's reemergence was marked by tragedy: the unexpected loss of his four-year-old daughter in a 2009 incident inside his home. This horrific misfortune made Tyson appear to be a more normal person. It also led many in the general public to sympathize with him because of his openness and candor about the events that led to his tragic loss. Tyson has also been very candid about his struggles with depression and thoughts of suicide, both very relatable conditions. As a result, Tyson was seen less as a member of an outgroup and more as a person who deserved empathy. In addition, he changed his life by being committed to sobriety and a healthy lifestyle, an effort that was documented and witnessed on popular TV shows, such as his 2011 appearance on *The Ellen DeGeneres Show*. This further solidified his status as a member of society who had changed and rehabilitated himself. He had rejoined the norms of society. In essence, Tyson moved to an ingroup status because his actions exemplified socially acceptable behaviors.

As mentioned above, Tyson had cameo appearances in *The Hangover* (2009) and *The Hangover Part II* (2011). Playing himself, he was still largely characterized as a bad boy, but this time it was in a comedic sense. Using Tyson as a parody removed some of the previous undesirable bad boy characterizations. Tyson also appeared on *The Tonight Show* with Jimmy Kimmel in 2017. In scenarios such as live talk television, he had opportunities to craft a more humorous persona. He became a more approachable character with his witty comments, charismatic personality, and relevant stories. Even the tribal tattoo on the left side of his face, which was initially seen as outlandish and emblematic of his already existing radical and aggressive identity, was normalized through its humorous depiction in *The Hangover Part II*.

It is apparent from Tyson's appearances in movies and television shows that he is still a relevant topic of discussion and still worthy of media coverage. To this day, media still refers to Tyson's physical strength as a metaphor to explain something that is strong and heavy hitting. For instance, in 2018, when Hurricane Florence hit the United States East Coast, reporters and meteorologists alike described the hurricane as having a "Mike Tyson–like punch" to explain the intensity of the storm's impact as it struck land. In social media, he was featured in a video that went viral after he fell off a hoverboard. The fall led to some back injuries, but the video received millions of views. This "epic fail" painted him, once again, as a normal, mortal guy and even added a comedic twist because he was the butt of the joke. Perhaps marking a culmination of Tyson's rebirth, as of 2019, a biopic of Tyson's life is reportedly in the works with actor Jamie Foxx set to play Tyson.

Concluding Thoughts on Tyson

As previously noted, Tyson's life has been riddled with unacceptable actions that have stigmatized him as a bad boy. He even labeled himself as the "baddest man on the planet," suggesting agreement with that identity. Other factors, nevertheless, also contributed to the creation of Tyson's label as a bad boy. By simply being a boxer, Tyson was automatically classified as aggressive, tough, and violent. This stigma led to his personal life being viewed as more likely to involve violence and other stereotypical negative activities. His stigmatized identity was reinforced when details about his relationship with his ex-wife Givens, which purportedly included domestic violence, were brought into the public realm. The media can set agendas, frame stories, and broadcast narratives in a way that exaggerates actions and commentary to create a compelling story and further villainize an individual, especially when that person is a black male celebrity. In sum, multiple factors aided in the construction of Tyson's bad boy persona and others who have been in the ring. Boxers are seen as tough and violent; they are rich and sexually active due to clusters of available women. Boxers frequently associate with others who are just as controversial and have also been branded as bad boys. Therefore, boxers are often projected as bad boys based upon their sport and the perks that come with success.

Even with this bad boy label, Tyson has managed to work hard to get a second chance at acceptance and approval. This rebirth can be attributed to a number of reasons. For one, Tyson was a great boxer; he became a legend by dominating his way to historic wins and did so unapologetically. And as much as the world may have wanted to expunge his legacy, greatness is a difficult thing to erase. Another reason for his redemption is his authenticity. Many people may not have agreed with his statements or approved of his rhetoric, but Tyson was himself to the core, and that included his brutal honesty. A quick internet search can lead one to several blogs that note authenticity and honesty as preferred and admirable traits in an individual. Tyson also strived to change his image in his modern-day media appearances. He has curtailed his use of obscenity; he has capitalized on his tough, bad boy image in a way that is more accepted by the mainstream (such as his role in *The Hangover* series); and he has communicated those changes and his personal growth quite effectively. For instance, Tyson has given advice that greatness constitutes being accepted by the people, not guarding oneself from the people. He has also acknowledged that being belligerent and fighting were not the best ways to make a statement. Tyson has additionally shared some motivational statements such as "I have to dream and reach for the stars, and if I miss a star then I grab a handful of clouds."

Boxing is still the sweet science. It is still capable of making one love the bad guy or wish for his downfall. Boxing still leaves spectators on the edge of their seats, wondering who will win, in what round, and with what decision. For a sport full of bad guys, the ability to accomplish so much is impressive. Tyson embodied the culture of boxing, both the good and the bad. He was a master scientist at the sweet science. He had a followership that was unbreakable, as well as a sea of doubters and nay-sayers. Tyson left people on the edge of their seats after every round; oftentimes, that was only one round. In the words of Martin Scorsese, "Mike Tyson's life is one of the most amazing American stories."

Tyson was a bad boy; he is a bad boy. And he cannot seem to completely outrun that label, though it is now reflected in a more positive light. For a majority of his life, he has been simultaneously celebrated and cursed. He transcended the highly stigmatized version of bad boy to become the iconic Hall-of-Famer bad boy. He is a cultural legend, not just within the boxing culture, but within the American culture. Tyson is still a force to be reckoned with and still weighs in as one of the most feared boxers in history.

Works Cited

Anderson, Dave. "Sports of The Times; The Humiliation of No. 922335 Mike Tyson." *The New York Times*, 29 Mar. 1992, www.nytimes.com/1992/03/29/sports/sports-of-the-times-the-humiliation-of-no-922335-mike-tyson.html.

Berger, Phil. "Tyson in Domestic Dispute." *The New York Times*, 4 Oct. 1988, www.nytimes.com/1988/10/04/sports/tyson-in-domestic-dispute.html.
Berkow, Ira. "BOXING; Tyson Remains An Object of Fascination." *The New York Times*, 21 May 2002, www.nytimes.com/2002/05/21/sports/boxing-tyson-remains-an-object-of-fascination.html.
_____. "Sports of The Times; Tyson Is a Role Model in Reverse." *The New York Times*, 11 Aug. 1991, www.nytimes.com/1991/08/11/sports/sports-of-the-times-tyson-is-a-role-model-in-reverse.html.
Blair, Alex. "Teddy Atlas argues why Mike Tyson wasn't a great fighter." News.com.au. 26 Sept. 2018, www.news.com.au/sport/boxing/teddy-atlas-argues-why-mike-tyson-wasnt-a-great-fighter/news-story/f335f1d85819ba67f41b00f6ede92cc3.
Bromley, Dennis Basil. *Reputation, Image and Impression Management*. John Wiley & Sons, 1993.
Eligon, John, and Brandon K. Thorp. "Missed in Coverage of Jack Johnson, the Racism Around Him." *The New York Times*, 24 May 2018, www.nytimes.com/2018/05/24/sports/jack-johnson-racism.html.
Eskenazi, Gerald. "The Bully Gets Bullied, And the Underdog Reigns." *The New York Times*, 11 Nov. 1996, www.nytimes.com/1996/11/11/sports/the-bully-gets-bullied-and-the-underdog-reigns.html.
Garnham, Emily. "Mike Tyson: The Movie Sparks Furious Backlash." Express.co.uk, 6 Apr. 2009, www.express.co.uk/entertainment/films/93800/Mike-Tyson-The-Movie-sparks-furious-backlash.
Goffman, Erving. *Stigma: Notes on the Management of Spoiled Identity*. Englewood Cliffs, NJ: Prentice-Hall, 1963.
Gottschalk, Peter, and Gabriel Greenberg. *Islamophobia: Making Muslims the Enemy*. Rowman & Littlefield, 2008.
Gross, Ken. "A Life on the Brink." PEOPLE.com, Time Inc, 26 Sept. 1988, people.com/archive/cover-story-a-life-on-the-brink-vol-30-no-13/.
Hogg, Michael A., and Scott A. Reid. "Social identity, Self-Categorization, and the Communication of Group Norms." *Communication Theory*, vol. 16, no. 1, 2006, pp. 7–30.
Knight, Jennifer L., Traci A. Giuliano, and Monica G. Sanchez-Ross. "Famous or Infamous? The Influence of Celebrity Status and Race on Perceptions of Responsibility for Rape." *Basic and Applied Social Psychology*, vol. 23, no. 3, 2001, pp. 183–90.
Linneweber, Colin. "Mike Tyson Had the Best Quote of the Past Decade." *Bleacher Report*, 18 Feb. 2010, bleacherreport.com/articles/348174-the-seven-best-quotes-of-the-2000s.
Lipsyte, Robert. "Will the Real Tyson Stand Up?" *The New York Times*, 28 June 1991, www.nytimes.com/1991/06/28/sports/robert-lipsyte-will-the-real-tyson-stand-up.html.
Lule, Jack. "The rape of Mike Tyson: Race, the press and symbolic types." *Critical Studies in Media Communication*, vol. 12, no. 2, 1995, pp. 176–195.
Mitchell, Kevin. "The madness of Mike Tyson." *The Guardian*, 26 Jan. 2002, www.theguardian.com/sport/2002/jan/27/boxing.comment.
Nelson, Jill. "Not Ready for Redemption." *The New York Times*, 17 June 1995, www.nytimes.com/1995/06/17/opinion/not-ready-for-redemption.html.
Scott, A. O. "Violence Embodied in a Boxer's Rise and Fall." *The New York Times*, 23 Apr. 2009, www.nytimes.com/2009/04/24/movies/24tyso.html?mtrref=www.google.com&gwh=B5 A22E3604D518A5D75F4CB0F54EC944&gwt=pay.
Sharpley-Whiting, T. Denean. "When a Black Woman Cries Rape: Discourses of Unrapeability, Intraracial Sexual Violence, and the *State of Indiana v. Michael Gerard Tyson*." In *Spoils of War: Women of Color, Cultures, and Revolutions*, edited by Renée T. White and Denean T. Sharpley-Whiting. Rowman & Littlefield, 1997, pp. 45–57.
Tajfel, Henri. "Social Psychology of Intergroup Relations." *Annual Review of Psychology*, vol. 33, no. 1, 1982, pp. 1–39.
Tannenbaum, Rob. "Mike Tyson on Ditching Club Life and Getting Sober." *Rolling Stone*, 4 Dec. 2013, www.rollingstone.com/culture/culture-news/mike-tyson-on-ditching-club-life-and-getting-sober-56592.
Tucker, Linda. "Blackballed: Basketball and Representations of the Black Male Athlete." *Amer-

ican Behavioral Scientist, vol. 47, no. 3, Nov. 2003, pp. 306–28, doi:10.1177/0002764203256189.

Worden, Alissa Pollitz, and Bonnie E. Carlson. "Attitudes and Beliefs About Domestic Violence: Results of a Public Opinion Survey: II. Beliefs about Causes." *Journal of Interpersonal Violence*, vol. 20, no. 10, 2005, pp. 1219–43.

About the Contributors

Brock T. **Adams** earned a Ph.D. in interpersonal communication from Louisiana State University and is assistant professor in professional sales at Weber State University. His research on listening and the adaptive misunderstandings through technology has been published in the *Journal of Language and Social Psychology*, as well as the *Journal of Social and Personal Relationships*.

Joseph M.M. **Aldinger** earned a Ph.D. from the State University of New York at Buffalo and is a Marion L. Brittain Fellow at Georgia Institute of Technology. He is the managing and technical editor for the *Journal for Cultural and Religious Theory*, where he published the article "Sport's Narratives: *The Crash Reel* and Disability Theory." His interdisciplinary research areas include business communication, digital pedagogy, disability studies, and early modern poetry.

Donna J. **Barbie** earned a Ph.D. from Emory University and is an associate dean of the College of Arts and Sciences and a professor of humanities and communication at Embry-Riddle Aeronautical University in Daytona Beach, Florida. Her publications in celebrity and cultural studies include the monograph *The Making of Sacagawea* and an edited collection, *The Tiger Woods Phenomenon*.

Sarah D. **Fogle** earned an MA from the University of Florida and is a professor of humanities and communication at Embry-Riddle Aeronautical University in Daytona Beach, Florida. She has published articles in *Crime Fiction and Film in the Sunshine State* and *The Tiger Woods Phenomenon*. She is a coeditor of *Minette Walters and the Meaning of Justice* and editor of *Martha Grimes Walks into a Pub*.

Joe **Gisondi** earned an MFA from Spalding University and is a professor of journalism at Eastern Illinois University. He regularly writes about sports, media and culture and has authored two books. *The Field Guide to Covering Sports* (2017) is used as a text for sports media classes across the country. *Monster Trek* (2015) investigates people who search for bigfoot across the United States.

Teresa Marie **Kelly** earned a BA and an MAT from Agnes Scott College and has taught at Purdue University Global since 2002. Her sports scholarship engages interdisciplinary approaches to teaching and learning using sports, studies of the role of sports narrative in the age of metrics, and the greater connections between sports and social issues. Her ongoing research explores themes relating to NASCAR and popular culture and the influence of iconic broadcaster Stuart Scott on the language of sports.

John C. **Lamothe** earned a Ph.D. from the University of Central Florida and is an associate professor of humanities and communication at Embry-Riddle Aeronautical University in Daytona Beach, Florida. He has written and spoken widely about a variety of issues related to athletics, including an essay in *The Tiger Woods Phenomenon*. His dissertation addresses how culture rhetorically constructs arguments about performance-enhancing technologies in sports. He is a coeditor of the forthcoming collection *Beyond Binaries: Trans Identities in Contemporary Culture*.

Ismael **Lopez Medel** earned a Ph.D. from Central European University and is an associate professor of communication at Azusa Pacific University in Azusa, California, where he designed and directs the undergraduate program in public relations. He has held academic and administrative positions in Spain and the United States and has had visiting teaching experiences across Europe. His research in the fields of advertising, social media, and public relations has been published internationally.

Steve **Master** earned an MS from Northwestern University's Medill School of Journalism and is an associate professor of communication and humanities at Embry-Riddle Aeronautical University in Daytona Beach, Florida. He has worked as a sportswriter for the *Daytona Beach News-Journal*, and as a columnist for *NASCAR Illustrated*. He has published an essay in *The Tiger Woods Phenomenon* and co-authored "Sally Jenkins Speaks Against NOW and for New Waves of Feminism" in *Studies in Popular Culture*.

Jessica **McKee** earned a Ph.D. from the University of South Florida and is an associate professor of humanities and communication at Embry-Riddle Aeronautical University in Daytona Beach, Florida, where she teaches courses on literature, film, music and culture. Her research explores representations of race and gender in contemporary culture. She is the coeditor, with Michael V. Perez, of the collection *Billie Holiday: Essays on the Artistry and Legacy* (2019).

Taylor Joy **Mitchell** earned a Ph.D. from the University of South Florida and is an associate professor of humanities at Embry-Riddle Aeronautical University in Daytona Beach, Florida. Her research explores the inextricable relationships among sexuality, gender, and race in popular media. She co-authored "Sally Jenkins Speaks Against NOW and for New Waves of Feminism" in *Studies in Popular Culture* and analyzes the so-called liberalization of sports media.

Brandy **Mmbaga** earned a Ph.D. from the University of Tennessee. Her areas of research include organizational behavior, receiver-based communication, social media and reputation. She teaches a variety of courses on leadership and business & professional development. Whenever possible, she incorporates sports as a context, studying the outcomes and role of social media within sports.

Nick **Mmbaga** earned a Ph.D. from the University of Tennessee. His teaching and research focus primarily on areas of entrepreneurship, reputation, and stigma. As a previously active boxer, he integrates the boxing context into his work of strategic business decisions and stigma.

About the Contributors

Lynnette **Porter** earned a Ph.D. from Bowling Green State University and is a professor in humanities and communication at Embry-Riddle Aeronautical University in Daytona Beach, Florida. She has authored or co-authored more than 20 books and 25 chapters, many about popular culture and fandom, and has been a frequent speaker at academic conferences and fan conventions internationally. She has been a contributing editor for *PopMatters* and an editor of *Studies in Popular Culture*.

Index

Aaron, Hank 99
ABC 61, 65, 115, 155, 156
addiction 4, 35, 37, 38, 40, 81, 86, 87, 214
advertisements 47, 69, 115, 139, 140, 142, 154–156, 186; California Milk Producers 154; Gatorade 115; Head and Shoulders 186; Nike 115, 188; Victoria's Secret 154–155
Aguirre, Mark 149
Albright, Madeline 157
Ali, Muhammad 157, 187
Allison, Bobby 130, 135
Allison, Davey 135, 141
Allison, Donnie 129–130
Alou, Felipe 100
American Civil Liberties Union (ACLU) 187
American dream 47, 180, 181, 204, 205
Amnesty International 188
Anderson, Garret 98
Anderson, Greg 101
apology 54, 55–57, 59, 65, 81, 103, 106–107, 119, 122, 123, 136, 158, 166
Armstrong, Lance 47, 55, 58, 68–69
Army 180, 188
Arnold, Patrick 101
arrests 5, 52, 53, 54, 61, 102, 118–119, 125, 170, 185, 209, 210; *see also* convictions
Arroyo, Bronson 98
Artest, Ron 53, 146
Associated Press 65, 100
Atlas, Teddy 213–214
Augusta National Golf Club 32, 33
Australian Professional Golf Association 34
autobiography 10, 15, 19, 20, 21, 54, 56, 73, 89, 120, 139, 140, 155, 170; *see also* memoir

badness 1–4, 120
Baiul, Oksana 12
Bakes, Anicka 155
Baldwin, James 182
ballet 15, 16, 18, 152
Balotelli, Mario 80
Barkley, Charles 52, 121

Barthes, Roland 198–199, 201
baseball 3, 5–6, 46, 47, 54, 95–109, 114, 131, 164, 179, 180; Little League World Series 46; *see also* Major League Baseball
Basillo, Carmen 209
basketball 3, 6, 44, 45, 46, 47, 52, 53, 121, 124, 146–159; Harlem Globetrotters 158; *see also* National Basketball Association
Baszler, Shayna 200
Bay-Area Laboratory Co-Operative (BALCO) 5, 48–51, 52, 53, 57, 101, 102, 106
Bean, Butter 157
Beatty, Ned 129
Belbin, Tanith 13
Belichick, Bill 117
Bell, Kimberly 102
Berbick, Trevor 209
Berenger, Tom 156
Bergeron, Tom 61
Best, George 90
bias 12, 125, 162–163, 166, 169, 172, 204, 211
bigotry 3, 180, 183; *see also* racism
Bilardo, Carlos 90
Biogenesis of America 103, 106
Black Panthers 187
Black Power Movement 182, 187
Blackman, James 163
blasting 172
bobsledding 14
Bochy, Bruce 117
Bonds, Barry 5–6, 58, 95–109
Boorstin, Daniel 157
Botha, Francois 210
boxing 4, 63, 148, 183, 204, 208–218; Fight of the Century 182–183; heavyweight 115, 182, 186, 202, 209, 211, 212, 213
Brady, Tom 113, 117, 185–186
Bridges, Jeff 129
Brock, Jim 104
Brown, Bobby 214
Brown, James 187
Brown, Jim 157

225

226 Index

Browne, Travis 202
Bryant, Kobe 53–54, 56, 57
Buck, Joe 106
Buckner, Bill 98
Bumgarner, Madison 117
Burger King 164
Burke, Cheryl 61
Busch, Kurt 128, 129, 143
Busch, Kyle 128, 129
Bush, Billy 64, 68
Bush, George 89
Bush, George W. 46
Byrd, James 159

Camus, Albert 124
Cano, Robinson 105
Canseco, Jose 47, 101
Cantona, Eric 80
Carlos, John 181–182
Carlos, Roberto 92
Carney, Jay 158
Castro, Fidel 87, 89
categorization theory 213
CBS 19, 33, 129, 155, 183
celebrity 1–4, 6, 8, 19, 22, 24, 25, 29, 41, 72, 152, 153, 155, 156–157, 159, 165, 168, 201, 211, 212, 214–215, 216, 217
Chamberlin, Wilt 155
Chambers, Dwain 49
Chávez, Hugo 89
Chen, Nathan 14, 23
Christiansen, Jayson 105
Christie, Linford 49
Church of Maradona 81, 91
Churchill, Winston 159
civil rights 157, 187
Clemens, Roger 108
Clemente, Javier 90, 91
Clinton, Hillary 186
CMT 157
CNBC 107
CNN 62, 158
coaches 10, 12, 13, 15–16, 17, 30, 32, 35, 36, 44, 47, 48, 50, 71, 72, 73, 74, 84, 91, 92, 104, 106, 107, 112, 114, 115, 116–117, 118, 122, 148, 149–150, 164, 165, 171, 179, 183, 184, 204, 205
Cobb, Ty 95–96, 99, 108, 109
Cochran, Johnny 50
codes of conduct 31, 76, 116, 179, 194; Game Operations Manual 179
Collins, Doug 188
commercials 6, 47, 84, 139, 140, 141, 142, 154, 155, 186; see also advertisements
commodification 153
Congress 101
Conte, Victor 48, 49, 50, 101
convictions 56, 72, 106, 172, 210, 211, 213; see also arrests
Cooper, Chris 48

Coppola, Guillermo 86, 88
Costas, Bob 147, 178
Costner, Kevin 95
Couric, Katie 102
Croce, Dosh 142
Croce, Jim 142
Cruijff, Hendrik 92
Cruise, Tom 129
Cruz, Ted 186
Cuomo, Chris 158
Curry, Stephen 116
cycling 47; Tour de France 47
Cyterspiller, Jorge 84

Dale Earnhardt Incorporated (DEI) 137, 138, 140
Daly, Bettye 36–37, 40
Daly, Chuck 149, 150
Daly, Dale 36
Daly, John 4–5, 8, 28–42
Daly, Paulette 36, 38
Daly, Sherrie 37
Deery, Kyle 74
Deford, Frank 147
Degeneres, Ellen 216
Delgado, Daniel 84
Diack, Lamine 57
Diamond, Dustin 157
Dilfer, Trent 176
Dillon, Austin 142
Dillon, Ty 142
DiMaggio, Joe 99
diplomacy 6, 157, 158
disability 7, 44, 45, 46, 196, 204, 205, 206
Doherty, Peter 82
dos Santos, Junior 115
Douglas, Gabby 71
Downey, Robert, Jr. 214
Drug Enforcement Administration (DEA) 103
Dukes, Jessmyn 200
Duncan, Tim 112
Durocher, Leo 114

E! 62, 75
Earnhardt, Dale, Jr. 127, 131, 137, 138, 139, 140, 142, 143
Earnhardt, Dale (Ralph), Sr. 1, 6, 8, 127–143; Intimidator 6, 127, 128–132, 134, 135, 136, 137, 138, 140, 142, 143
Earnhardt, Ralph 130, 139
Earnhardt, Teresa 137, 139, 143
Electra, Carmen 155
Elliott, Bill 34
Embiid, Joel 120–121
endorsements 47, 66, 154–155; see also sponsors
Ervin, Anthony 76
ESPN 13, 16, 65, 66, 71, 102, 107, 138, 170–171, 176, 178, 181

Index

fans 2, 4, 5, 6, 9, 11, 12, 15, 16–17, 23, 24, 25, 29, 32, 33, 39–40, 41, 45, 48, 52, 53, 54, 57, 58, 62, 70, 76, 77, 83, 87, 88, 89, 90, 91, 92, 93, 96, 97, 99, 103, 105, 106, 107, 108, 120, 122, 128, 129–130, 131, 132, 133, 134–137, 139, 140–142, 162–163, 165, 166–172, 175, 176, 178, 179, 180, 181, 183, 197, 201
Favre, Brett 135
Fédération Internationale de Football Association (FIFA) 81, 82, 89, 91, 92, 157
Federer, Roger 123
Feherty, David 39, 40
femininity 7, 13, 15, 24, 25, 47, 152, 195, 196, 202, 203–206
Ferlaino, Corriano 91
Ferrell, Will 129
Figgins, Chone 98
figure skating 4, 9–25; Grand Prix 10; U.S. Junior Championship 10; U.S. National Championship 20; Worlds 10, 20; *see also* Olympics
finances 8, 9, 62, 88, 120, 154, 168, 187, 210
Fisher, Jimbo 112, 171
Flacco, Joe 112
Flair, Ric 200
Flake, Jeff 177–178, 179
Flutie, Doug 117, 127
football 3, 4, 6–7, 16–18, 46, 76, 82, 85, 91, 112, 114, 124, 148, 163, 164, 165, 166, 167, 170, 171, 172, 176–177, 179, 183–184, 186, 188; *see also* National Collegiate Athletic Association; National Football League
Football Association 81, 82, 84
Foreman, George 212
Foucault, Michel 195, 200, 203
Foudy, Julie 63
Fowler, Ricky 32
Fox 137, 138–139
Fox News 158, 176
Fox Sports 1, 107
Fox Sports Australia 64
Foxx, Jamie 217
France, Bill, Jr. 139
Frasier, Joe 209
Frasier, Marvis 209

Galindo, Rudy 20
Gammons, Peter 102
gangsta 151
Garnett, Kevin 112
Gatorade Player of the Year 47
Geer, Jill 56
gender 2, 3, 4, 6, 8, 9–10, 12, 16, 17, 18–19, 23, 25, 71, 154, 158, 182, 195–196, 203, 204, 206, 213
Giambi, Jason 102
Giambi, Jeremy 102
Gibson, Kirk 98, 127
Gilmore, Gary 67
Ginsburg, Ruth Bader 122, 185

Givens, Robin 210–211, 217
Glamazon 195
golf 4, 28–42, 55, 57, 75, 76; Masters 31, 32, 33; Open Championship 31; Players Championship 36; U.S. Open 28, 33, 122, 123; *see also* Professional Golf Association
golf courses 28, 31, 32, 33, 34, 55; Augusta National Golf Course 32, 33; Bay Hill 28, 33; Old Course (St. Andrews) 31; Pebble Beach 28; Royal Liverpool 28
Goodell, Roger 120, 179
Gordon, Jeff 128, 129, 133, 134
Graham, Trevor 48
Gray, Jim 215
Graziano, Rocky 209
Green, Draymond 112
Green, Mitch 213
Grondona, Julio 91
Gulati, Sunil 117
gymnastics 14, 71

Hall of Fame 31, 52, 97, 103, 106, 108–109, 114, 121, 129, 130, 146, 151, 184, 185, 200, 218; Naismith Memorial Basketball Hall of Fame 52, 151; National Association for Stock Car Racing Hall of Fame 129, 130; National Baseball Hall of Fame 108–109; National Basketball Association Hall of Fame 146; World Golf Hall of Fame 31
Hamilton, Scott 22–23
Hannity, Sean 176
Harding, Tanya 11, 12
Hardy, Greg 119–120
Harmon, Butch 36
Harper, Ron 150
Harrison, Rodney 176
Harvick, Kevin 142
Havelange, Joao 91
HBO 157
Helton, Mike 139
Hernandez, Aaron 172
heroes 1, 2, 4, 6, 9, 29, 39, 57, 58, 66, 68, 69, 89, 91, 93, 125, 127, 129, 133, 135, 136, 157, 162, 163, 171, 182, 201; sports hero 9, 66, 68, 69, 127, 162, 163, 171
Hill, Brian 150
hip-hop 74, 151
Hogan, Hulk 146, 157, 199
Hogan, Paul 214
Holmes, Holly 200
Holyfield, Evander 210, 213
Hornung, Paul 185–186
Hubbell, Carl 95
Hunter, C.J. 49–50

Ibrahimovic, Zlatan 80
ice dancing 18
identity 9–10, 12, 19, 25, 31, 81, 129, 152, 167, 170, 171, 172, 177, 195, 200, 208, 213, 214–215, 217; Do Nothin' Bitches (DNB) 7, 196,

202–203, 204, 206; femininely badass absolute abled-bodiness 7, 194, 196, 202, 203–206; gender 9–10, 19
incarceration 37, 52, 56, 76, 176, 212, 215, 224; *see also* prison
Ingram, Laura 158
International Association of Athletics Federation 57
International Boxing Federation (IBF) 209
International Olympic Committee (IOC) 45, 49, 54, 55, 64, 113
Irvin, Ernie 136
Iverson, Alan 71, 146, 151

Jackson, Elroy, Jr. 129
Jackson, Phil 150, 157
Jackson, "Shoeless" Joe 95–96, 99, 108, 109
Jacobs, Regina 49
James, Lebron 112, 116, 119, 158
James, Rick 214
Jarrett, Dale 135
Jeffries, James 182–183
Jenkins, Malcolm 115
Jeter, Derek 98, 105, 135
Jett, Joan 200
Jimmy the Greek 183
Johnson, Ben 49
Johnson, Jack 182, 211
Johnson, Jimmie 127, 128, 129
Johnson, Junior 129
Jones, Bobby 32
Jones, Cullen 76
Jones, Marion 2, 5, 44–59
Jordan, Michael 147, 150, 151–152, 154, 157; "The Jordan Rules" 149
Joy, Mike 138–139
Juan Carlos I 90
Judge, Aaron 119
judo 194, 195, 204–205; World Judo Championship 194
Junior Olympic Games 209

Kaepernick, Colin 3, 7, 8, 115, 158, 175–189
Karas, Kenneth M. 52–54
Kaufman, Sarah 197–198
Kent, Jeff 104–105
Kentucky Derby 22, 24
Kenworthy, Gus 19
Kerrigan, Nancy 11, 12
Kerry, John 158
Keselowski, Brad 128
Kim, Jong-un 157, 158, 159
Kimmel, Jimmy 217
King, Billie Jean 157
King, Martin Luther 181, 183
Kinsman, Erica 165, 168–169, 170
kneeling (taking a knee) 175, 180, 187, 188
Knight, Suge 214
Knowles, Beyoncé 206
Kulwicki, Alan 135

Laimbeer, Bill 149
Lauer, Matt 64–65
Layden, Elmer 179
Leach, Mike 171
Lee, Spike 214
Lewis, Carl 49
Lewis, Lennox 215
Lezak, Jason 76
Lincecum, Tim 117
Liotta, Ray 95
Lipinski, Tara 22, 23, 24
Lochte, Ryan 5, 8, 61–77
Lombardi, Vince 114
lone wolf 204–205
Loud Mouth Golf 32, 33
Louis, Joe 183
Louis XIV 151
Lucas, John 150
Luckovich, Mike 140
Lysacek, Evan 12, 13–14, 16

Madonna 155, 156
Maduro, Nicolás 89
Mafia 80, 88
Mahorn, Ric 149
Mailer, Norman 67
Major League Baseball 54, 81, 96, 97, 100, 102, 103, 105, 106, 107, 164; American League 96; American League Championship Series 98; Anaheim Angels 98; Atlanta Braves 128; Baltimore Orioles 101; Boston Red Sox 98, 124; Brooklyn Dodgers 180; Chicago Cubs 99; Chicago White Sox 95; Cincinnati Reds 54; Cy Young Award 117; Miami Marlins 107; Most Valuable Player (MVP) 97, 102, 103, 104, 117; New York Giants 97; New York Yankees 97, 98, 105, 106, 119, 124; 1909 World Series 96; 1919 World Series 95, 96, 97, 108; Oakland A's 95; Pittsburgh Pirates 97, 104; St. Louis Cardinals 95, 99, 100; San Francisco Giants 97, 98, 100, 101, 104–105, 107, 117; Seattle Mariners 97, 102; Silver Slugger award 97; Texas Rangers 97, 164; 2002 World Series 98; 2009 World Series 97; 2014 World Series 117
Malcolm X 181
Malone, Karl 157
Manley, Dwight 154, 157
Maradona, Diego 5, 7, 80–93
marathons 46, 113; Boston 46; New York 46
Marines 67, 68
Maris, Roger 99
Markgraf, Kate 116
Marlin, Sterling 138
Marta 116
masculinity 10, 12–18, 20, 24–25, 151, 154, 176, 202, 203
Mathews, Stanley 82
Mattingly, Don 107

Index

Maxwell, Vernon 146
McCain, John 102, 177–178, 179
McDowell, Graham 28
McEwen, John 49
McGwire, Mark 99, 100, 108
McReynolds, Larry 138
McVeigh, Timothy 67
memoir 29, 33, 34, 35, 37, 40, 73, 116, 124, 194, 199; *see also* autobiography
Menotti, Cesar 90
Messi, Lionel 83, 90, 92
Meyers, Chocolate 139
military 85, 150, 176, 177, 178, 179, 180, 182, 184, 188
military academies 177; Naval Academy 177; West Point 177
Mitchell, Andrea 224
Mixed Martial Arts (MMA) 4, 195, 196, 197, 198, 200, 204, 206
Montgomery, Tim 48, 49, 50
Moon, Warren 184
moral rigor 67–68, 70, 71, 77
MTV 155, 156

Nabokov, Vladimir 123–124
narratives 1, 6, 7, 11, 30, 68, 69, 70, 81, 151, 169, 170, 178, 184, 196, 204, 205, 206, 211, 214, 216, 217; false narratives 170
national anthem 71, 89, 175, 176, 177, 178–180, 181, 182, 188; *see also* "The Star-Spangled Banner"
National Association for Stock Car Racing (NASCAR) 6, 127–131, 132, 133, 134–135, 136–143; Cup Series 127, 128, 131, 134, 135, 142, 143; Cup Series Championships 127, 128, 131; Daytona 500 127, 129, 130, 133, 135, 136–137, 138, 139, 142; National Sportsman Division Champion 130; Pepsi 400 134; Speed Weeks 135, 137, 140; Winston All-Star Race 132; Winston Cup 131, 132, 135; Xfinity series 142
National Baseball League (NBL) 108
National Basketball Association (NBA) 52, 81, 112, 115–116, 119, 120, 146, 148, 149, 150, 151, 155, 156, 159; All-Star team 52, 97, 150; All Defensive Team 150; Boston Celtics 149; Chicago Bulls 146, 149, 150, 151, 152; Dallas Mavericks 146; Defensive Player of the Year 150; Detroit Pistons 53, 146, 147, 148, 149, 151; Los Angeles Lakers 54, 57, 146, 149, 153, 155; San Antonio Spurs 146, 149, 150
National Collegiate Athletic Association (NCAA) 100, 124; Atlantic Coast Conference (ACC) 170; Atlantic Coast Conference Championships 164; Auburn University 164; Clemson University 112, 163, 165; College Football National Championship 163; College Football Playoff 164, 170; Dartmouth College 166; Florida State University 112, 163, 168, 172; Gators 163, 172; Heisman trophy 163, 164, 165, 168, 185–186; Princeton University 166, 186; Seminoles 163, 164, 168, 172; Southeastern Conference (SEC) 170–171; Tigers 163; University of Florida 163, 172; Washington State University 171
National Football League (NFL) 13, 17, 53, 81, 100, 112, 113, 115, 117, 119–120, 164, 168, 175–176, 177–179, 181, 182, 184, 185, 186–187, 188; Atlanta Falcons 178; Baltimore Ravens 119; Carolina Panthers 119, 175; Houston Oilers 179; Jacksonville Jaguars 112, 117; Minnesota Vikings 46; New England Patriots 117, 172; Oakland Raiders 149; Philadelphia Eagles 115; quarterback 7, 112, 113, 117, 163–164, 166, 167, 168, 169, 171, 175, 176, 180, 181, 183–184, 185, 186, 188; San Francisco 49ers 175–176, 181; Super Bowl 114, 117, 181, 183, 186; Tampa Bay Buccaneers 164, 166; Washington Redskins 183
nationalism 81, 114
Natural Hair Movement 187
Navy 179
NBA Properties 149
NBC 21, 22, 23, 24, 25, 64, 137, 155, 156, 176
Neymar Júnior 85
NFL Nation 181
Nicklaus, Jack 30
Niners Nation 175
Nixon, Richard 157
Norris, Ty 137
notoriety 2, 4, 5, 9, 19, 29, 47, 48, 74, 96, 105, 138, 208, 214
Novitsky, Jeff 49, 51
Nunes, Amanda 200

Obama, Barack 158, 159
Obama, Michelle 122
objectification 154
Olympics 14, 16, 17, 20, 21, 23, 24, 25, 47, 48, 49, 50, 51, 52, 55, 57, 61, 62, 63, 64–65, 69, 70–71, 73, 74, 75, 76, 100, 114, 116, 157, 181, 182, 194, 205; 1964 Summer 73; 1968 Summer 73, 181–182; 1988 Summer 49; 1992 Summer 47; 1992 Winter 52; 1996 Winter 52; protest 61, 181–182; 2000 Summer 48, 50, 51, 57; 2004 Summer 50, 57, 74, 116, 205; 2006 Winter 23; 2008 Summer 69, 194; 2010 Winter 17, 20, 24; 2012 Summer 55, 64, 67; 2014 Winter 21; 2016 Summer 24, 61, 62, 63, 64–65, 70–71, 75; 2018 Winter 25; 2020 Summer 76, 100
Osaka, Naomi 122–123
otherness 16, 147, 148, 151, 153
Ott, Mel 95

Palmeiro, Rafael 101, 108
Palmer, Arnold 39
Paralympics 44–45; 2000 Games 44

patriotism 81, 114, 175, 177–178, 179, 180, 181, 182, 188, 189
Pedro, Jim, Sr. 205
Pelé 82, 85–86, 90, 91, 92
Pereira, Thiago 63
performance-enhancing drugs (PEDs) 45, 46–47, 48, 49–50, 51, 52, 53, 54, 56, 58, 99, 100–101, 102, 103, 104, 106, 107, 108, 109, 222; anabolic steroids 48, 49, 101, 102; human growth hormone (HGH) 101, 102, 103; Mitchell Report 102; Primobolan 102; testosterone cream 49, 101, 103; tetrahydrogestrinone (THG) 48–49, 101
Perón, Juan 88
Peter Pan syndrome 68
Petty, Richard 127, 130, 141
Petty, Tom 34
Phelps, Michael 62, 63, 66, 67, 69, 75
ping pong 45, 157
Piper, Rowdy Roddy 195
Pippen, Scottie 146, 150
Pixar 129
Platini, Michel 92
Polamalu, Troy 186
Popovich, Gregg (Pop) 115–116
Price, Nick 21
prison 52, 53, 54–55, 89, 211, 212–213; see also incarceration
Professional Golf Association (PGA) 4, 29–31, 32, 33–34, 36, 38, 39, 53; Championship 4, 29; Tour 29, 30, 33, 34, 36, 39, 53
Publix 165

race 2, 3, 4, 8, 19, 20, 71, 72, 147–148, 149, 151, 154, 183, 204, 213, 214–215
race tracks 6, 129, 130, 132, 133, 135, 136, 137, 138, 139, 140, 141, 143; Charlotte Motor Speedway 132; Daytona International Speedway 134–137, 141; Talladega Motor Speedway 135, 137
racial oppression 176
racism 7, 9, 89, 96, 116, 148, 184; Jim Crow 176, 180; see also bigotry
Ramos, Carlos 122–123
Ramsey, Jalen 112
Reed, Kayla Rae 76
Reid, Eric 115, 175
religion 81, 91, 175, 204, 215, 216; Christianity 23, 215; Islam 178, 215–216
reputational spillover 214
reputations 2, 5, 6, 7, 9, 10, 23, 31, 48, 50, 51, 62, 63, 66, 74, 88, 96, 109, 133, 148, 149, 153, 163, 200, 209, 210, 213, 214, 215, 222
Reynolds, Burt 129
Ribagorda, Carlos 44, 45
Rice, Ray 119
Richard Childress Racing (RCR) 131, 140, 142
Richardson, Bill 158, 159
Rickey, Branch 180
Riggs, Bobby 183

Rippon, Adam 19, 20
Rivera, Mariano 105
Robinson, David 149
Robinson, Jackie 180–181, 182
Robinson, Ray 209
Rockne, Knute 114
Rodman, Dennis 1, 6, 8, 68, 146–159
Rodman Group 154
Rodriguez, Alex 5, 95–109
Rogers, Kenny 129
role model 1, 12, 18–22, 25, 53, 121–122, 202
Romanowski, Bill 48
Ronaldo, Cristiano 85
Rose, Pete 54, 58, 69, 107, 109
Rourke, Mickey 156
Rousey, Ronda 1–2, 3, 7, 194–206
Rozelle, Pete 179
Ruiz, Rosie 46
Rummenigge, Karl-Heinz 92
Ruth, Babe 96, 99, 179
Ryan, Greg 116–117

Savarese, Lou 210
Schollander, Don 73
Schrader, Kenny 134, 138
Scorsese, Martin 218
Scurry, Brianna 116–117
SEC Television Network 170
Selig, Bud 103
sexual orientation 4, 8, 9–10, 12, 15, 18–19, 20, 21, 25, 153, 155, 204; bisexuality 152, 155; heterosexuality 153, 154, 195; homosexuality 10, 18–22, 24, 115, 152–153
sexuality 10, 20, 154, 155, 222
Shafir, Marina 200
Shapton, Leanne 73
Sharapova, Maria 47
Silva, Anderson 47
Silverstein, Rob 24
Sinagra, Cristina 88
slavery 147, 176
slaves 147–148, 176
Smith, Calvin 49
Smith, Onterrio 46
Smith, Timmie 181–182
soccer 5, 6, 63, 69, 80–86, 88, 89, 90, 91, 92, 112, 113, 115, 116–117, 120, 121, 122, 123, 124, 148; Al Was 92; Argentinos Juniors 83–84, 92; Athletic de Bilbao 90; Barcelona 83, 84, 86, 87, 89, 90–91; Boca Juniors 83; Cebollitas 84; Deportivo Mandiyu 92; Deportivo Riestra 92; Dorados of Sinaloa 92; Estudiantes 90; Fujairah 92; goalkeeper 81, 89, 112, 113, 114, 115, 116, 117, 122, 123–124; Golden Glove Award 114, 117; Manchester United 90; Marseille 91; Napoli 83, 88, 89, 91; 1978 World Cup 85, 90; 1979 Youth World Cup 85; 1982 World Cup 90, 91; 1983 Spanish Cup 90; 1986 World Cup 80, 84, 91; 1990 World Cup 83, 87; 1994 World

Cup 87; 1999 World Cup 116, 117; Real Madrid 81, 90; River 84; 2010 World Cup 91, 92; 2015 World Cup 119; UEFA Champions League 84; U.S. Women's National Team 114, 116
Solo, Hope 6, 8, 69, 112–125
Sosa, Sammy 99–100, 101, 108
SPEED TV (FS1) 137
Spitz, Mark 62
sponsors 29, 36, 37, 66, 68, 84, 128, 130, 134, 135, 137, 139, 142, 204; Airweave 66; California Milk Producers 154; Carl's Jr. 154; Comfort Inn 154; Converse 154; Gentle Hair Remover 66; Goodyear 142, 143; Hooters 36, 135; Kodak 154; Nike 115, 188; Oakley 154; Ralph Lauren 66; Speedo USA 66; Syneron-Candela 66; Victoria's Secret 154–155; Wilson 37
Sport Spectator Identification Scale (SSIS) 166–167
Sprewell, Latrell 146, 151
"The Star-Spangled Banner" 178–182; *see also* national anthem
Stefano, Di 82, 90
Stern, David 150
steroids 46, 47, 48, 49, 58, 95, 97, 99–100, 101–103, 108, 109, 113, 177; *see also* performance-enhancing drugs
Stevens, Jerramy 118
Stewart, Tony 128, 138
Stojko, Elvis 14
Strikeforce 197–198
swimming 4, 5, 45, 61, 62–63, 64–66, 67, 70, 71, 72, 73, 74, 75, 76, 195

Tate, Miesha 197–199, 200
Taylor, Lawrence 53
tennis 122–123, 183; Battle of the Sexes 183; Grand Slam 47; U.S. Open 122, 123
Thiem, Dominic 123
Thomas, Frank 107
Thomas, Isaiah 149
Thompson, Neil 128
Thomson-Garland, Rosemarie 196
Thorogood, George 149
Title IX 165
Toth, Kevin 49
track and field 4, 5, 44, 45, 47, 49, 51, 54, 55, 56, 59; USA Outdoor Championships 47
Travis, Clay 185
Troy, Gregg 73
Trump, Donald 64, 115, 116, 156, 158, 159
Tuivasa, Tui 115
Tupac 214
Turner, Brock 72
Tyson, Mike 7, 8, 208–218

Ultimate Fighting Championship (UFC) 47, 115, 195, 196, 197, 198, 199, 200–201, 202, 203, 206, 207

Union of European Football Associations (UEFA) 84
United Soccer League 115; Orange County Blues 115
U.S. Anti-Doping Agency (USADA) 48, 50, 75, 100
U.S. Figure Skating Association (USFSA) 10–12, 13, 16, 17, 23, 25
U.S. Olympic Committee (USOC) 10, 49
U.S. Soccer Federation (USSF) 112, 116, 117, 121
U.S. Tennis Federation 123
U.S. Track and Field Association (USATF) 45, 49
USA Judo 204, 205
USA Swimming 66

Valdano, Jorge 84, 85, 92
Valente, James 101
Van Damme, Jean-Claude 156
VH1 155
Vice Media 157
Vick, Michael 76–77, 187
Vidal, Gore 67
Villafañe, Claudia 88
villainy 1, 2, 4, 6, 7, 11, 57, 93, 107, 109, 116, 125, 134, 135, 136, 196, 201, 208, 217
Vincent, Fay 100

Wallace, Mike 47, 53
Wallace, Rusty 132, 135, 141
Walters, Barbara 210
Waltrip, Darrell (DW) 133, 137, 138, 139, 141
Waltrip, Michael (Mikey) 139, 140
Waltrip, Stevie 133
war 67, 176, 177, 178, 179, 182, 183, 185; Civil War 176–177, 183; Falklands War 80; Vietnam War 179; war on terror 179; World War II 179, 182
Warren, Elizabeth 122
Washington, Desiree 210–211, 212
Watson, Bubba 28
Weir, Johnny 4, 8, 9–25
Weiss, Michael 14
Wheeler, Humpy 130
White, Dana 185, 198, 207
White, Kelli 49
Williams, Doug 183
Williams, Serena 115, 122–123
Williams, Ted 100
Williams, Venus 115
Wilson, Owen 129
Winston, Jameis 6–7, 8, 162–172
Wolfe, Tom 129
Woods, Tiger 28, 29, 36, 41, 53, 55, 57, 76, 134
World Boxing Association (WBA) 209
World Boxing Council (WBC) 209
World Wrestling Entertainment (WWE) 119, 195, 199, 201, 202

WrestleMania 202
wrestling 6, 68, 119, 146, 157, 195, 198, 199–202, 204

Yarborough, Cale 129–130

Zidane, Zinedine 92
Zoeller, Fuzzy 31, 39, 40, 41
Zoff, Dino 89